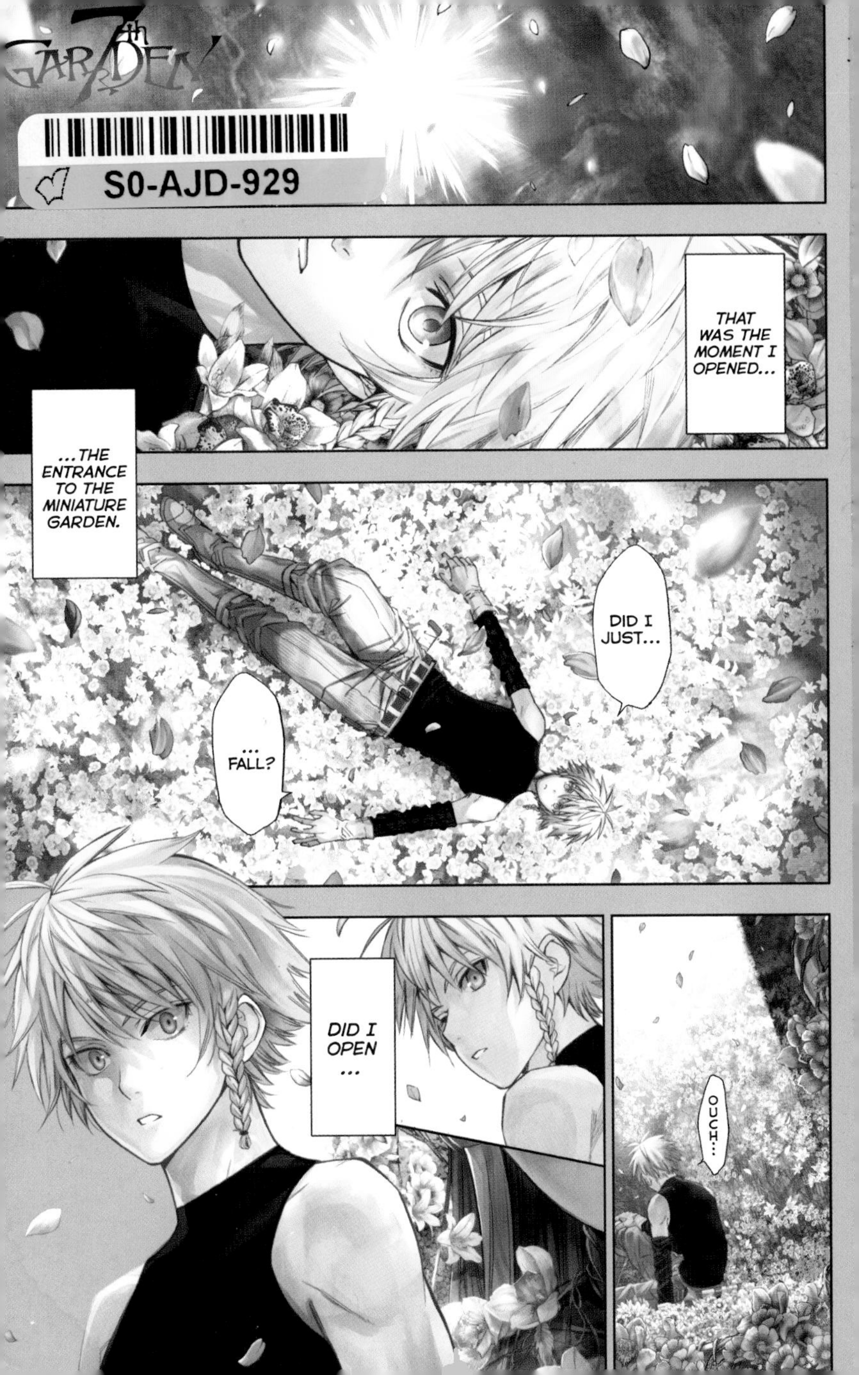
7th GARDEN
THAT WAS THE MOMENT I OPENED...
...THE ENTRANCE TO THE MINIATURE GARDEN.
DID I JUST...
...FALL?
OUCH...
DID I OPEN ...

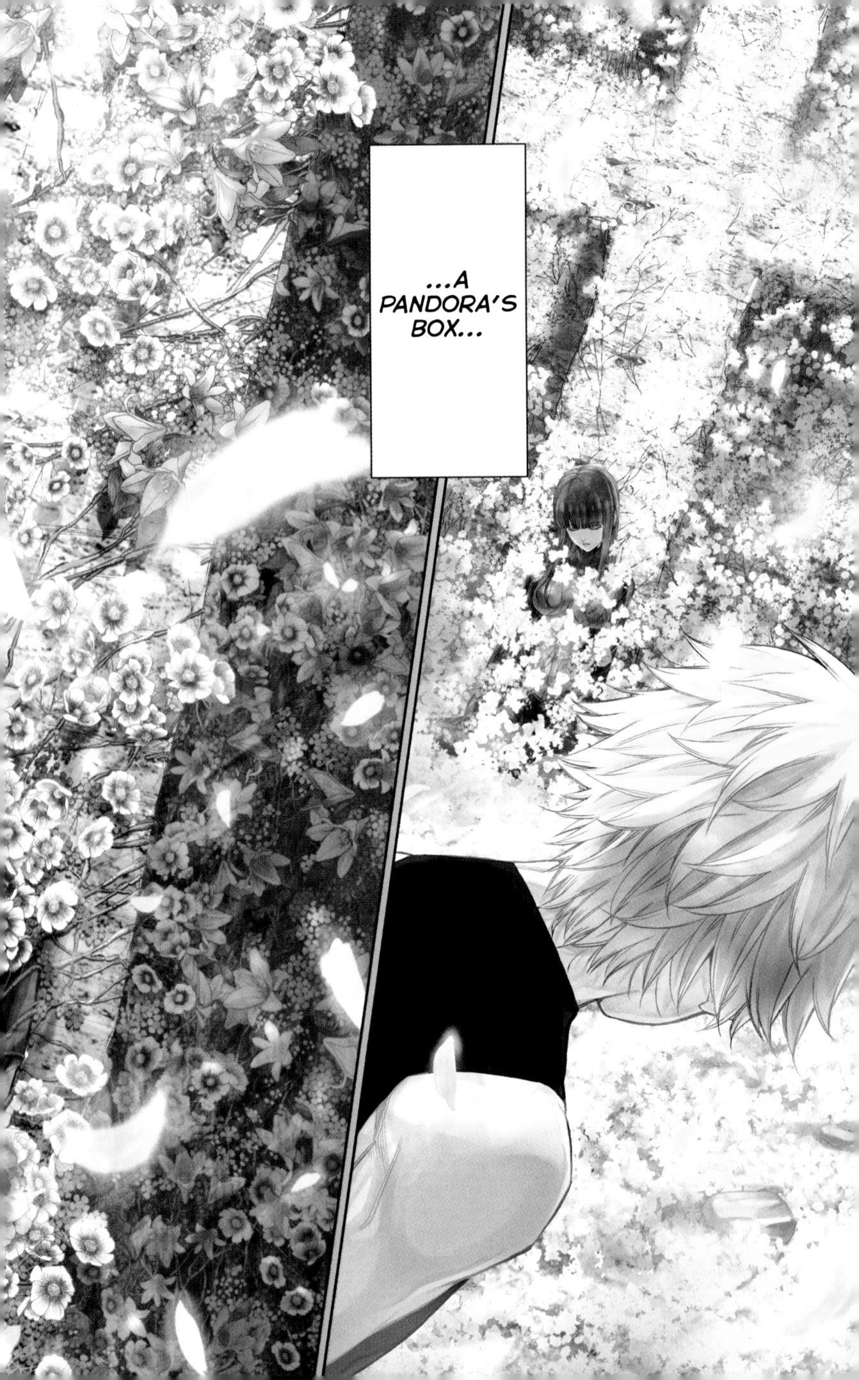
...A PANDORA'S BOX...

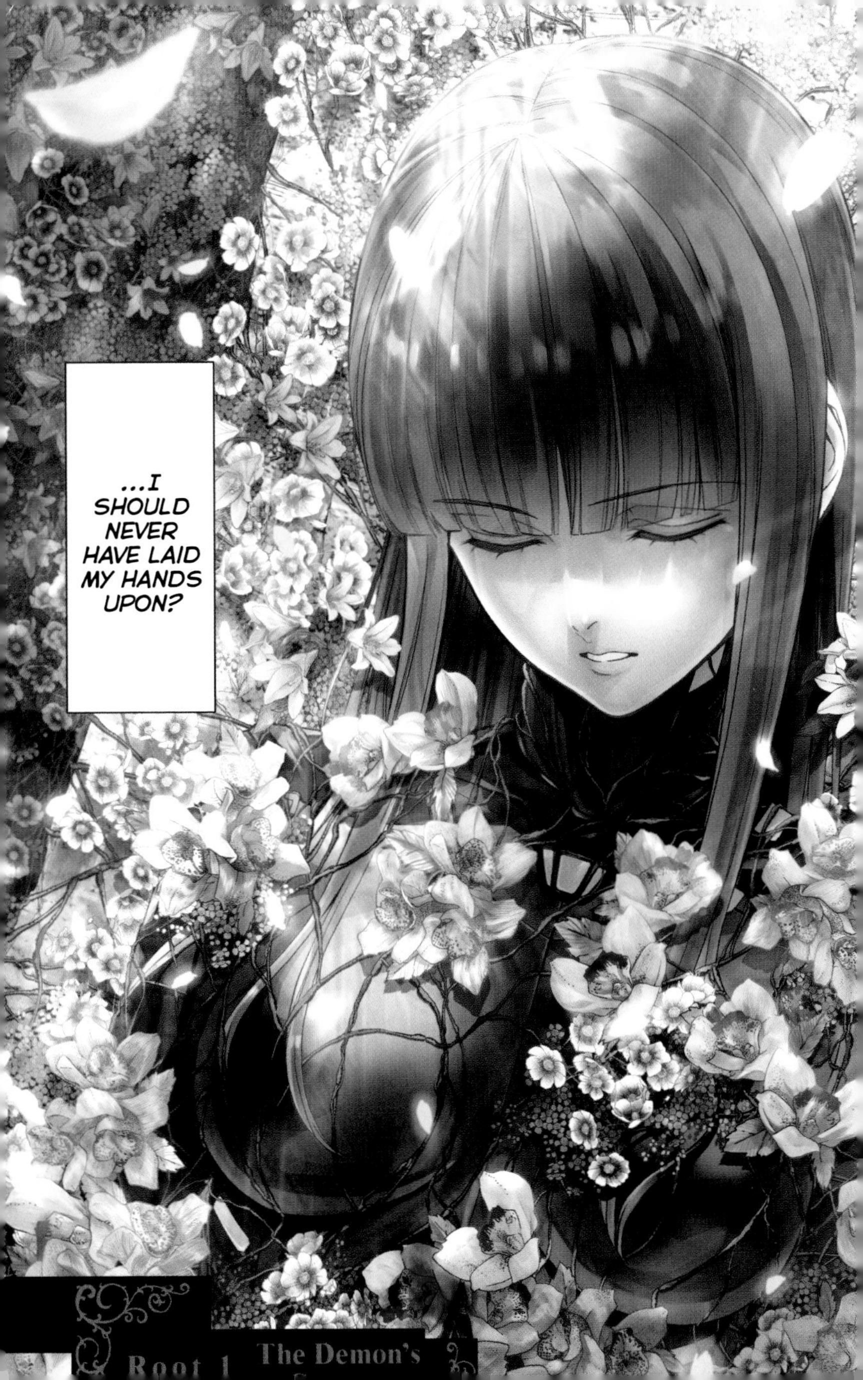
...I SHOULD NEVER HAVE LAID MY HANDS UPON?
Root 1
The Demon's

God created the stars...

...filled them with figurines...

...and created a miniature garden.

7thGARDEN

CONTENTS

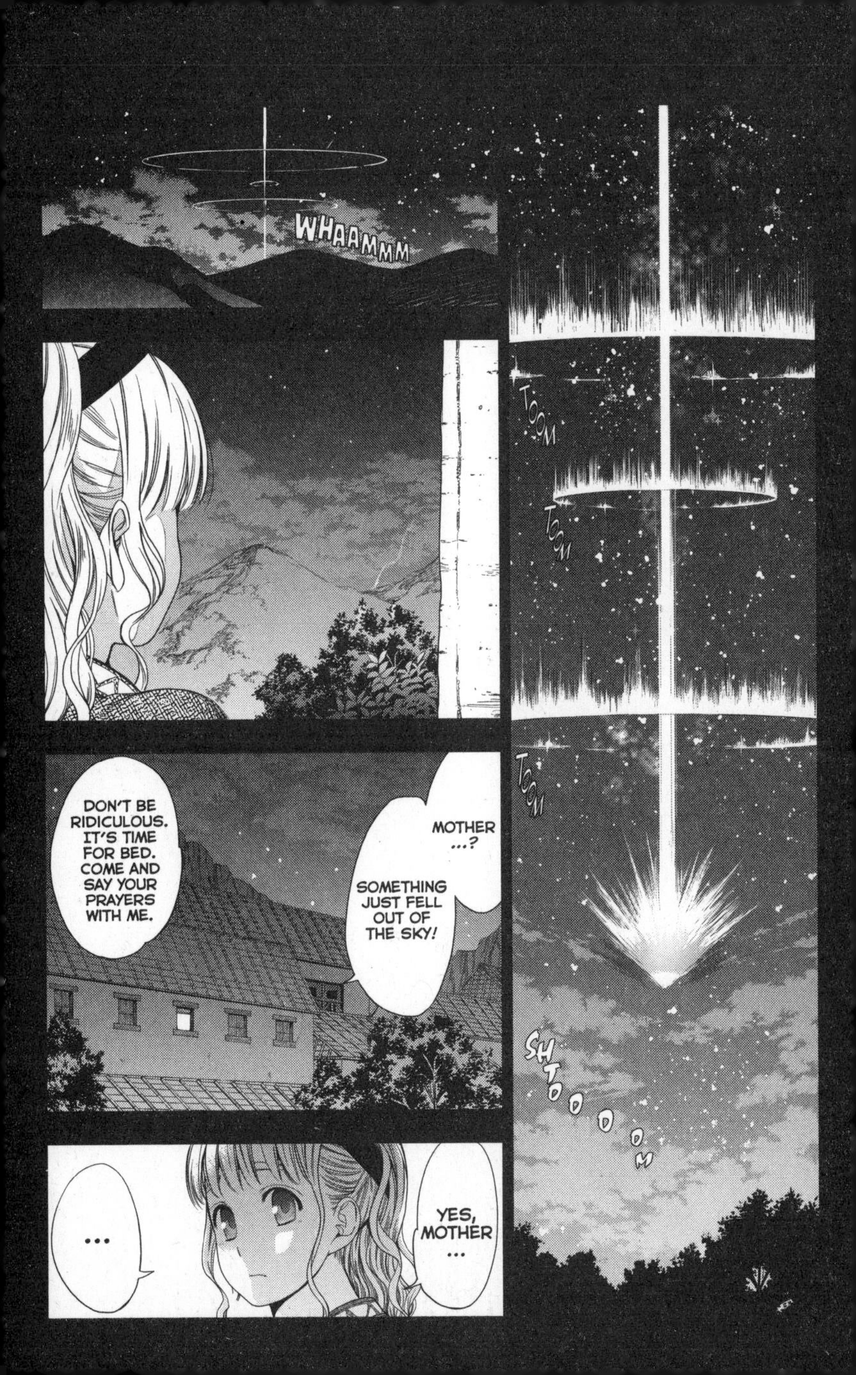
TOOM
TOOM
TOOM
SHTOOOOOM
WHAAMMM
MOTHER ...?
SOMETHING JUST FELL OUT OF THE SKY!
DON'T BE RIDICULOUS. IT'S TIME FOR BED. COME AND SAY YOUR PRAYERS WITH ME.
YES, MOTHER ...
...

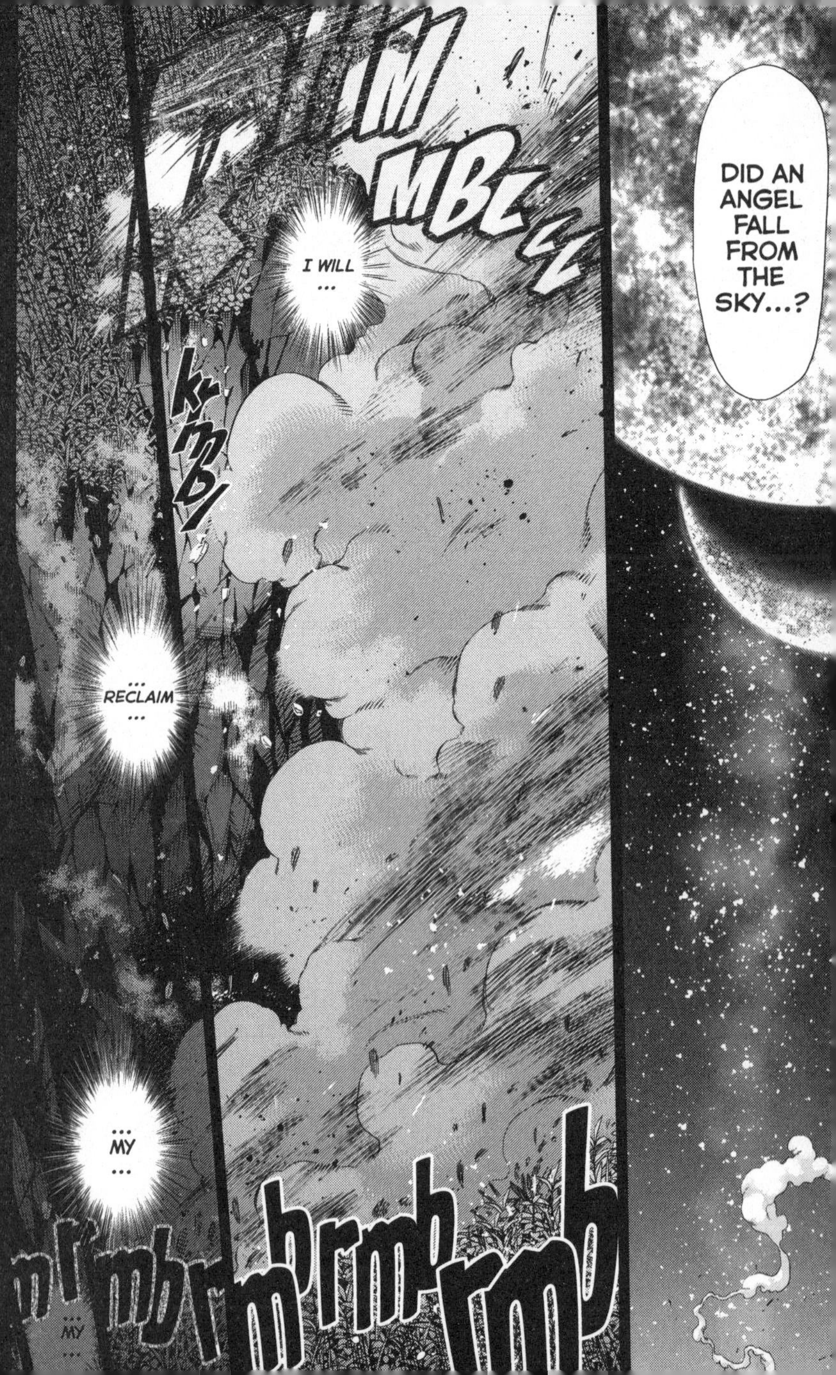
DID AN ANGEL FALL FROM THE SKY...?
I WILL ...
... RECLAIM ...
... MY ...
... MY ...

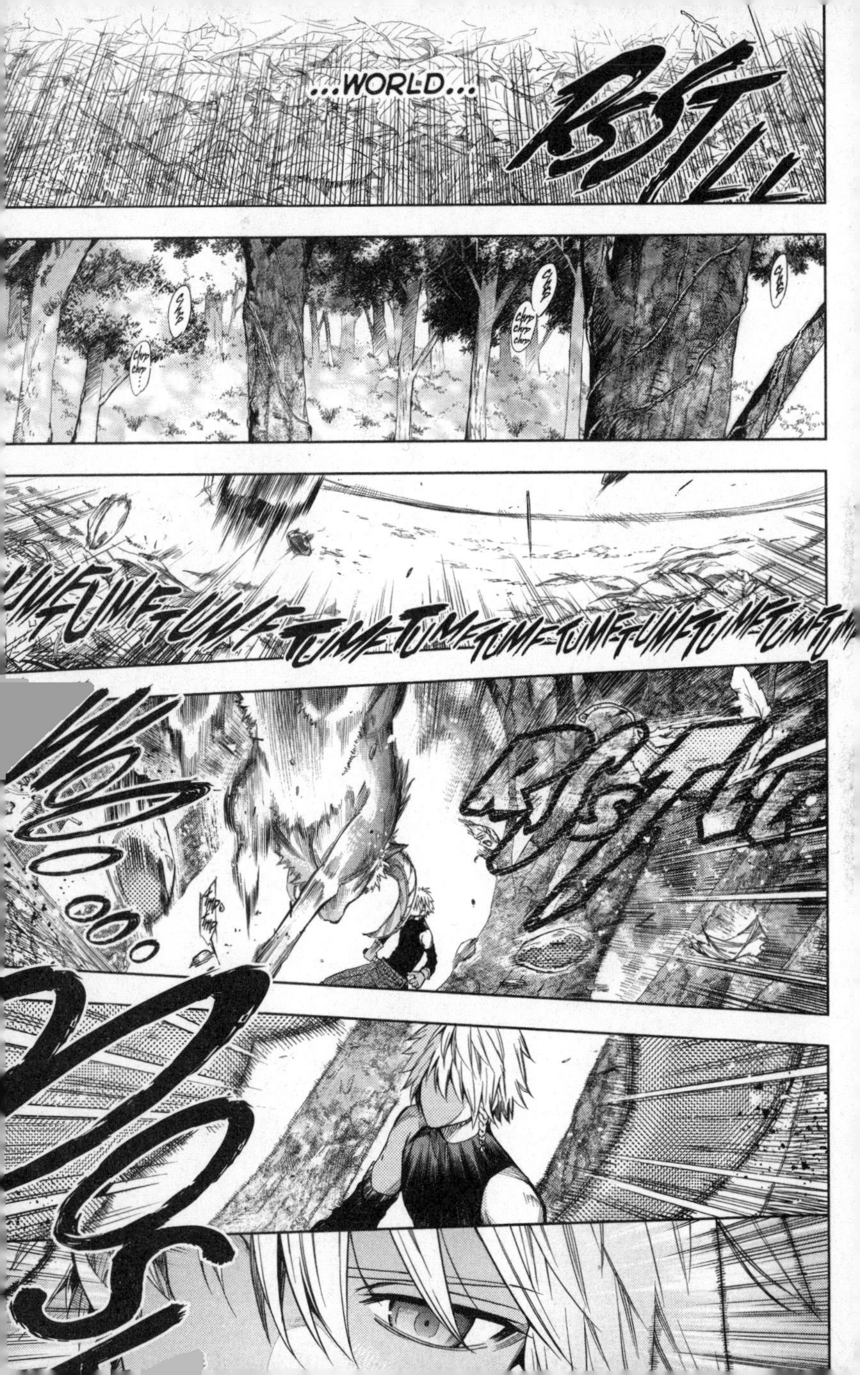
...WORLD...
chirp chirp chirp
chirp chirp...
TUMF TUMF TUMF TUMF TUMF TUMF TUMF TUMF TUMF TUMF

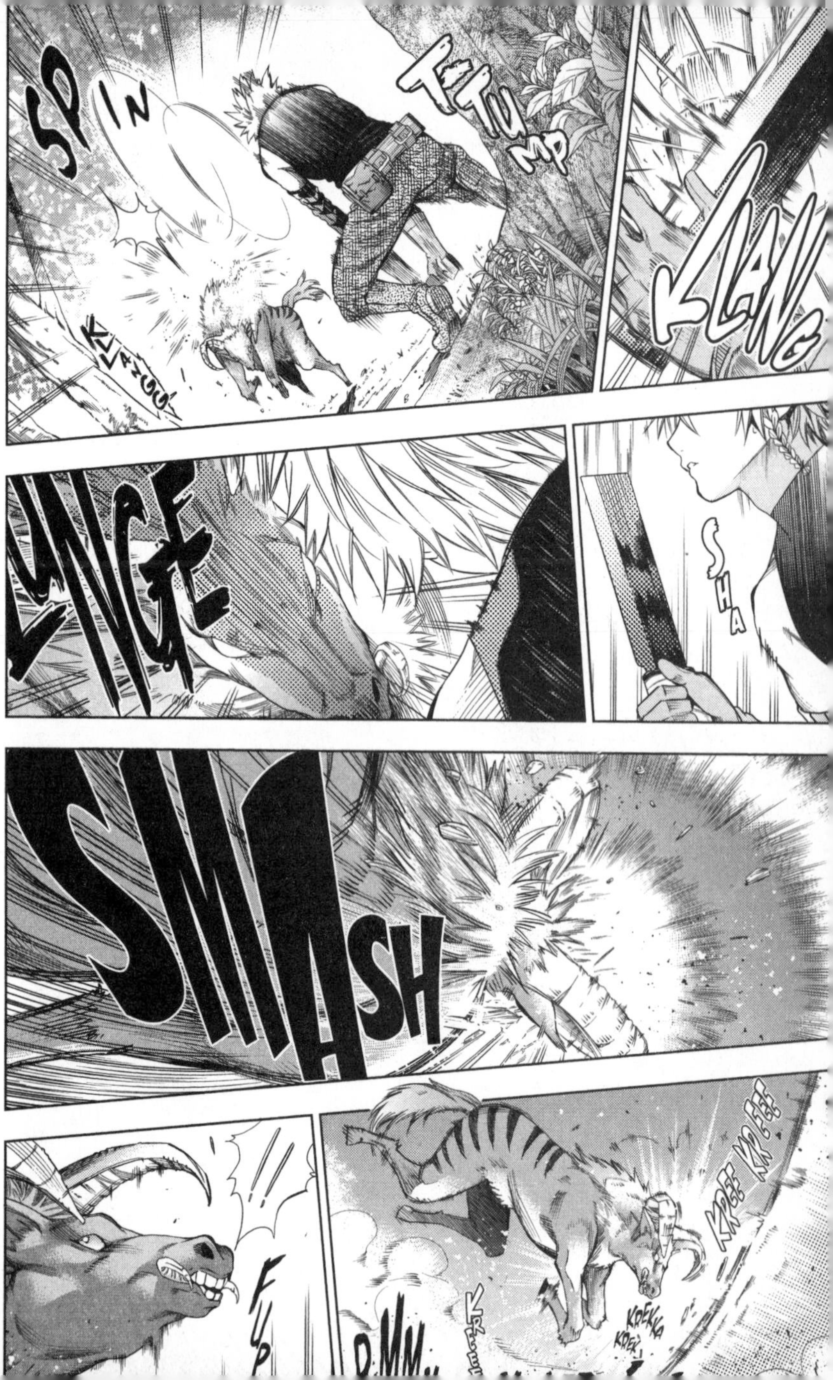
KLANG
TATUMP
SPIN
KYAGU
!
SHA
UNGE
SMASH
KREE KREE KREEE
KREKKA
KREK!
KREEE
DMM..
FUP
!!

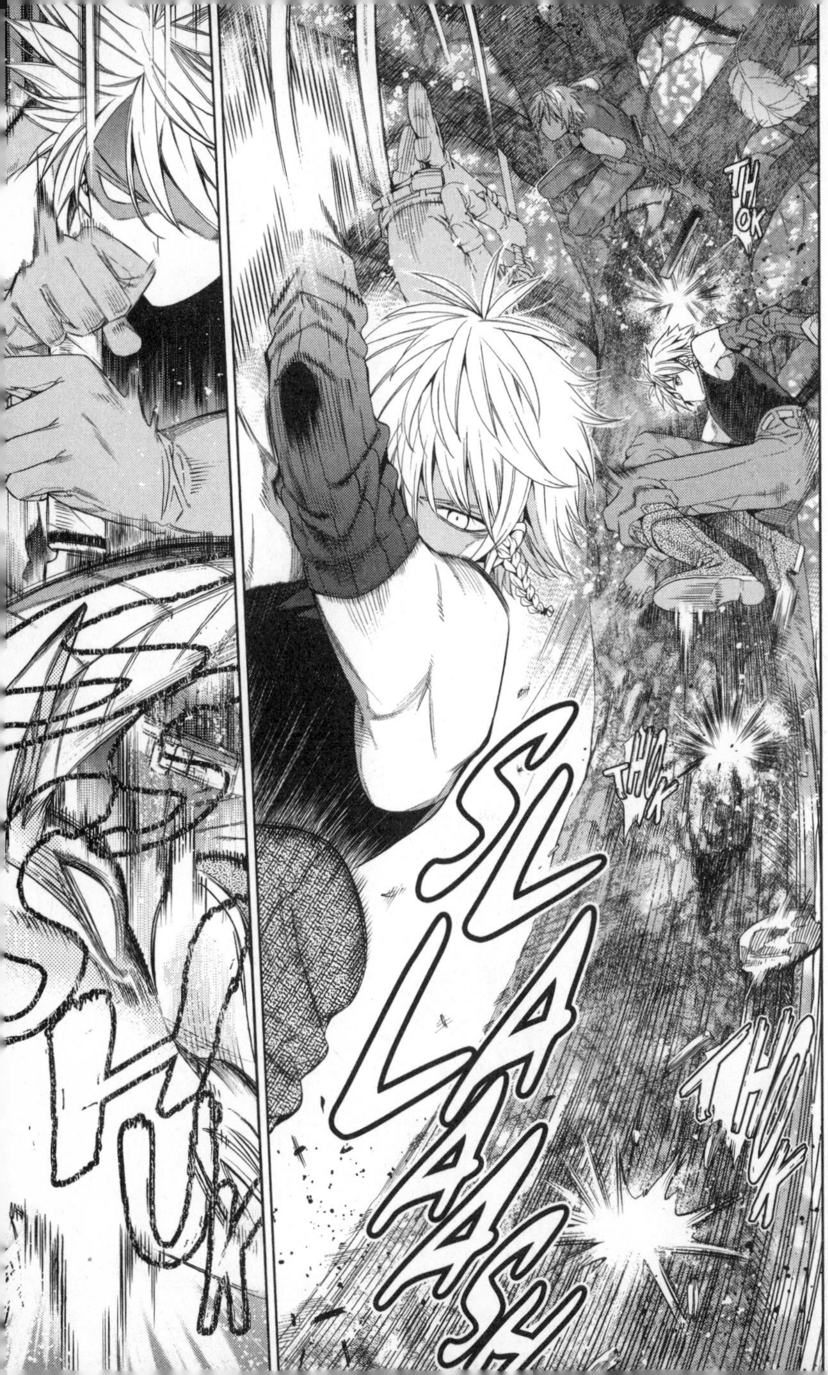
THOK
THOK
THOK
SLAAASH

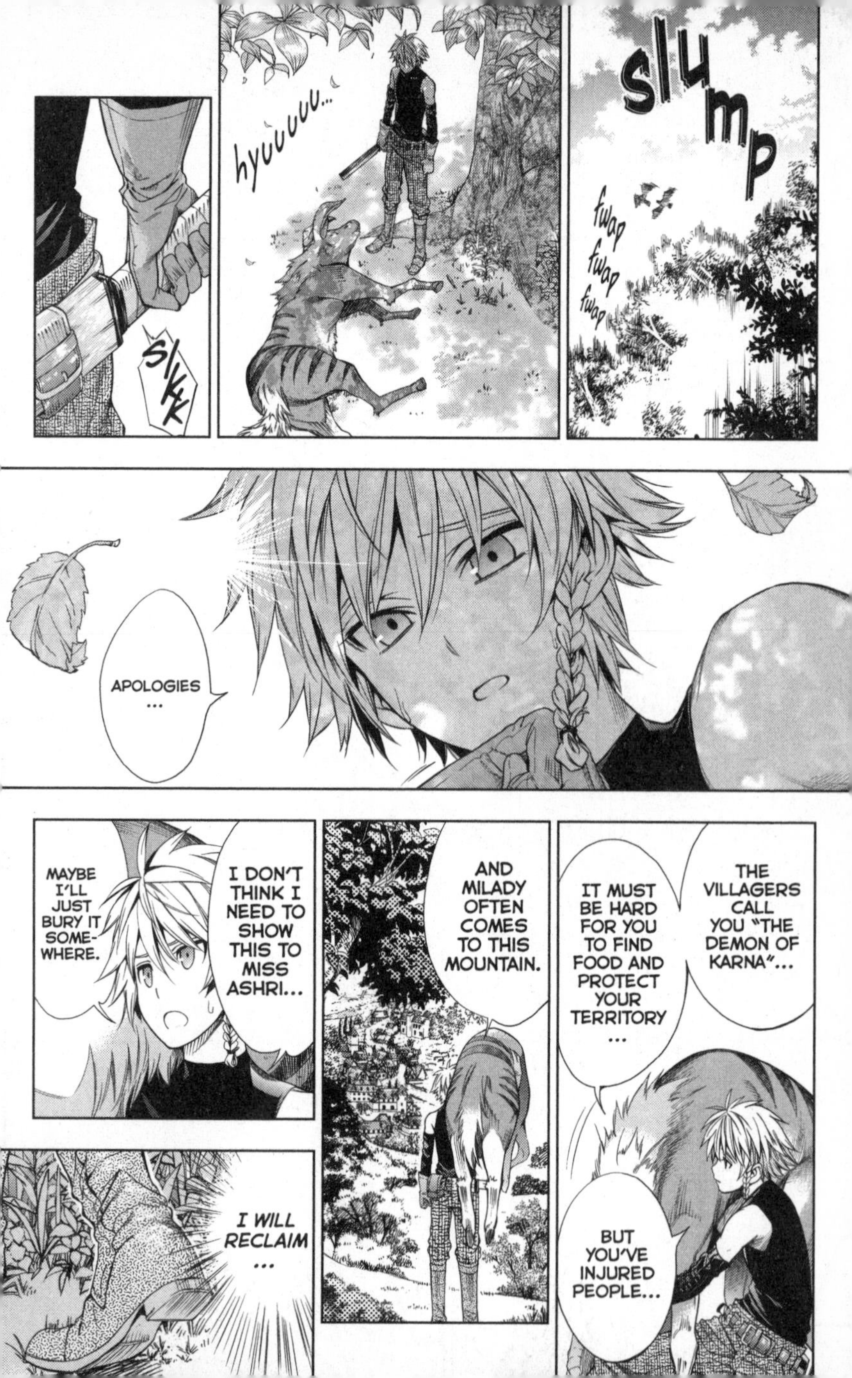
slump
fwap fwap fwap
hyuuuuu...
SLIKK
APOLOGIES ...
THE VILLAGERS CALL YOU "THE DEMON OF KARNA"...
IT MUST BE HARD FOR YOU TO FIND FOOD AND PROTECT YOUR TERRITORY ...
BUT YOU'VE INJURED PEOPLE...
AND MILADY OFTEN COMES TO THIS MOUNTAIN.
I DON'T THINK I NEED TO SHOW THIS TO MISS ASHRI...
MAYBE I'LL JUST BURY IT SOME-WHERE.
I WILL RECLAIM ...

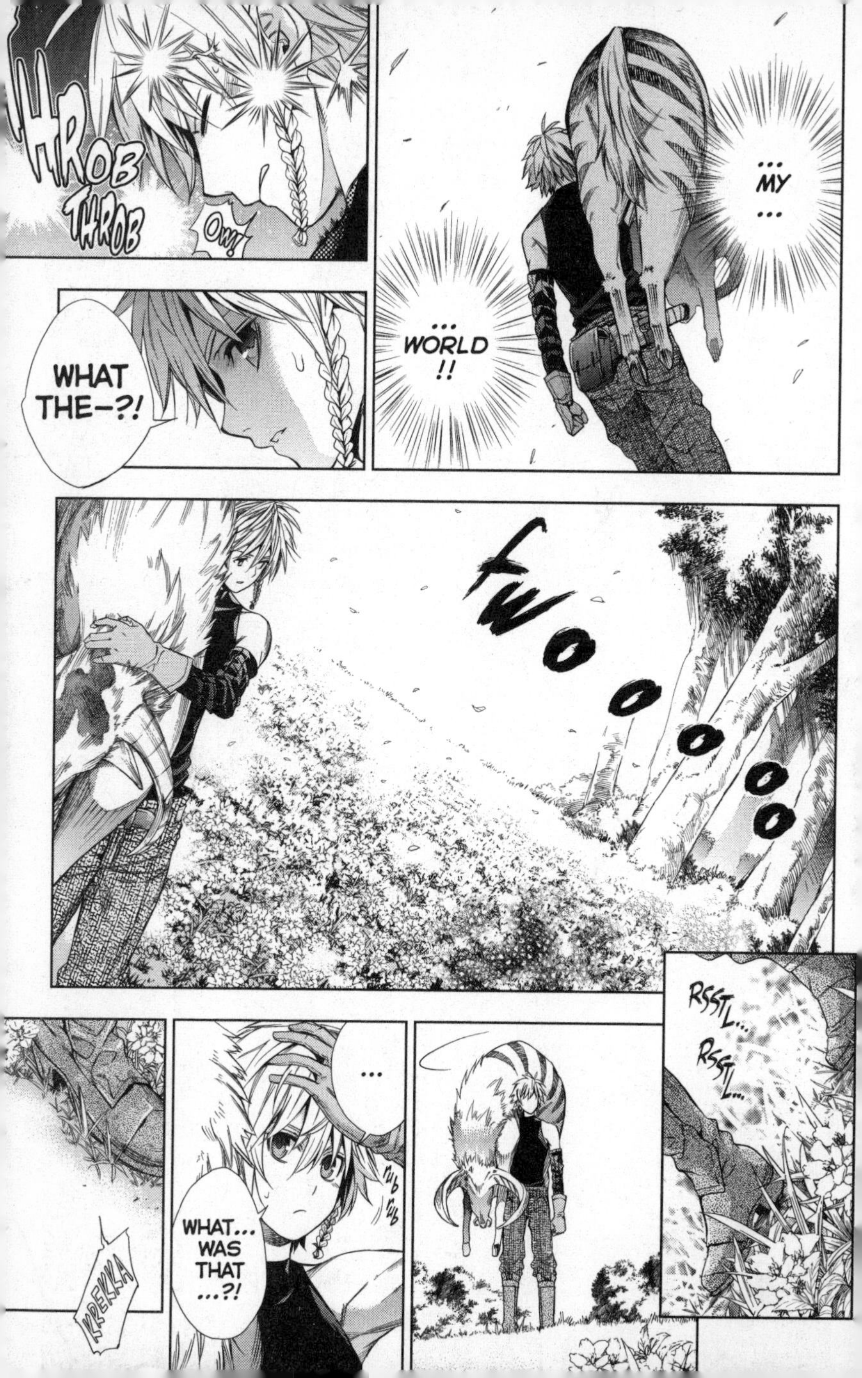

...MY...
...WORLD!!
THROB THROB
OW!
WHAT THE-?!
fwoooooo
RSSTL... RSSTL...
...
rub rub
WHAT... WAS THAT...?!
KREKKA

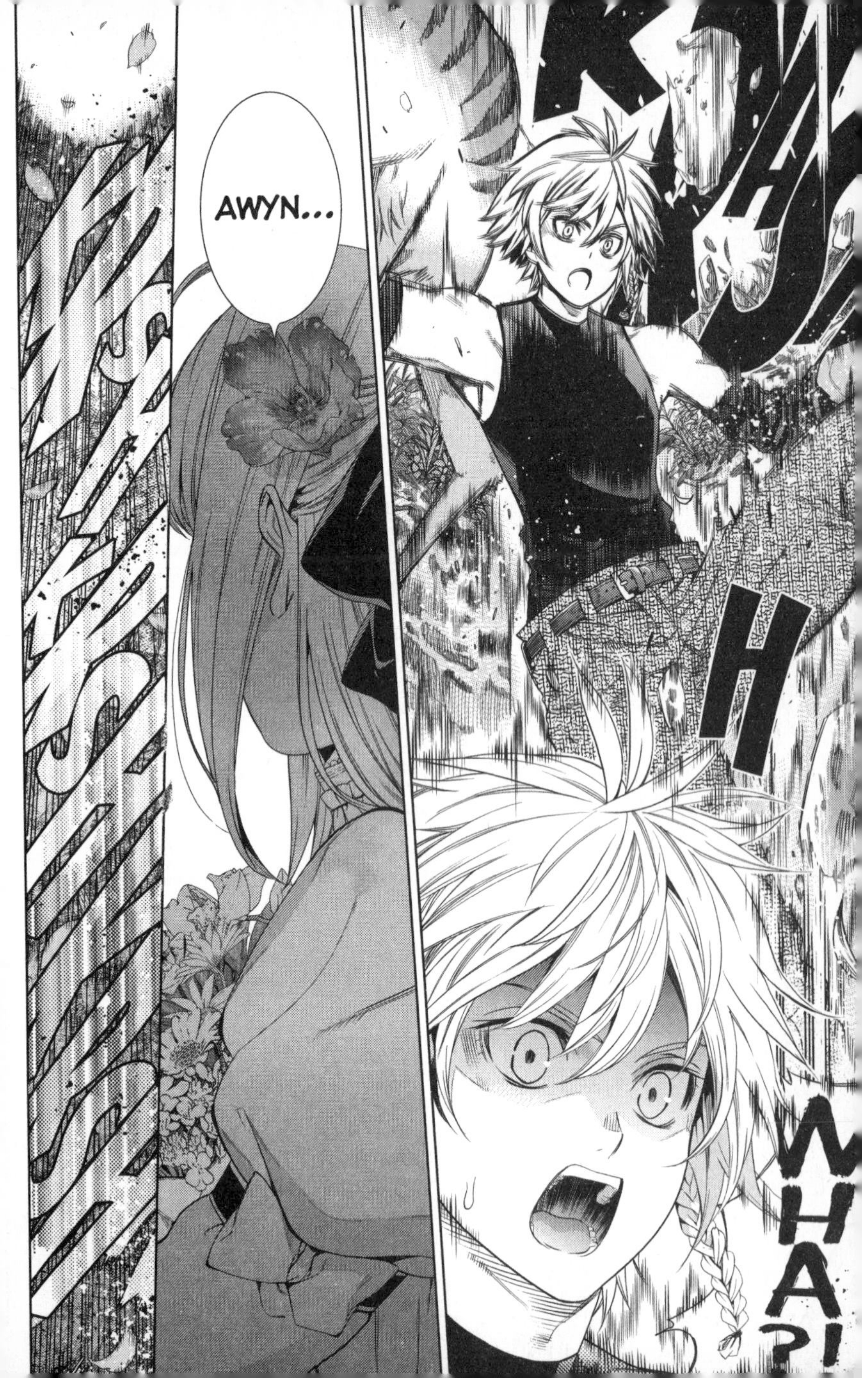
WHA?!
AWYN...

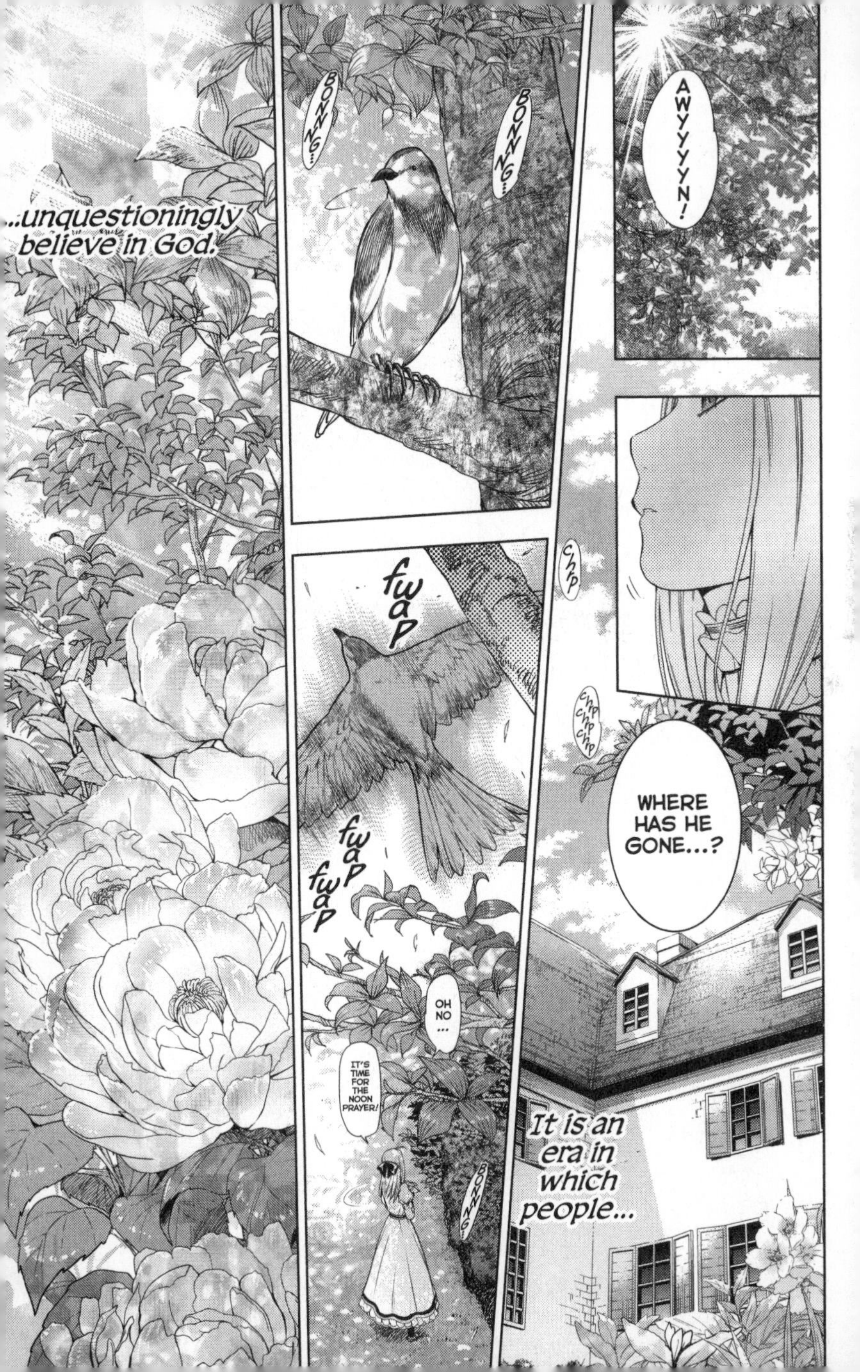
AWYYYYN!
BONNNG...
BONNNG...
Chirp
chirp chirp chirp
WHERE HAS HE GONE...?
fwap
fwap
fwap
OH NO...
IT'S TIME FOR THE NOON PRAYER!
BONNNG...
It is an era in which people...
...unquestioningly believe in God.

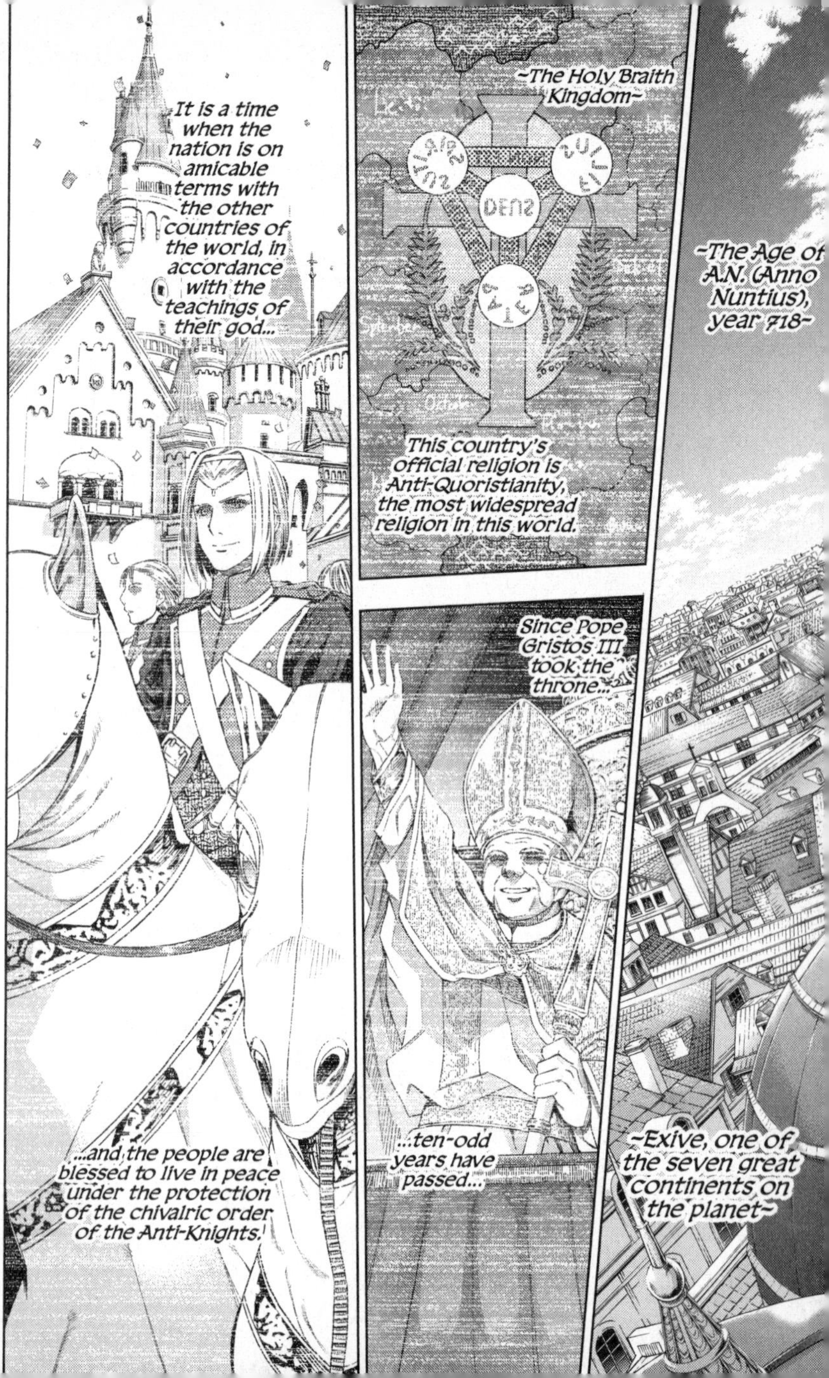
~The Age of A.N. (Anno Nuntius), year 718~
~Exive, one of the seven great continents on the planet~
~The Holy Braith Kingdom~
This country's official religion is Anti-Quoristianity, the most widespread religion in this world.
Since Pope Gristos III took the throne...
...ten-odd years have passed...
It is a time when the nation is on amicable terms with the other countries of the world, in accordance with the teachings of their god...
...and the people are blessed to live in peace under the protection of the chivalric order of the Anti-Knights.

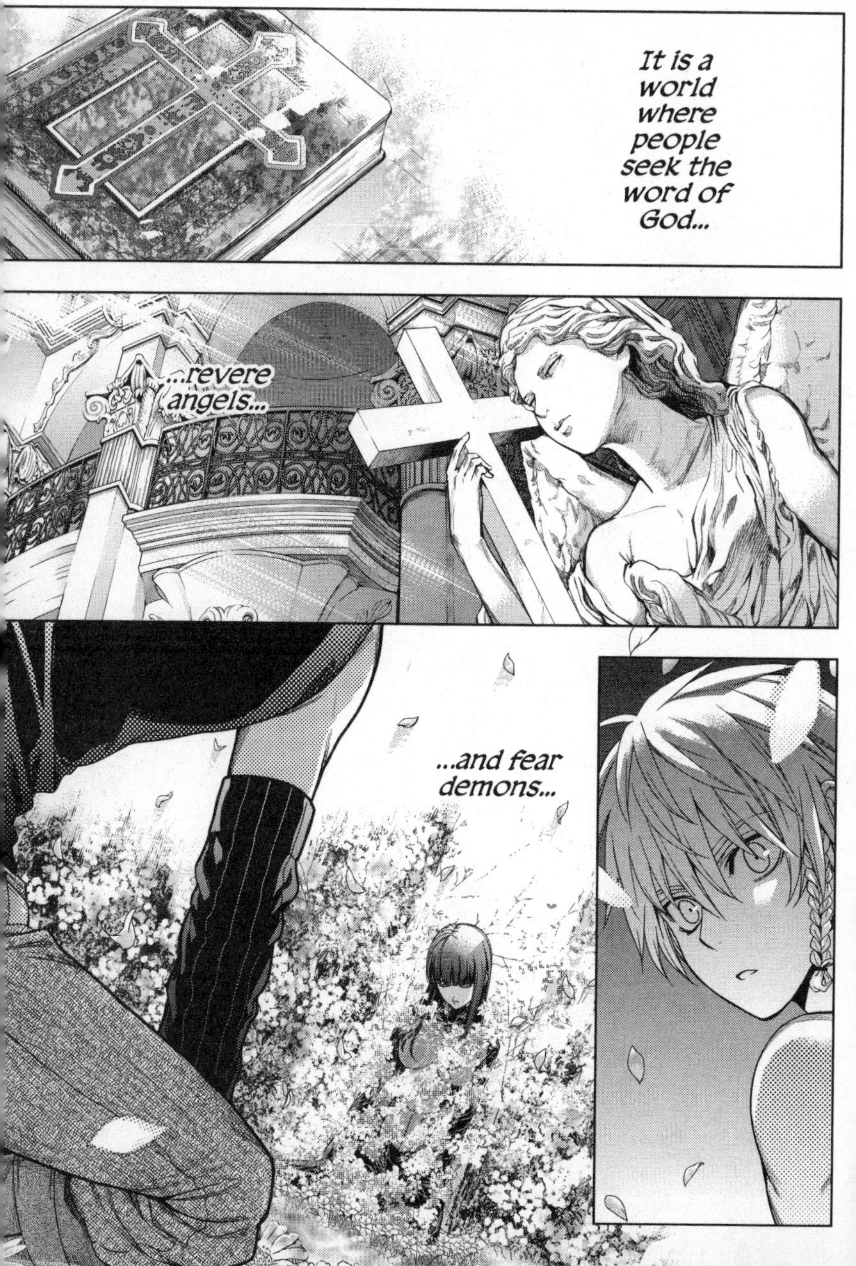
It is a world where people seek the word of God...
...revere angels...
...and fear demons...

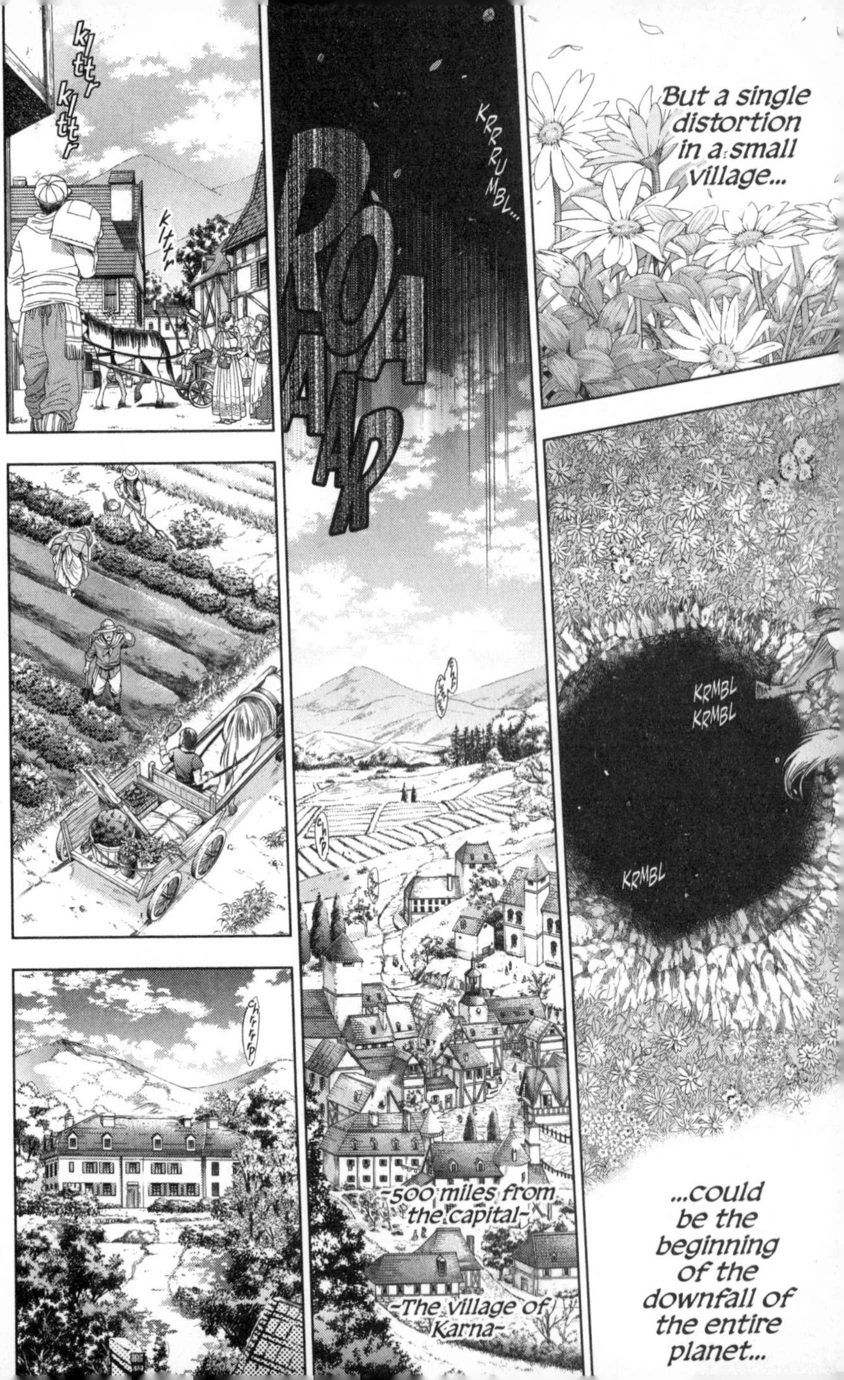
But a single distortion in a small village...
KRMBL KRMBL
KRMBL
...could be the beginning of the downfall of the entire planet...
KRRRUMBL...
ROAAAP
~500 miles from the capital~
~The village of Karna~
klttr klttr
klttr
chrrrp

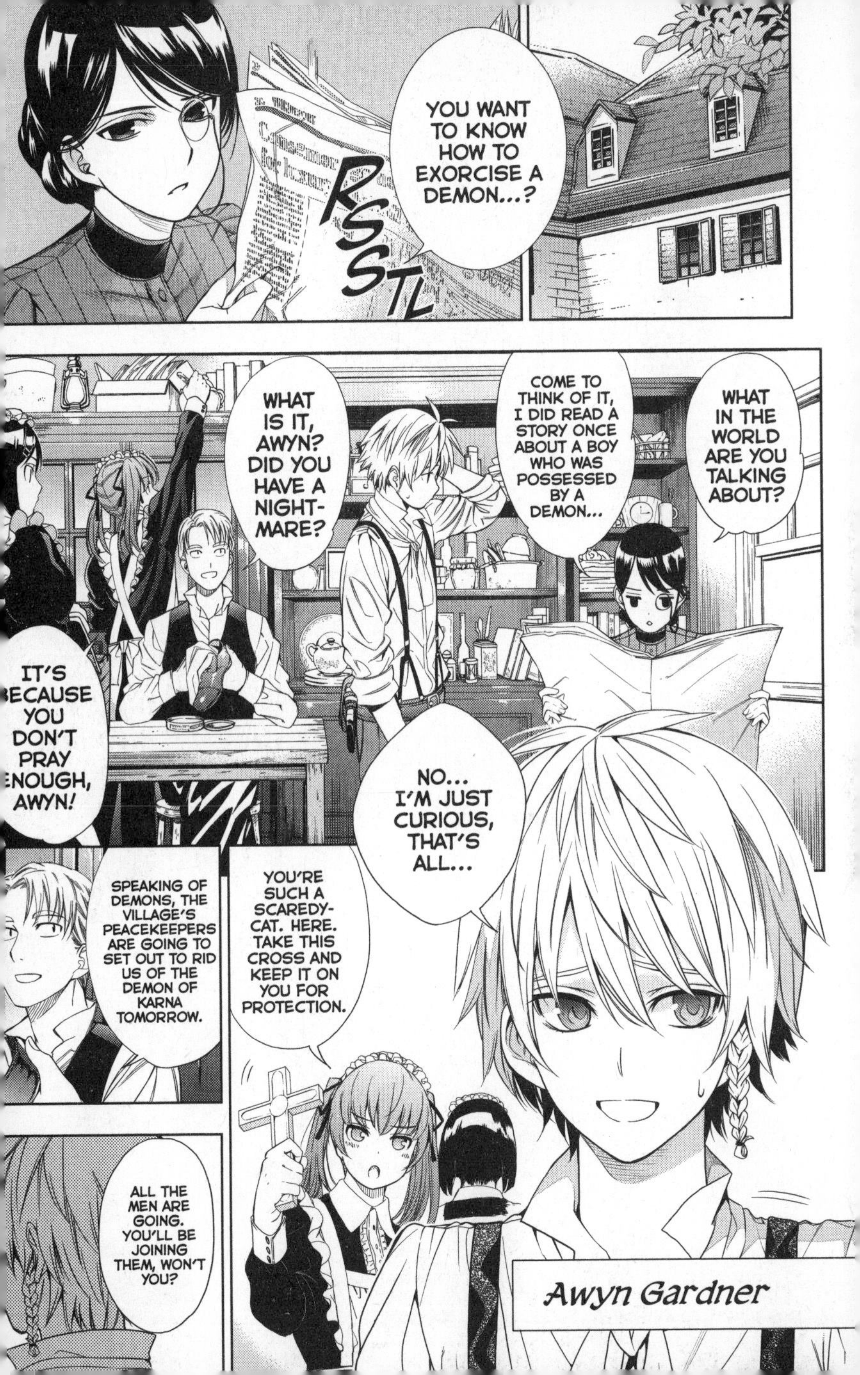
YOU WANT TO KNOW HOW TO EXORCISE A DEMON...?
RSSTL
WHAT IN THE WORLD ARE YOU TALKING ABOUT?
COME TO THINK OF IT, I DID READ A STORY ONCE ABOUT A BOY WHO WAS POSSESSED BY A DEMON...
WHAT IS IT, AWYN? DID YOU HAVE A NIGHT-MARE?
IT'S ECAUSE YOU DON'T PRAY ENOUGH, AWYN!
NO... I'M JUST CURIOUS, THAT'S ALL...
YOU'RE SUCH A SCAREDY-CAT. HERE. TAKE THIS CROSS AND KEEP IT ON YOU FOR PROTECTION.
Awyn Gardner
SPEAKING OF DEMONS, THE VILLAGE'S PEACEKEEPERS ARE GOING TO SET OUT TO RID US OF THE DEMON OF KARNA TOMORROW.
ALL THE MEN ARE GOING. YOU'LL BE JOINING THEM, WON'T YOU?

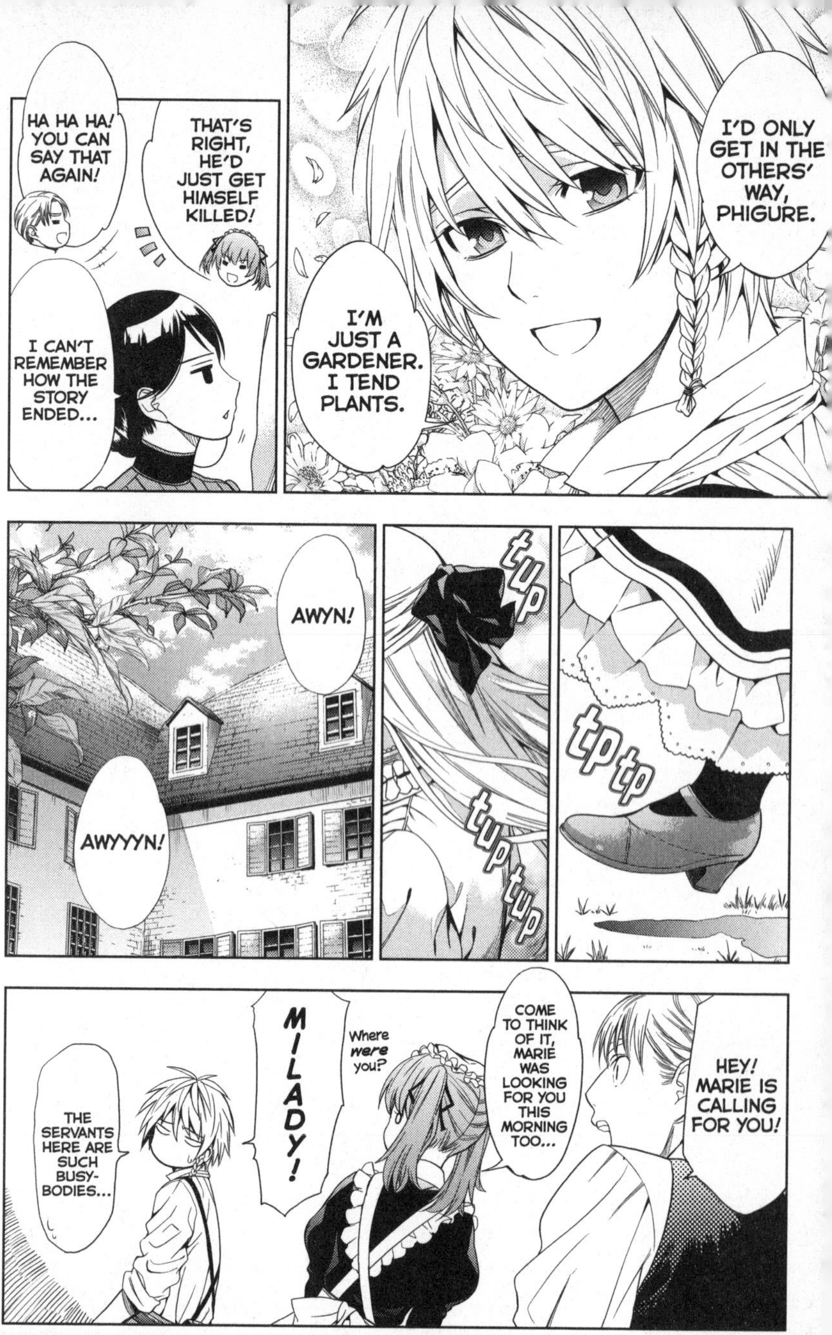
I'D ONLY GET IN THE OTHERS' WAY, PHIGURE.
I'M JUST A GARDENER. I TEND PLANTS.
THAT'S RIGHT, HE'D JUST GET HIMSELF KILLED!
HA HA HA! YOU CAN SAY THAT AGAIN!
I CAN'T REMEMBER HOW THE STORY ENDED...
tp tp
tup tup tup tup
AWYN!
AWYYYN!
HEY! MARIE IS CALLING FOR YOU!
COME TO THINK OF IT, MARIE WAS LOOKING FOR YOU THIS MORNING TOO...
Where *were* you?
MILADY!
THE SERVANTS HERE ARE SUCH BUSY-BODIES...

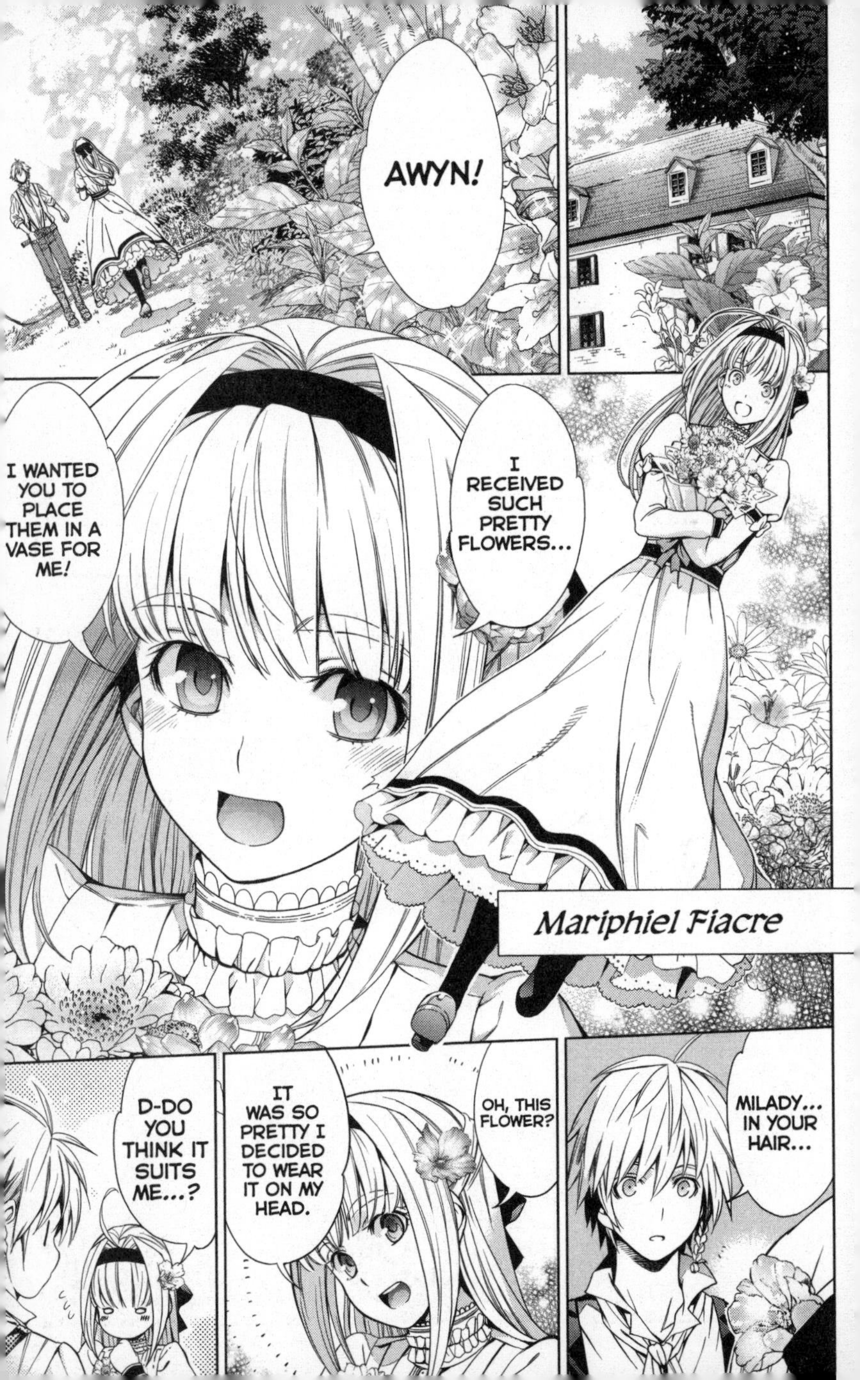
AWYN!
I RECEIVED SUCH PRETTY FLOWERS...
I WANTED YOU TO PLACE THEM IN A VASE FOR ME!
Mariphiel Fiacre
MILADY... IN YOUR HAIR...
OH, THIS FLOWER?
IT WAS SO PRETTY I DECIDED TO WEAR IT ON MY HEAD.
D-DO YOU THINK IT SUITS ME...?

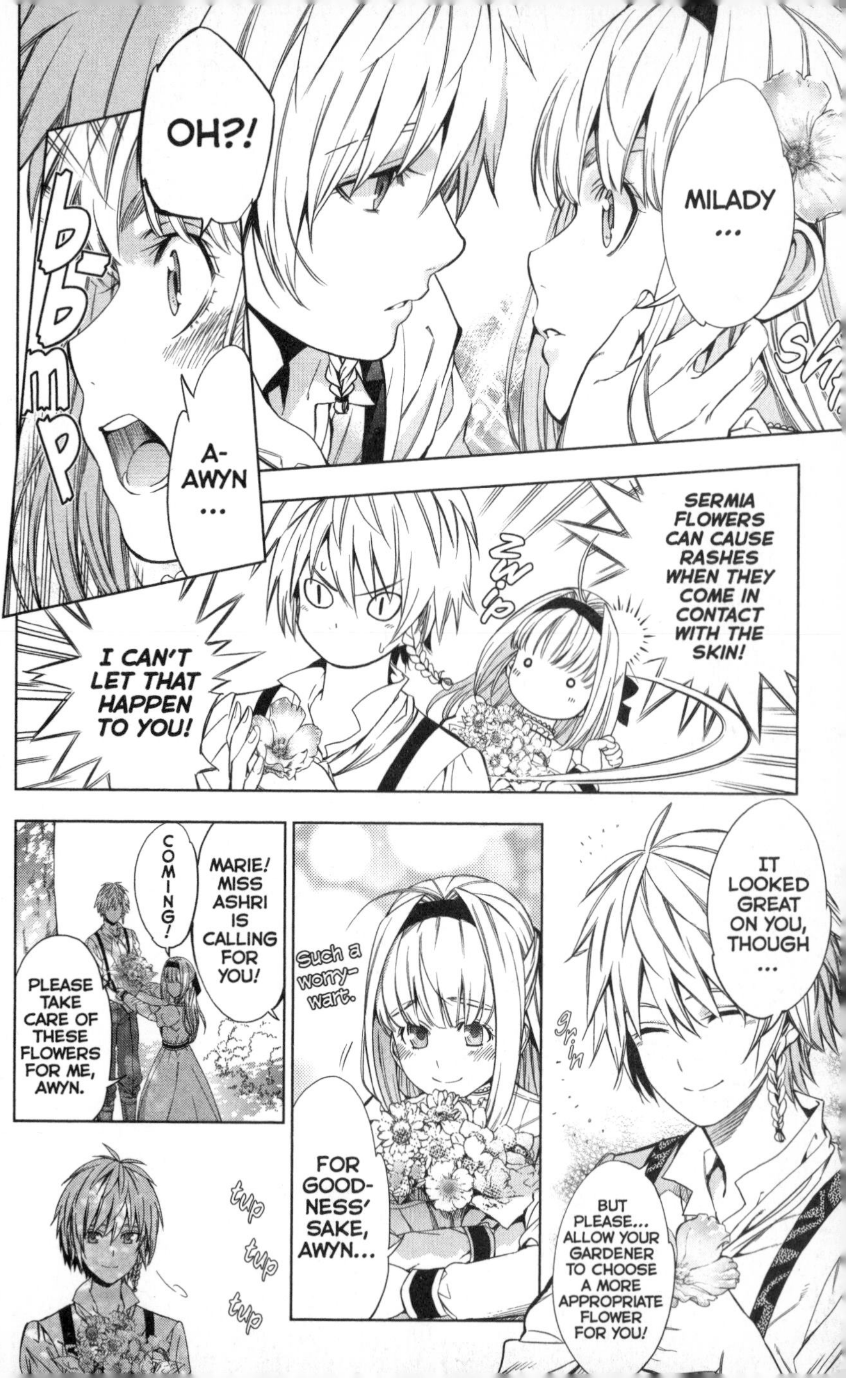
MILADY ...
OH?!
b-bmp
A- AWYN ...
SERMIA FLOWERS CAN CAUSE RASHES WHEN THEY COME IN CONTACT WITH THE SKIN!
whip
I CAN'T LET THAT HAPPEN TO YOU!
IT LOOKED GREAT ON YOU, THOUGH ...
grin
BUT PLEASE... ALLOW YOUR GARDENER TO CHOOSE A MORE APPROPRIATE FLOWER FOR YOU!
Such a worry-wart.
FOR GOODNESS' SAKE, AWYN...
MARIE! MISS ASHRI IS CALLING FOR YOU!
COMING!
PLEASE TAKE CARE OF THESE FLOWERS FOR ME, AWYN.
tup
tup
tup

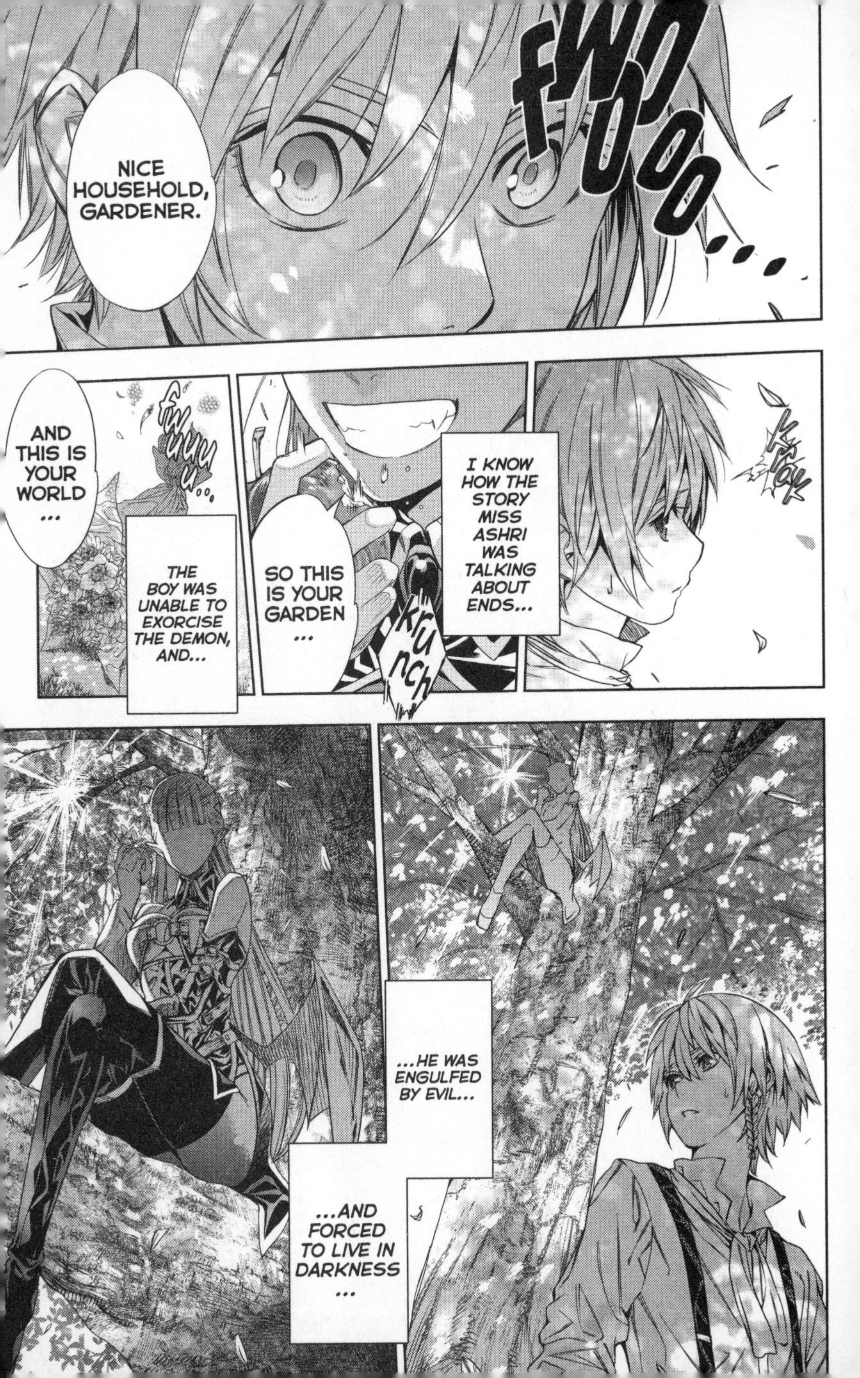
FWOOOO...
NICE HOUSEHOLD, GARDENER.
I KNOW HOW THE STORY MISS ASHRI WAS TALKING ABOUT ENDS...
SO THIS IS YOUR GARDEN ...
krunch
fwuuuuu...
AND THIS IS YOUR WORLD ...
THE BOY WAS UNABLE TO EXORCISE THE DEMON, AND...
...HE WAS ENGULFED BY EVIL...
...AND FORCED TO LIVE IN DARKNESS ...

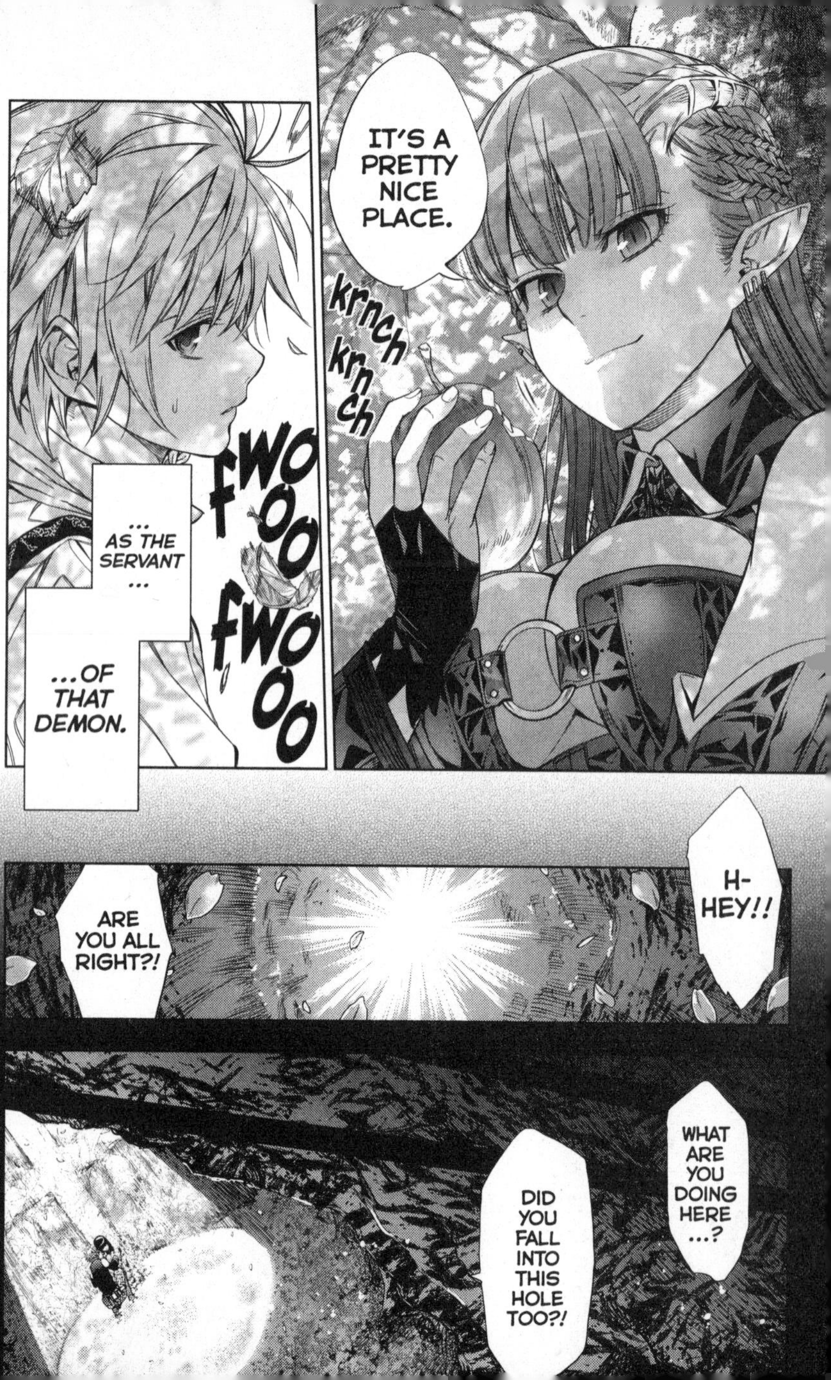
IT'S A PRETTY NICE PLACE.
krnch krnch
FWOO FWOO
... AS THE SERVANT ...
...OF THAT DEMON.
H-HEY!!
ARE YOU ALL RIGHT?!
WHAT ARE YOU DOING HERE ...?
DID YOU FALL INTO THIS HOLE TOO?!

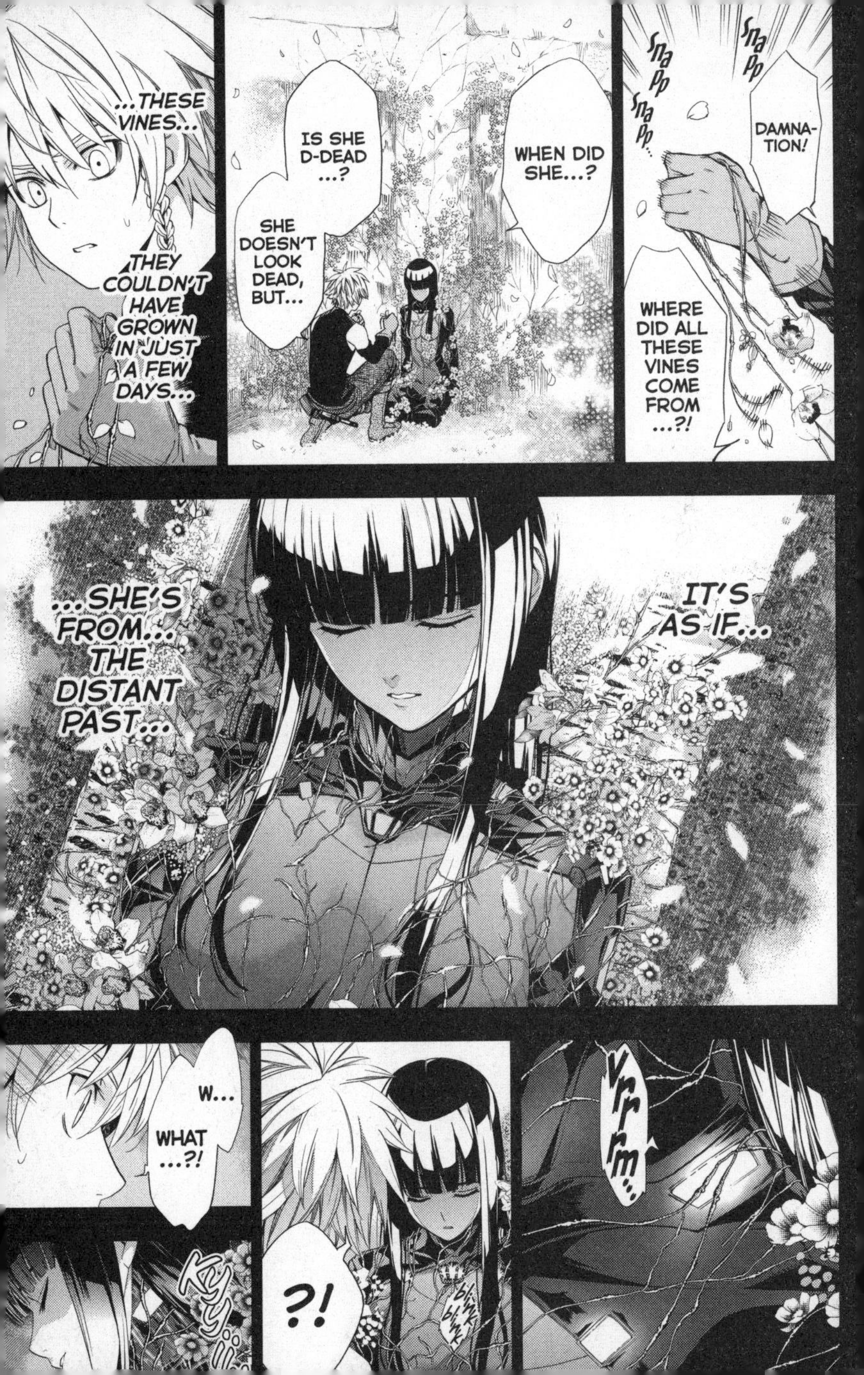
Snapp
Snapp...
Snapp
DAMNA-TION!
WHERE DID ALL THESE VINES COME FROM ...?!
WHEN DID SHE...?
IS SHE D-DEAD ...?
SHE DOESN'T LOOK DEAD, BUT...
...THESE VINES...
THEY COULDN'T HAVE GROWN IN JUST A FEW DAYS...
IT'S AS IF...
...SHE'S FROM... THE DISTANT PAST...
Vrrrm...
blink blink
?!
W...
WHAT ...?!

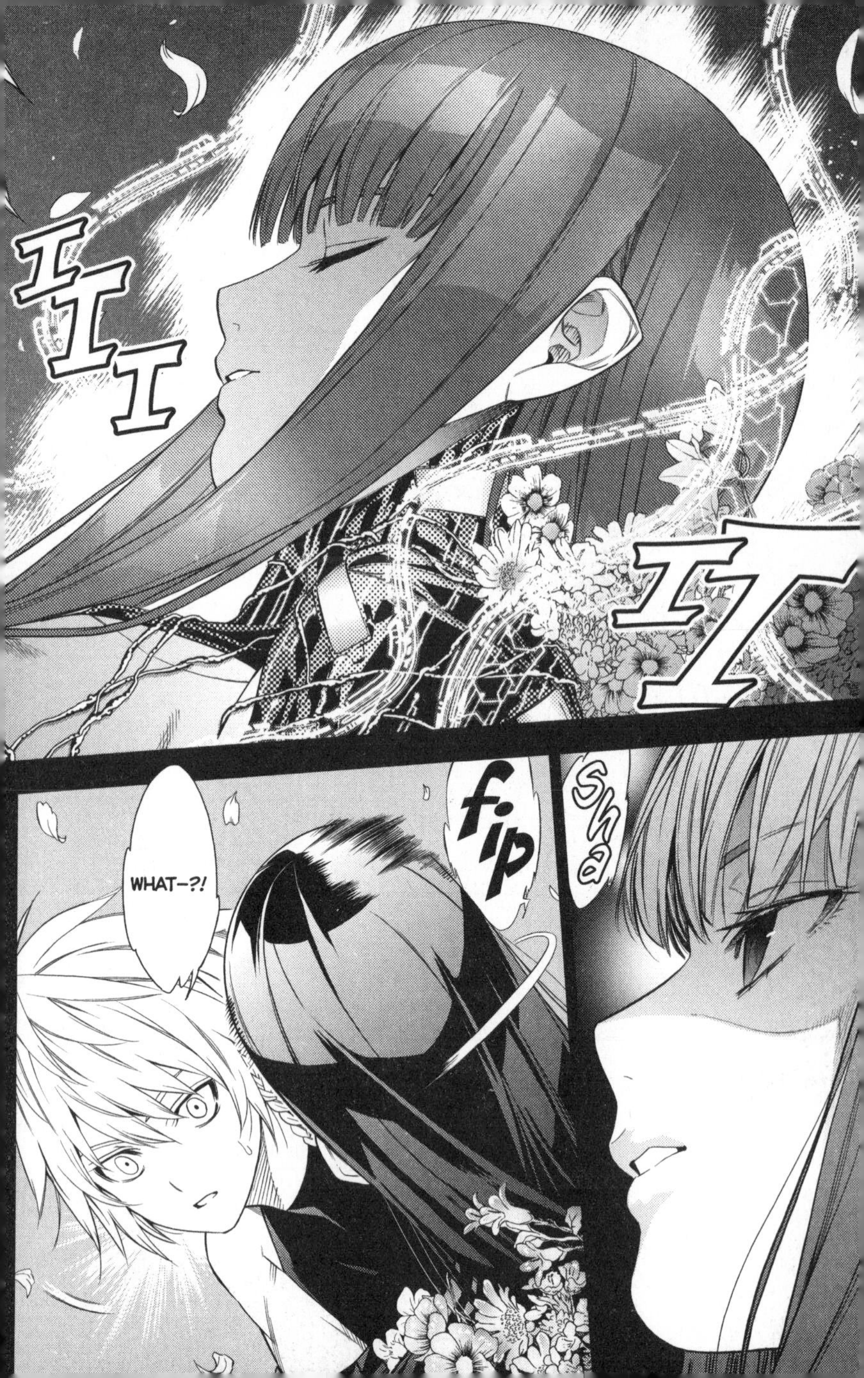
II
III
sha
fip
WHAT—?!

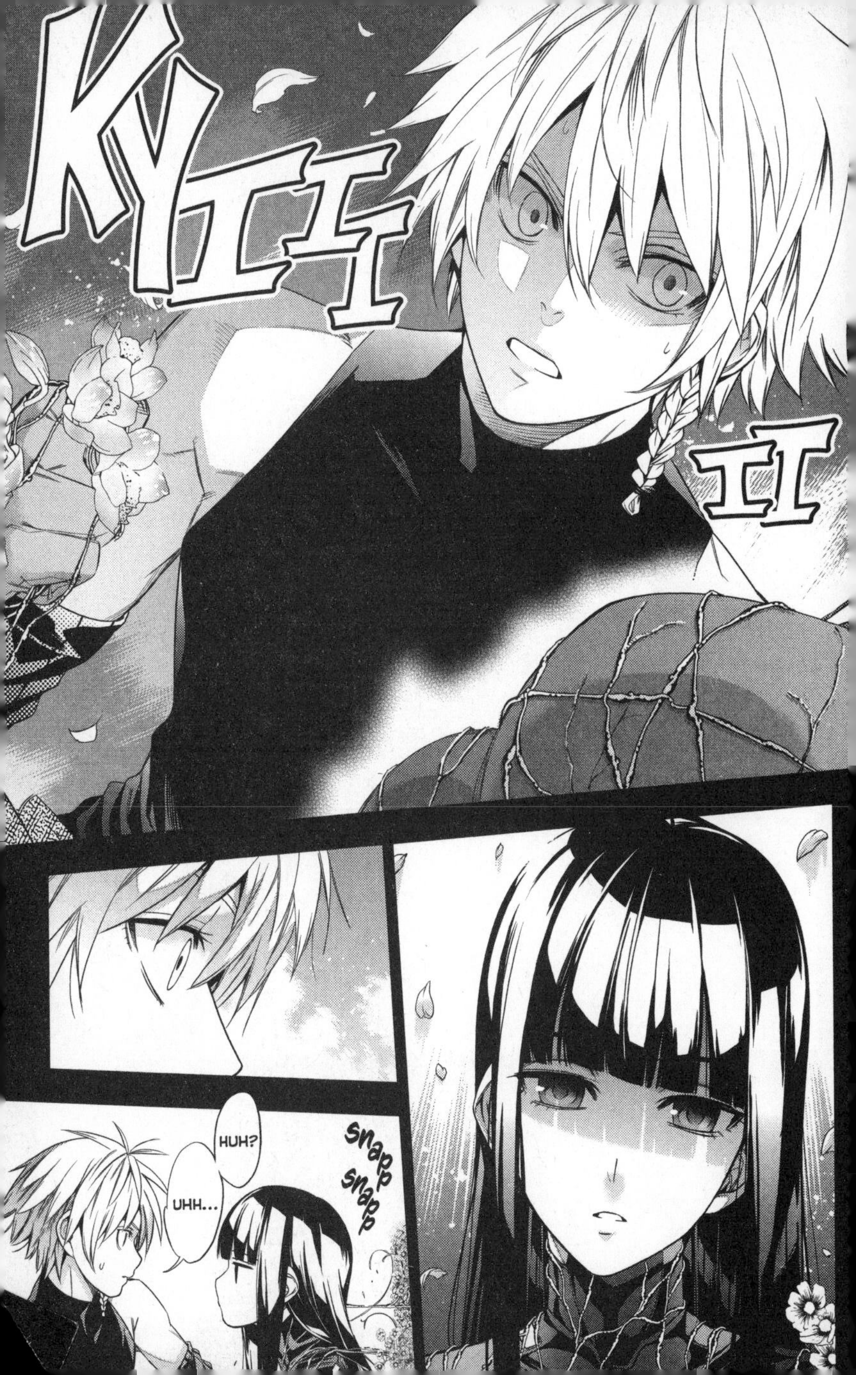
KYIIII
II
snapp snapp
HUH?
UHH...

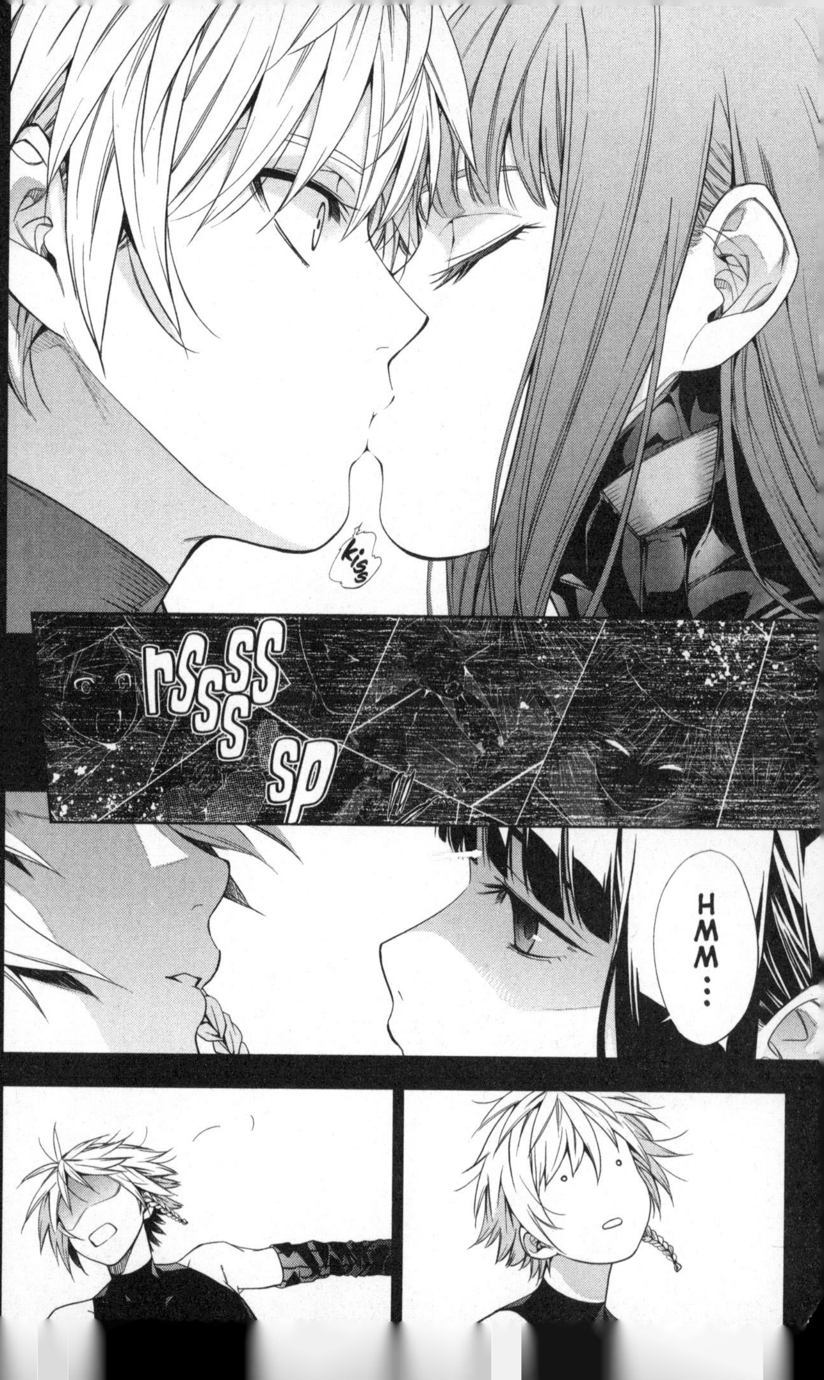
kiss
rSSSSS
sp
HMM...

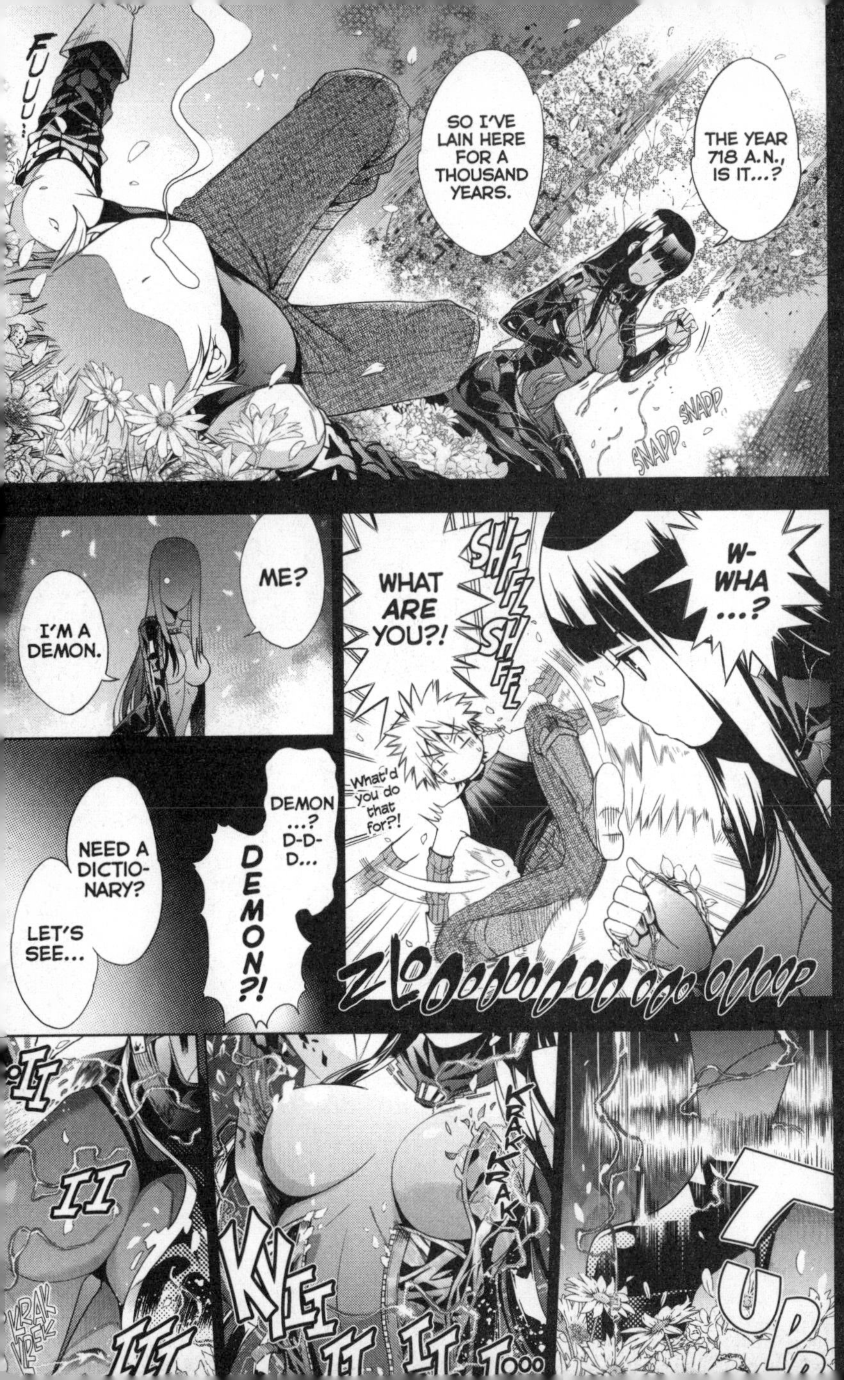
THE YEAR 718 A.N., IS IT...?
SO I'VE LAIN HERE FOR A THOUSAND YEARS.
SNAPP SNAPP
FUUUU...
W-WHA...?
WHAT ARE YOU?!
SHFFL SHFFL
What'd you do that for?!
ZLOOOOOOOOOOOOOOOP
ME?
I'M A DEMON.
DEMON...? D-D-D...
DEMON?!
NEED A DICTIONARY?
LET'S SEE...
T
UP
KRAK KRAK KRAK
KNII IT IT IT TOOO
II
II
KRAK KREK

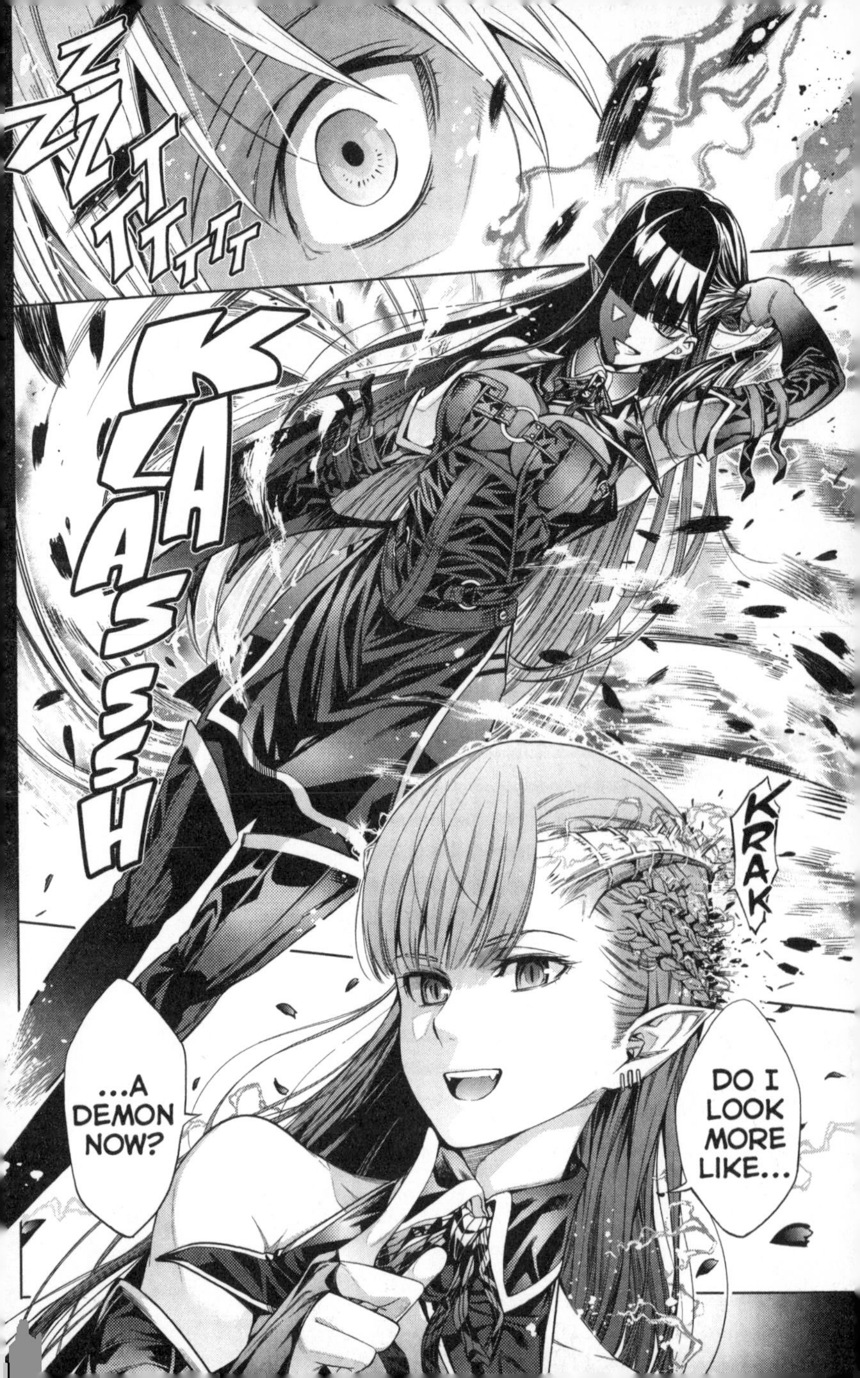
ZZZTTTTTT
KLASSSH
KRAK
DO I LOOK MORE LIKE...
...A DEMON NOW?

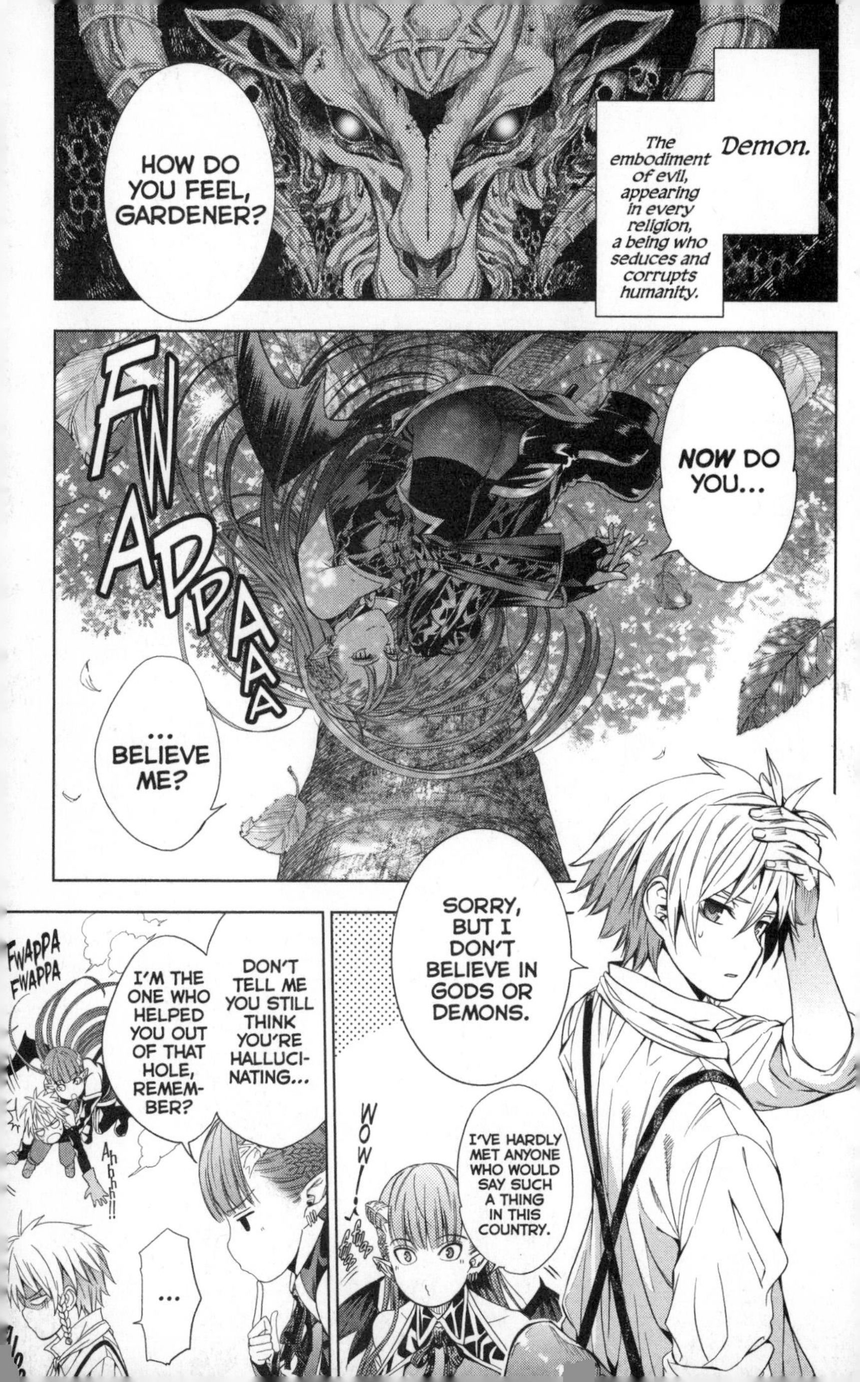
Demon.
The embodiment of evil, appearing in every religion, a being who seduces and corrupts humanity.
HOW DO YOU FEEL, GARDENER?
FWAPPAAA
NOW DO YOU...
...BELIEVE ME?
SORRY, BUT I DON'T BELIEVE IN GODS OR DEMONS.
WOW!
I'VE HARDLY MET ANYONE WHO WOULD SAY SUCH A THING IN THIS COUNTRY.
FWAPPA FWAPPA
DON'T TELL ME YOU STILL THINK YOU'RE HALLUCI-NATING...
I'M THE ONE WHO HELPED YOU OUT OF THAT HOLE, REMEM-BER?
...

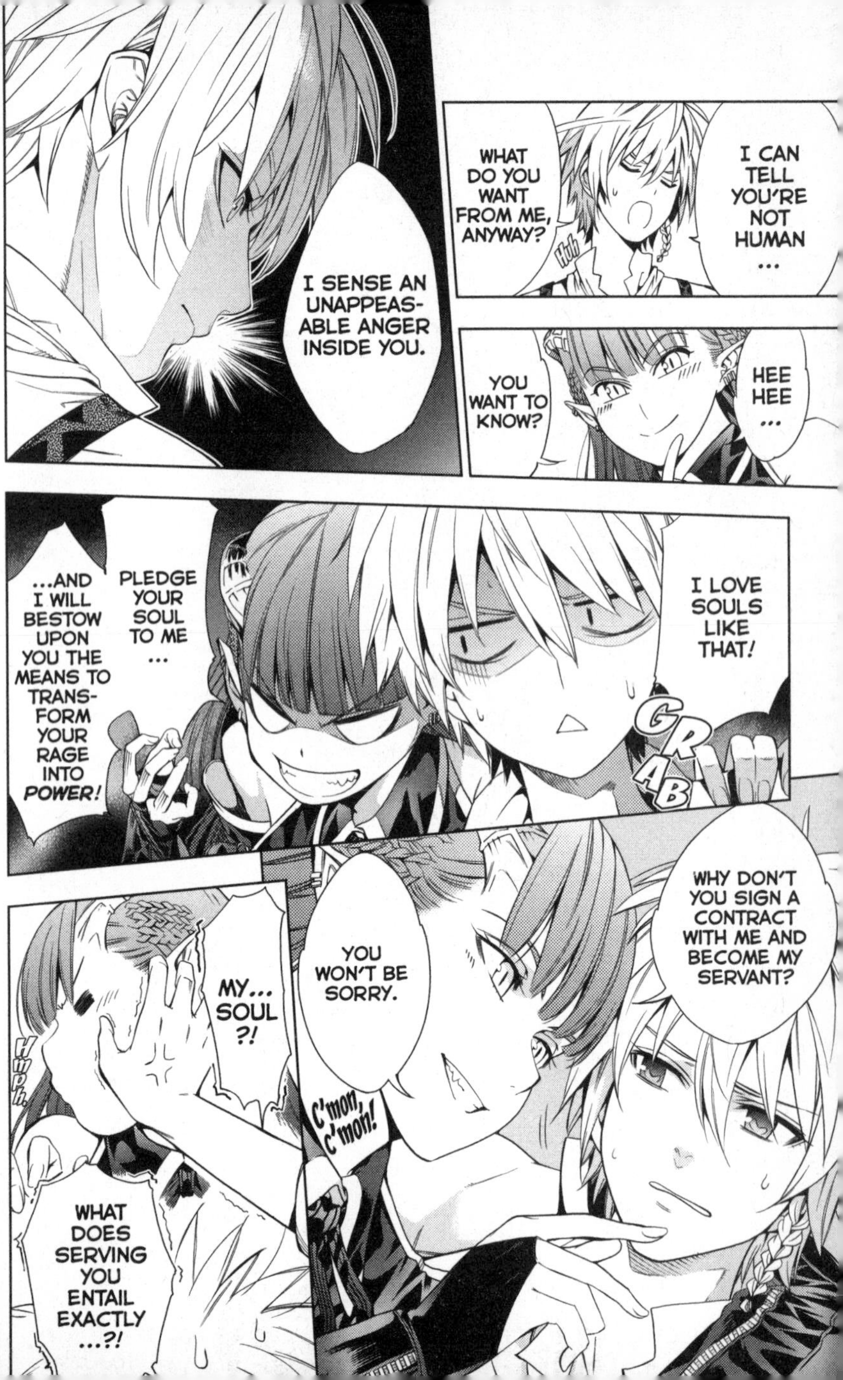
I CAN TELL YOU'RE NOT HUMAN ...
Huh
WHAT DO YOU WANT FROM ME, ANYWAY?
HEE HEE ...
YOU WANT TO KNOW?
I SENSE AN UNAPPEASABLE ANGER INSIDE YOU.
I LOVE SOULS LIKE THAT!
GRAB
PLEDGE YOUR SOUL TO ME ...
...AND I WILL BESTOW UPON YOU THE MEANS TO TRANSFORM YOUR RAGE INTO POWER!
WHY DON'T YOU SIGN A CONTRACT WITH ME AND BECOME MY SERVANT?
YOU WON'T BE SORRY.
C'mon, c'mon!
MY... SOUL ?!
Hmph
WHAT DOES SERVING YOU ENTAIL EXACTLY ...?!

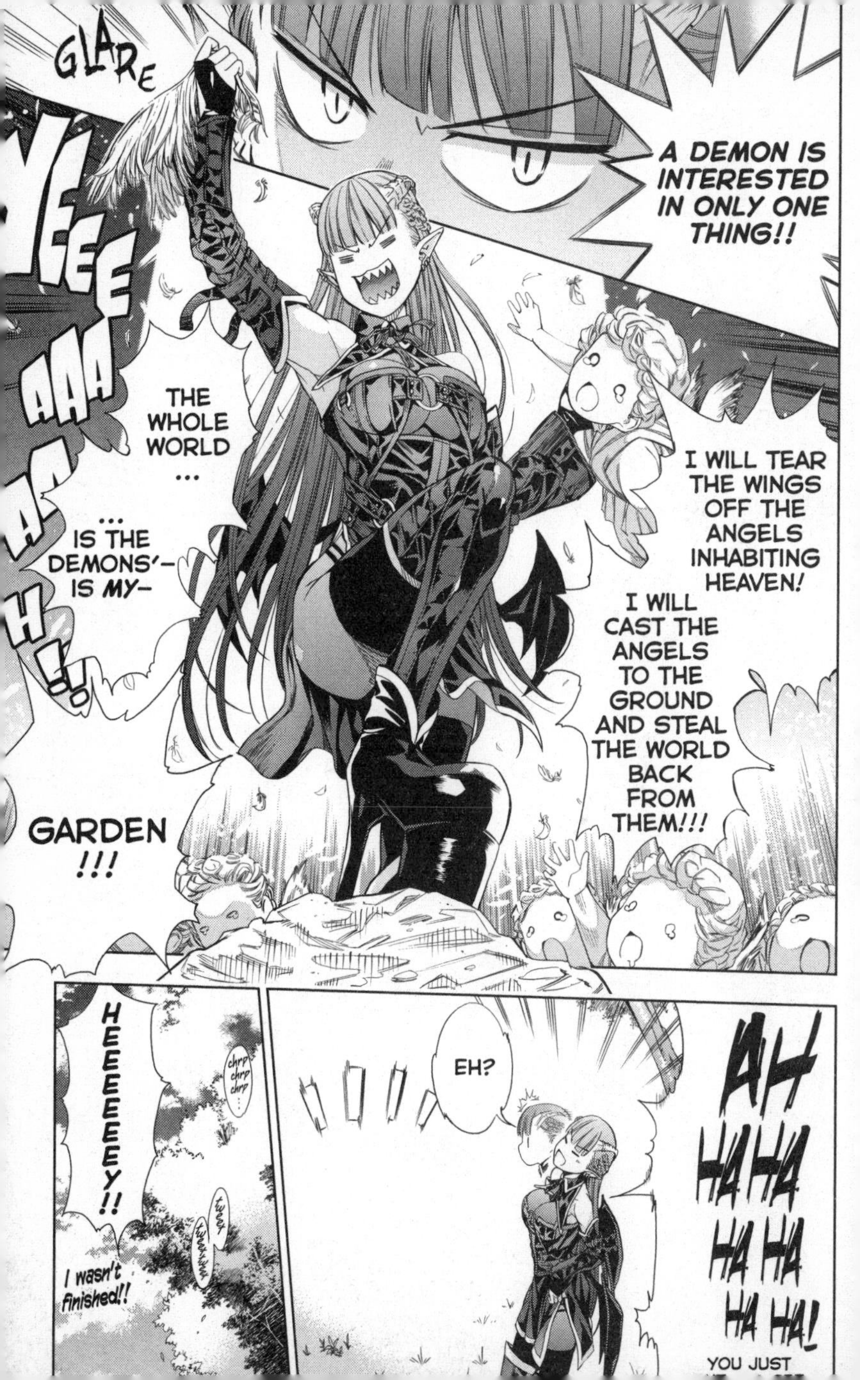
A DEMON IS INTERESTED IN ONLY ONE THING!!
GLARE
YEEEEAAAAAAH!!
I WILL TEAR THE WINGS OFF THE ANGELS INHABITING HEAVEN!
I WILL CAST THE ANGELS TO THE GROUND AND STEAL THE WORLD BACK FROM THEM!!!
THE WHOLE WORLD...
...IS THE DEMONS'— IS *MY*—
GARDEN!!!
AH HA HA HA HA HA HA HA!
YOU JUST
EH?
HEEEEEEEY!!
chrp chrp chrp...
tweet tweeeeeet
I wasn't finished!!

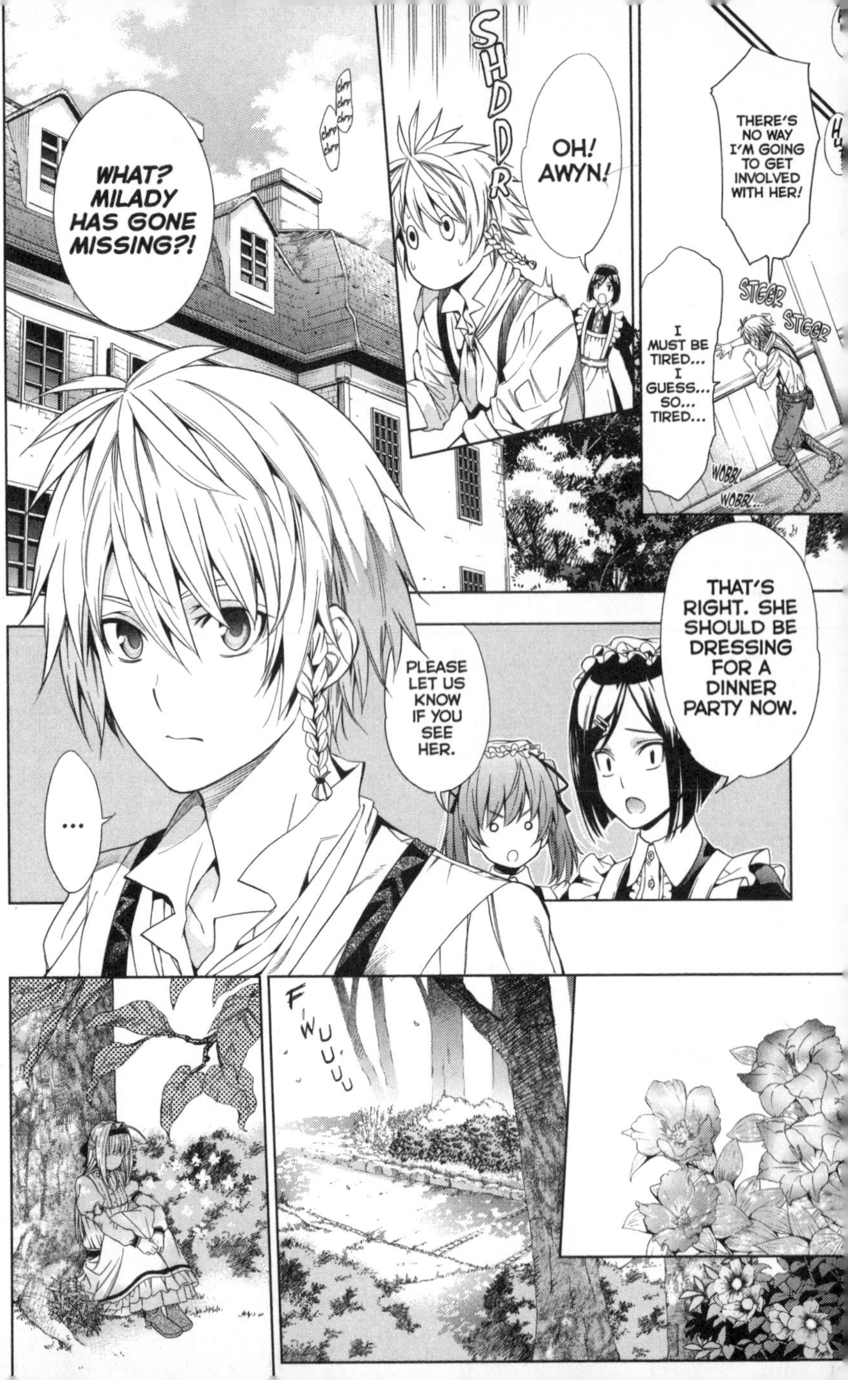
THERE'S NO WAY I'M GOING TO GET INVOLVED WITH HER!
STGGR STGGR
I MUST BE TIRED... I GUESS... SO... TIRED...
WOBBL WOBBL...
SHDDR
OH! AWYN!
WHAT? MILADY HAS GONE MISSING?!
THAT'S RIGHT. SHE SHOULD BE DRESSING FOR A DINNER PARTY NOW.
PLEASE LET US KNOW IF YOU SEE HER.
...
FWUUUU

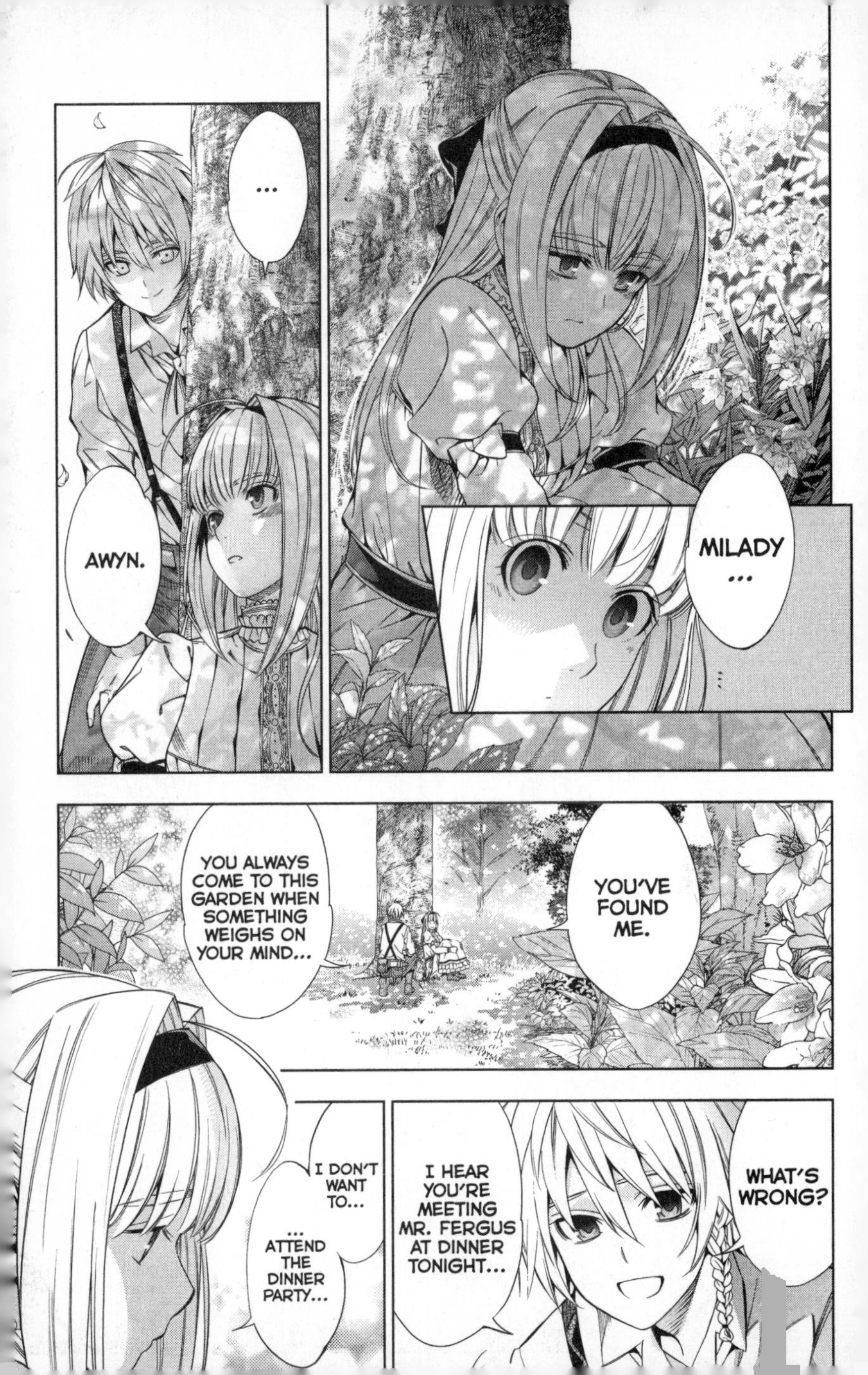
MILADY ...
...
AWYN.
YOU'VE FOUND ME.
YOU ALWAYS COME TO THIS GARDEN WHEN SOMETHING WEIGHS ON YOUR MIND...
WHAT'S WRONG?
I HEAR YOU'RE MEETING MR. FERGUS AT DINNER TONIGHT...
I DON'T WANT TO...
... ATTEND THE DINNER PARTY...

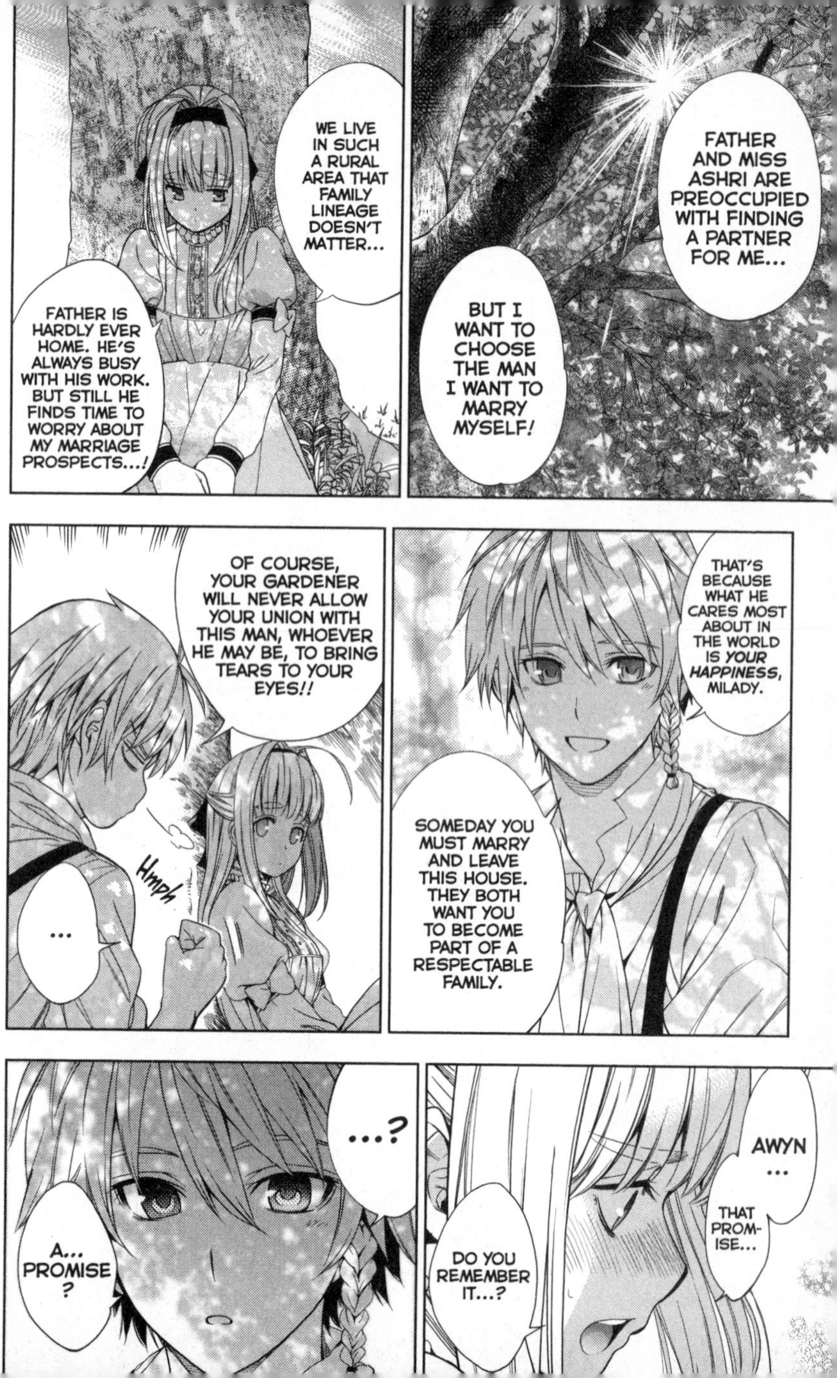
FATHER AND MISS ASHRI ARE PREOCCUPIED WITH FINDING A PARTNER FOR ME...
BUT I WANT TO CHOOSE THE MAN I WANT TO MARRY MYSELF!
WE LIVE IN SUCH A RURAL AREA THAT FAMILY LINEAGE DOESN'T MATTER...
FATHER IS HARDLY EVER HOME. HE'S ALWAYS BUSY WITH HIS WORK. BUT STILL HE FINDS TIME TO WORRY ABOUT MY MARRIAGE PROSPECTS...!
THAT'S BECAUSE WHAT HE CARES MOST ABOUT IN THE WORLD IS *YOUR HAPPINESS*, MILADY.
SOMEDAY YOU MUST MARRY AND LEAVE THIS HOUSE. THEY BOTH WANT YOU TO BECOME PART OF A RESPECTABLE FAMILY.
OF COURSE, YOUR GARDENER WILL NEVER ALLOW YOUR UNION WITH THIS MAN, WHOEVER HE MAY BE, TO BRING TEARS TO YOUR EYES!!
Hmph
...
AWYN ...
THAT PROMISE...
DO YOU REMEMBER IT...?
...?
A... PROMISE ?

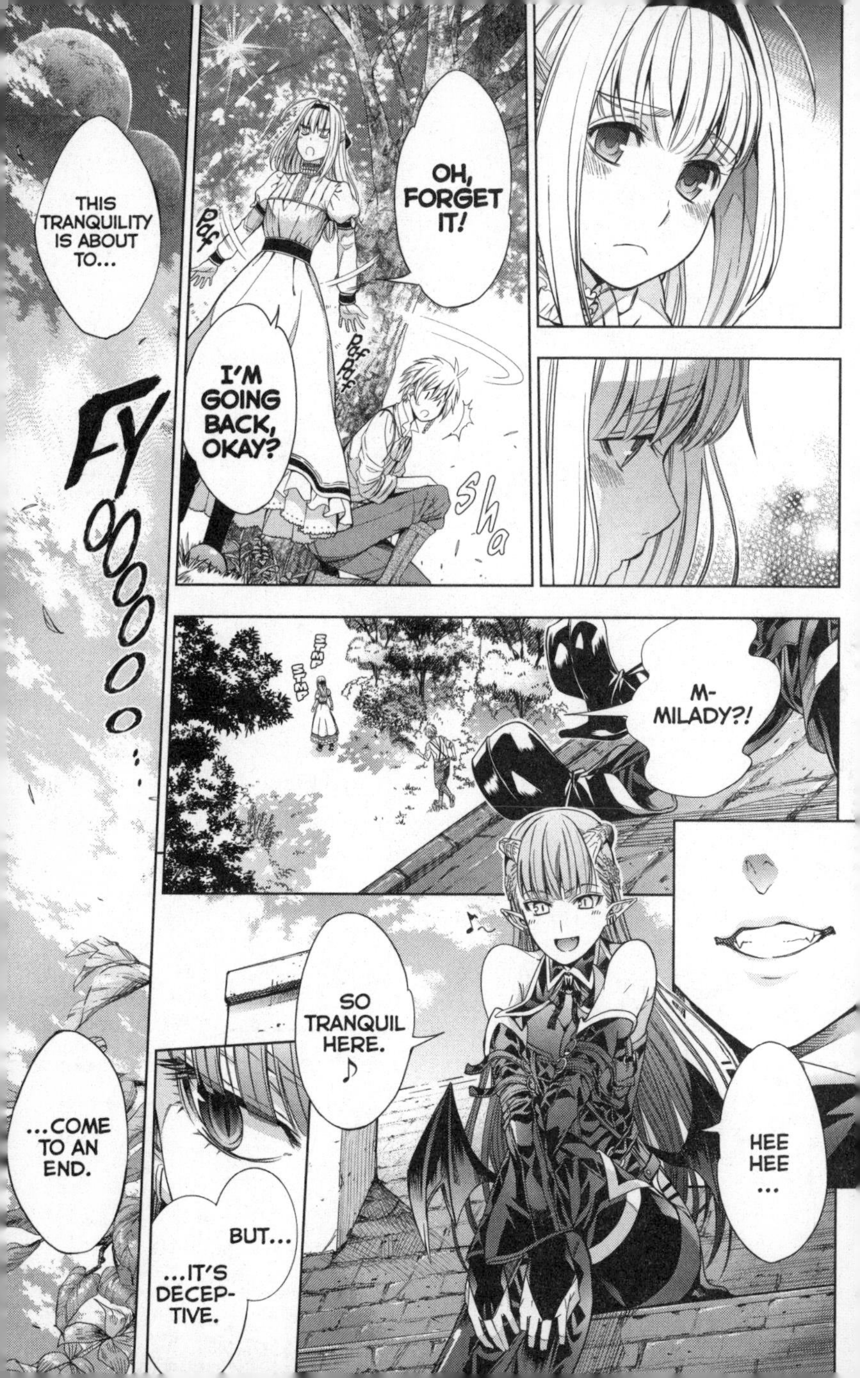
OH, FORGET IT!
Paf
I'M GOING BACK, OKAY?
Paf paf
sha
M-MILADY?!
STMP STMP
HEE HEE...
SO TRANQUIL HERE. ♪
BUT...
...IT'S DECEPTIVE.
THIS TRANQUILITY IS ABOUT TO...
FYOOOOOO...
...COME TO AN END.

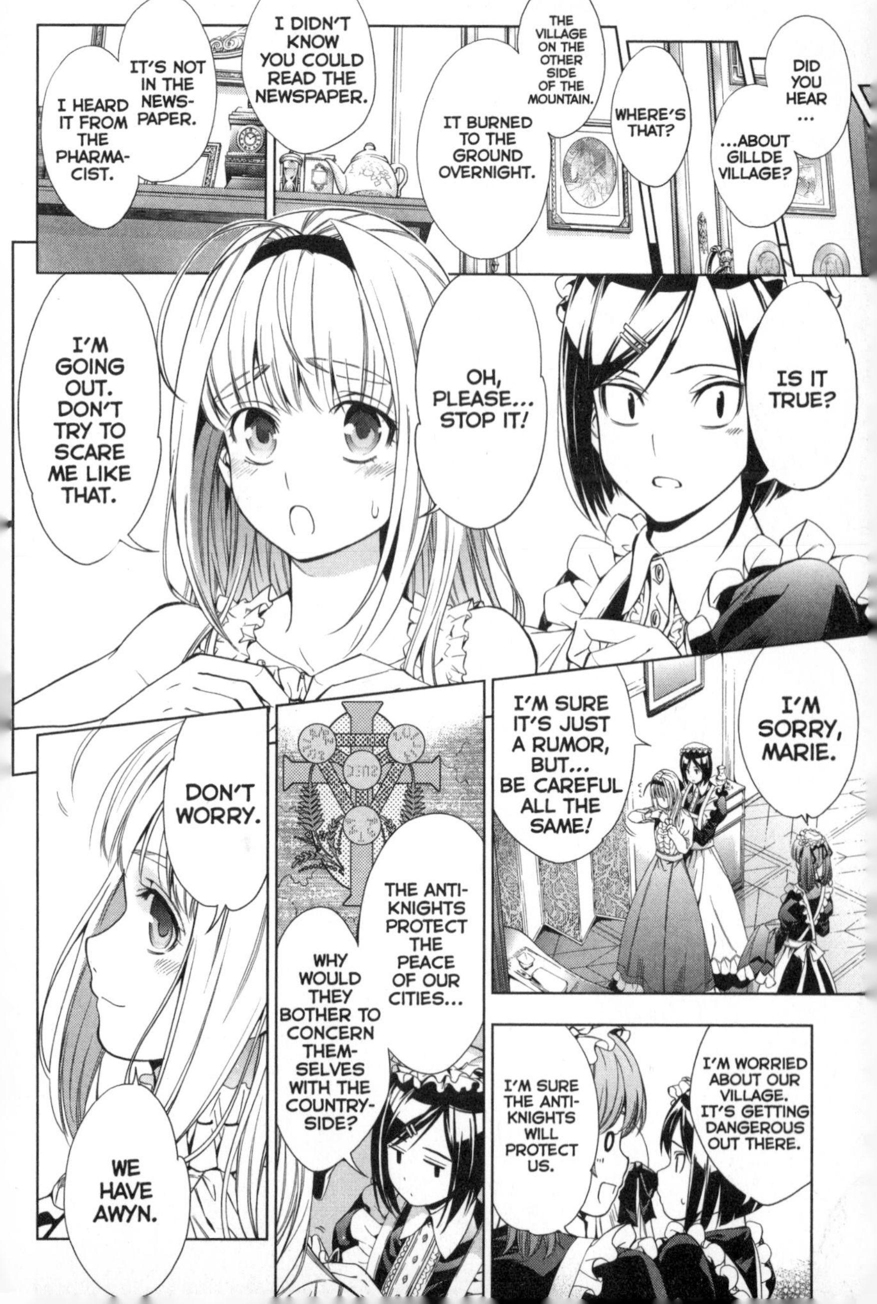
DID YOU HEAR ...
...ABOUT GILLDE VILLAGE?
WHERE'S THAT?
THE VILLAGE ON THE OTHER SIDE OF THE MOUNTAIN.
IT BURNED TO THE GROUND OVERNIGHT.
I DIDN'T KNOW YOU COULD READ THE NEWSPAPER.
IT'S NOT IN THE NEWS-PAPER.
I HEARD IT FROM THE PHARMA-CIST.
IS IT TRUE?
OH, PLEASE... STOP IT!
I'M GOING OUT. DON'T TRY TO SCARE ME LIKE THAT.
I'M SORRY, MARIE.
I'M SURE IT'S JUST A RUMOR, BUT... BE CAREFUL ALL THE SAME!
I'M WORRIED ABOUT OUR VILLAGE. IT'S GETTING DANGEROUS OUT THERE.
I'M SURE THE ANTI-KNIGHTS WILL PROTECT US.
THE ANTI-KNIGHTS PROTECT THE PEACE OF OUR CITIES...
WHY WOULD THEY BOTHER TO CONCERN THEM-SELVES WITH THE COUNTRY-SIDE?
DON'T WORRY.
WE HAVE AWYN.

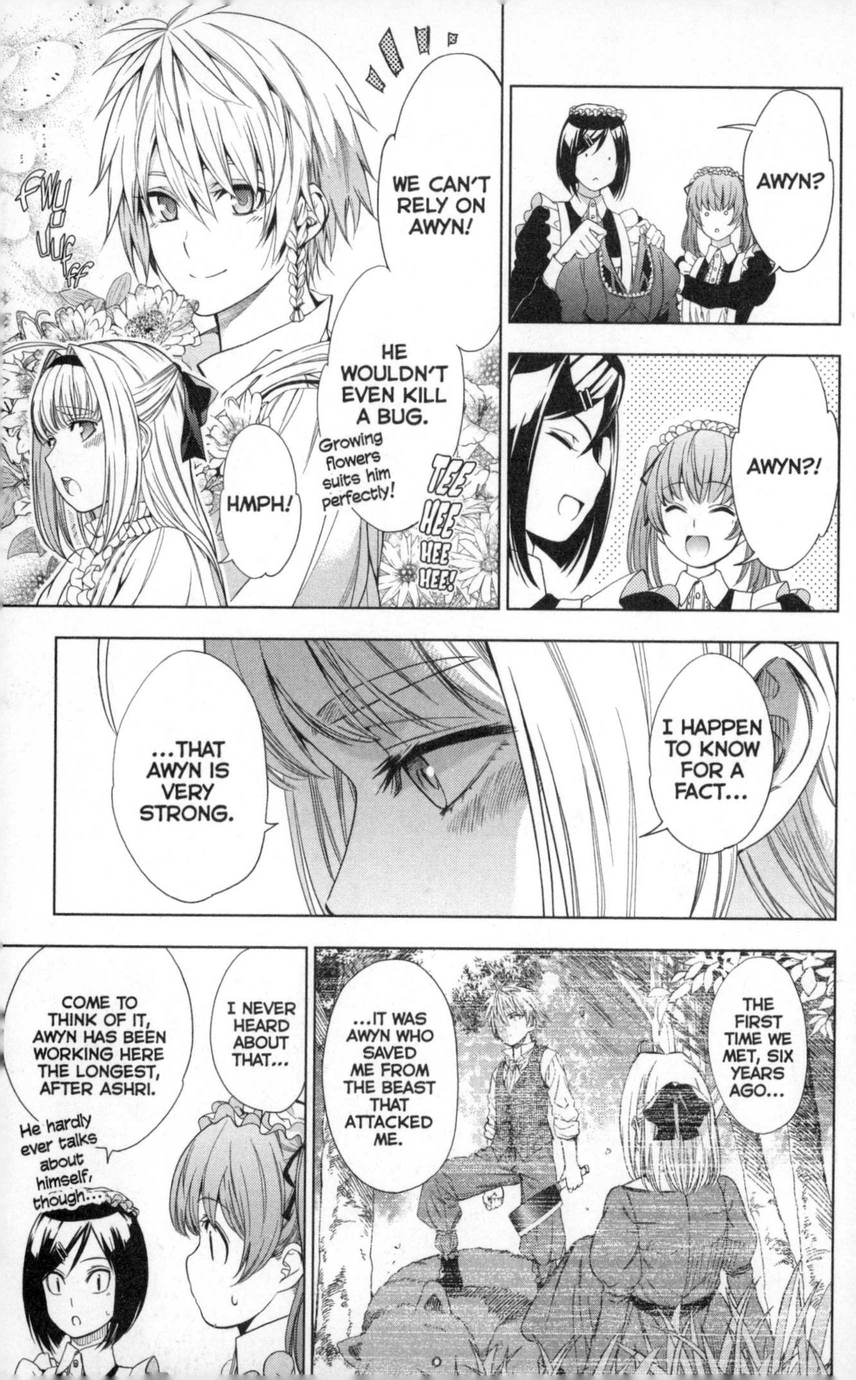
AWYN?
AWYN?!
WE CAN'T RELY ON AWYN!
HE WOULDN'T EVEN KILL A BUG.
Growing flowers suits him perfectly!
TEE HEE HEE HEE!
HMPH!
I HAPPEN TO KNOW FOR A FACT...
...THAT AWYN IS VERY STRONG.
THE FIRST TIME WE MET, SIX YEARS AGO...
...IT WAS AWYN WHO SAVED ME FROM THE BEAST THAT ATTACKED ME.
I NEVER HEARD ABOUT THAT...
COME TO THINK OF IT, AWYN HAS BEEN WORKING HERE THE LONGEST, AFTER ASHRI.
He hardly ever talks about himself, though...

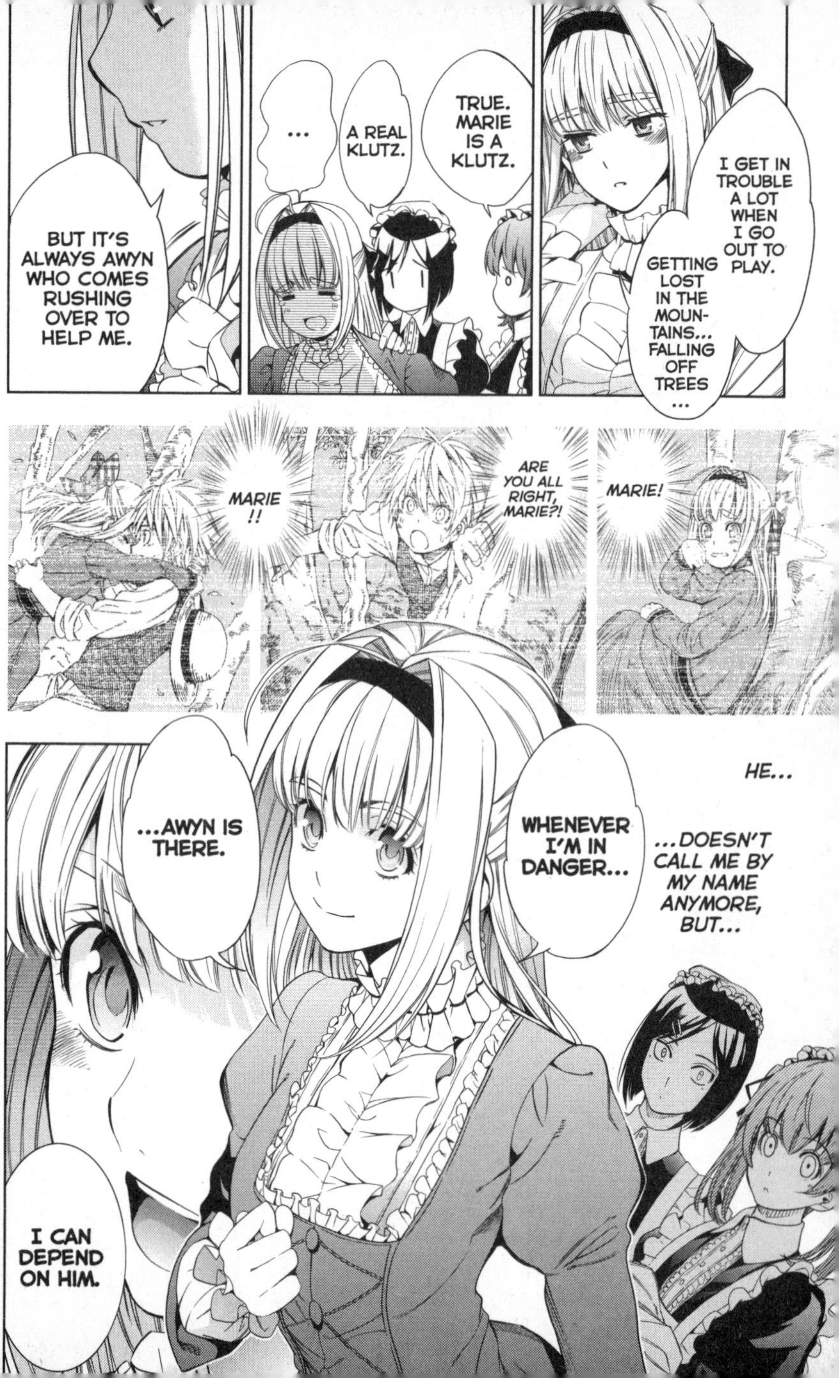
I GET IN TROUBLE A LOT WHEN I GO OUT TO PLAY.
GETTING LOST IN THE MOUNTAINS... FALLING OFF TREES...
TRUE. MARIE IS A KLUTZ.
A REAL KLUTZ.
...
BUT IT'S ALWAYS AWYN WHO COMES RUSHING OVER TO HELP ME.
MARIE!
ARE YOU ALL RIGHT, MARIE?!
MARIE !!
HE...
...DOESN'T CALL ME BY MY NAME ANYMORE, BUT...
WHENEVER I'M IN DANGER...
...AWYN IS THERE.
I CAN DEPEND ON HIM.

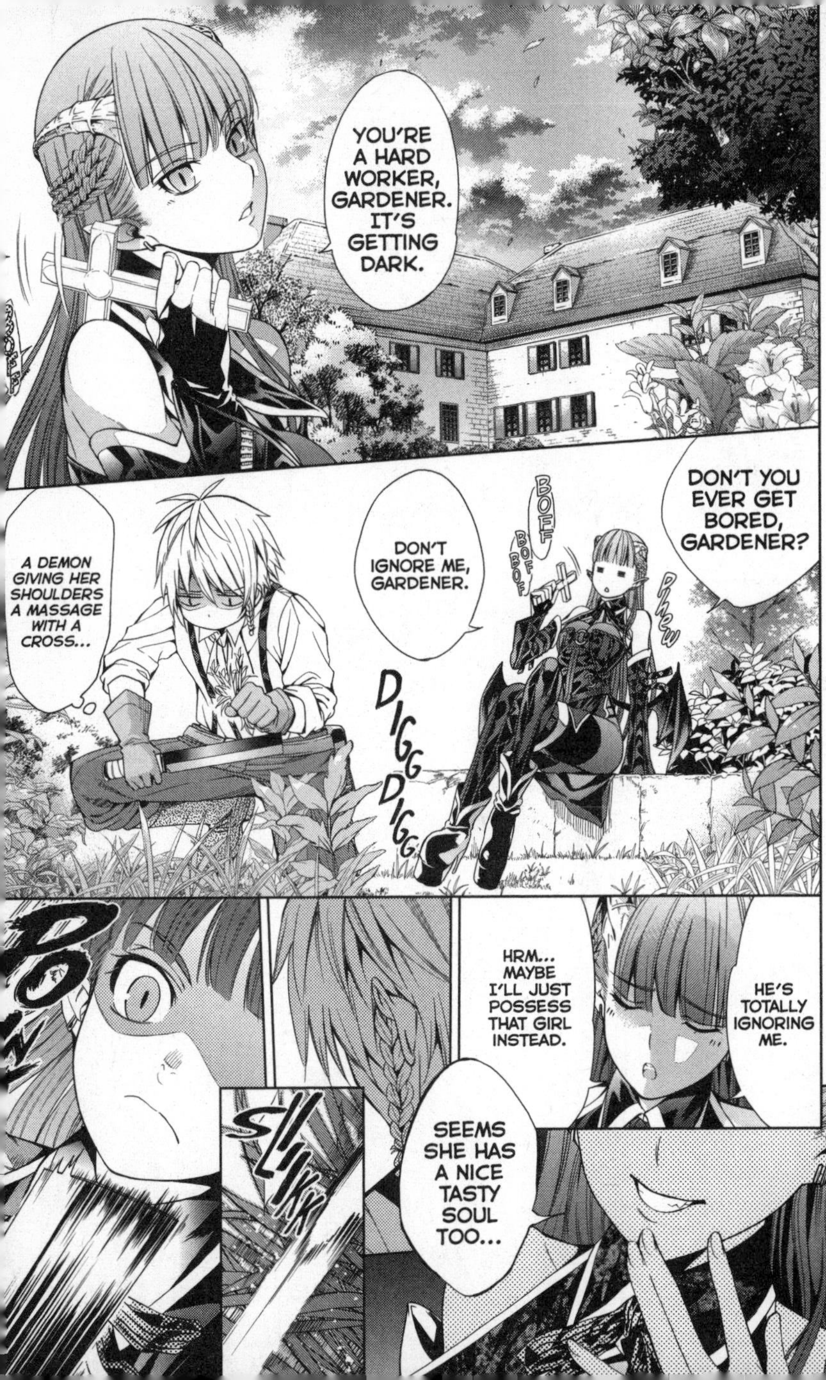
YOU'RE A HARD WORKER, GARDENER. IT'S GETTING DARK.
DON'T YOU EVER GET BORED, GARDENER?
BOFF
BOFF BOFF
PHEW
DON'T IGNORE ME, GARDENER.
DIGG DIGG DIGG
A DEMON GIVING HER SHOULDERS A MASSAGE WITH A CROSS...
HE'S TOTALLY IGNORING ME.
HRM... MAYBE I'LL JUST POSSESS THAT GIRL INSTEAD.
SEEMS SHE HAS A NICE TASTY SOUL TOO...
SLIKK

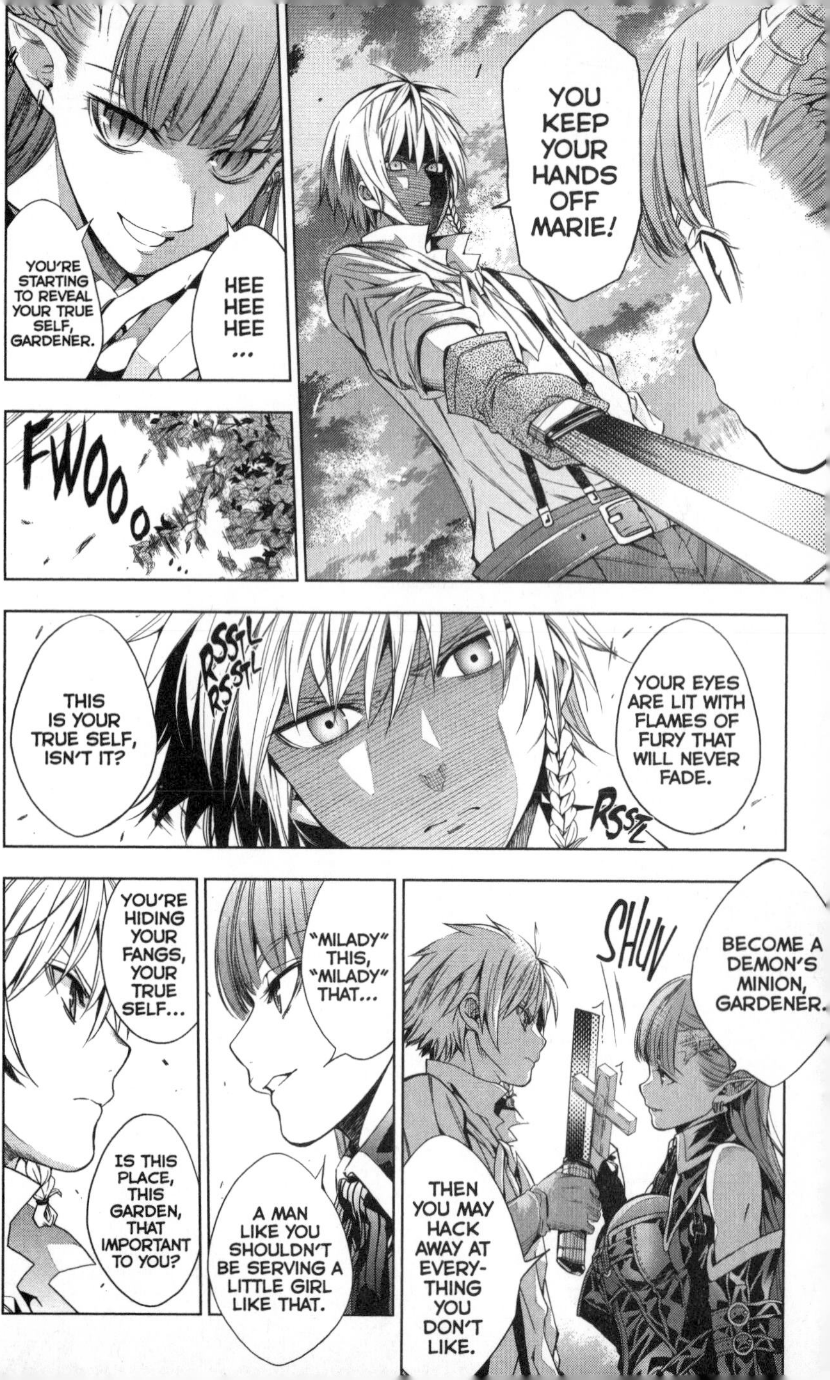
YOU KEEP YOUR HANDS OFF MARIE!
HEE HEE HEE...
YOU'RE STARTING TO REVEAL YOUR TRUE SELF, GARDENER.
FWOOO...
YOUR EYES ARE LIT WITH FLAMES OF FURY THAT WILL NEVER FADE.
RSSTL
RSSTL RSSTL
THIS IS YOUR TRUE SELF, ISN'T IT?
BECOME A DEMON'S MINION, GARDENER.
SHUV
THEN YOU MAY HACK AWAY AT EVERY-THING YOU DON'T LIKE.
"MILADY" THIS, "MILADY" THAT...
A MAN LIKE YOU SHOULDN'T BE SERVING A LITTLE GIRL LIKE THAT.
YOU'RE HIDING YOUR FANGS, YOUR TRUE SELF...
IS THIS PLACE, THIS GARDEN, THAT IMPORTANT TO YOU?

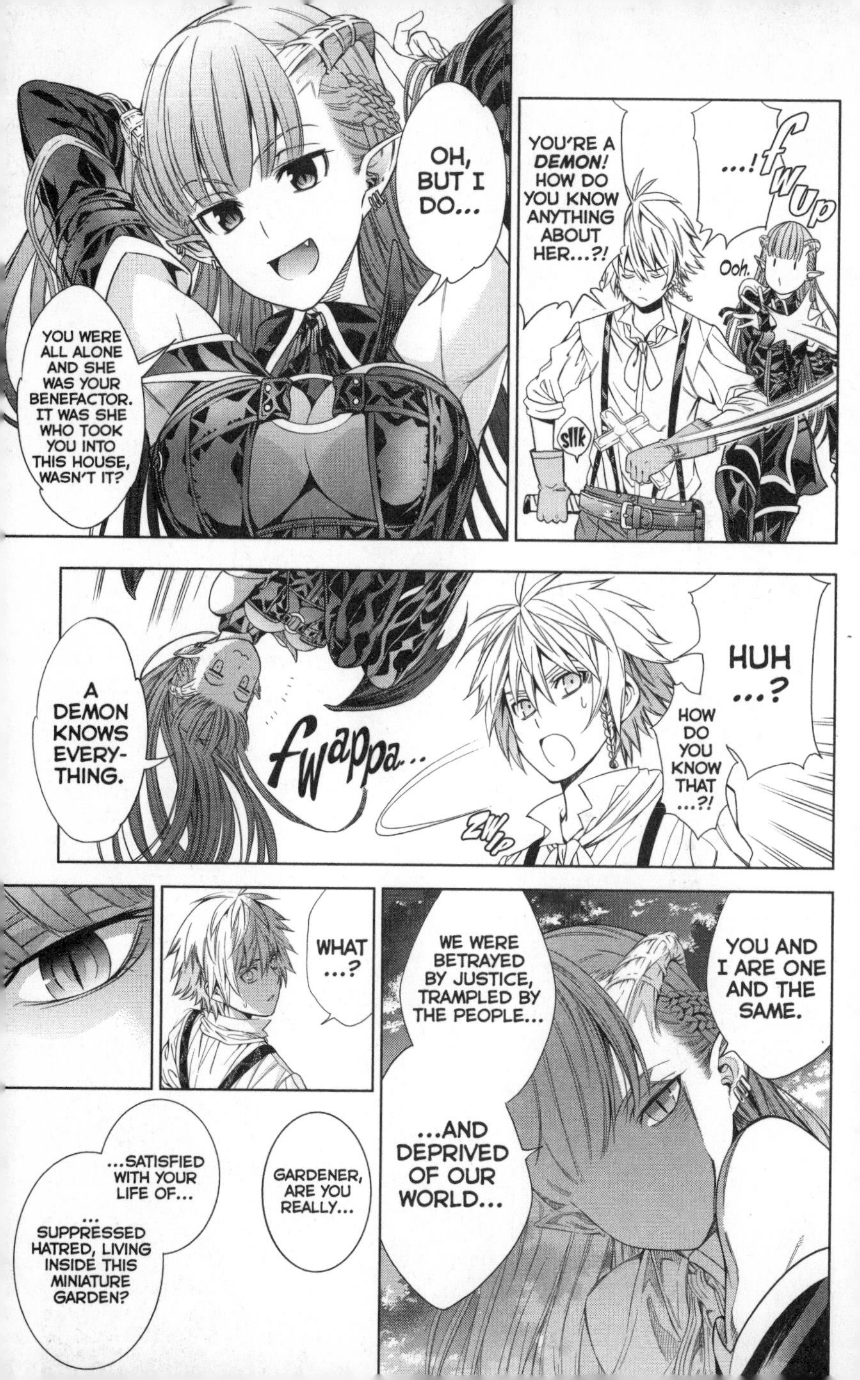
...!
fwup
YOU'RE A *DEMON!* HOW DO YOU KNOW ANYTHING ABOUT HER...?!
Ooh.
sllk
OH, BUT I DO...
YOU WERE ALL ALONE AND SHE WAS YOUR BENEFACTOR. IT WAS SHE WHO TOOK YOU INTO THIS HOUSE, WASN'T IT?
HUH ...?
HOW DO YOU KNOW THAT ...?!
zwip
fwappa...
A DEMON KNOWS EVERY-THING.
YOU AND I ARE ONE AND THE SAME.
WE WERE BETRAYED BY JUSTICE, TRAMPLED BY THE PEOPLE...
...AND DEPRIVED OF OUR WORLD...
WHAT ...?
GARDENER, ARE YOU REALLY...
...SATISFIED WITH YOUR LIFE OF...
... SUPPRESSED HATRED, LIVING INSIDE THIS MINIATURE GARDEN?

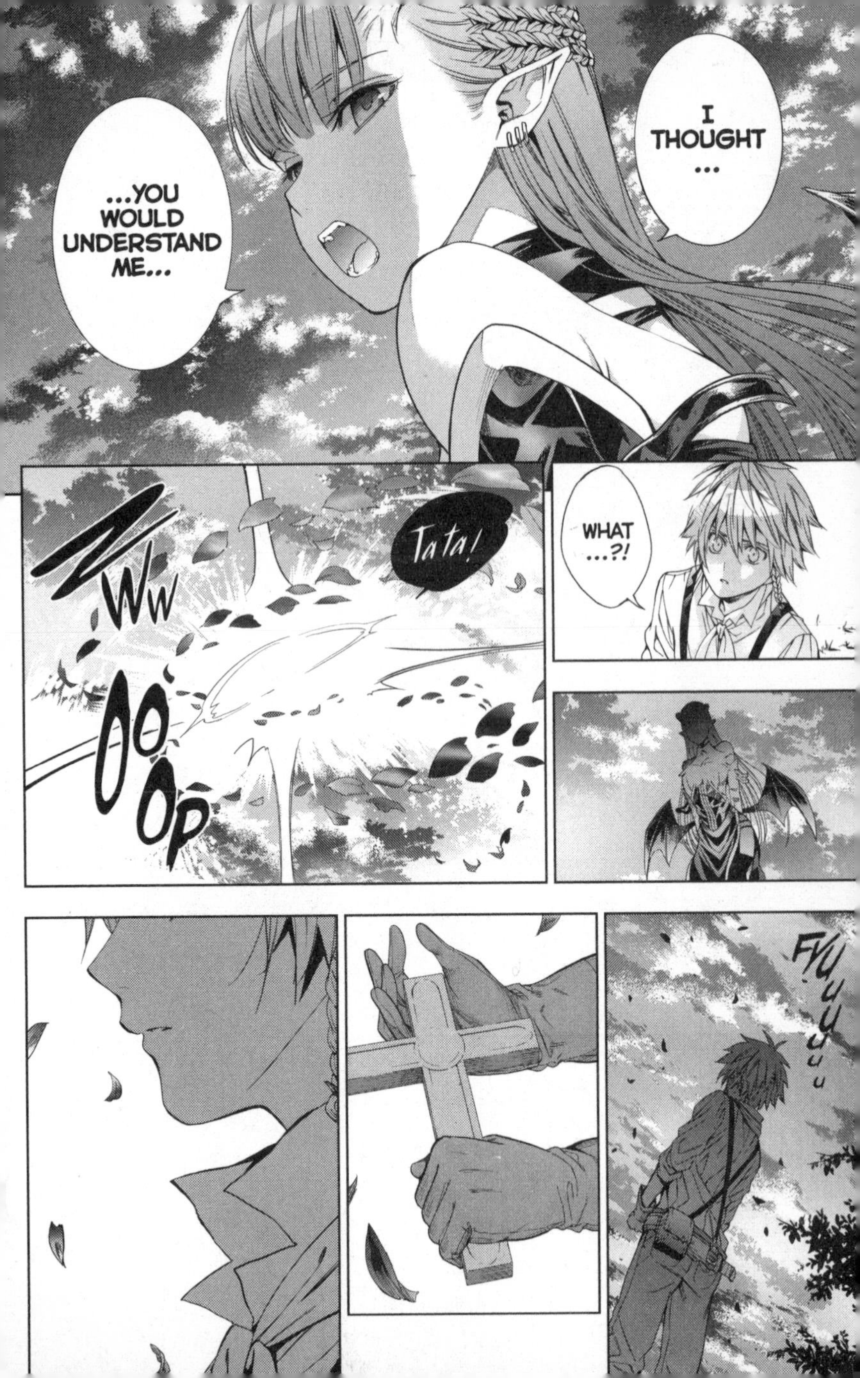
I THOUGHT ...
...YOU WOULD UNDERSTAND ME...
WHAT ...?!
Tata!
WWOOOOP
FYUUUUUU

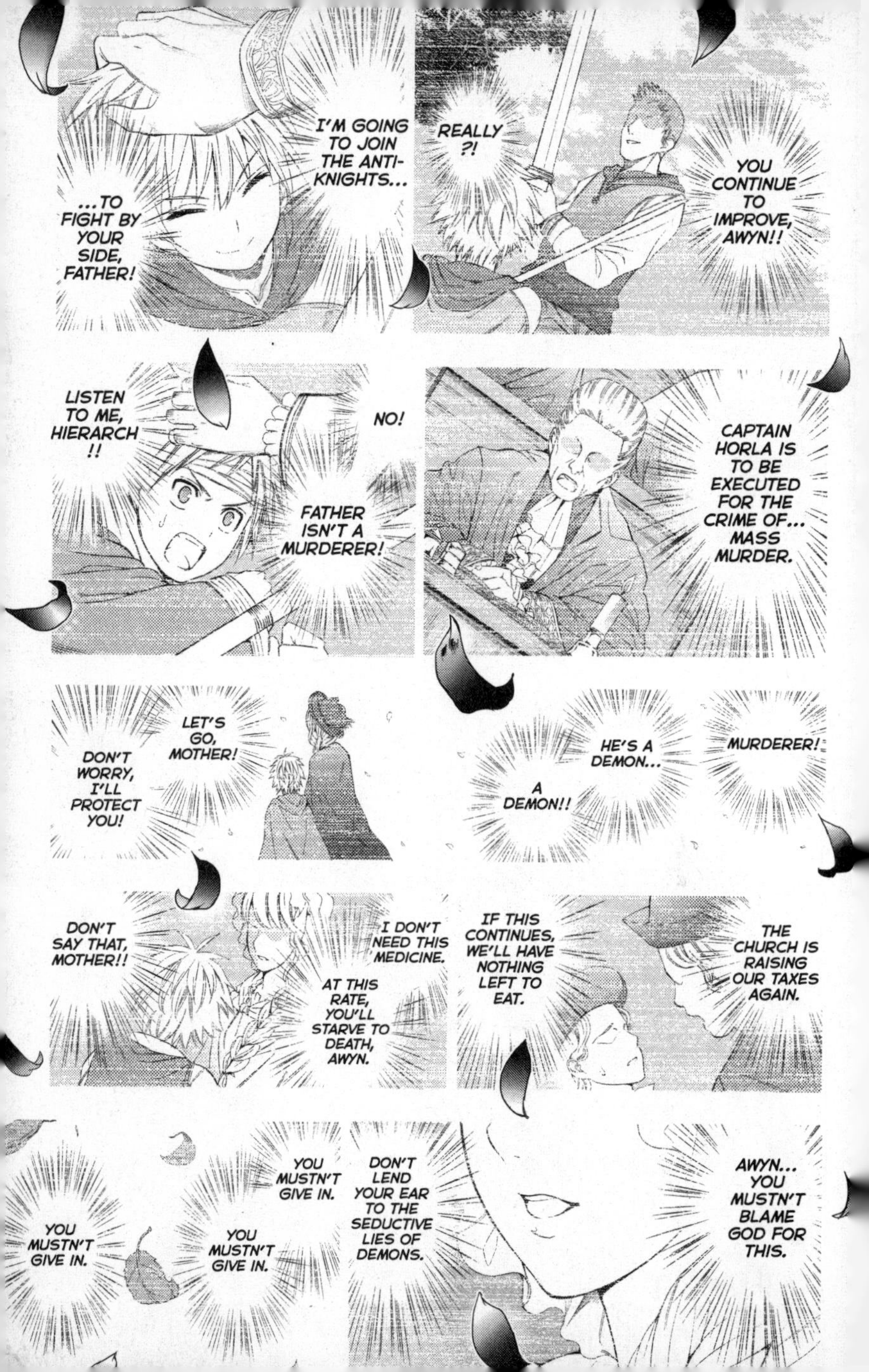
YOU CONTINUE TO IMPROVE, AWYN!!
REALLY ?!
I'M GOING TO JOIN THE ANTI-KNIGHTS...
...TO FIGHT BY YOUR SIDE, FATHER!
CAPTAIN HORLA IS TO BE EXECUTED FOR THE CRIME OF... MASS MURDER.
NO!
FATHER ISN'T A MURDERER!
LISTEN TO ME, HIERARCH !!
MURDERER!
HE'S A DEMON...
A DEMON!!
LET'S GO, MOTHER!
DON'T WORRY, I'LL PROTECT YOU!
THE CHURCH IS RAISING OUR TAXES AGAIN.
IF THIS CONTINUES, WE'LL HAVE NOTHING LEFT TO EAT.
I DON'T NEED THIS MEDICINE.
AT THIS RATE, YOU'LL STARVE TO DEATH, AWYN.
DON'T SAY THAT, MOTHER!!
AWYN... YOU MUSTN'T BLAME GOD FOR THIS.
DON'T LEND YOUR EAR TO THE SEDUCTIVE LIES OF DEMONS.
YOU MUSTN'T GIVE IN.
YOU MUSTN'T GIVE IN.
YOU MUSTN'T GIVE IN.

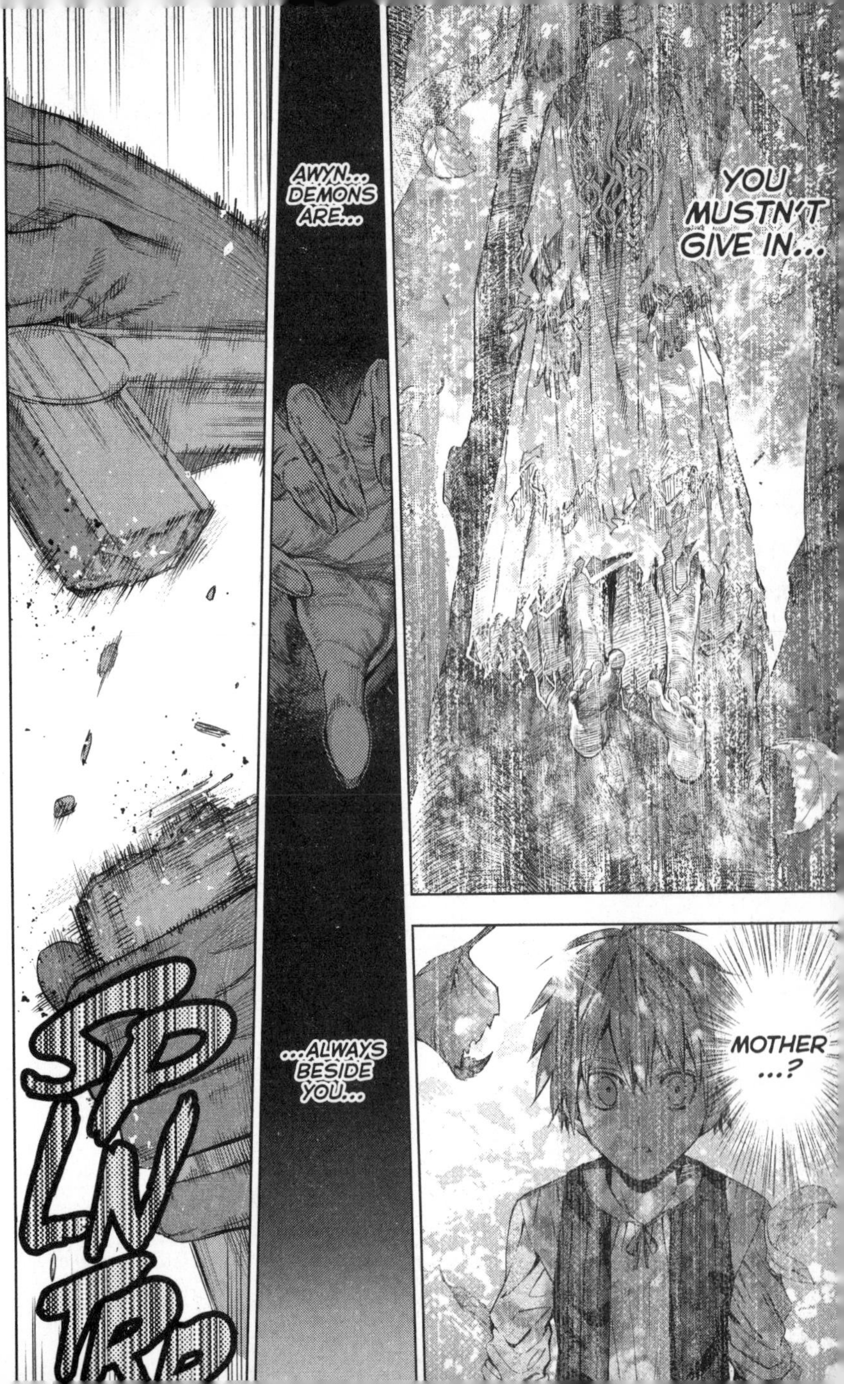
YOU MUSTN'T GIVE IN...
MOTHER ...?
AWYN... DEMONS ARE...
...ALWAYS BESIDE YOU...
SPLNTR

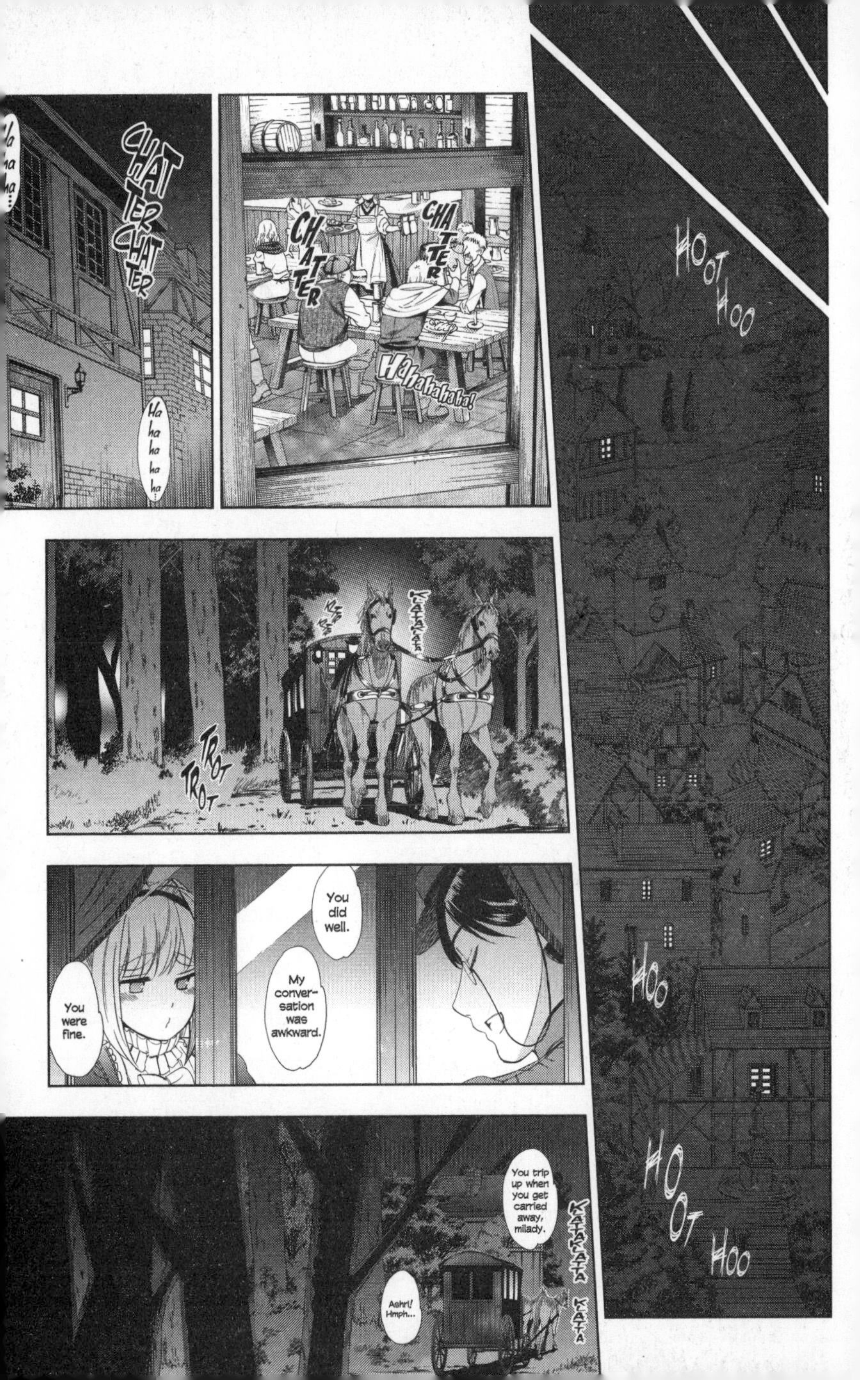
HOOT HOO
HOO
HOOT HOO
CHATTER
CHATTER
Hahahahaha!
CHATTER CHATTER
Ha ha ha ha ha...
Ha ha ha...
KATAKATA
TROT TROT
You did well.
My conversation was awkward.
You were fine.
You trip up when you get carried away, milady.
KATAKATA KATA
Ashri! Hmph...

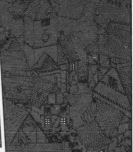

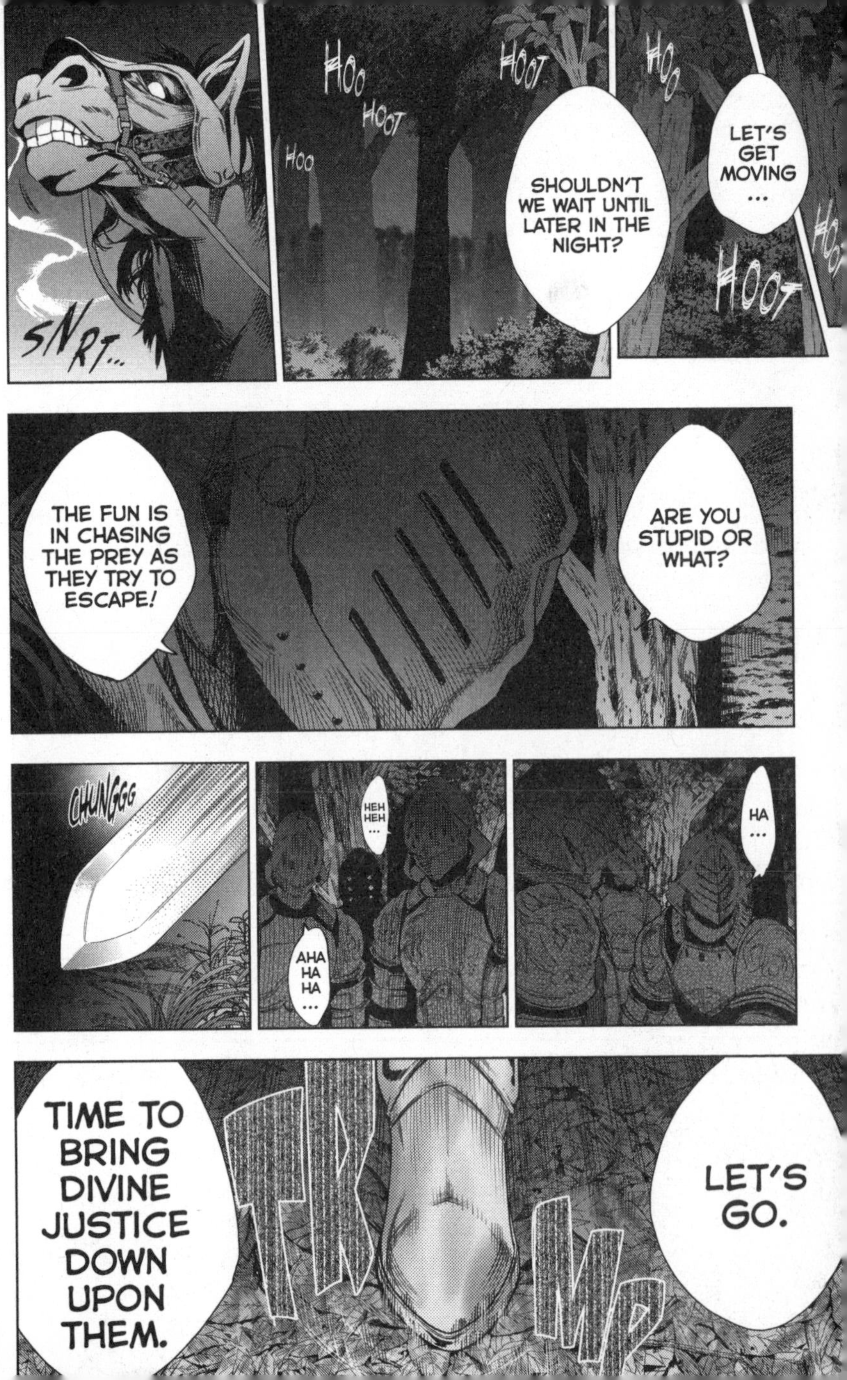
HOO
LET'S GET MOVING ...
HOOT
HOO
HOOT
SHOULDN'T WE WAIT UNTIL LATER IN THE NIGHT?
HOO
HOOT
HOO
SNRT...
ARE YOU STUPID OR WHAT?
THE FUN IS IN CHASING THE PREY AS THEY TRY TO ESCAPE!
HA ...
HEH HEH ...
AHA HA HA ...
CHUNGGG
LET'S GO.
THMP
TIME TO BRING DIVINE JUSTICE DOWN UPON THEM.

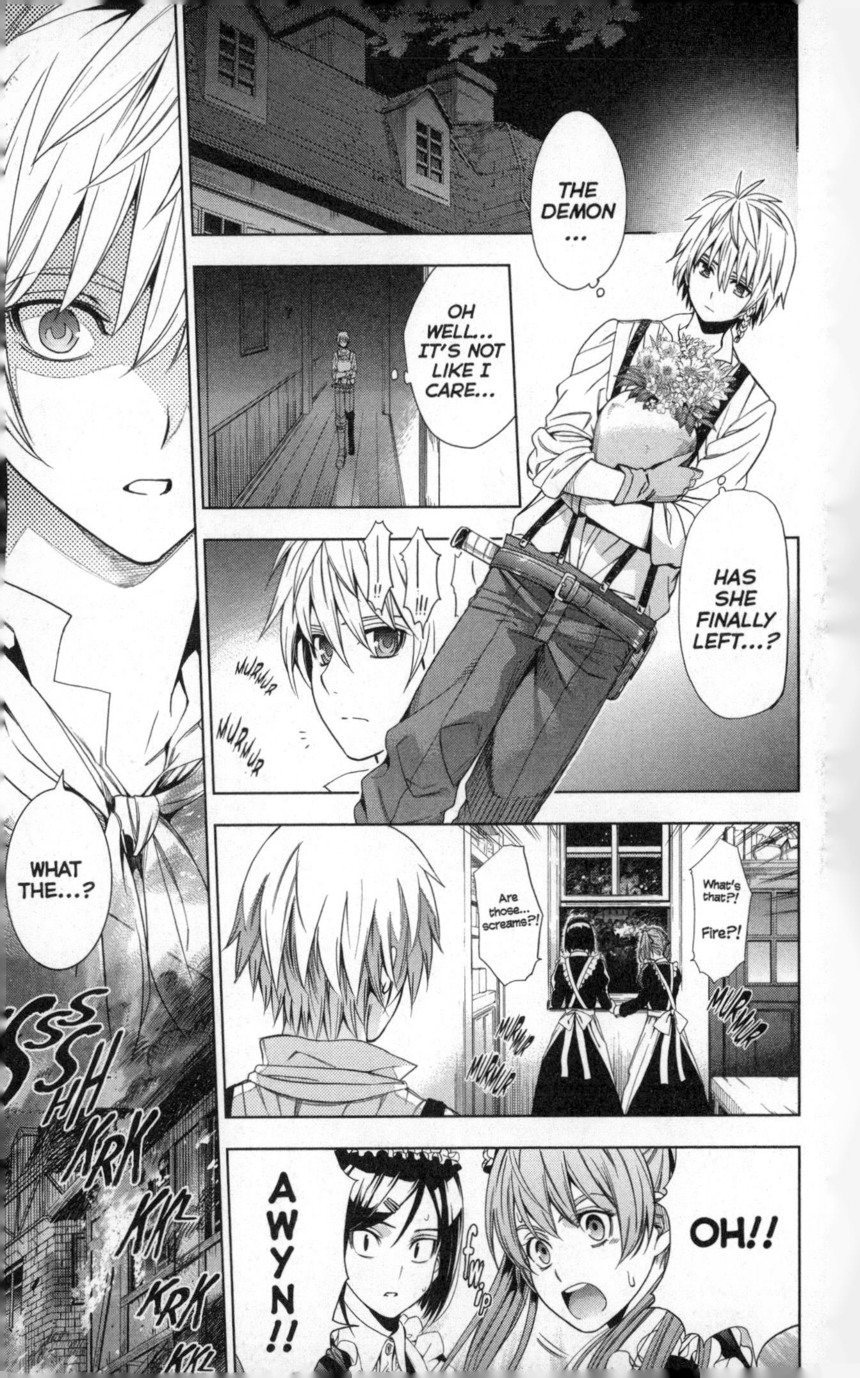
THE DEMON...
HAS SHE FINALLY LEFT...?
OH WELL... IT'S NOT LIKE I CARE...
!!
!!!
MURMUR
MURMUR
What's that?!
Fire?!
Are those... screams?!
MURMUR
MURMUR
MURMUR
OH!!
fwip
AWYN!!
WHAT THE...?
SSSSHH
KRK
KRK
KRK
KRK

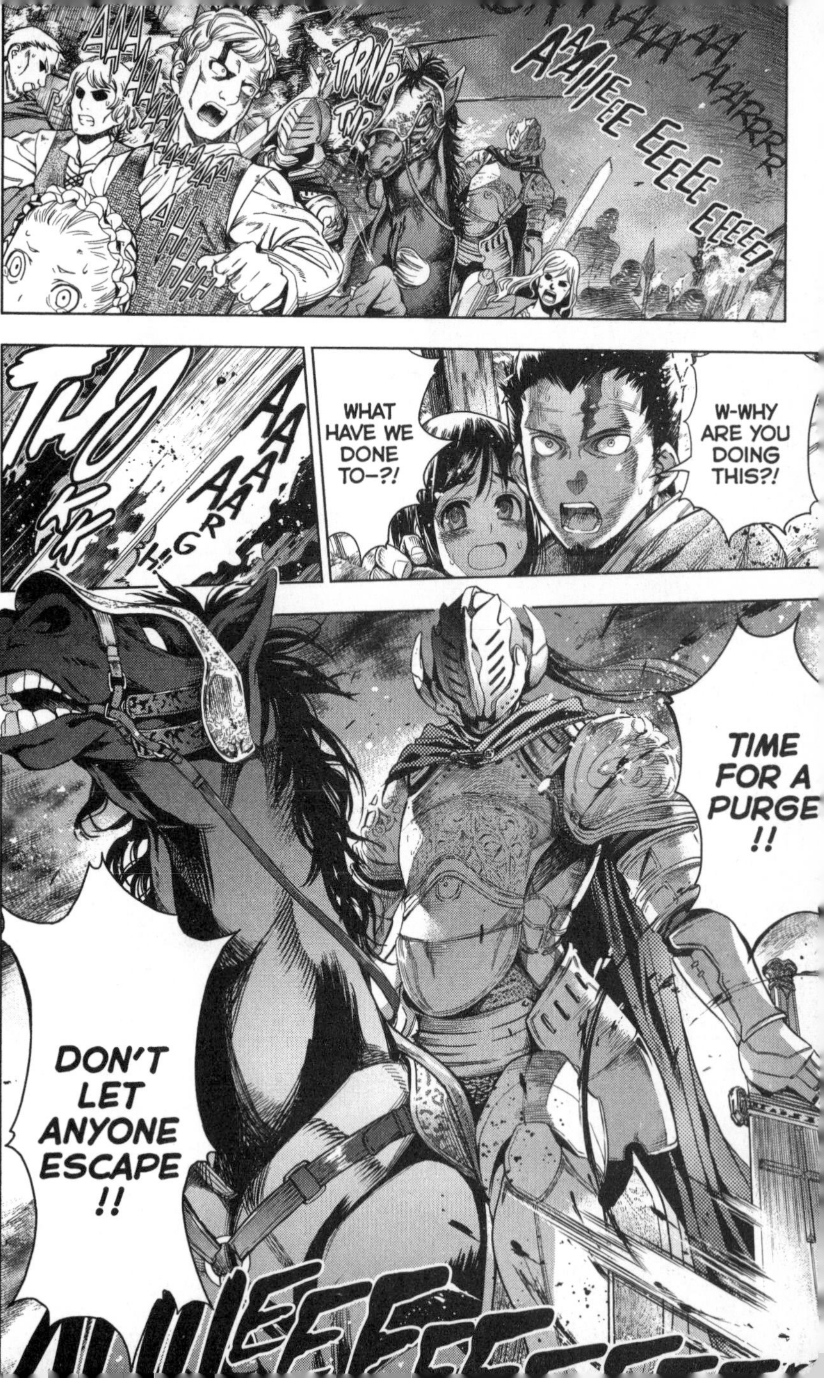
AAAIIEEE EEEEE EEEEE!
TRMP TMP
W-WHY ARE YOU DOING THIS?!
WHAT HAVE WE DONE TO-?!
AAAAARRGH!!
TIME FOR A PURGE!!
DON'T LET ANYONE ESCAPE!!

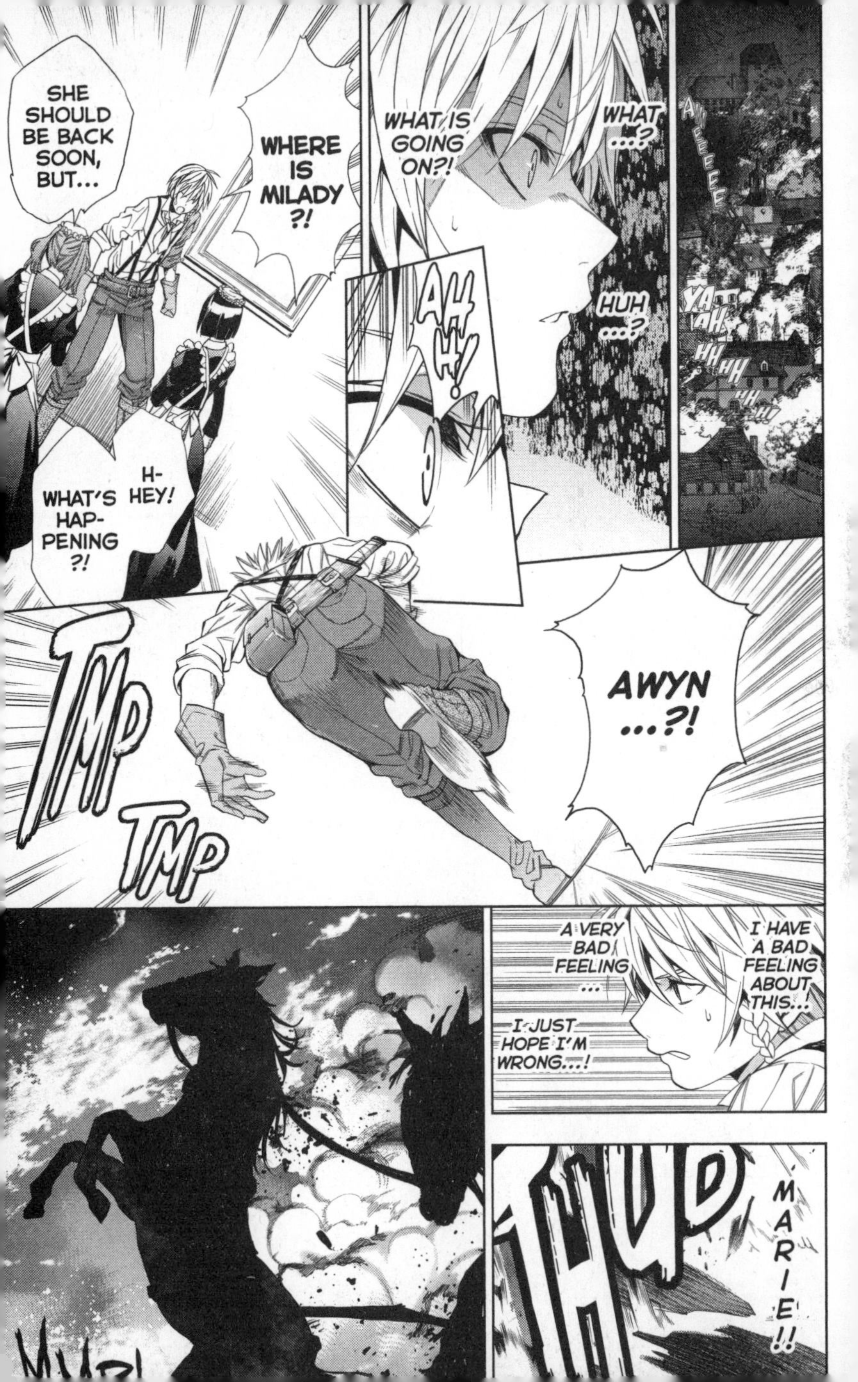
AIEEEEEE
YAAAHHHHHHH!
WHAT...?
HUH...?
WHAT IS GOING ON?!
AHH!
WHERE IS MILADY?!
SHE SHOULD BE BACK SOON, BUT...
H-HEY!
WHAT'S HAPPENING?!
AWYN...?!
TMP
TMP
I HAVE A BAD FEELING ABOUT THIS...!
A VERY BAD FEELING...
I JUST HOPE I'M WRONG...!
THUD
MARIE!!

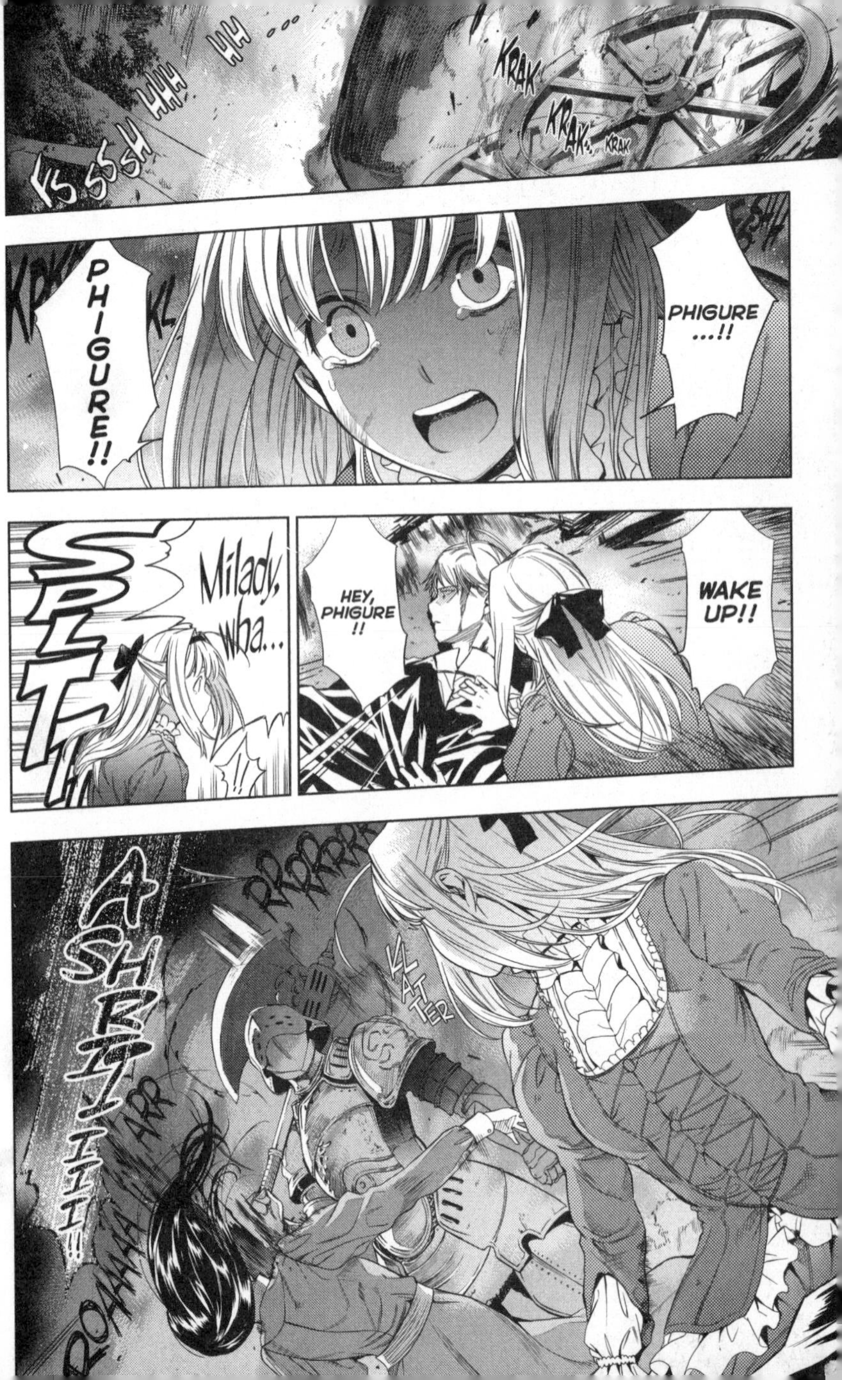
KRAK
KRAK
KRAK...
KRAK
FSSSSH
PHIGURE ...!!
PHIGURE!!
WAKE UP!!
HEY, PHIGURE !!
Milady, wha...
!!
SPLT

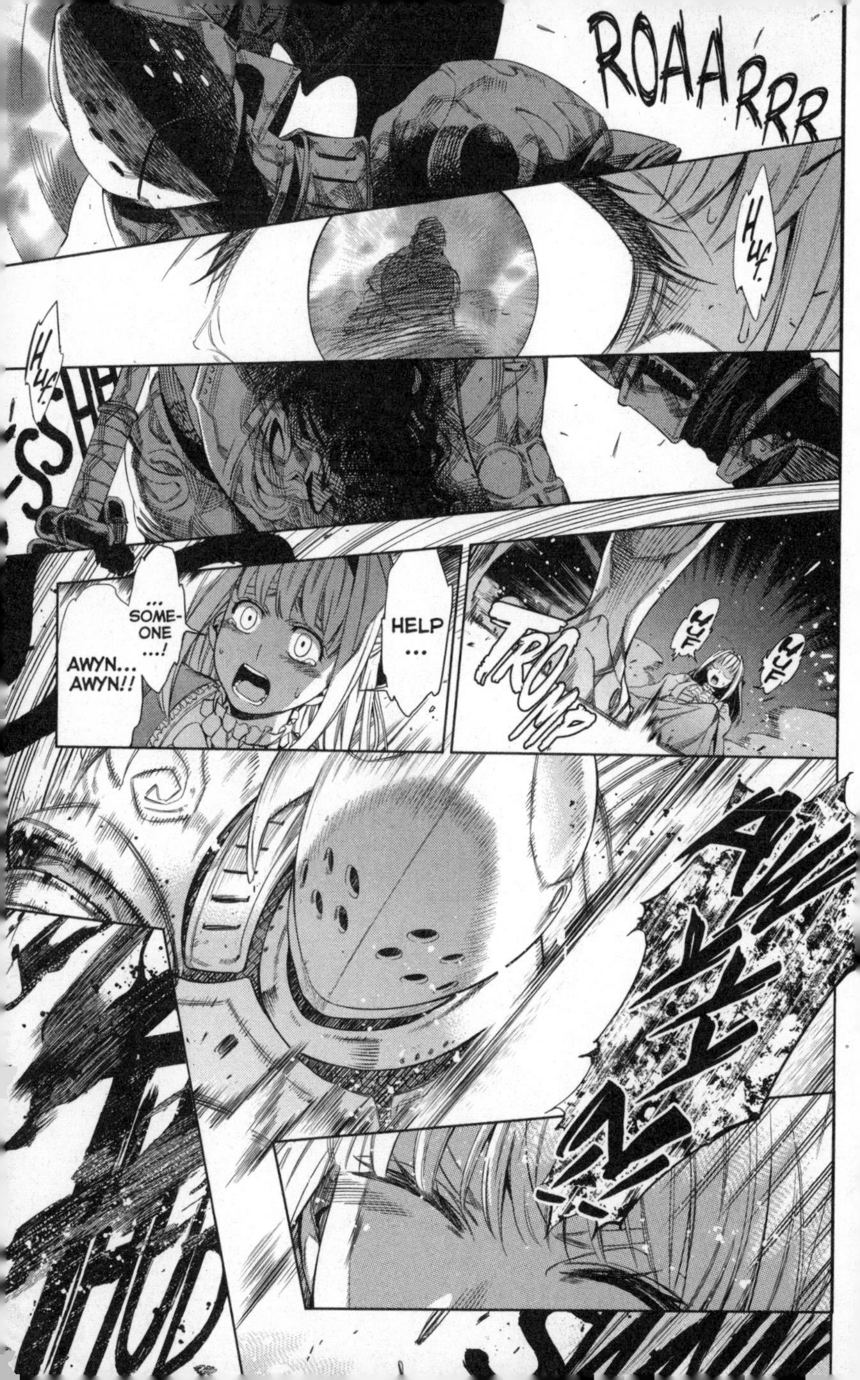
ROAAARRR
Huf.
Huf.
HUF
HUF
TROMP
HELP ...
... SOME-ONE ...!
AWYN... AWYN!!

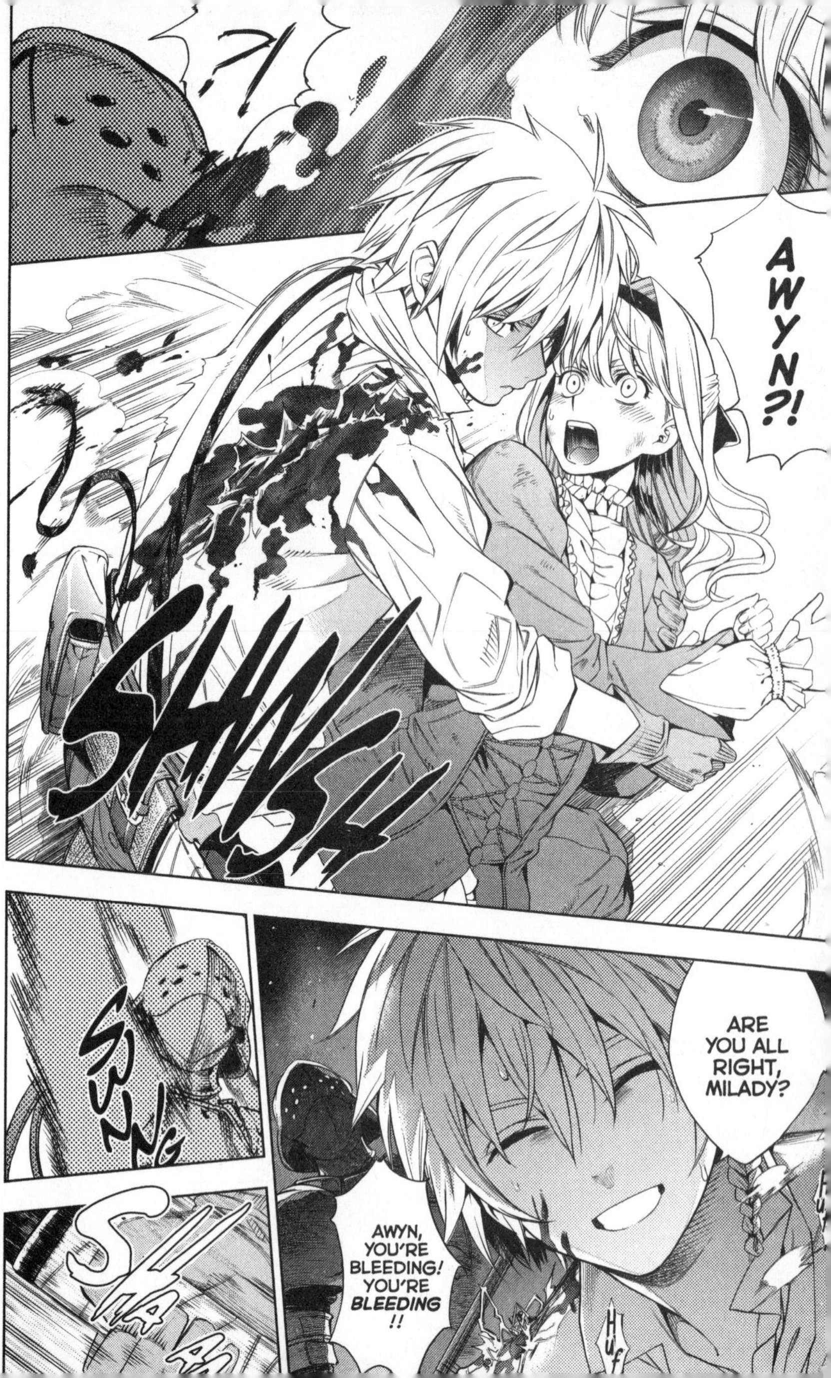
AWYN?!
..?!
SHWSH
ARE YOU ALL RIGHT, MILADY?
AWYN, YOU'RE BLEEDING! YOU'RE BLEEDING!!
HUF
SWUNG
SHAA

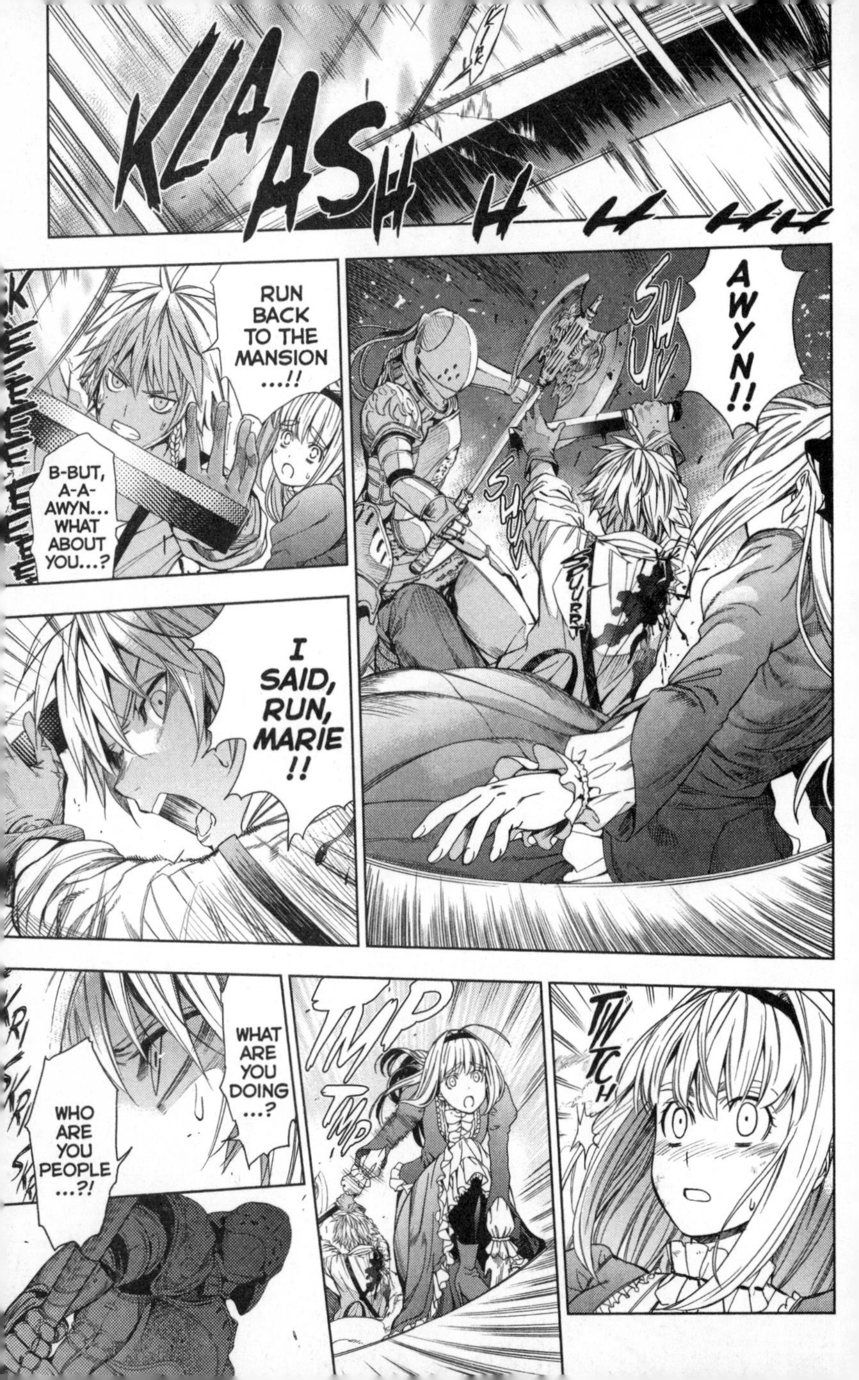
KLAASH HHHHH
AWYN!!
SHUV
SHU
SPUURRT
RUN BACK TO THE MANSION ...!!
B-BUT, A-A-AWYN... WHAT ABOUT YOU...?
KSHEEEEEE
I SAID, RUN, MARIE !!
TWITCH
TMP
TMP
WHAT ARE YOU DOING ...?
WHO ARE YOU PEOPLE ...?!
SHRI SHRI

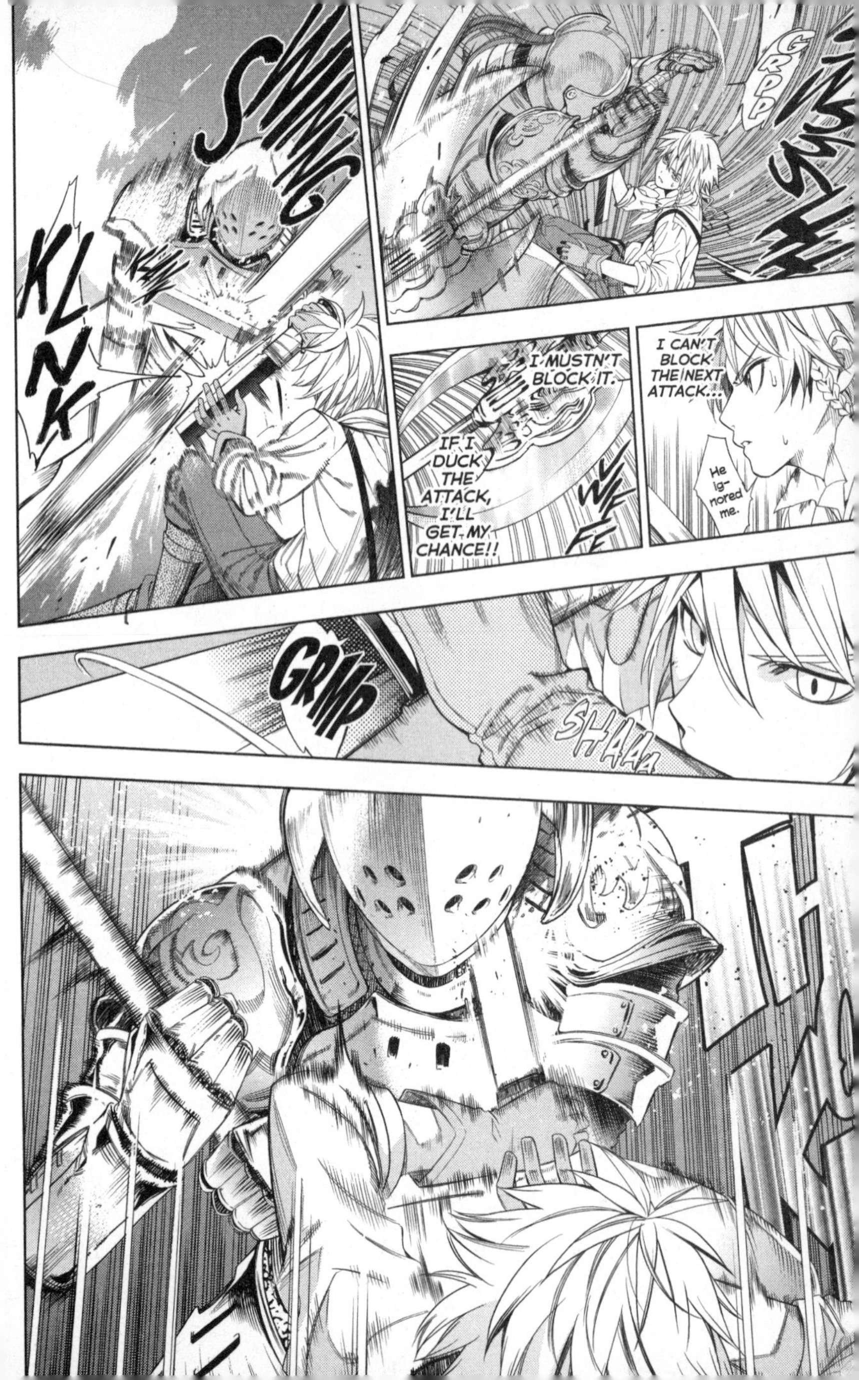
GRPP
SWISHH
I CAN'T BLOCK THE NEXT ATTACK...
He ignored me.
I MUSTN'T BLOCK IT.
IF I DUCK THE ATTACK, I'LL GET MY CHANCE!!
WFF
SWING
KLNK
GRMP
SHAAA

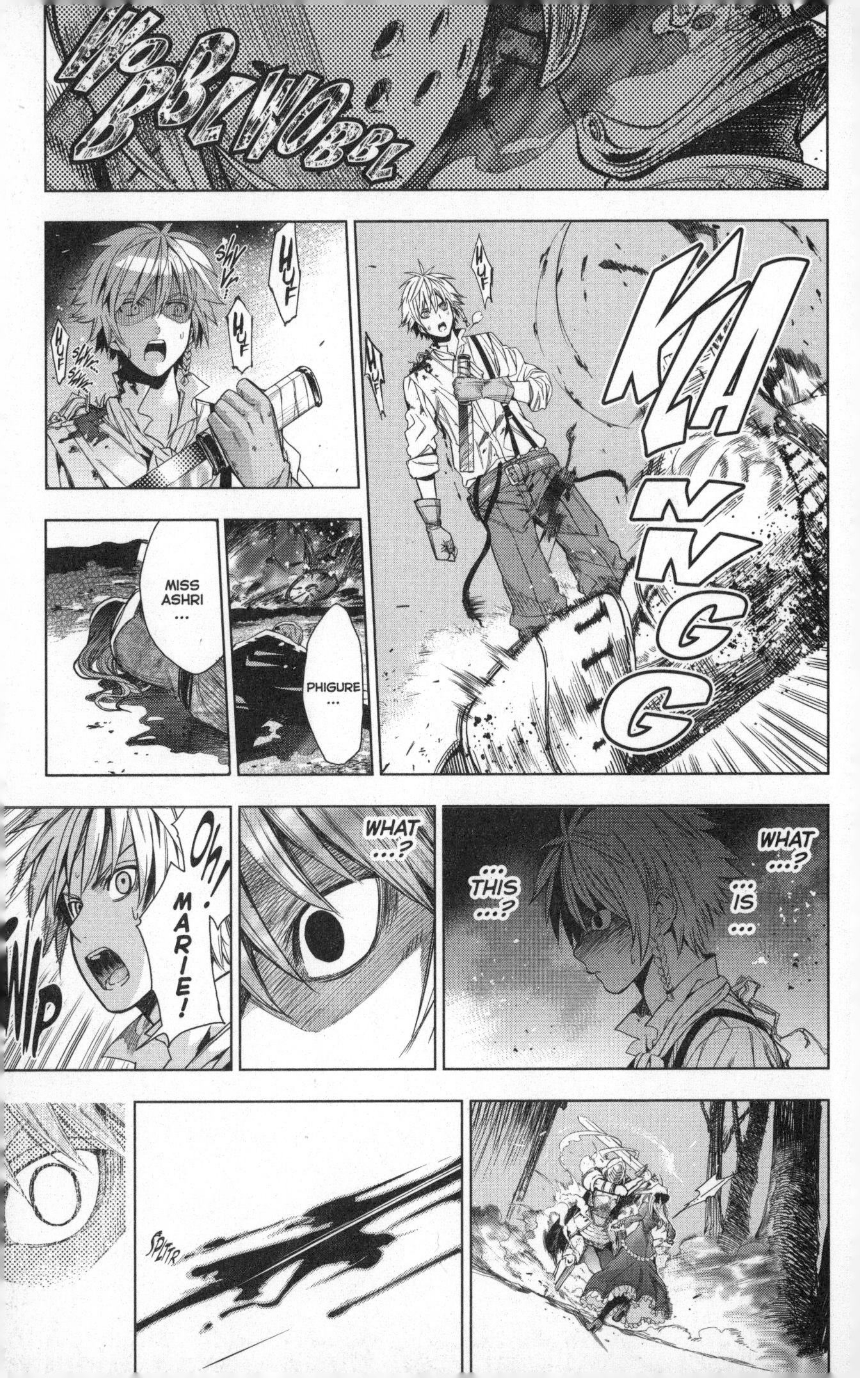
WOBBL WOBBL
KLANNNGG
HUF
HUF
HUF
SHVV
HUF
HUF
HUF
SHVV SHVV
PHIGURE
...
MISS ASHRI
...
WHAT
...?
...
IS
...
...
THIS
...?
WHAT
...?
Oh!
MARIE!
WHIP
SPLTTR

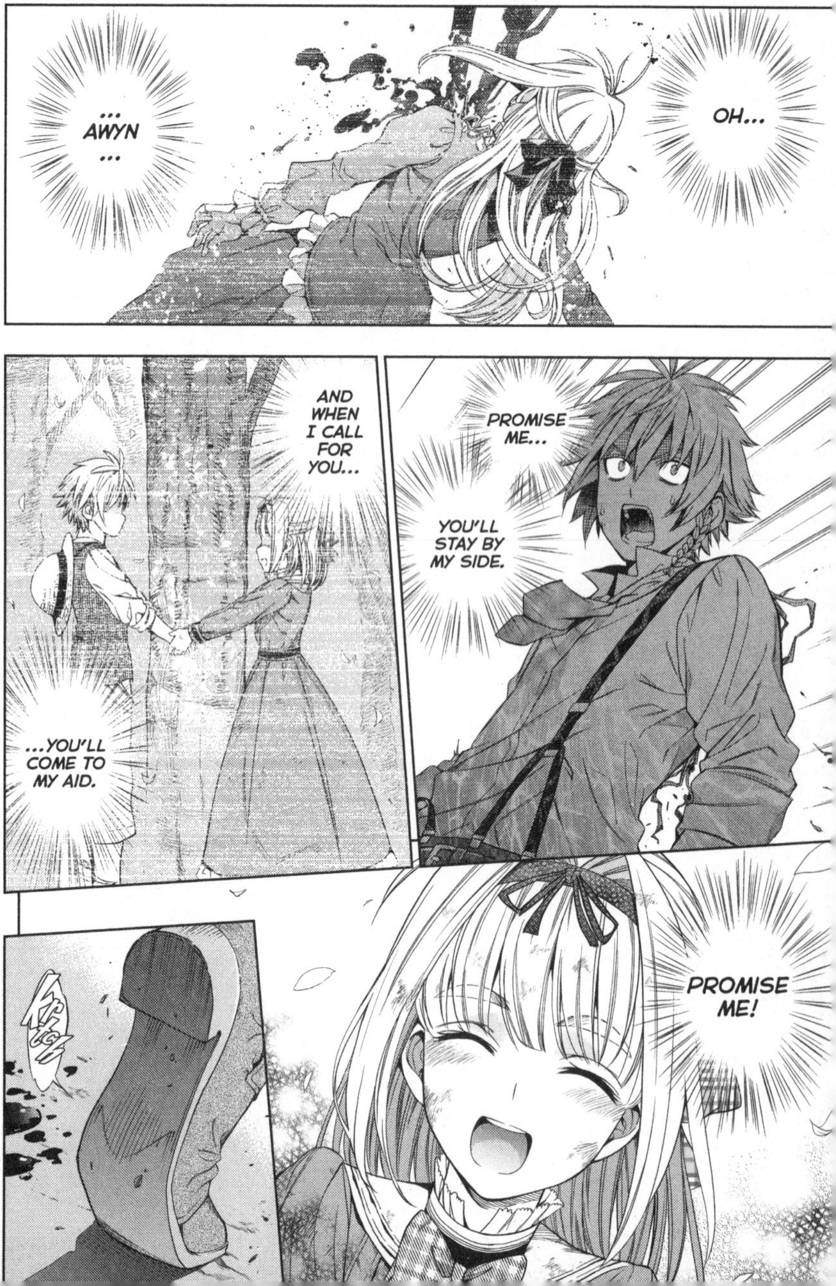
OH...
...AWYN...
PROMISE ME...
YOU'LL STAY BY MY SIDE.
AND WHEN I CALL FOR YOU...
...YOU'LL COME TO MY AID.
PROMISE ME!
KRTCH!!

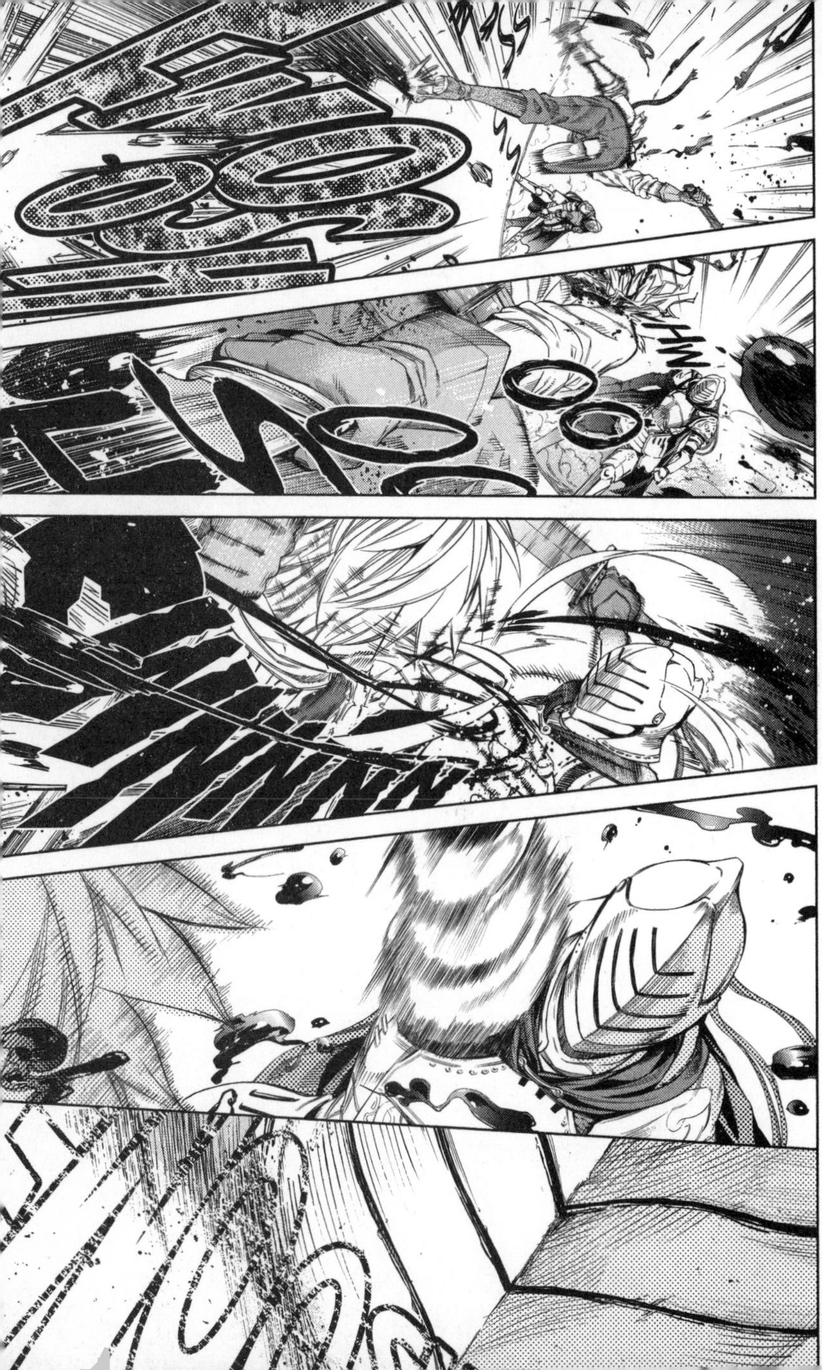

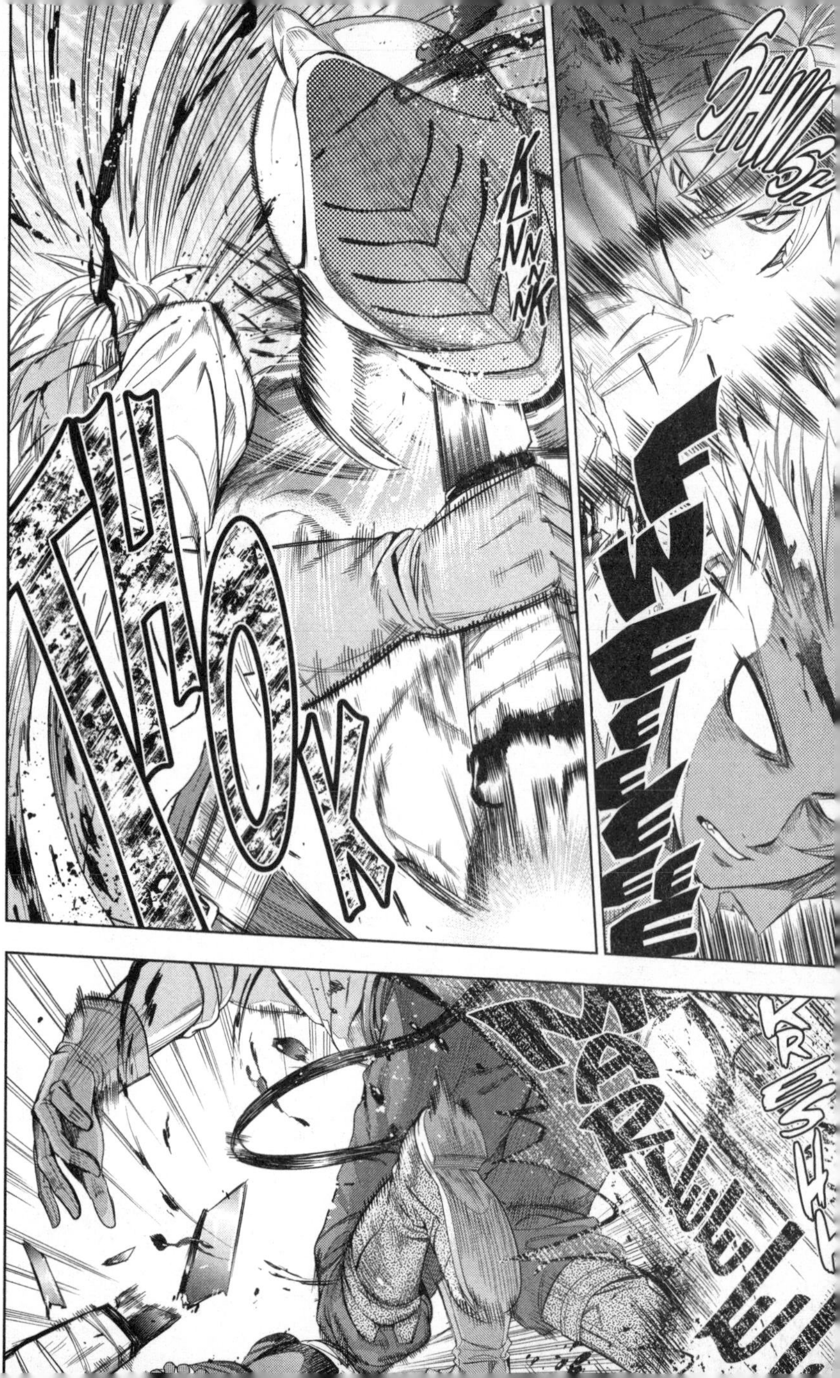
FWEEEEEEE
KLNNNNK
THOK

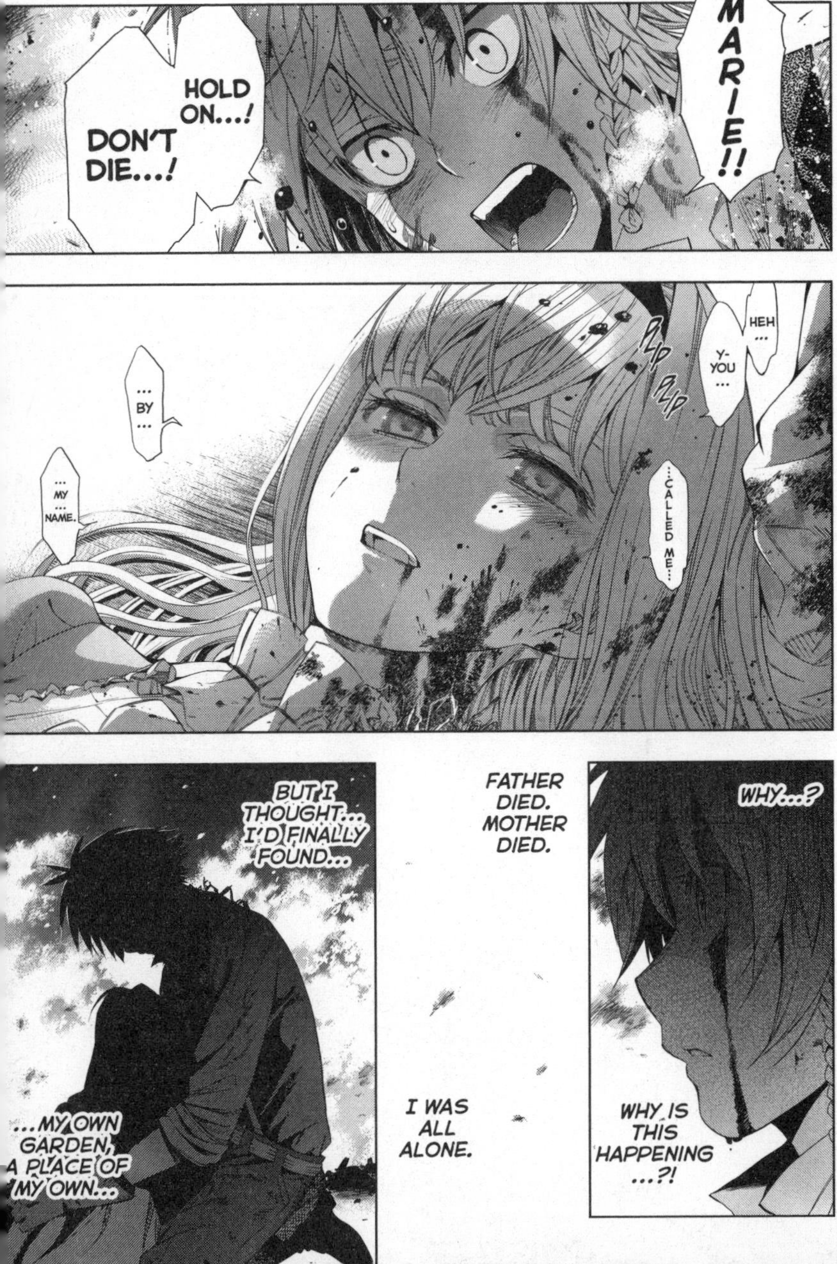
MARIE!!
HOLD ON...!
DON'T DIE...!
HEH...
Y-YOU...
...CALLED ME...
...BY...
...MY... NAME.
WHY...?
WHY IS THIS HAPPENING...?!
FATHER DIED. MOTHER DIED.
I WAS ALL ALONE.
BUT I THOUGHT... I'D FINALLY FOUND...
...MY OWN GARDEN, A PLACE OF MY OWN...

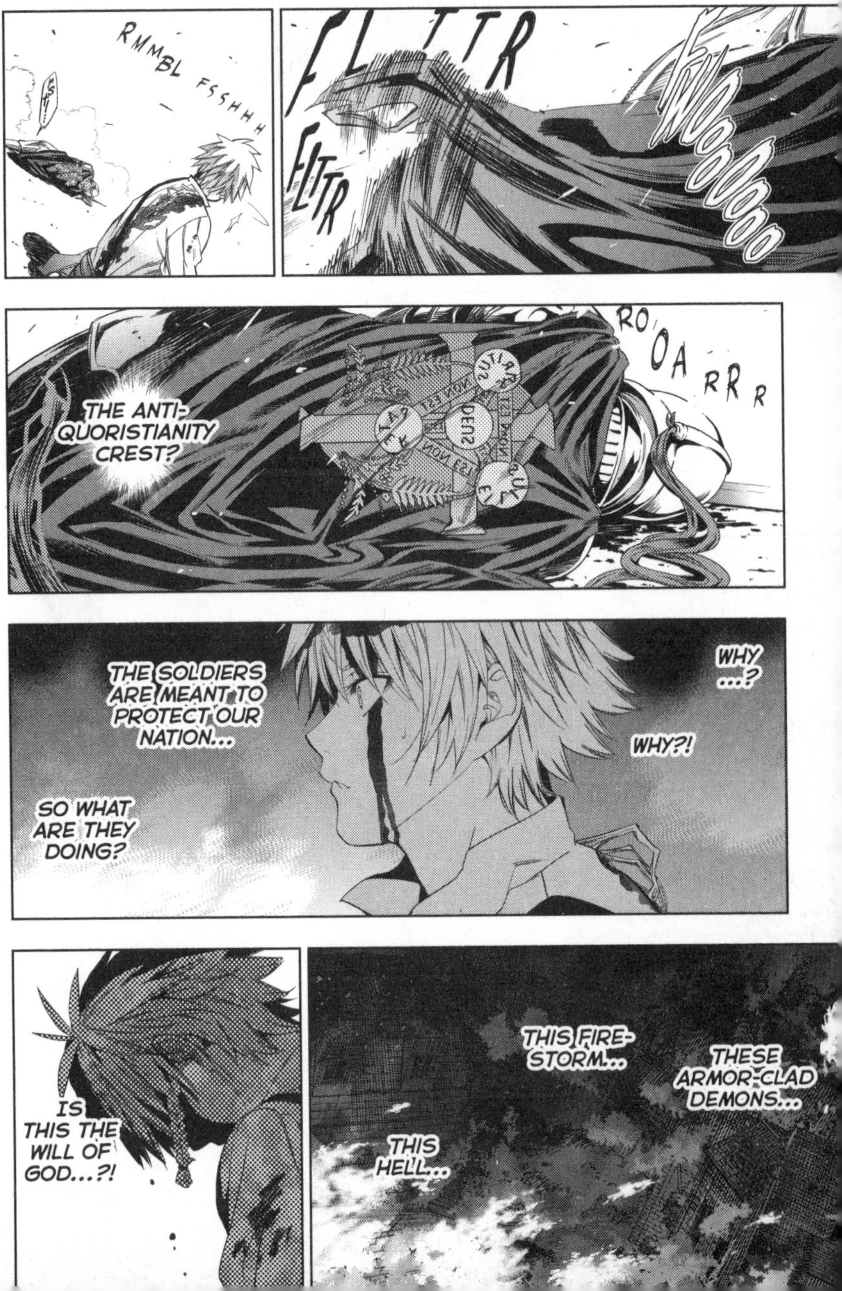
FLTTR
FLTTR
FWOOOOOOO
RMMBL
FSSHHH
ROOARRRR
THE ANTI-QUORISTIANITY CREST?
WHY...?
WHY?!
THE SOLDIERS ARE MEANT TO PROTECT OUR NATION...
SO WHAT ARE THEY DOING?
THESE ARMOR-CLAD DEMONS...
THIS FIRE-STORM...
THIS HELL...
IS THIS THE WILL OF GOD...?!

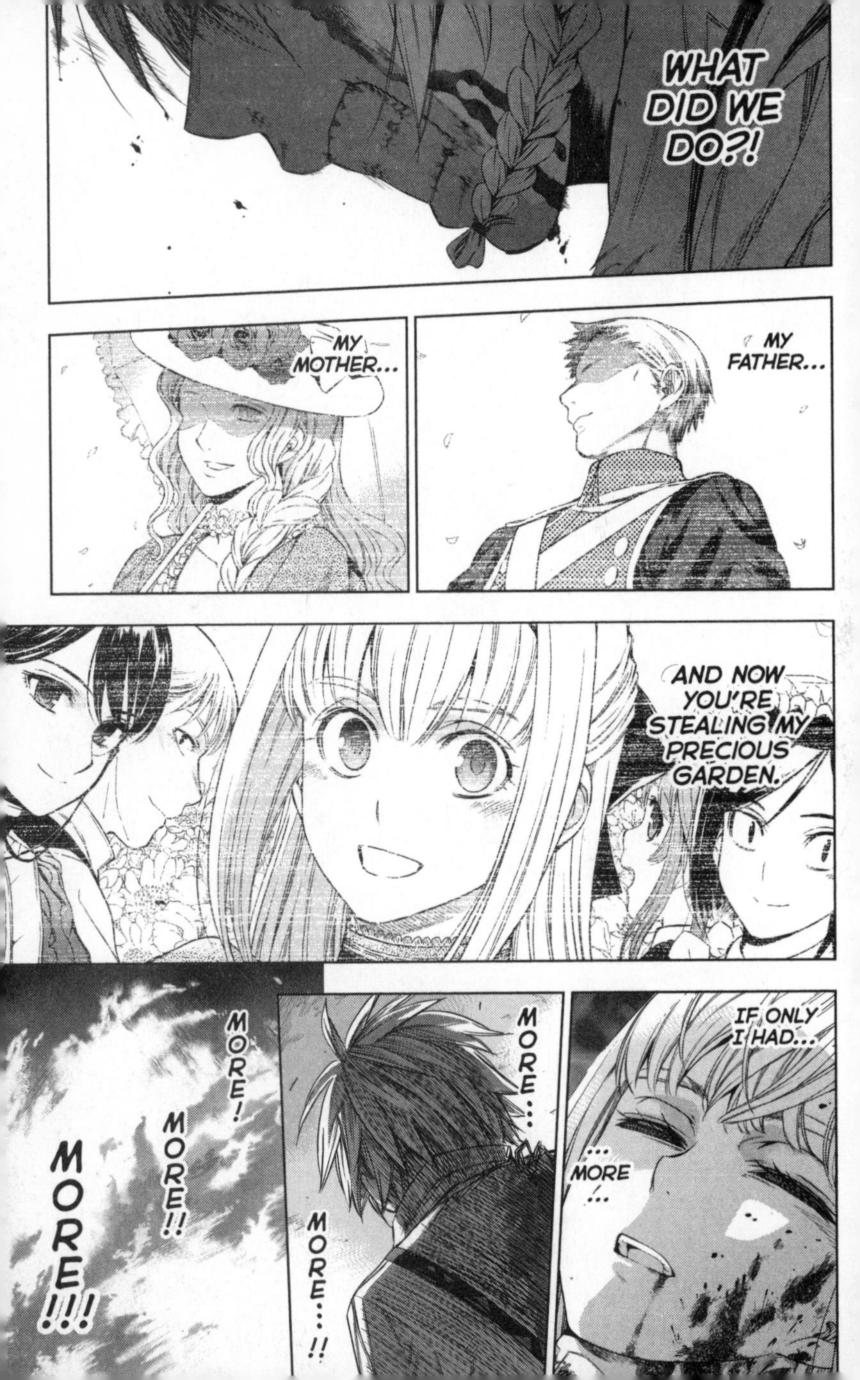
WHAT DID WE DO?!
MY FATHER...
MY MOTHER...
AND NOW YOU'RE STEALING MY PRECIOUS GARDEN.
IF ONLY I HAD...
...MORE...
MORE...
MORE...!!
MORE!
MORE!!
MORE!!!

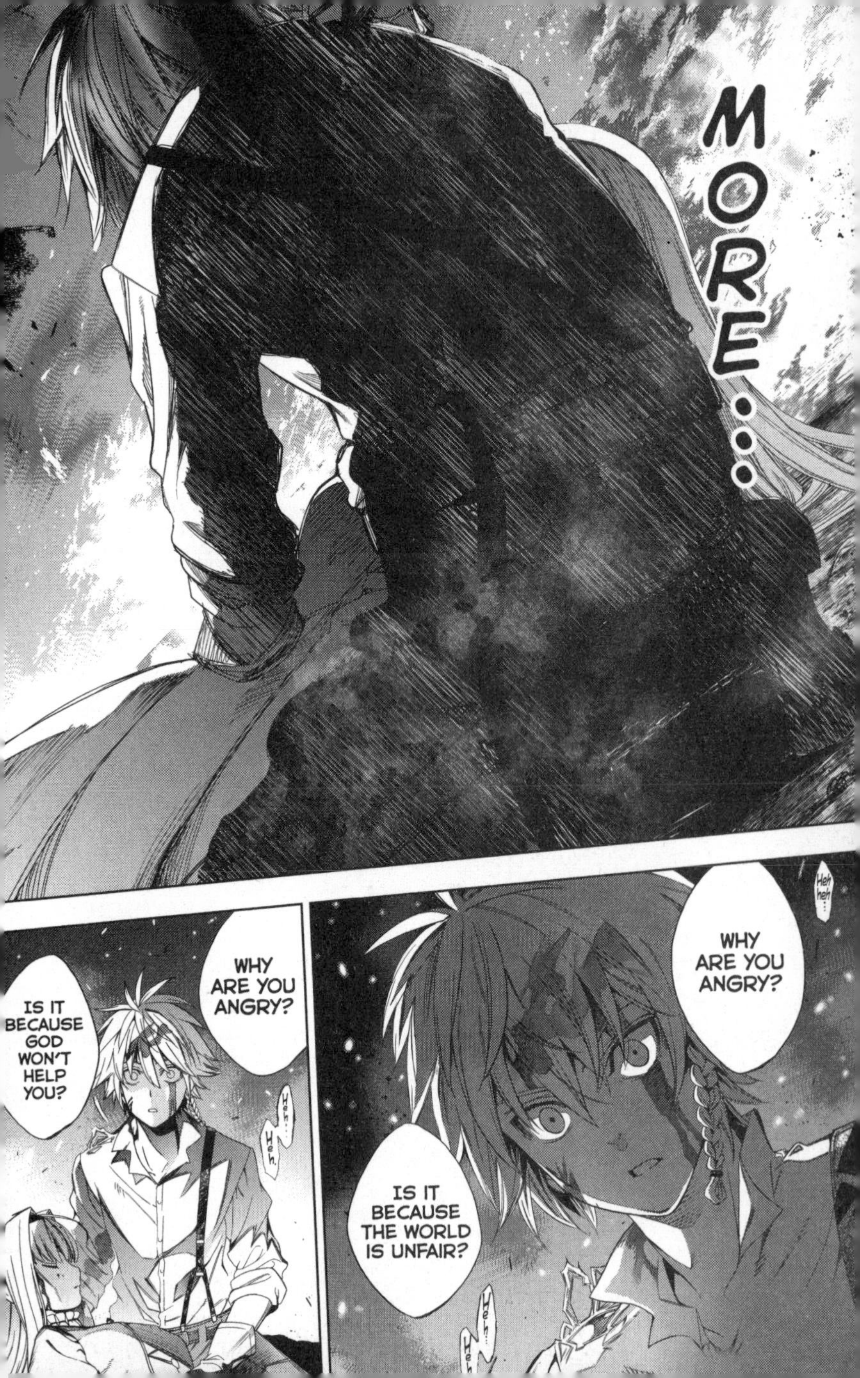
MORE...
Heh heh...
WHY ARE YOU ANGRY?
IS IT BECAUSE THE WORLD IS UNFAIR?
Heh...
WHY ARE YOU ANGRY?
IS IT BECAUSE GOD WON'T HELP YOU?
Heh...
Heh.

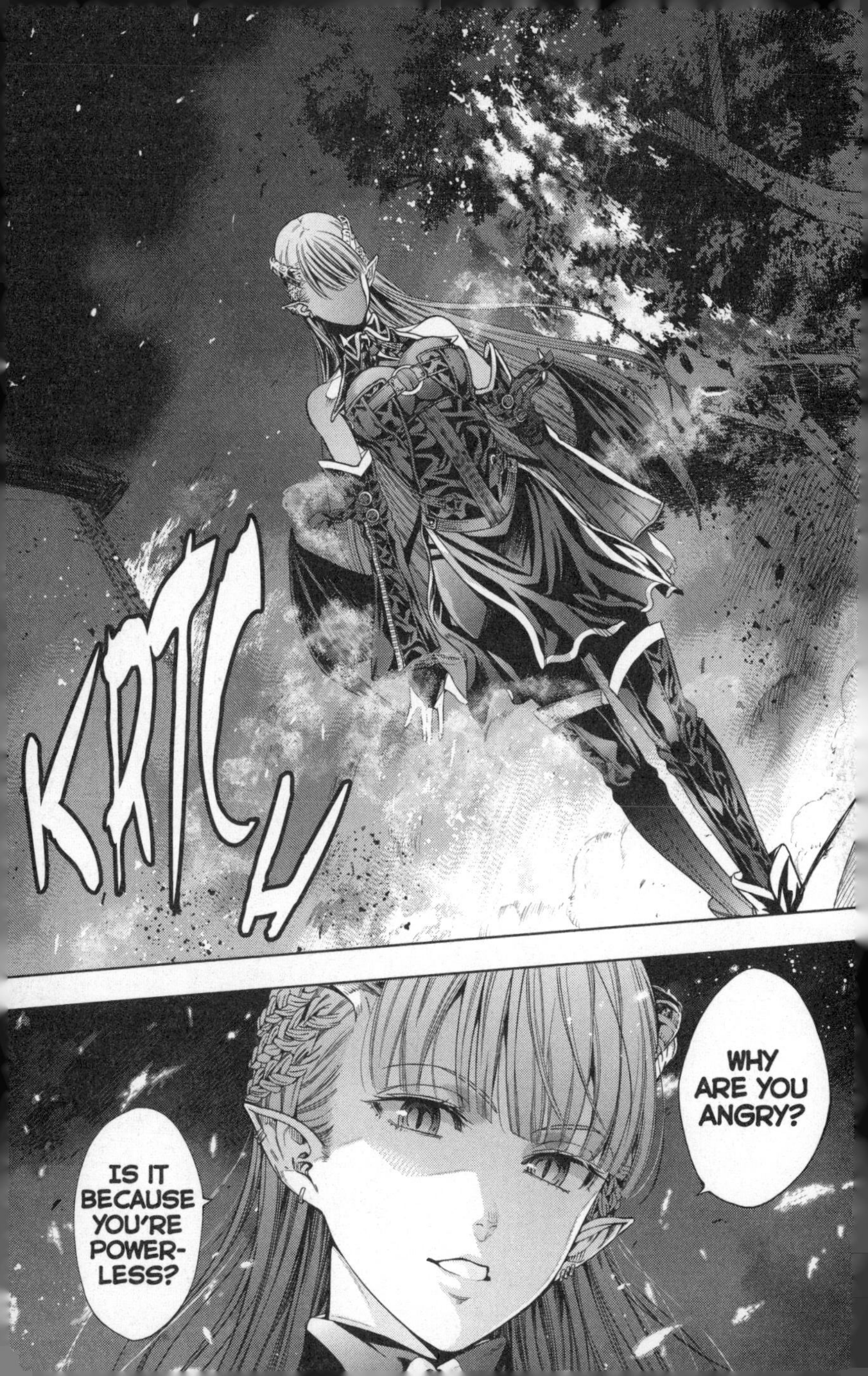
KRTCH
WHY ARE YOU ANGRY?
IS IT BECAUSE YOU'RE POWER-LESS?

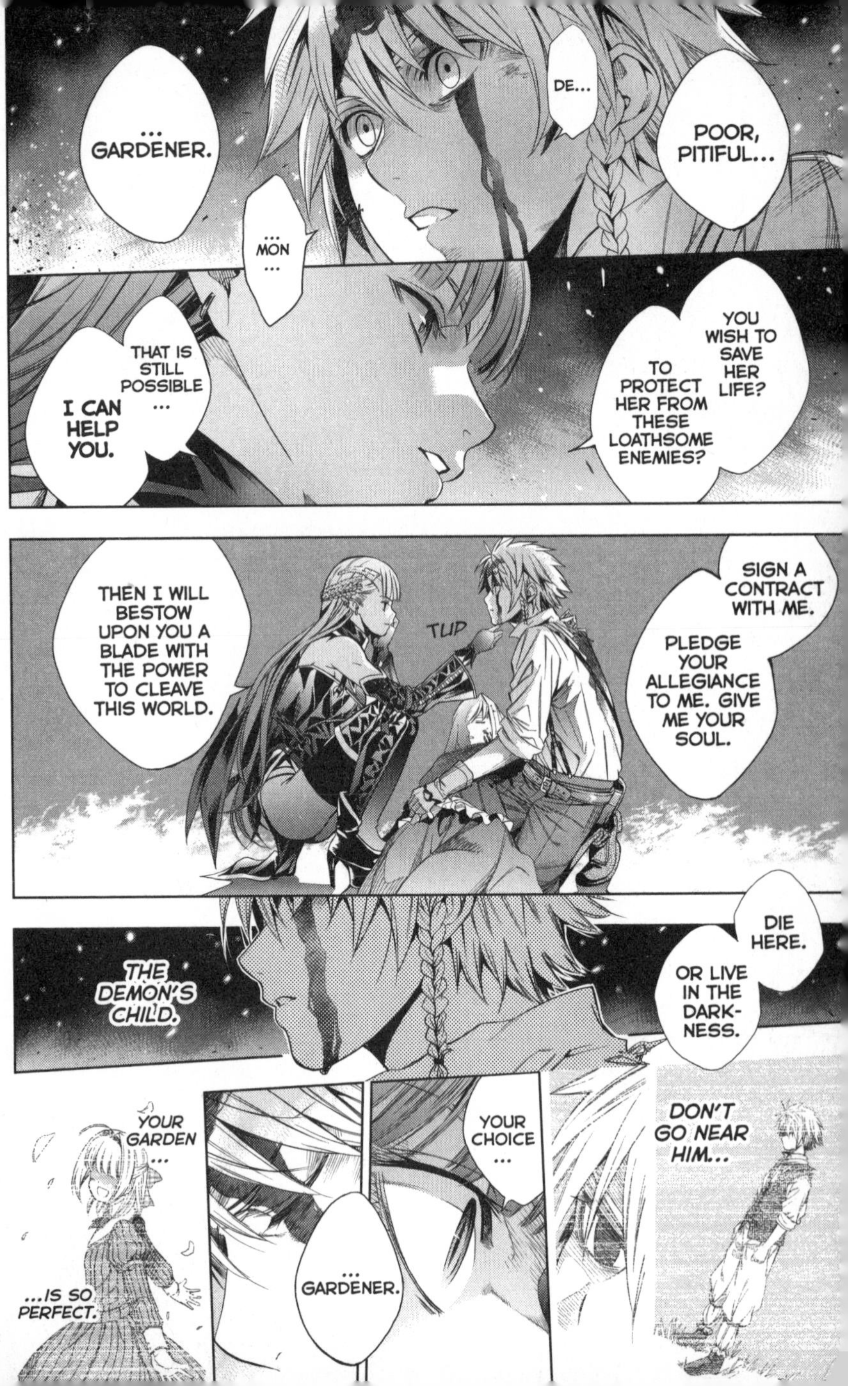
POOR, PITIFUL...
DE...
...GARDENER.
...MON...
YOU WISH TO SAVE HER LIFE?
TO PROTECT HER FROM THESE LOATHSOME ENEMIES?
THAT IS STILL POSSIBLE...
I CAN HELP YOU.
SIGN A CONTRACT WITH ME.
PLEDGE YOUR ALLEGIANCE TO ME. GIVE ME YOUR SOUL.
TUP
THEN I WILL BESTOW UPON YOU A BLADE WITH THE POWER TO CLEAVE THIS WORLD.
DIE HERE.
OR LIVE IN THE DARK-NESS.
THE DEMON'S CHILD.
DON'T GO NEAR HIM...
YOUR CHOICE...
...GARDENER.
YOUR GARDEN...
...IS SO PERFECT.

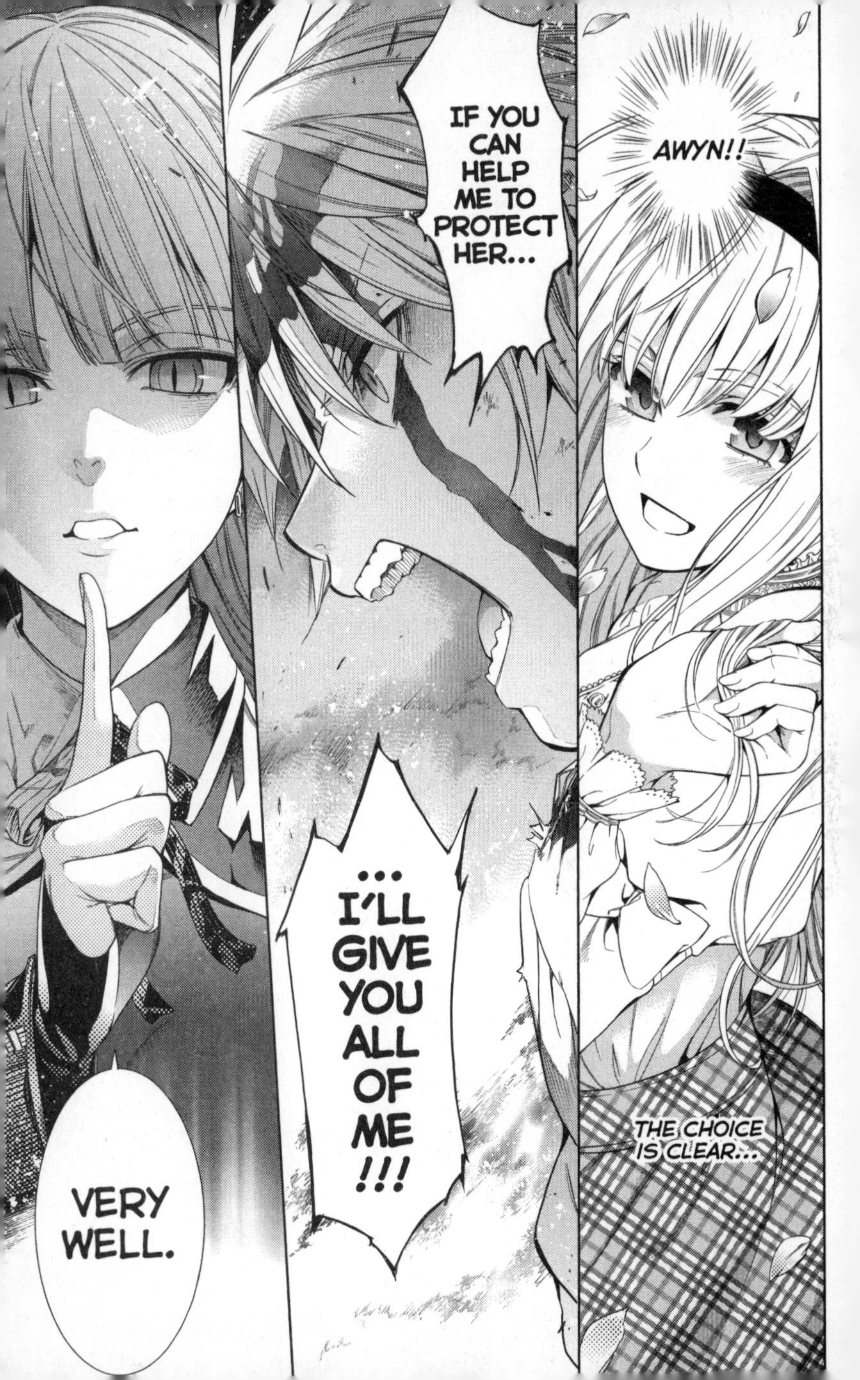
AWYN!!
THE CHOICE IS CLEAR...
IF YOU CAN HELP ME TO PROTECT HER...
...I'LL GIVE YOU ALL OF ME!!!
VERY WELL.

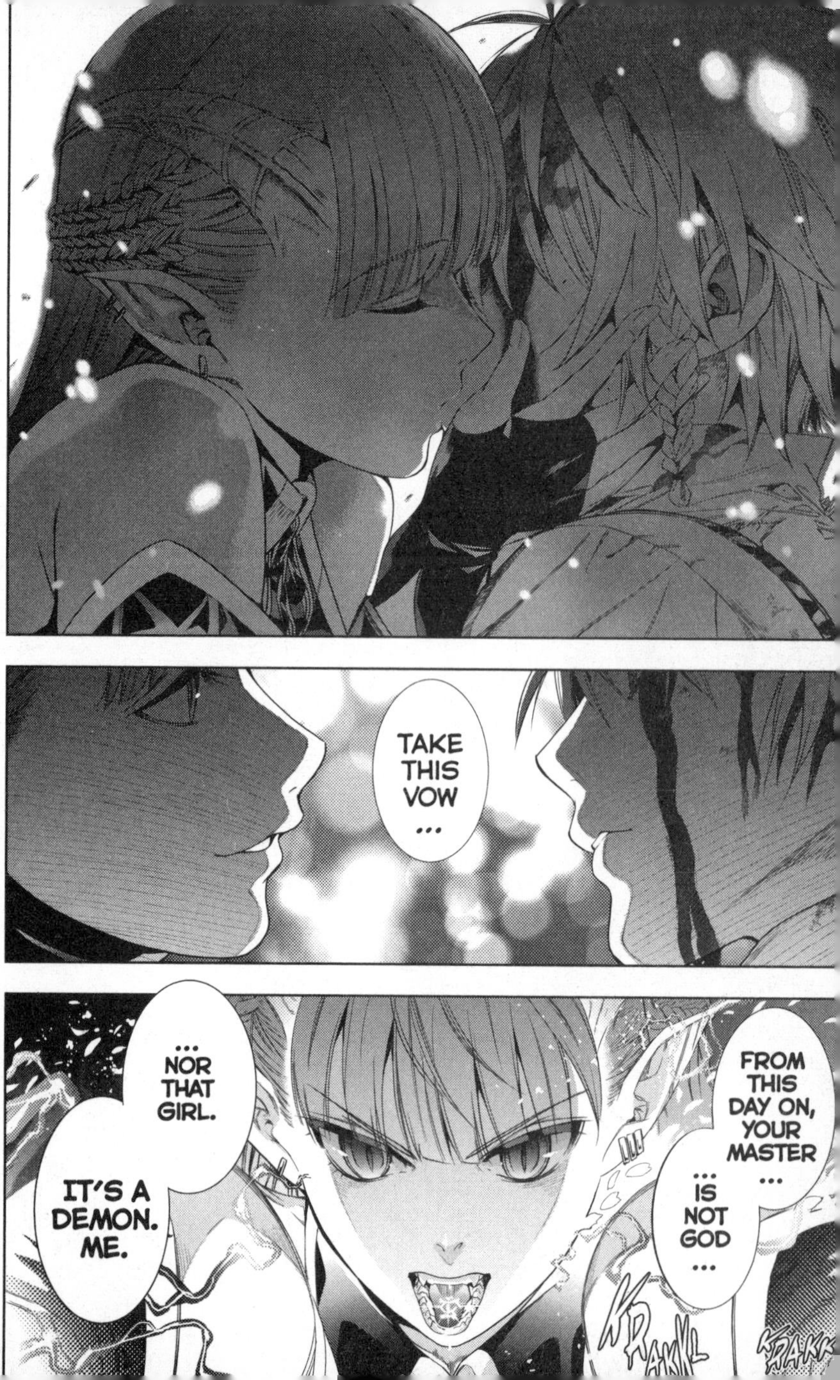
TAKE THIS VOW ...
FROM THIS DAY ON, YOUR MASTER ...
... IS NOT GOD ...
... NOR THAT GIRL.
IT'S A DEMON. ME.
KRAKK
KRAKKL

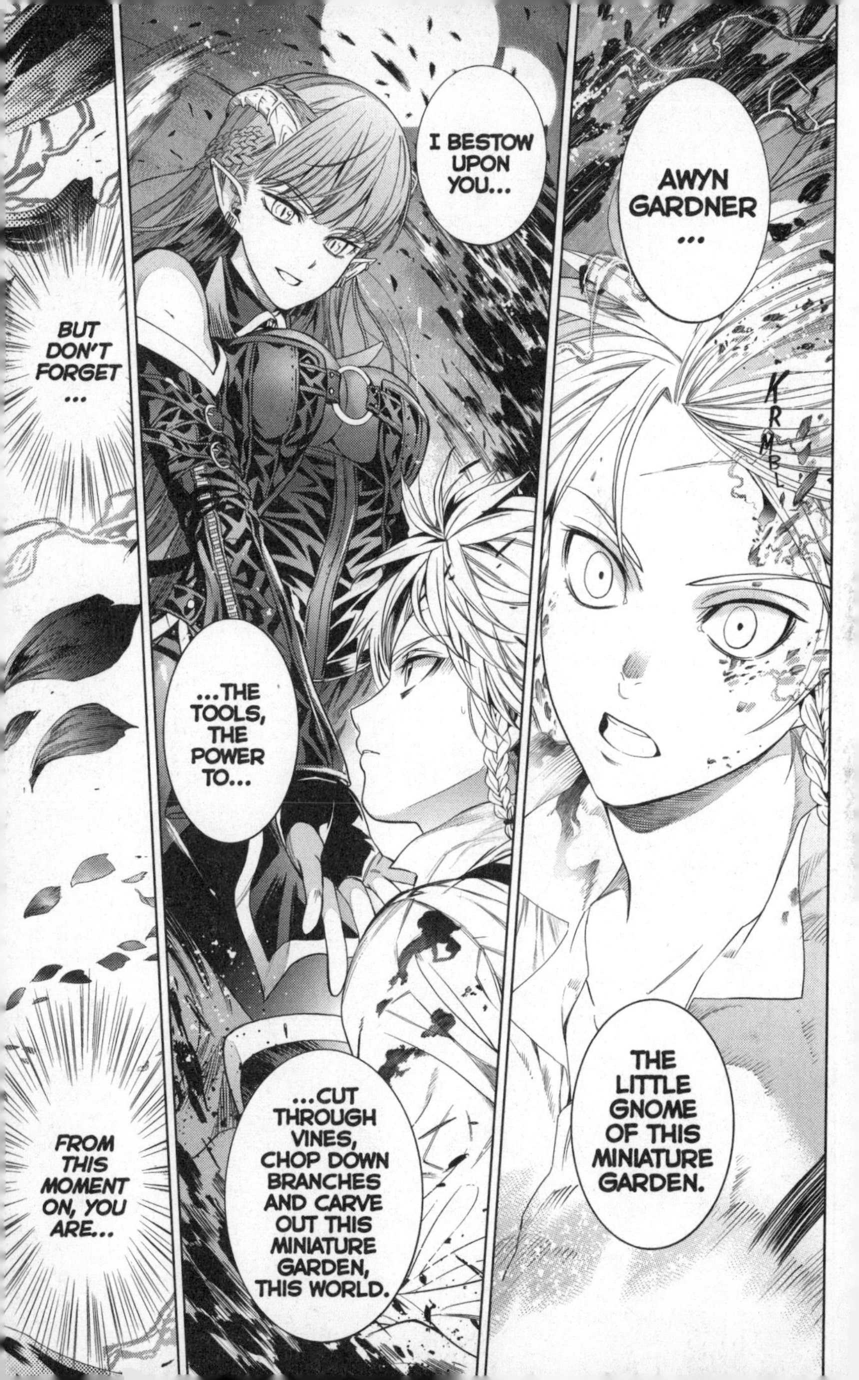
AWYN GARDNER ...
KRMBL
THE LITTLE GNOME OF THIS MINIATURE GARDEN.
I BESTOW UPON YOU...
...THE TOOLS, THE POWER TO...
...CUT THROUGH VINES, CHOP DOWN BRANCHES AND CARVE OUT THIS MINIATURE GARDEN, THIS WORLD.
BUT DON'T FORGET ...
FROM THIS MOMENT ON, YOU ARE...

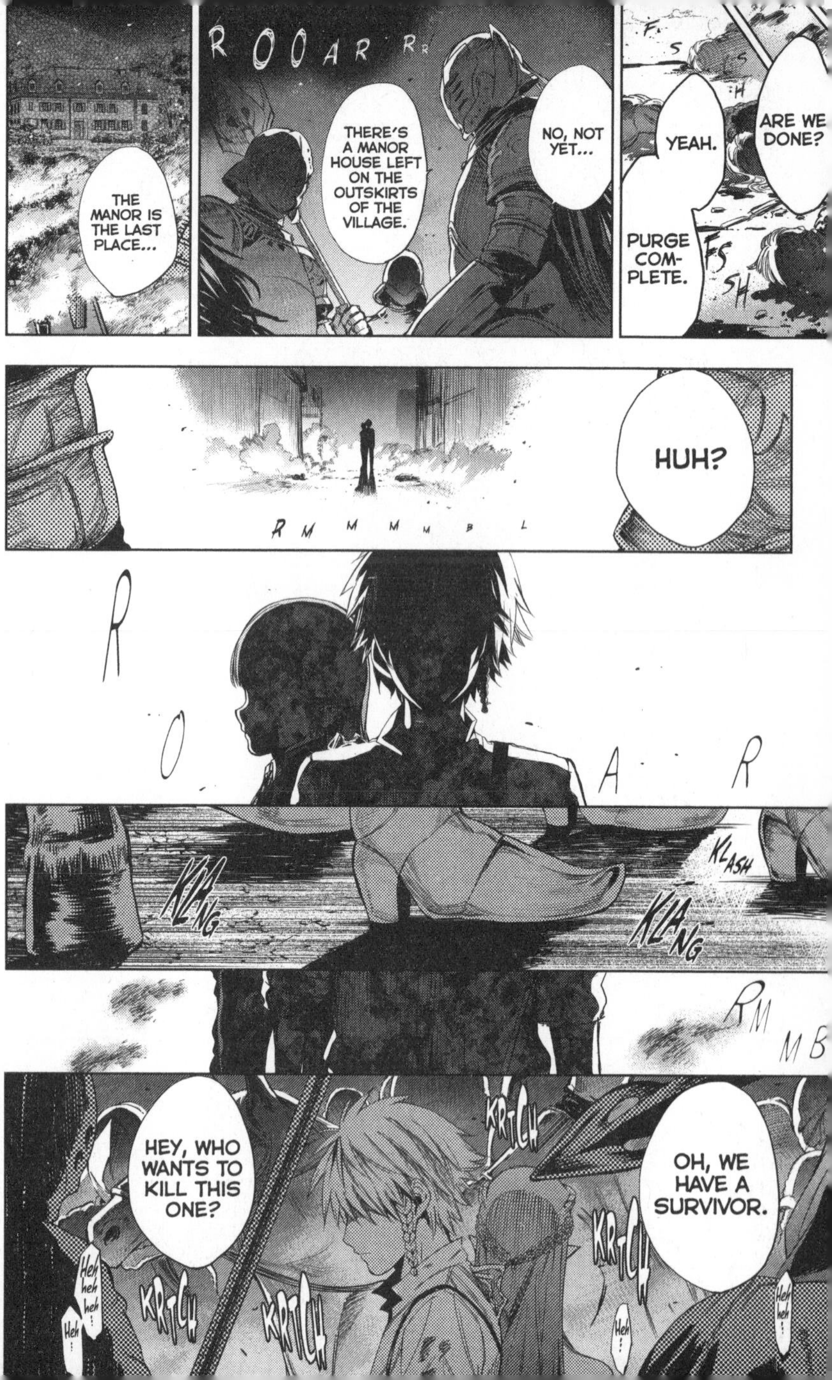
FSSH
ARE WE DONE?
YEAH.
PURGE COMPLETE.
FSSH
ROOARRR
NO, NOT YET...
THERE'S A MANOR HOUSE LEFT ON THE OUTSKIRTS OF THE VILLAGE.
THE MANOR IS THE LAST PLACE...
HUH?
RMMMMBL
ROAR
KLASH
KLANG
KLANG
RMMB
KRTCH
OH, WE HAVE A SURVIVOR.
Heh heh...
KRTCH
Heh...
HEY, WHO WANTS TO KILL THIS ONE?
KRTCH
KRTCH
Heh heh heh... Heh...

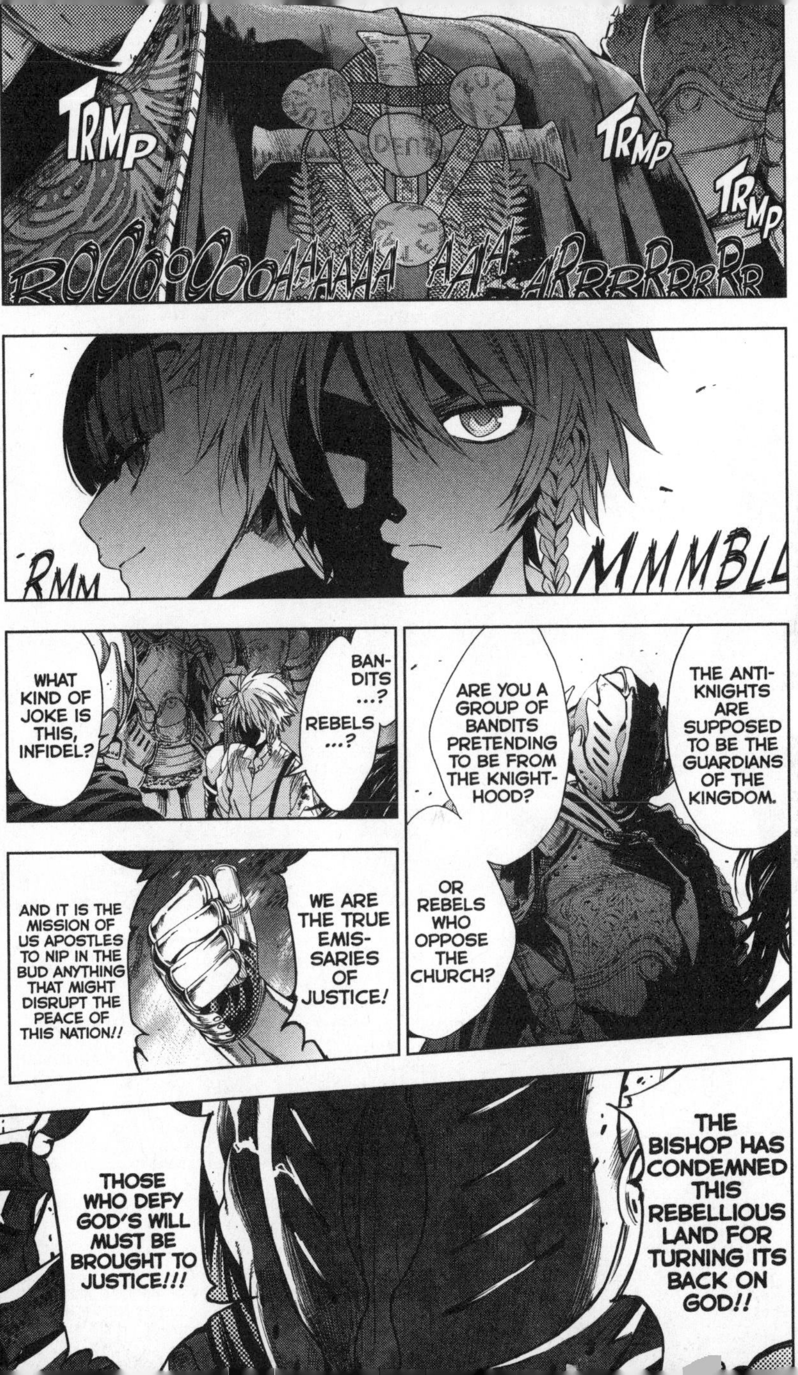
TRMP
TRMP
TRMP
ROOOOOOOOAAAAAA AAA ARRRRRRRR
MMMBLL
RMM
THE ANTI-KNIGHTS ARE SUPPOSED TO BE THE GUARDIANS OF THE KINGDOM.
ARE YOU A GROUP OF BANDITS PRETENDING TO BE FROM THE KNIGHTHOOD?
OR REBELS WHO OPPOSE THE CHURCH?
BANDITS ...? REBELS ...?
WHAT KIND OF JOKE IS THIS, INFIDEL?
WE ARE THE TRUE EMISSARIES OF JUSTICE!
AND IT IS THE MISSION OF US APOSTLES TO NIP IN THE BUD ANYTHING THAT MIGHT DISRUPT THE PEACE OF THIS NATION!!
THE BISHOP HAS CONDEMNED THIS REBELLIOUS LAND FOR TURNING ITS BACK ON GOD!!
THOSE WHO DEFY GOD'S WILL MUST BE BROUGHT TO JUSTICE!!!

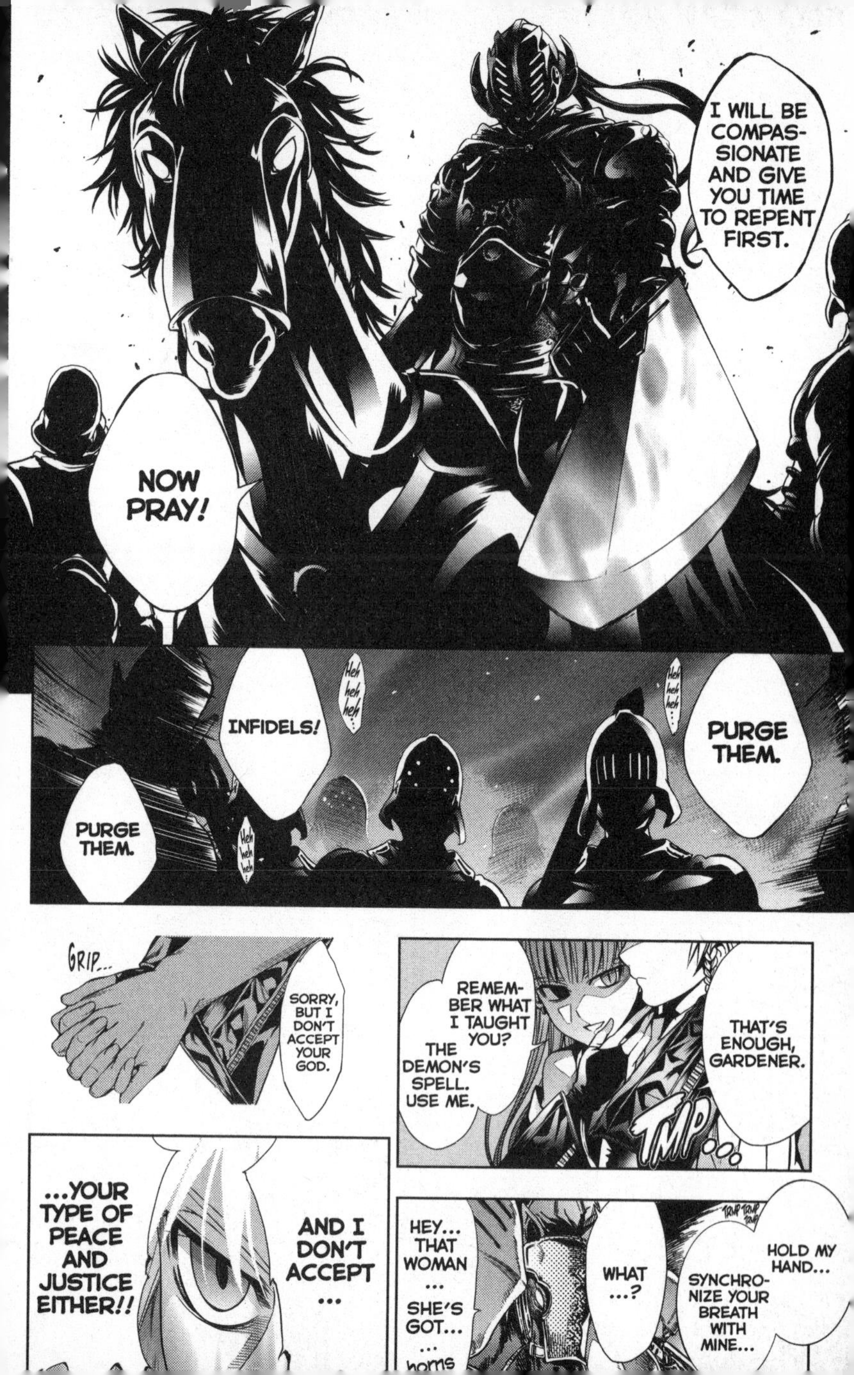
I WILL BE COMPASSIONATE AND GIVE YOU TIME TO REPENT FIRST.
NOW PRAY!
Heh heh heh...
PURGE THEM.
Heh heh heh...
INFIDELS!
Heh heh heh...
PURGE THEM.
THAT'S ENOUGH, GARDENER.
TMP...
REMEMBER WHAT I TAUGHT YOU? THE DEMON'S SPELL. USE ME.
GRIP...
SORRY, BUT I DON'T ACCEPT YOUR GOD.
TRMP TRMP TRMP
HOLD MY HAND... SYNCHRONIZE YOUR BREATH WITH MINE...
WHAT...?
HEY... THAT WOMAN... SHE'S GOT... ...horns
AND I DON'T ACCEPT...
...YOUR TYPE OF PEACE AND JUSTICE EITHER!!

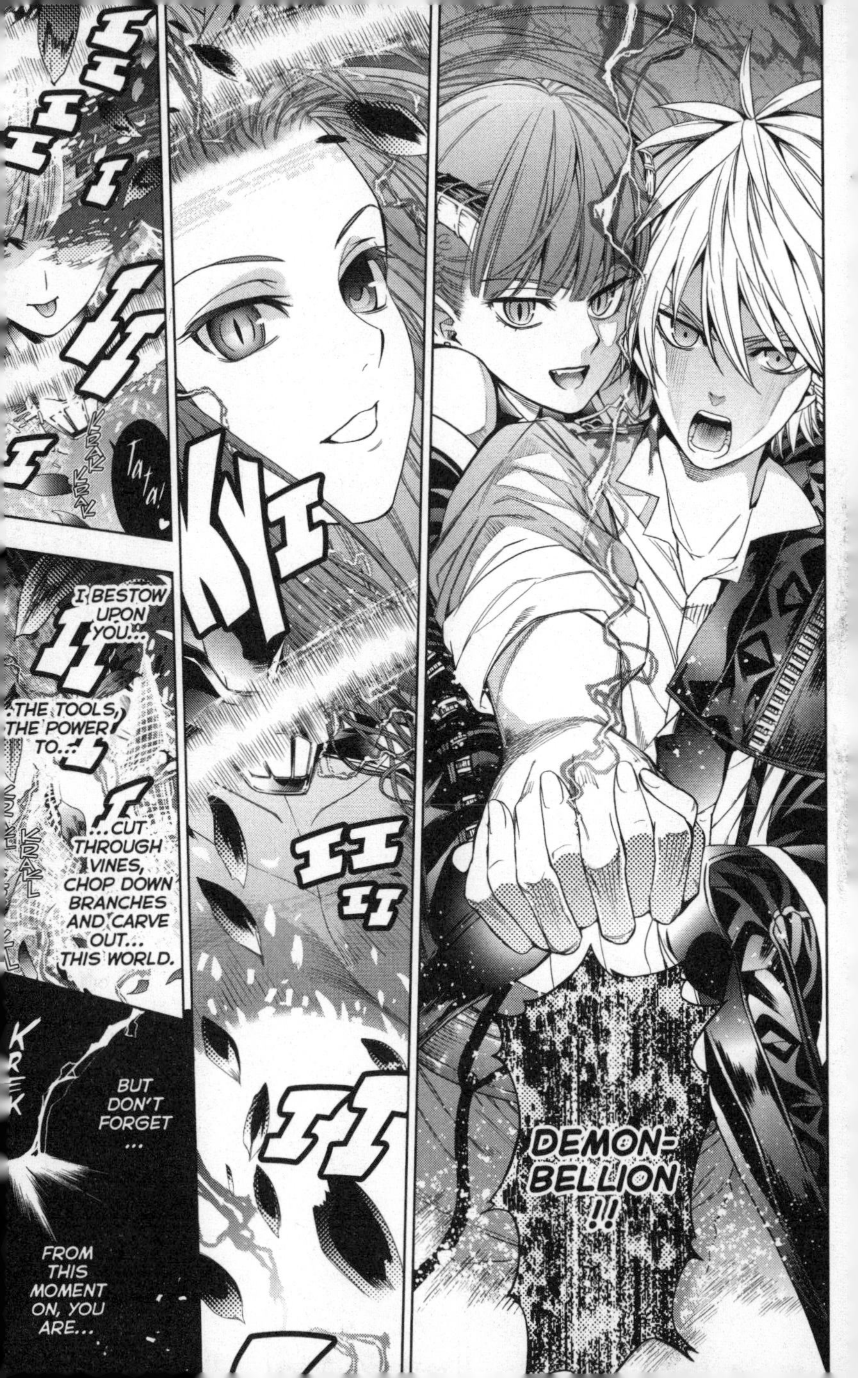
DEMON-BELLION!!
Ta ta!
KRAK KRAK KRAK
I BESTOW UPON YOU...
...THE TOOLS, THE POWER TO...
...CUT THROUGH VINES, CHOP DOWN BRANCHES AND CARVE OUT... THIS WORLD.
KREK
BUT DON'T FORGET ...
FROM THIS MOMENT ON, YOU ARE...

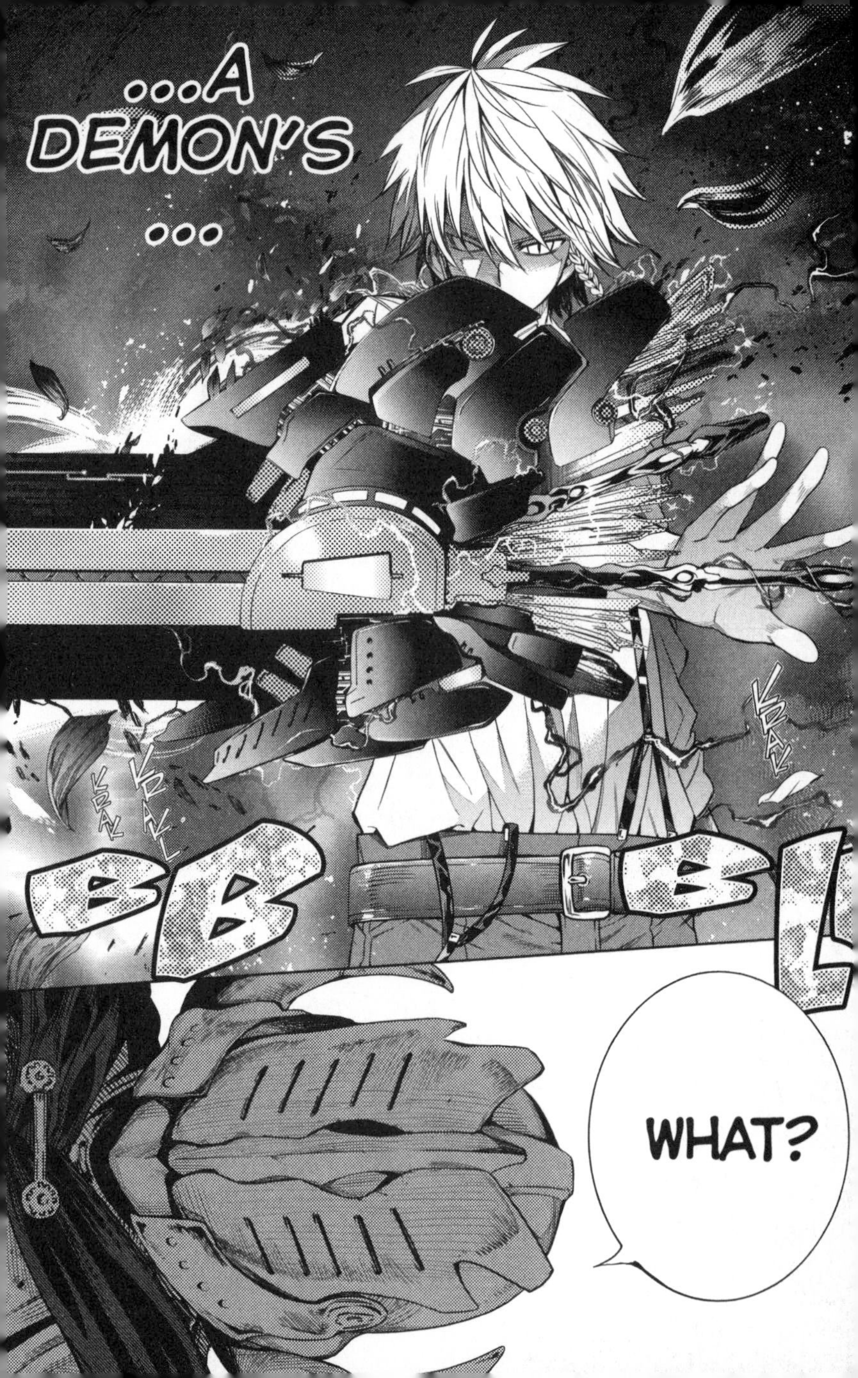
...A DEMON'S ...
KRAK
KRAKL
KRAK
BB
BL
WHAT?

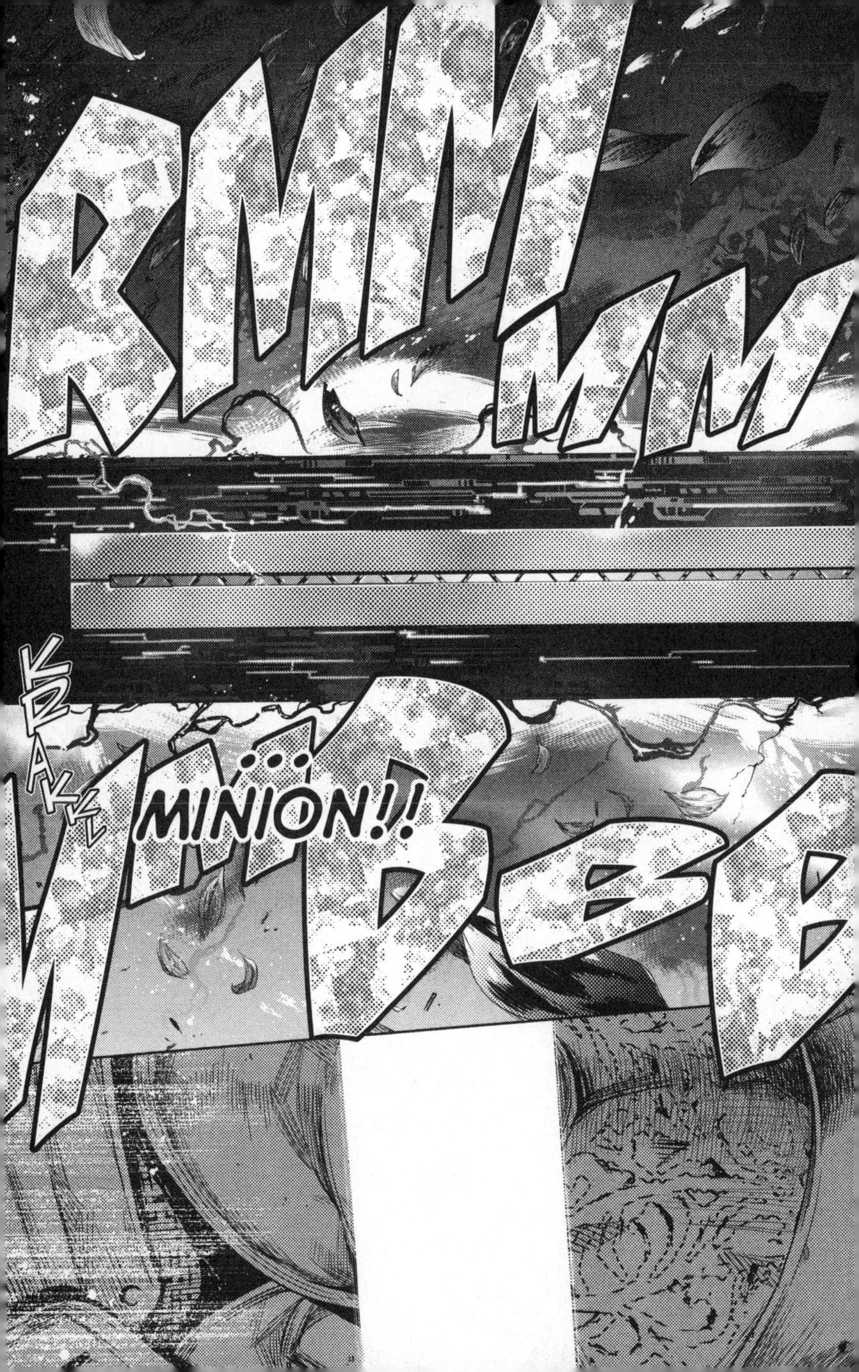
KRAKKL
...MINION!!

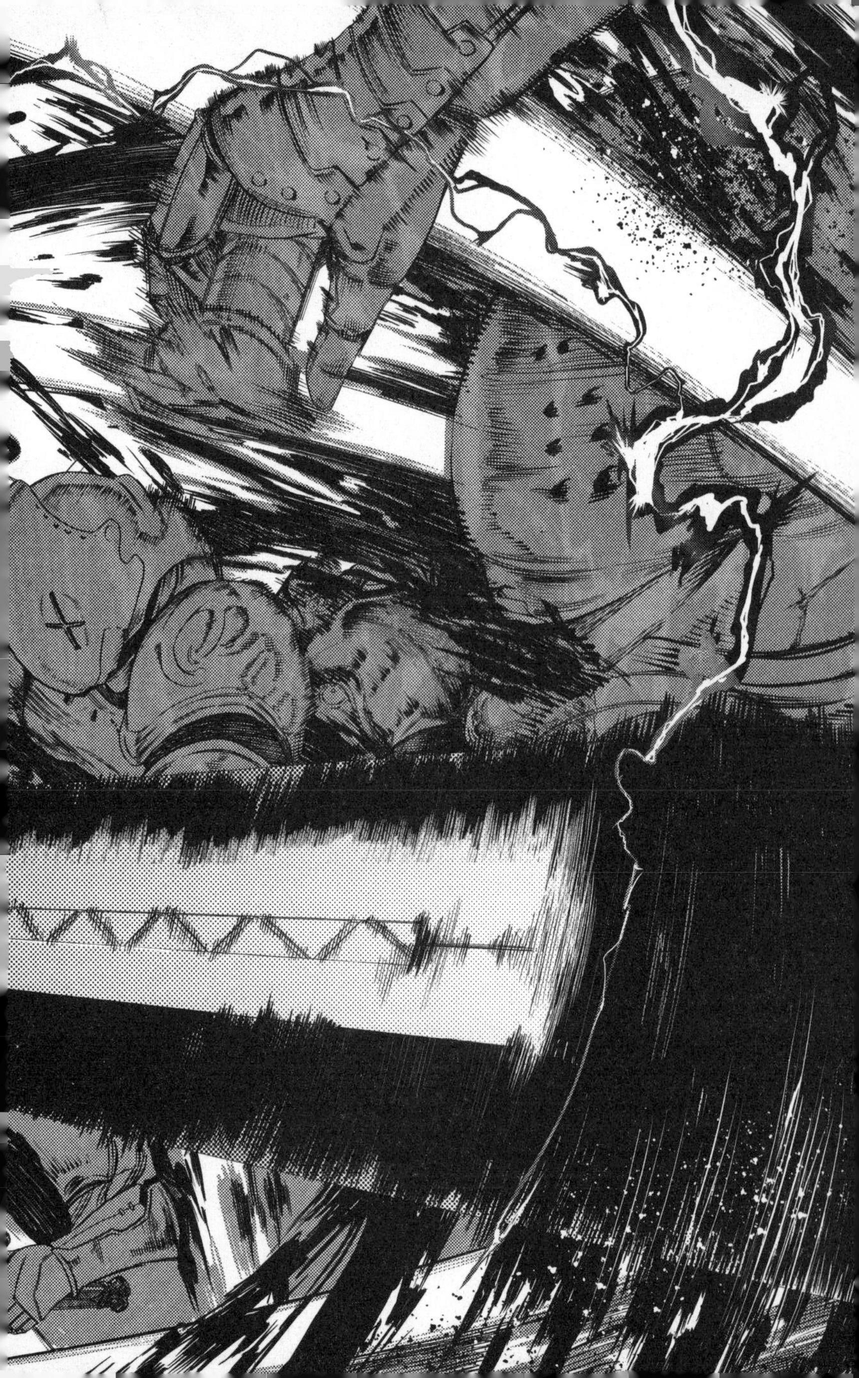

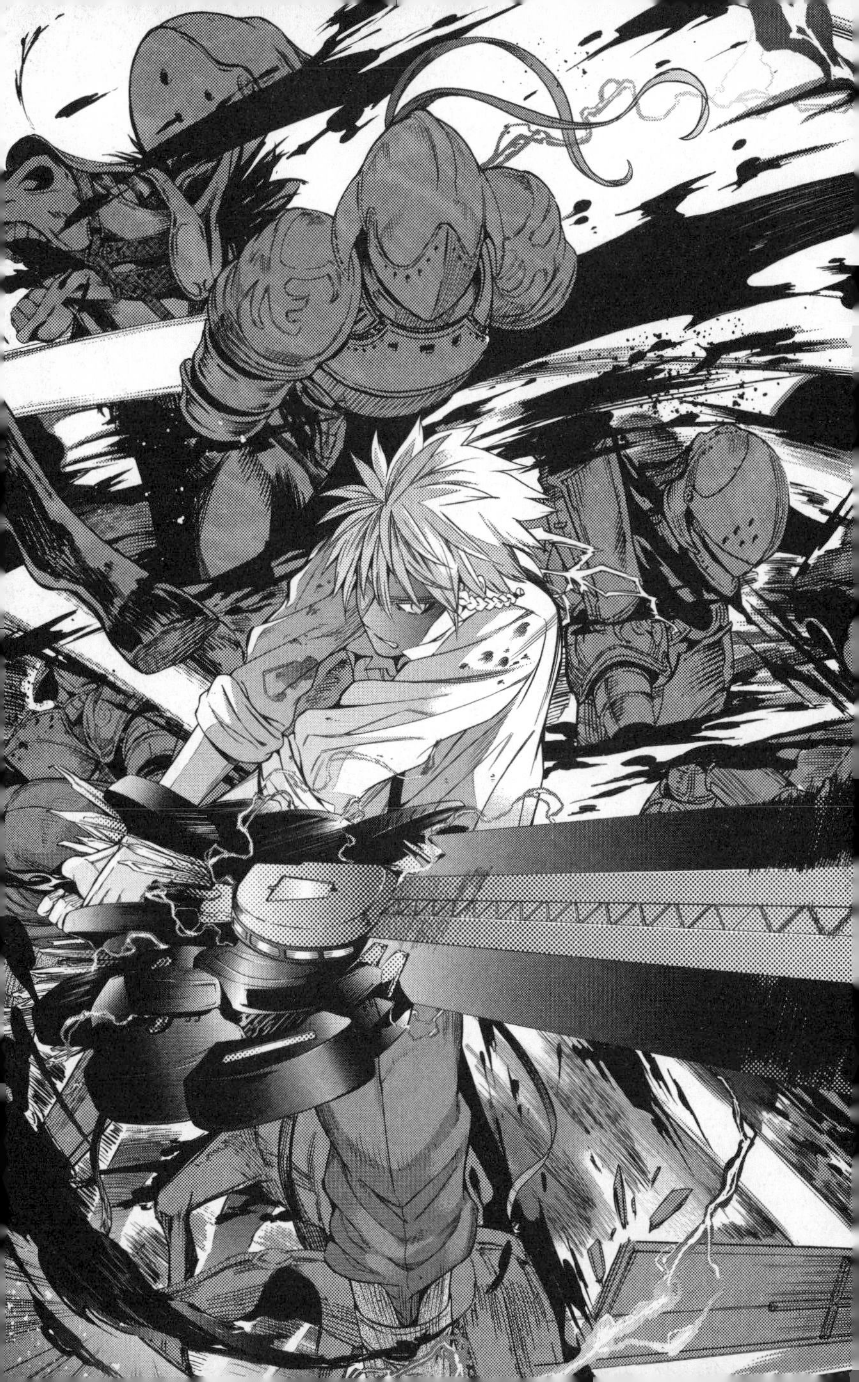

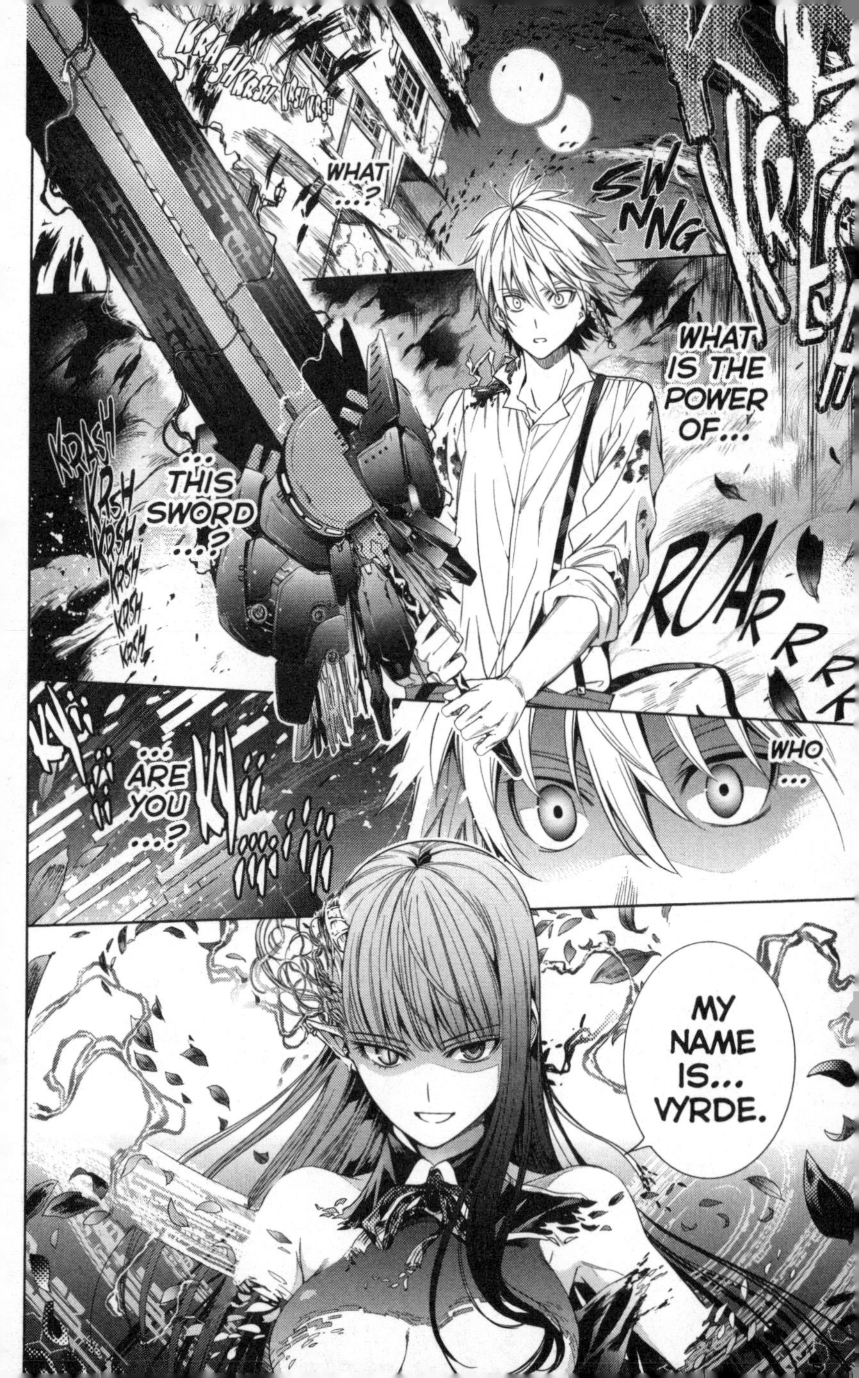
SWNNG
WHAT...?
KRASHKRSH KRSH KRSH
WHAT IS THE POWER OF...
ROARRRRK
...THIS SWORD...?
KRASH KRSH KRSH KRSH KRSH KRSH
WHO...
...ARE YOU...?
MY NAME IS... VYRDE.

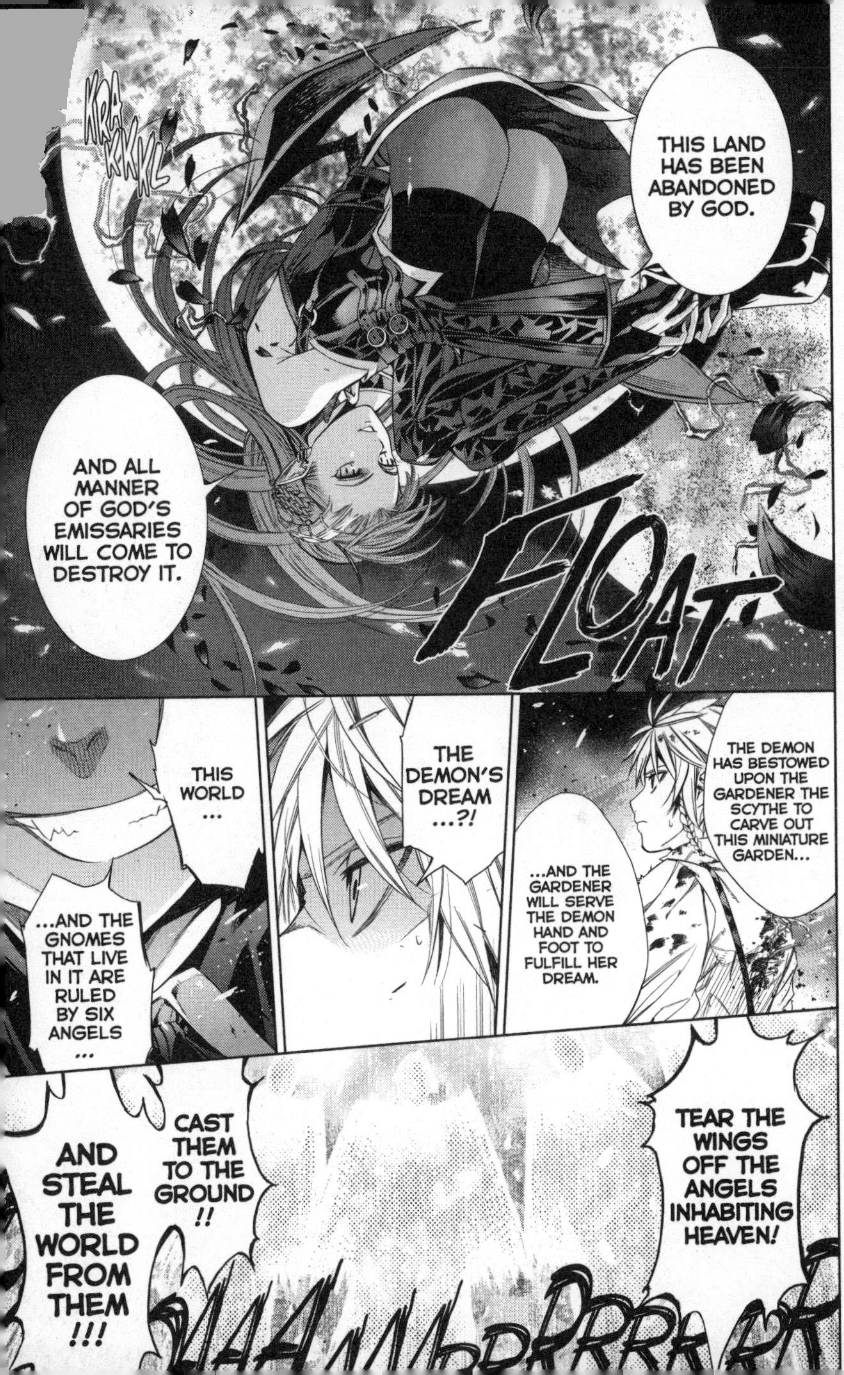
THIS LAND HAS BEEN ABANDONED BY GOD.
KRAKKKL
AND ALL MANNER OF GOD'S EMISSARIES WILL COME TO DESTROY IT.
FLOAT
THE DEMON HAS BESTOWED UPON THE GARDENER THE SCYTHE TO CARVE OUT THIS MINIATURE GARDEN...
...AND THE GARDENER WILL SERVE THE DEMON HAND AND FOOT TO FULFILL HER DREAM.
THE DEMON'S DREAM ...?!
THIS WORLD ...
...AND THE GNOMES THAT LIVE IN IT ARE RULED BY SIX ANGELS ...
TEAR THE WINGS OFF THE ANGELS INHABITING HEAVEN!
CAST THEM TO THE GROUND !!
AND STEAL THE WORLD FROM THEM !!!

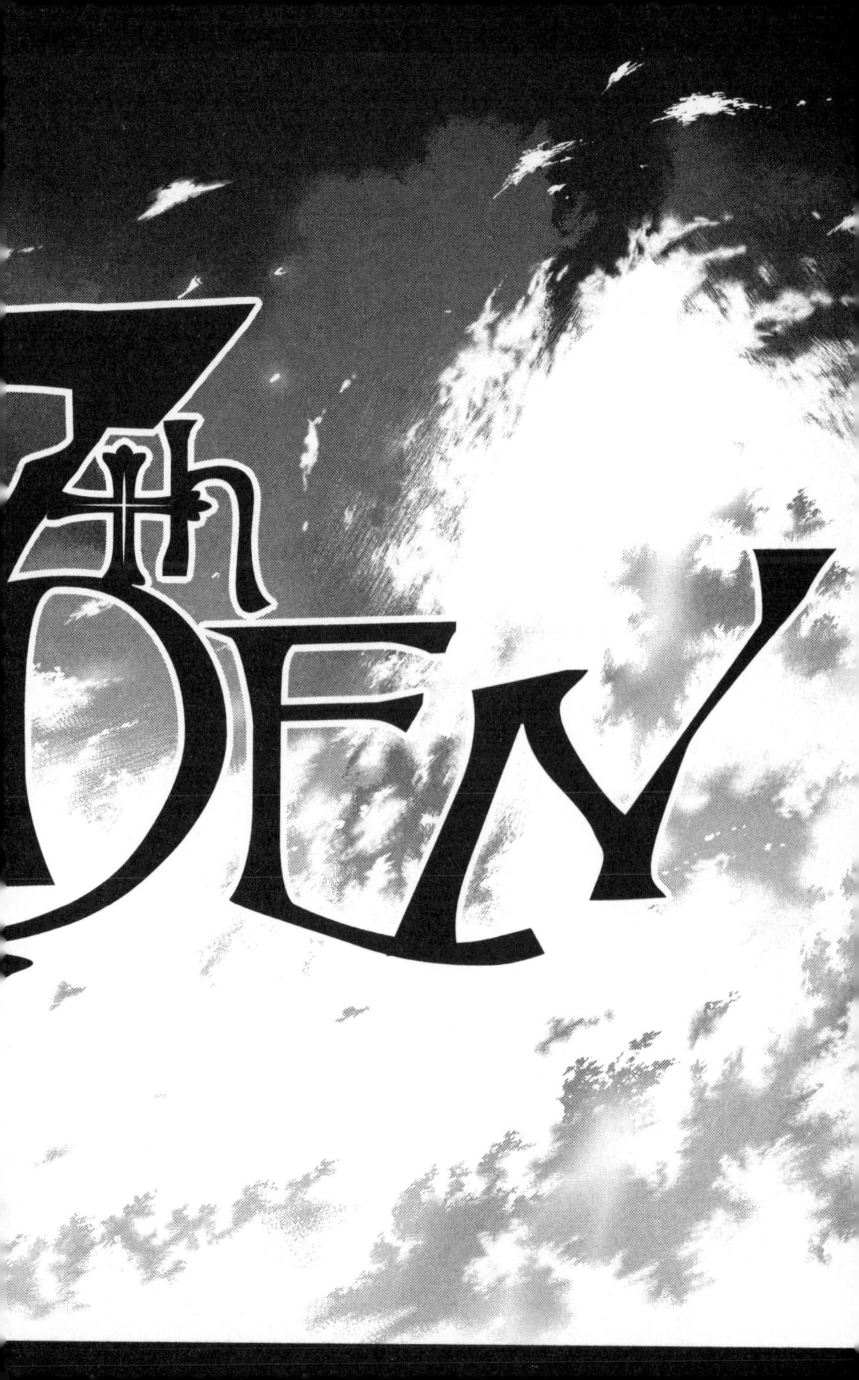
7th
DEV

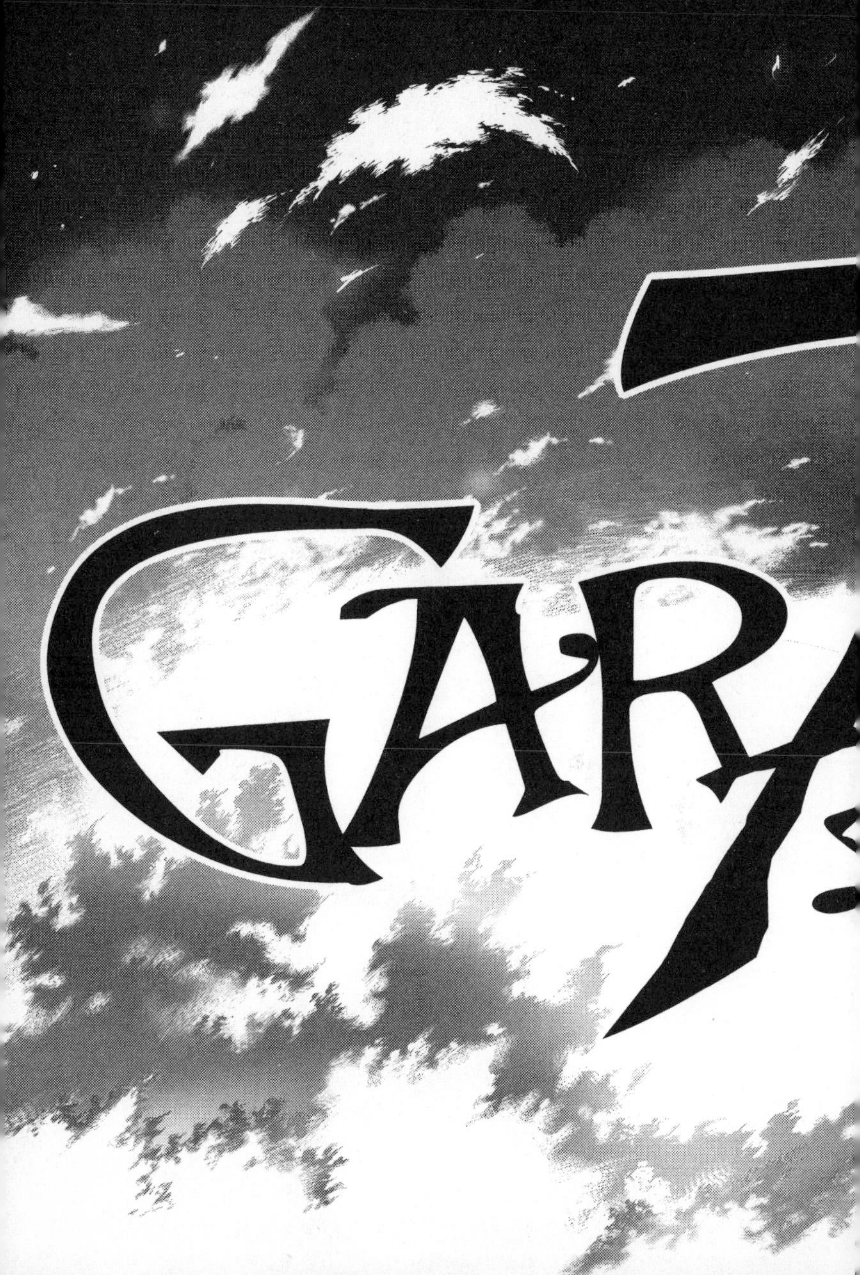

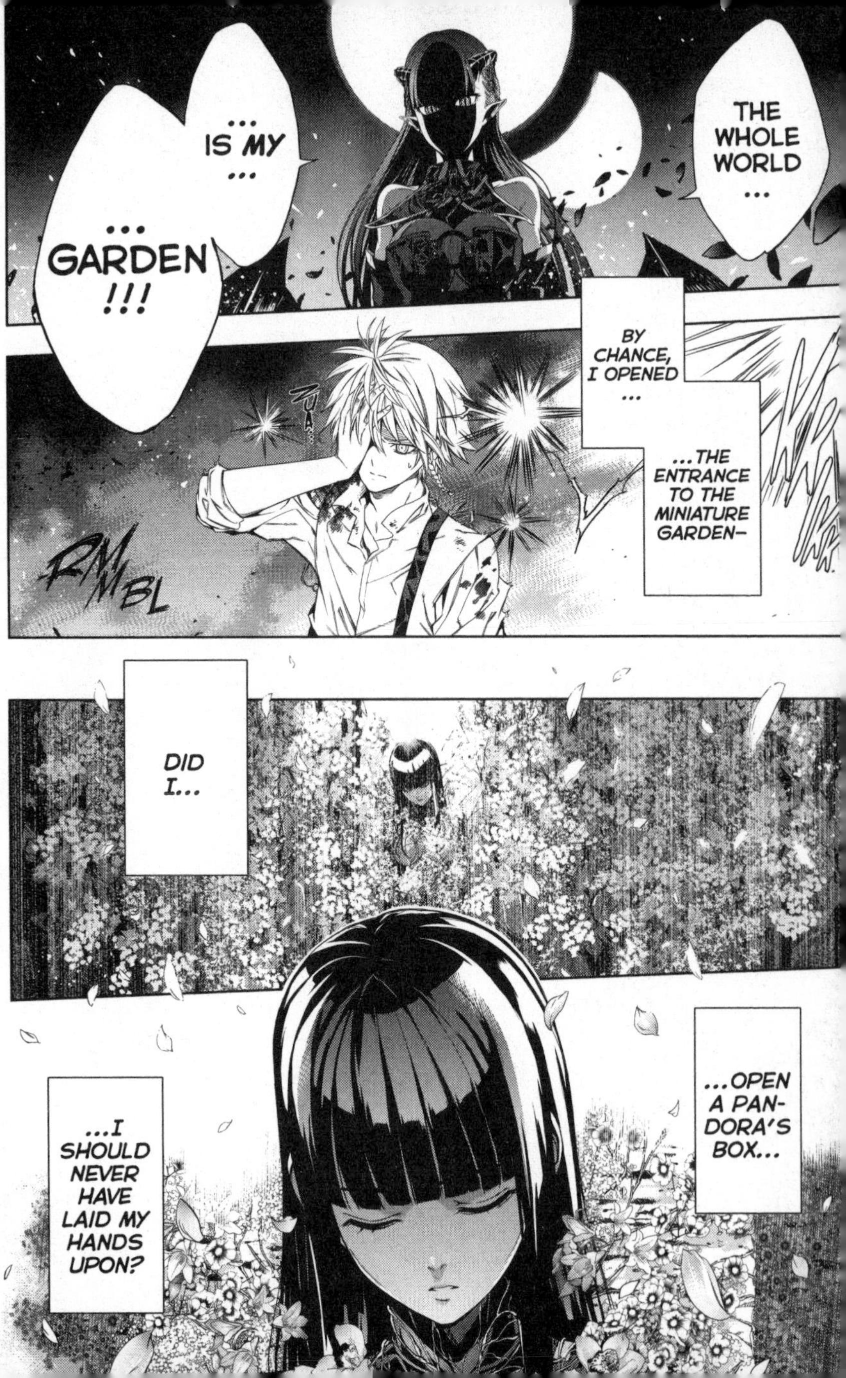
THE WHOLE WORLD ...
... IS MY ...
... GARDEN !!!
BY CHANCE, I OPENED ...
...THE ENTRANCE TO THE MINIATURE GARDEN—
ZUA...
RMMBL
DID I...
...OPEN A PAN-DORA'S BOX...
...I SHOULD NEVER HAVE LAID MY HANDS UPON?

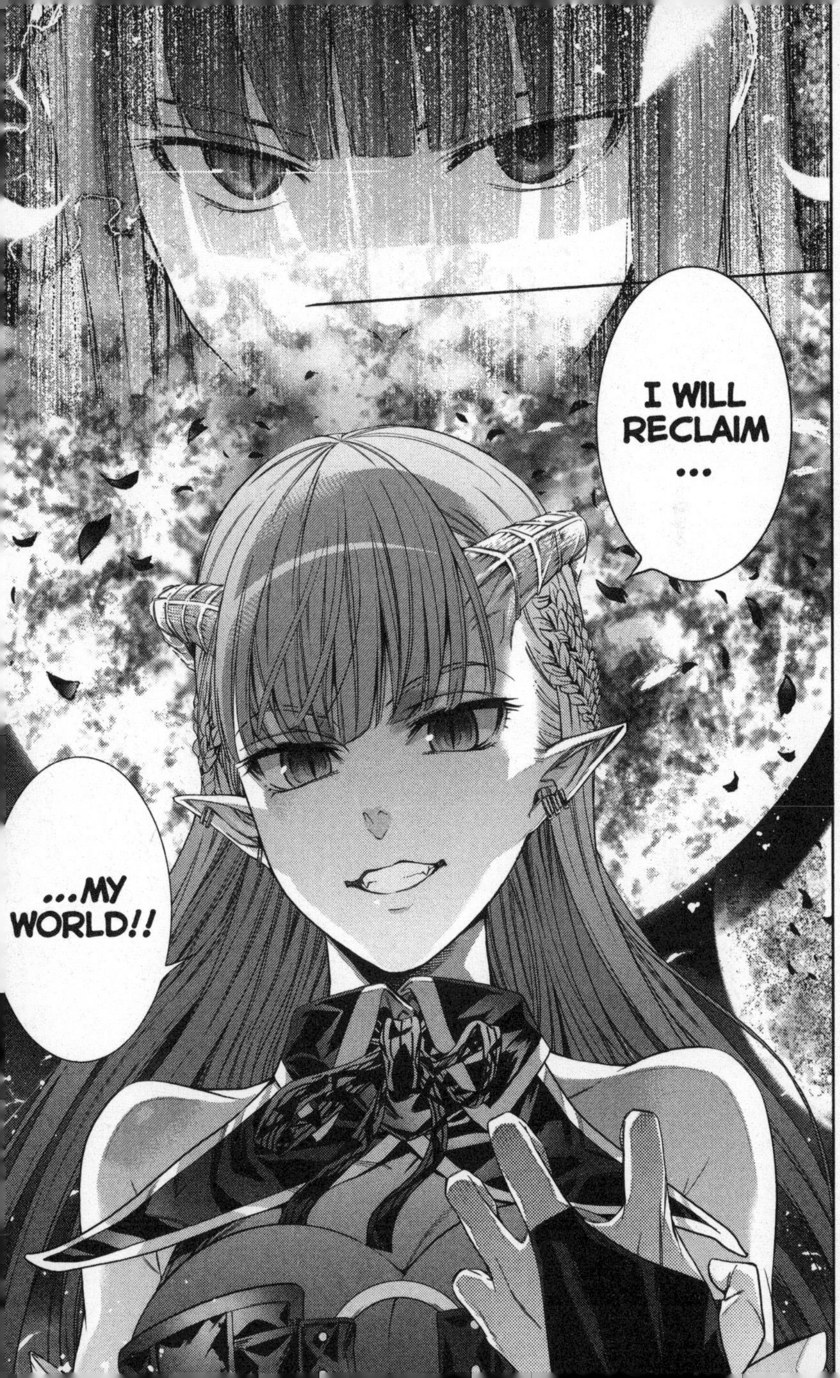
I WILL RECLAIM ...
...MY WORLD!!

7th GARDEN

1

MITSU IZUMI

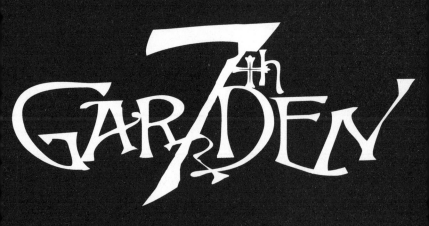

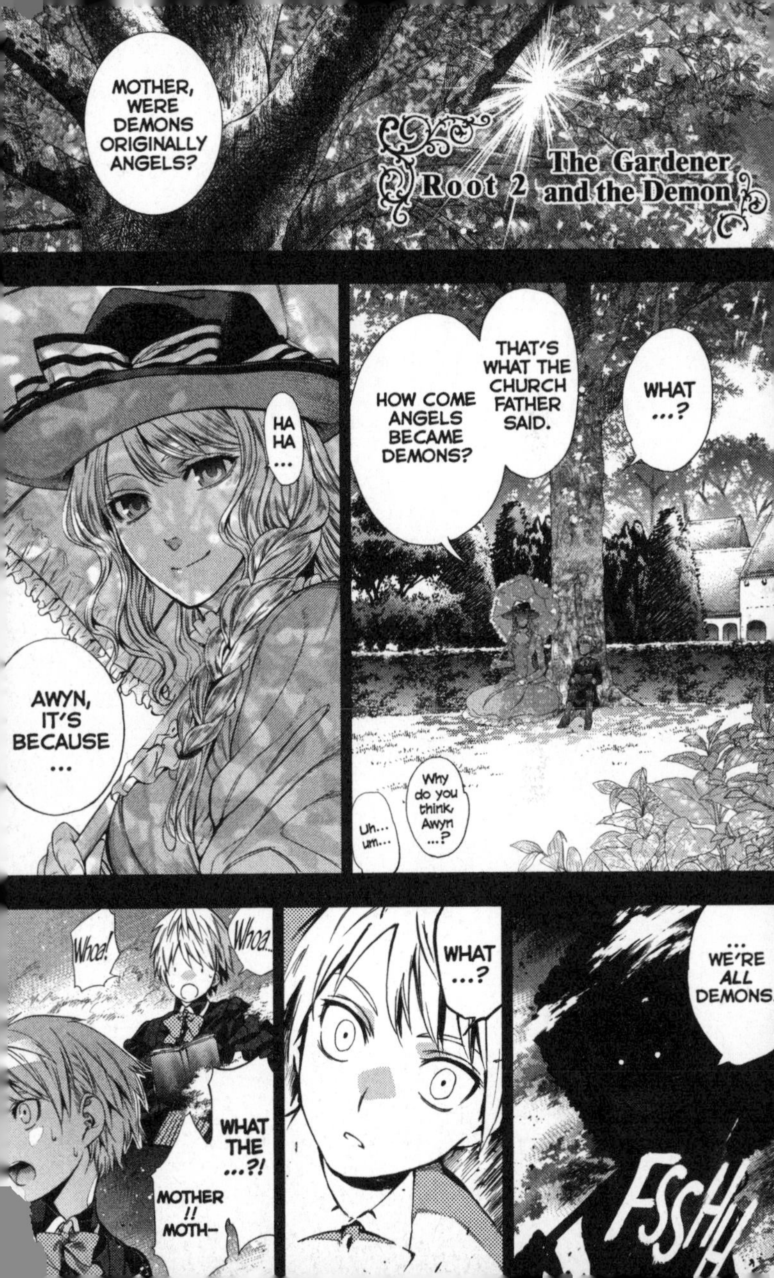
Root 2 The Gardener and the Demon
MOTHER, WERE DEMONS ORIGINALLY ANGELS?
WHAT...?
THAT'S WHAT THE CHURCH FATHER SAID.
HOW COME ANGELS BECAME DEMONS?
Why do you think, Awyn...?
Uh... um...
HA HA...
AWYN, IT'S BECAUSE...
...WE'RE ALL DEMONS.
FSSH
WHAT...?
Whoa...
Whoa!
WHAT THE...?!
MOTHER!! MOTH-

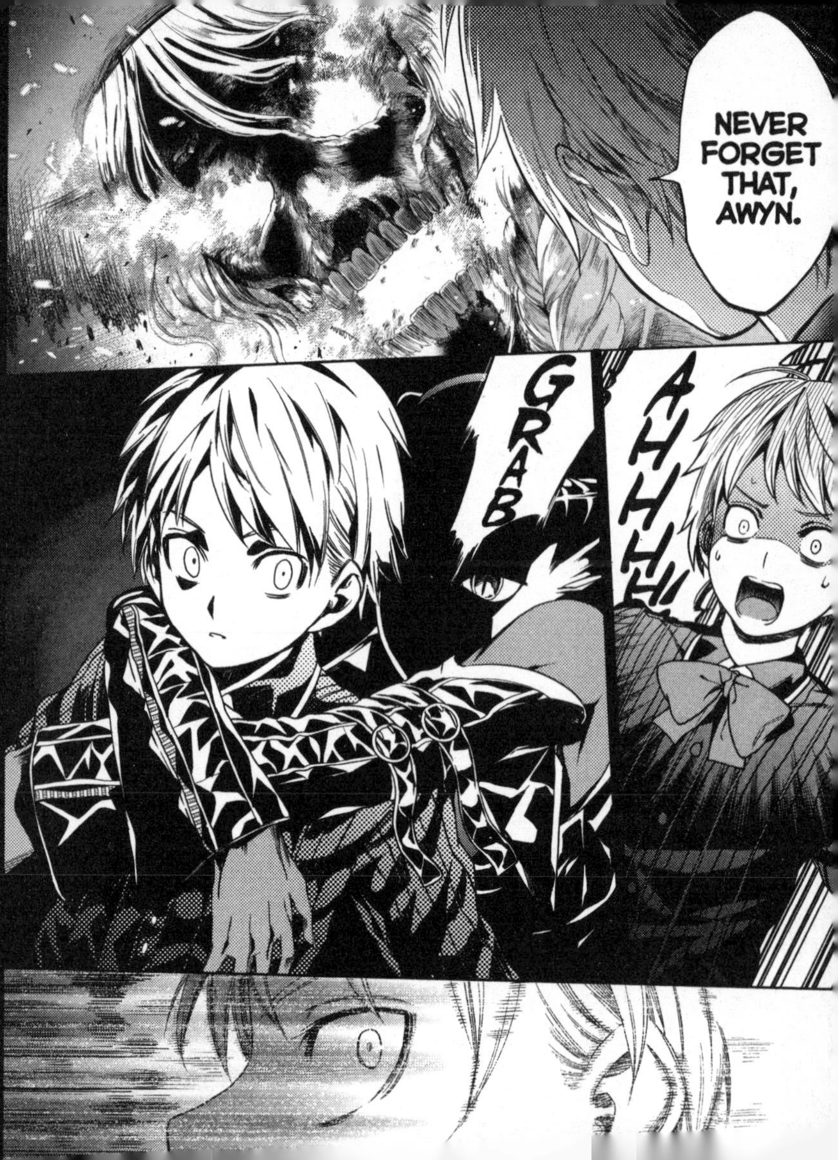
NEVER FORGET THAT, AWYN.
AHHHH!!
GRAB

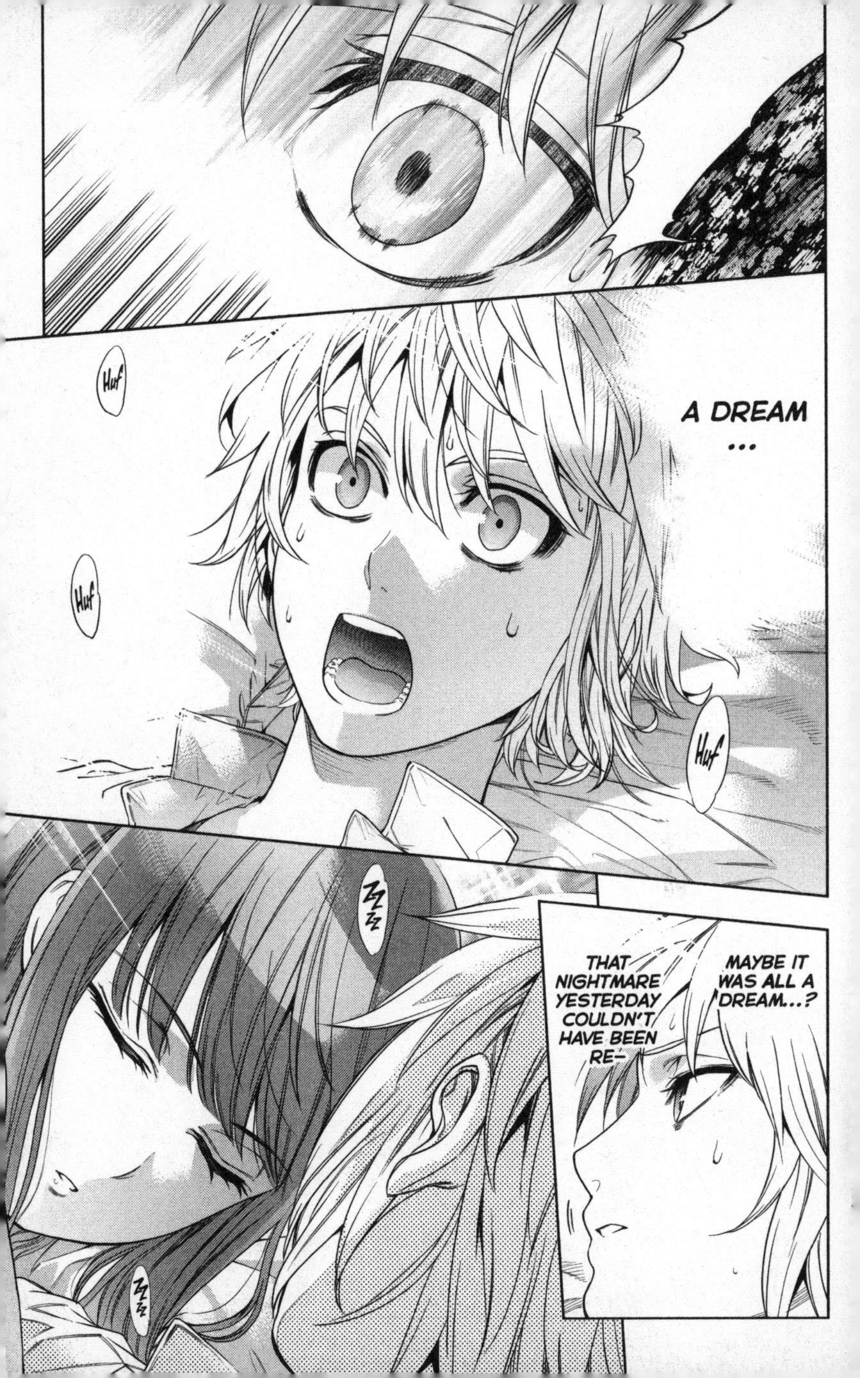
A DREAM ...
Huf
Huf
Huf
MAYBE IT WAS ALL A DREAM...?
THAT NIGHTMARE YESTERDAY COULDN'T HAVE BEEN RE—
ZZZ
ZZZ

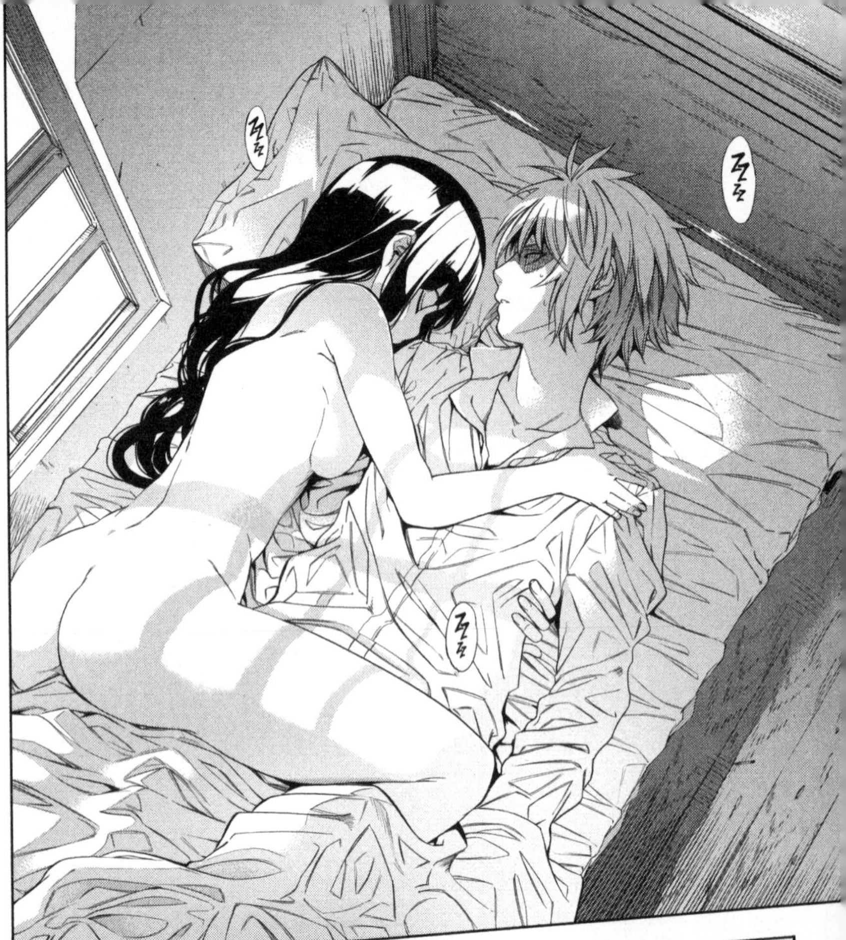
Zzz
Zzz
Zzz

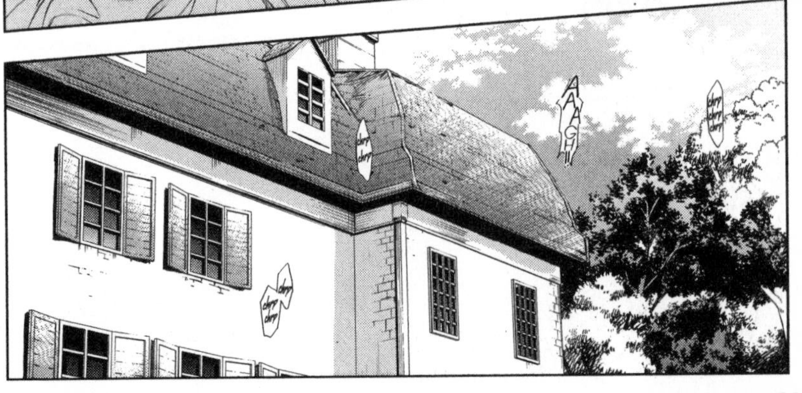
chirp chirp chirp
AAAGH!!
chirp chirp
chirp chirp chirp

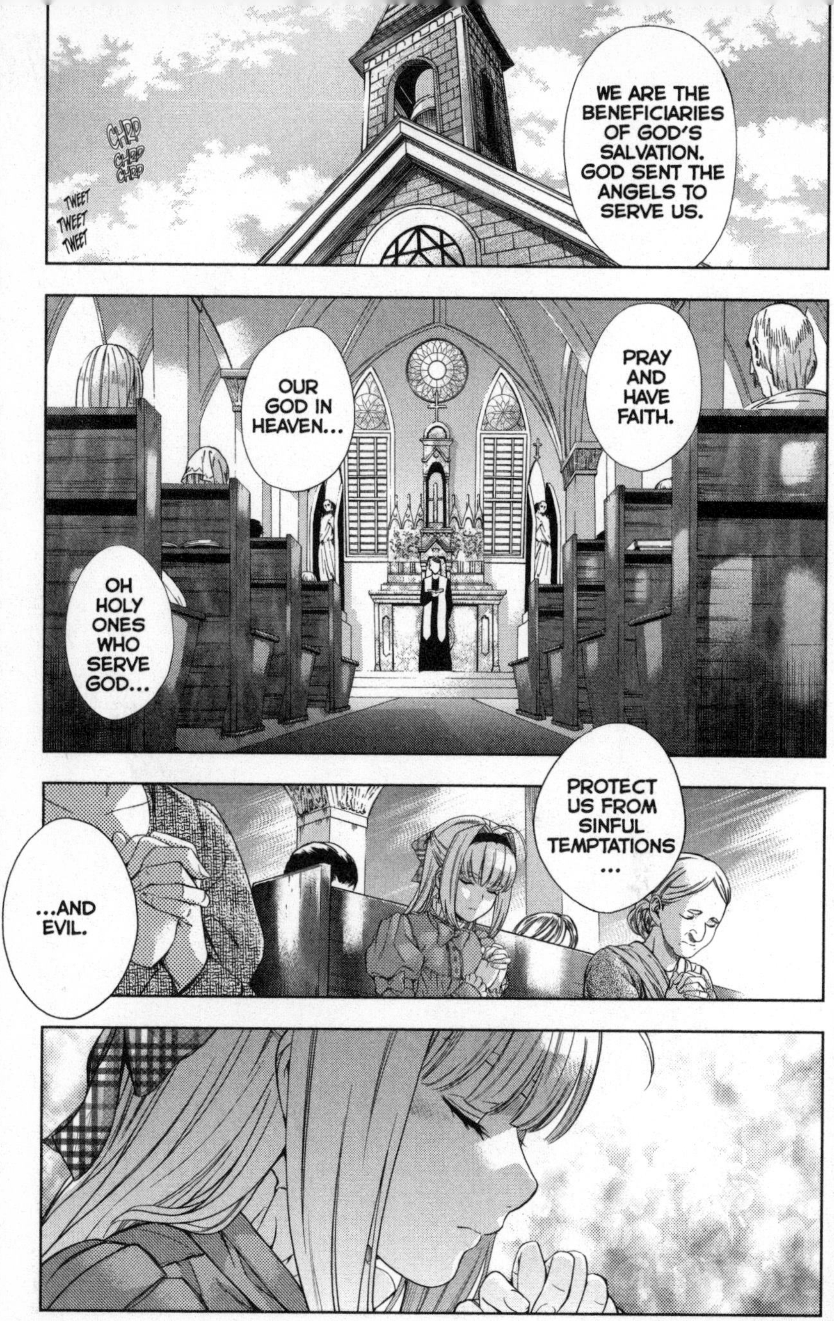
WE ARE THE BENEFICIARIES OF GOD'S SALVATION. GOD SENT THE ANGELS TO SERVE US.
CHRP CHRP CHRP
TWEET TWEET TWEET
PRAY AND HAVE FAITH.
OUR GOD IN HEAVEN...
OH HOLY ONES WHO SERVE GOD...
PROTECT US FROM SINFUL TEMPTATIONS...
...AND EVIL.

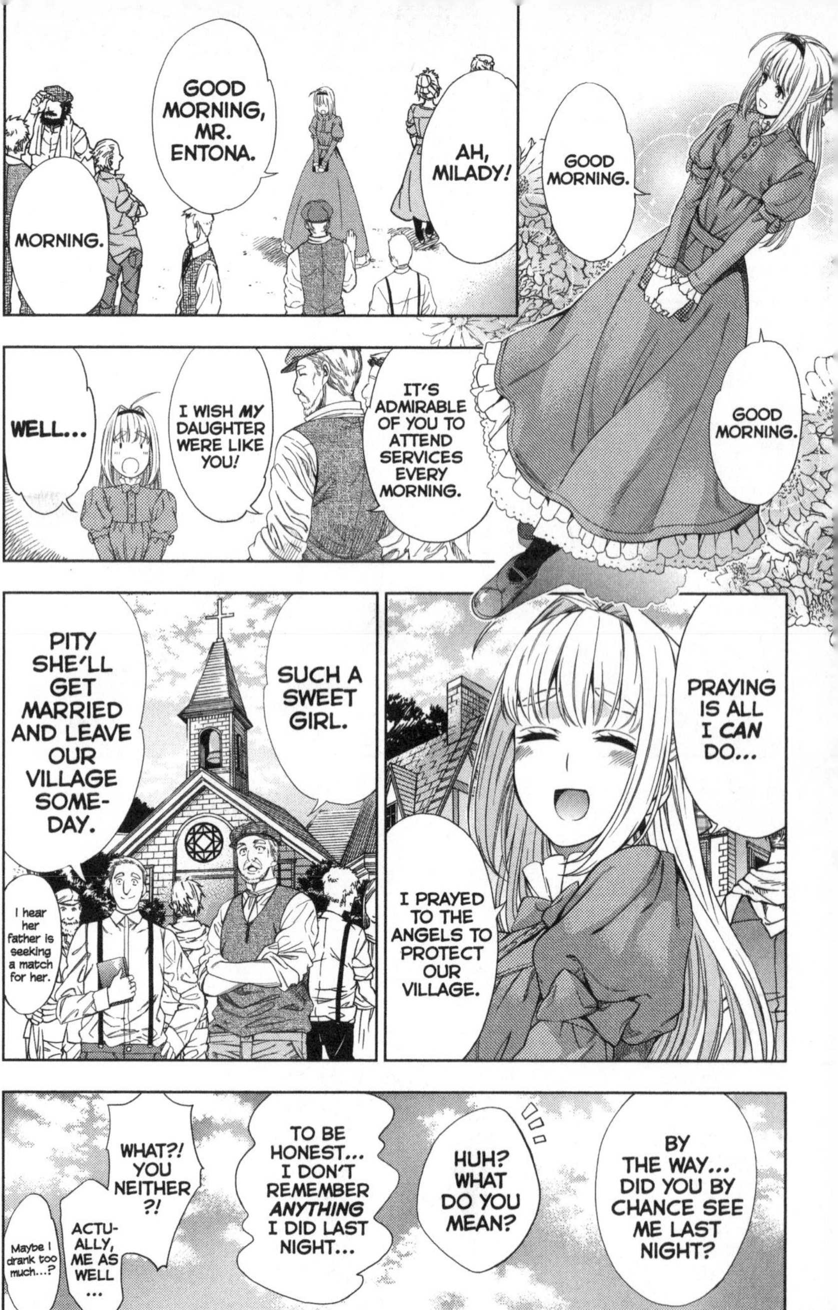
GOOD MORNING.
GOOD MORNING.
AH, MILADY!
GOOD MORNING, MR. ENTONA.
MORNING.
IT'S ADMIRABLE OF YOU TO ATTEND SERVICES EVERY MORNING.
I WISH *MY* DAUGHTER WERE LIKE YOU!
WELL...
PRAYING IS ALL I *CAN* DO...
I PRAYED TO THE ANGELS TO PROTECT OUR VILLAGE.
SUCH A SWEET GIRL.
PITY SHE'LL GET MARRIED AND LEAVE OUR VILLAGE SOME-DAY.
I hear her father is seeking a match for her.
BY THE WAY... DID YOU BY CHANCE SEE ME LAST NIGHT?
HUH? WHAT DO YOU MEAN?
TO BE HONEST... I DON'T REMEMBER *ANYTHING* I DID LAST NIGHT...
WHAT?! YOU NEITHER?!
ACTU-ALLY, ME AS WELL...
Maybe I drank too much...?

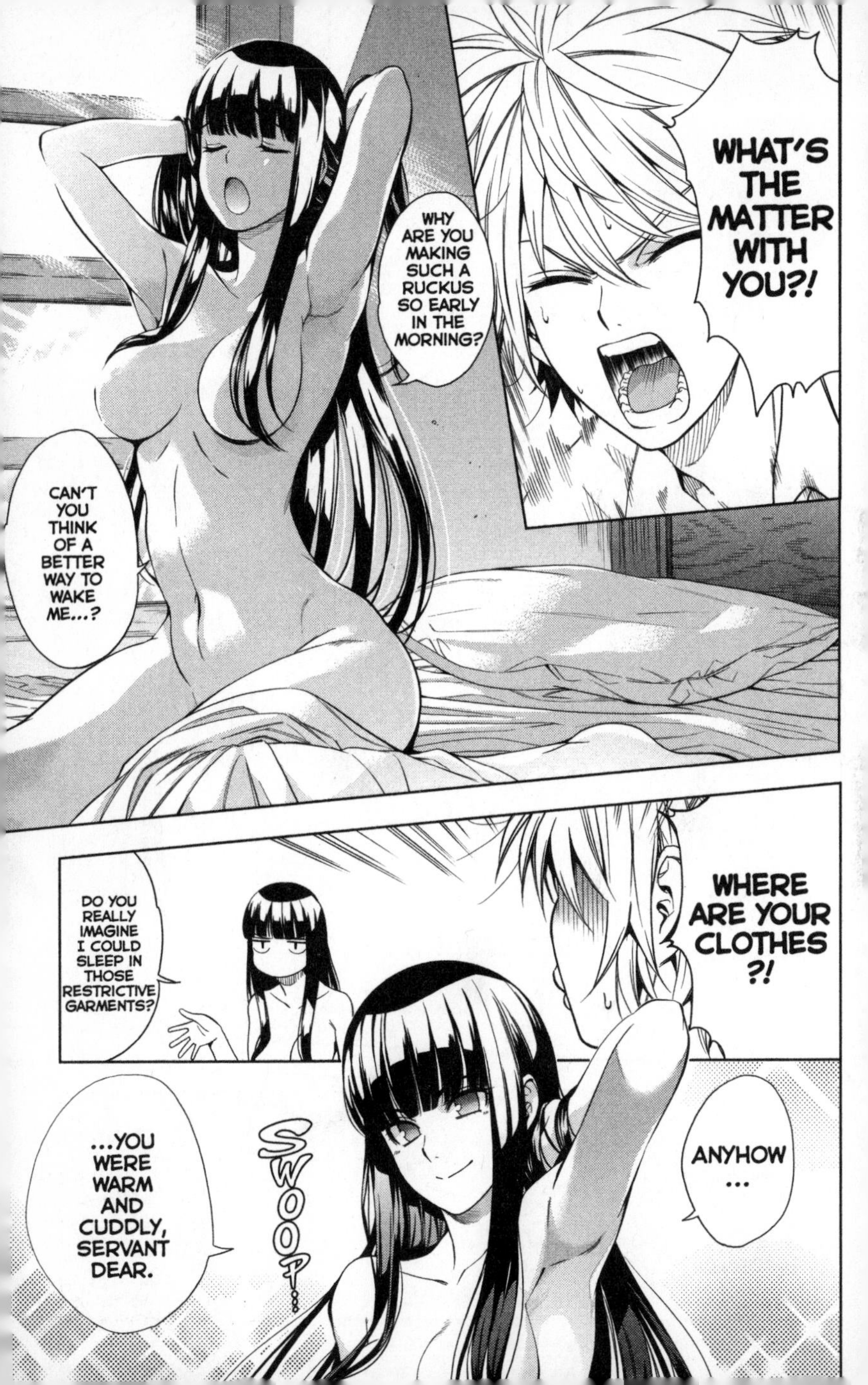
WHAT'S THE MATTER WITH YOU?!
WHY ARE YOU MAKING SUCH A RUCKUS SO EARLY IN THE MORNING?
CAN'T YOU THINK OF A BETTER WAY TO WAKE ME...?
WHERE ARE YOUR CLOTHES?!
DO YOU REALLY IMAGINE I COULD SLEEP IN THOSE RESTRICTIVE GARMENTS?
ANYHOW...
SWOOP...
...YOU WERE WARM AND CUDDLY, SERVANT DEAR.

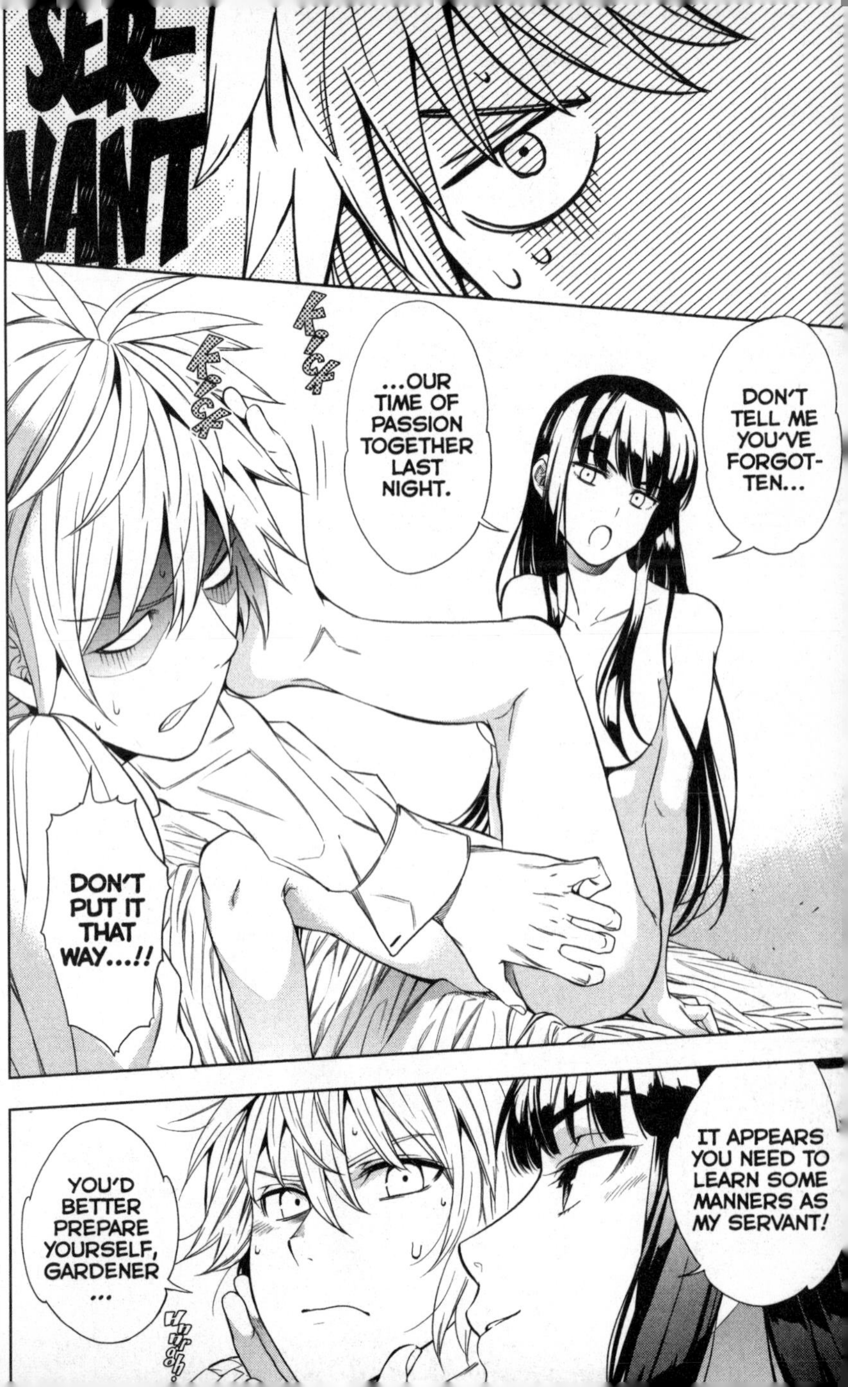
SER-VANT
DON'T TELL ME YOU'VE FORGOT-TEN...
...OUR TIME OF PASSION TOGETHER LAST NIGHT.
KICK KICK
DON'T PUT IT THAT WAY...!!
IT APPEARS YOU NEED TO LEARN SOME MANNERS AS MY SERVANT!
YOU'D BETTER PREPARE YOURSELF, GARDENER ...
Hnrrgh!

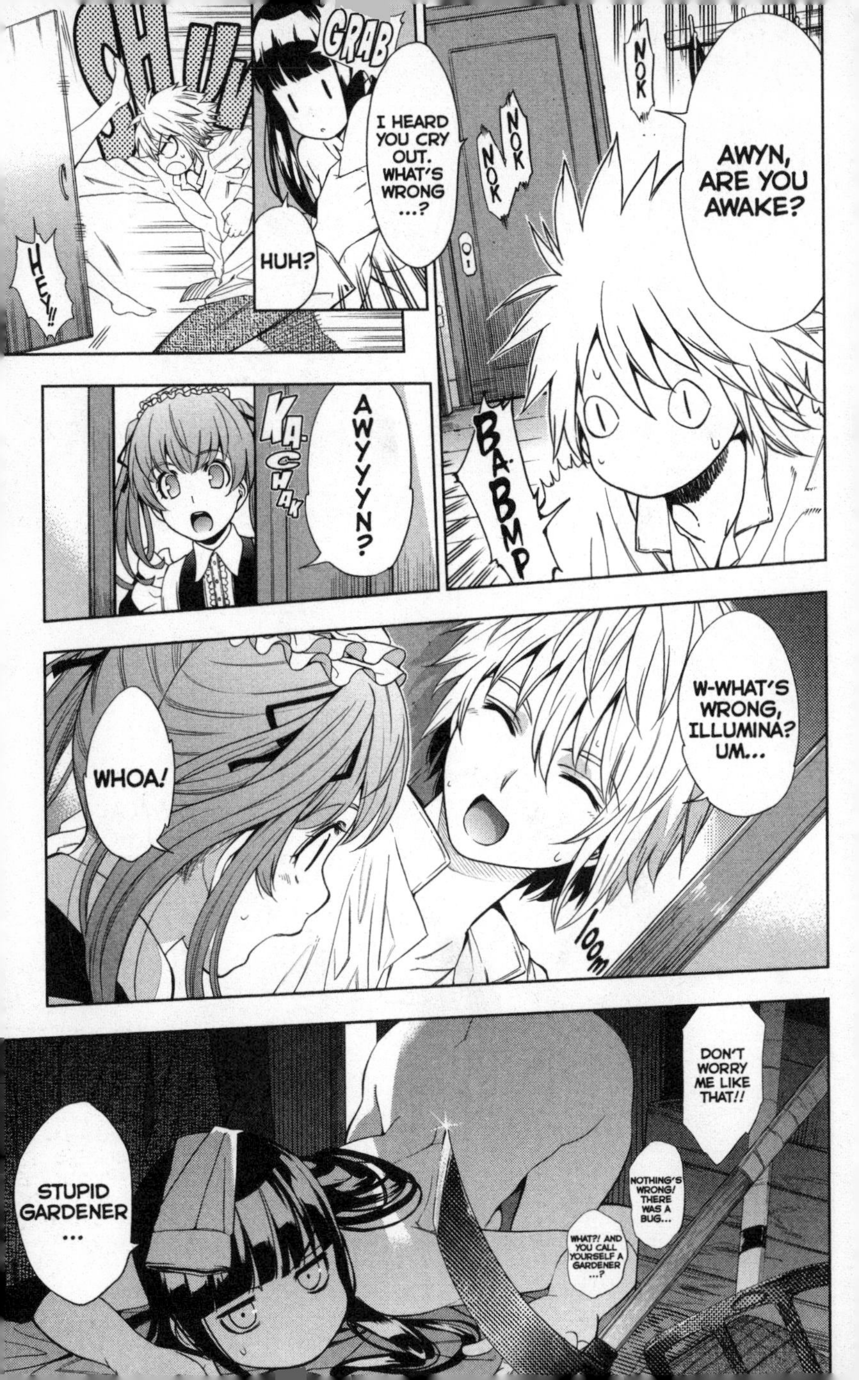
NOK
NOK
NOK
AWYN, ARE YOU AWAKE?
BABMP
GRAB
I HEARD YOU CRY OUT. WHAT'S WRONG...?
HUH?
HEY!!
KA-CHAK
AWYYYN?
W-WHAT'S WRONG, ILLUMINA? UM...
WHOA!
loom
DON'T WORRY ME LIKE THAT!!
NOTHING'S WRONG! THERE WAS A BUG...
WHAT?! AND YOU CALL YOURSELF A GARDENER...?
STUPID GARDENER...

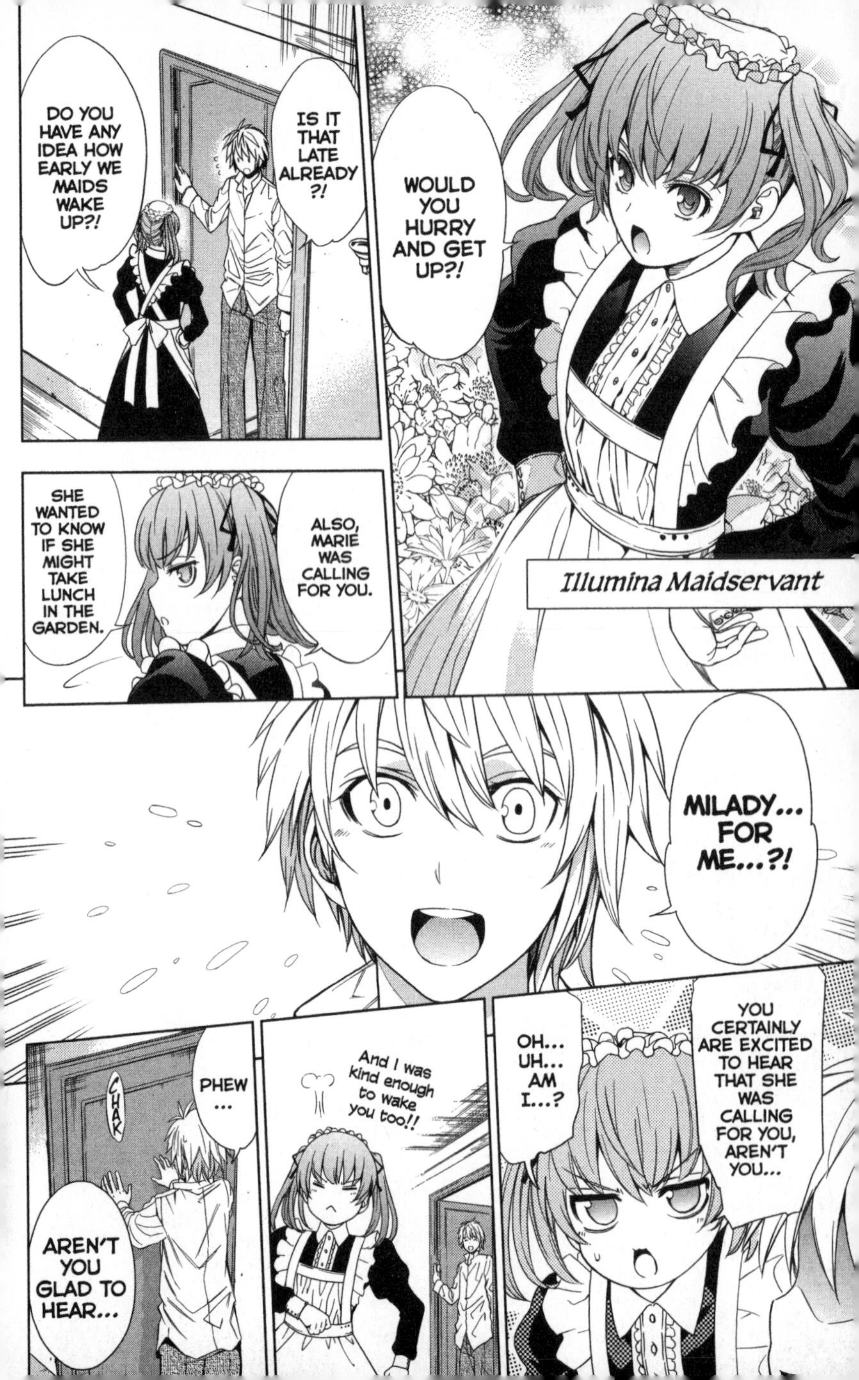
WOULD YOU HURRY AND GET UP?!
Illumina Maidservant
IS IT THAT LATE ALREADY?!
DO YOU HAVE ANY IDEA HOW EARLY WE MAIDS WAKE UP?!
ALSO, MARIE WAS CALLING FOR YOU.
SHE WANTED TO KNOW IF SHE MIGHT TAKE LUNCH IN THE GARDEN.
MILADY... FOR ME...?!
YOU CERTAINLY ARE EXCITED TO HEAR THAT SHE WAS CALLING FOR YOU, AREN'T YOU...
OH... UH... AM I...?
And I was kind enough to wake you too!!
PHEW ...
CHAK
AREN'T YOU GLAD TO HEAR...

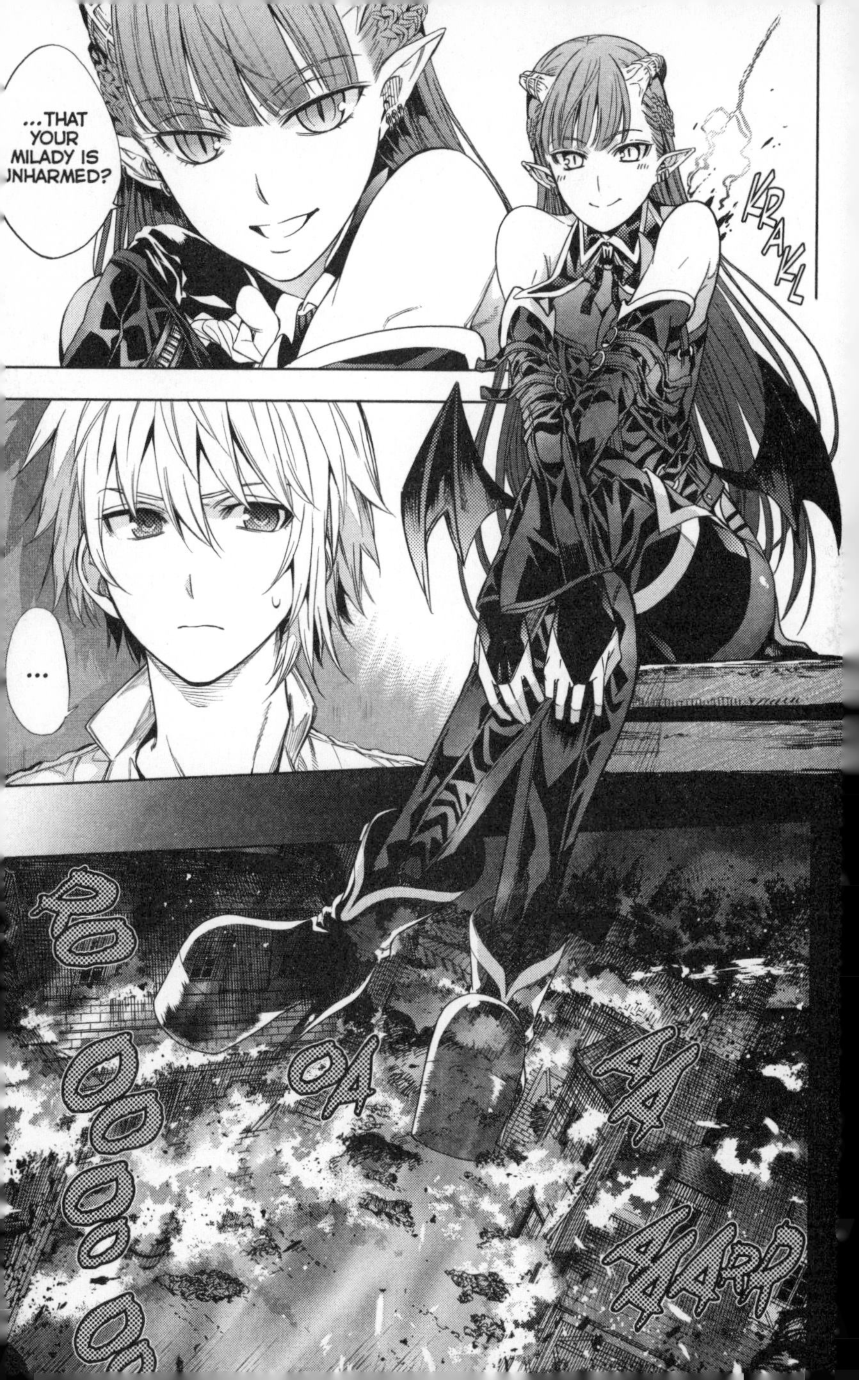
KRAKL
...THAT YOUR MILADY IS UNHARMED?
...
ROOOOOO
OA
AAAARR

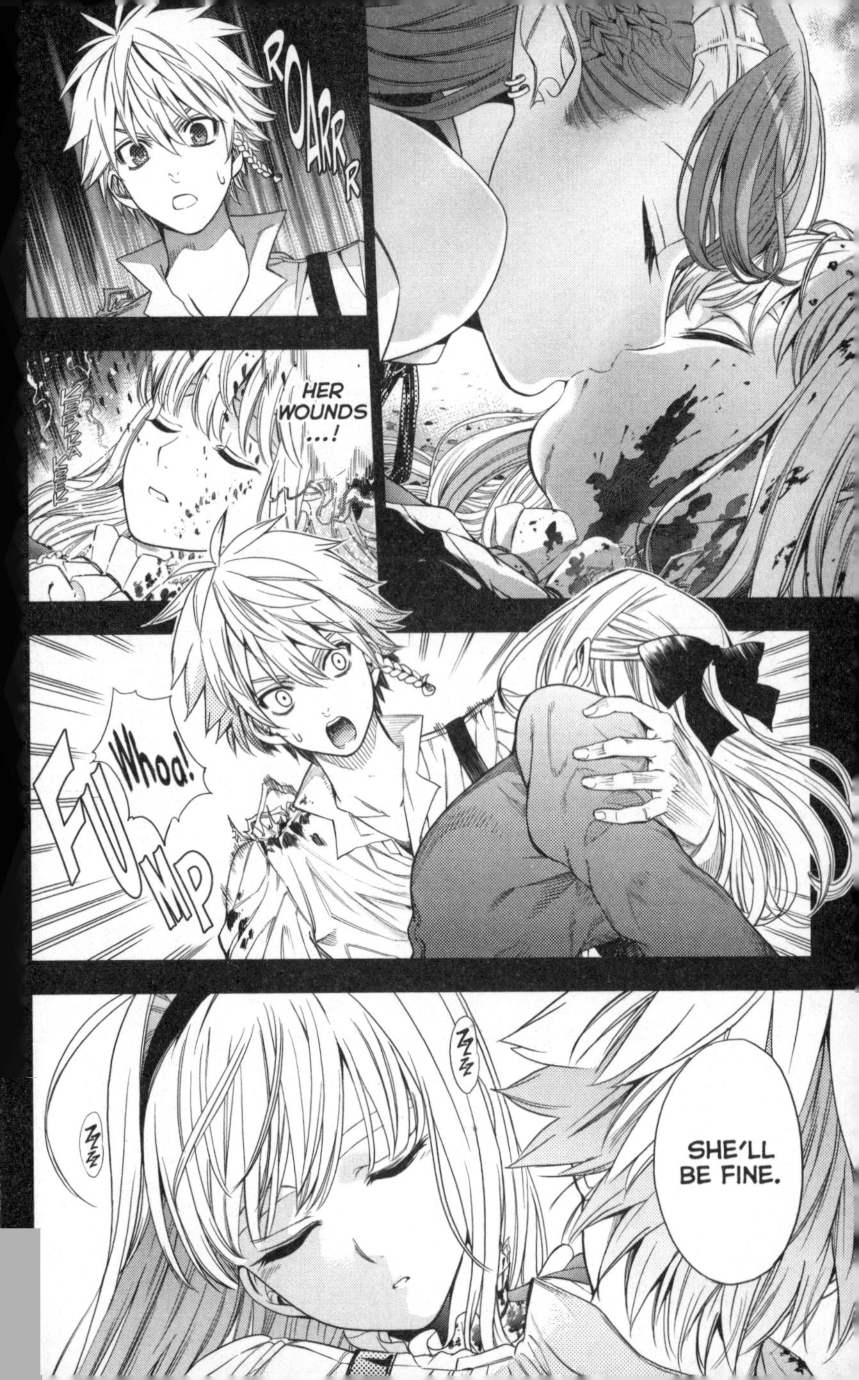
ROARRR
HER WOUNDS ...!
Whoa!
FLUMP
SHE'LL BE FINE.
ZZZ
ZZZ

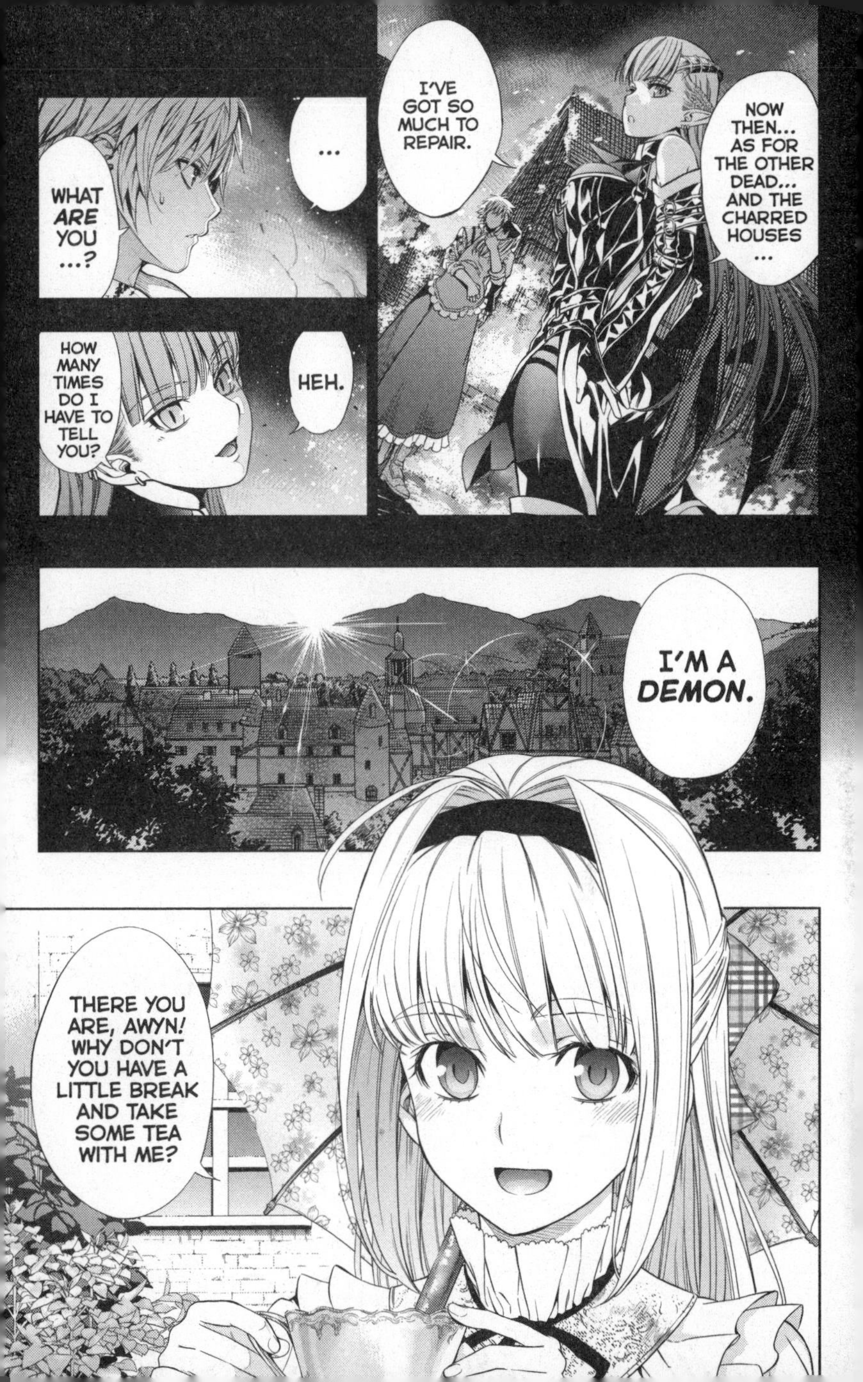
NOW THEN... AS FOR THE OTHER DEAD... AND THE CHARRED HOUSES...
I'VE GOT SO MUCH TO REPAIR.
...
WHAT *ARE* YOU...?
HEH.
HOW MANY TIMES DO I HAVE TO TELL YOU?
I'M A *DEMON*.
THERE YOU ARE, AWYN! WHY DON'T YOU HAVE A LITTLE BREAK AND TAKE SOME TEA WITH ME?

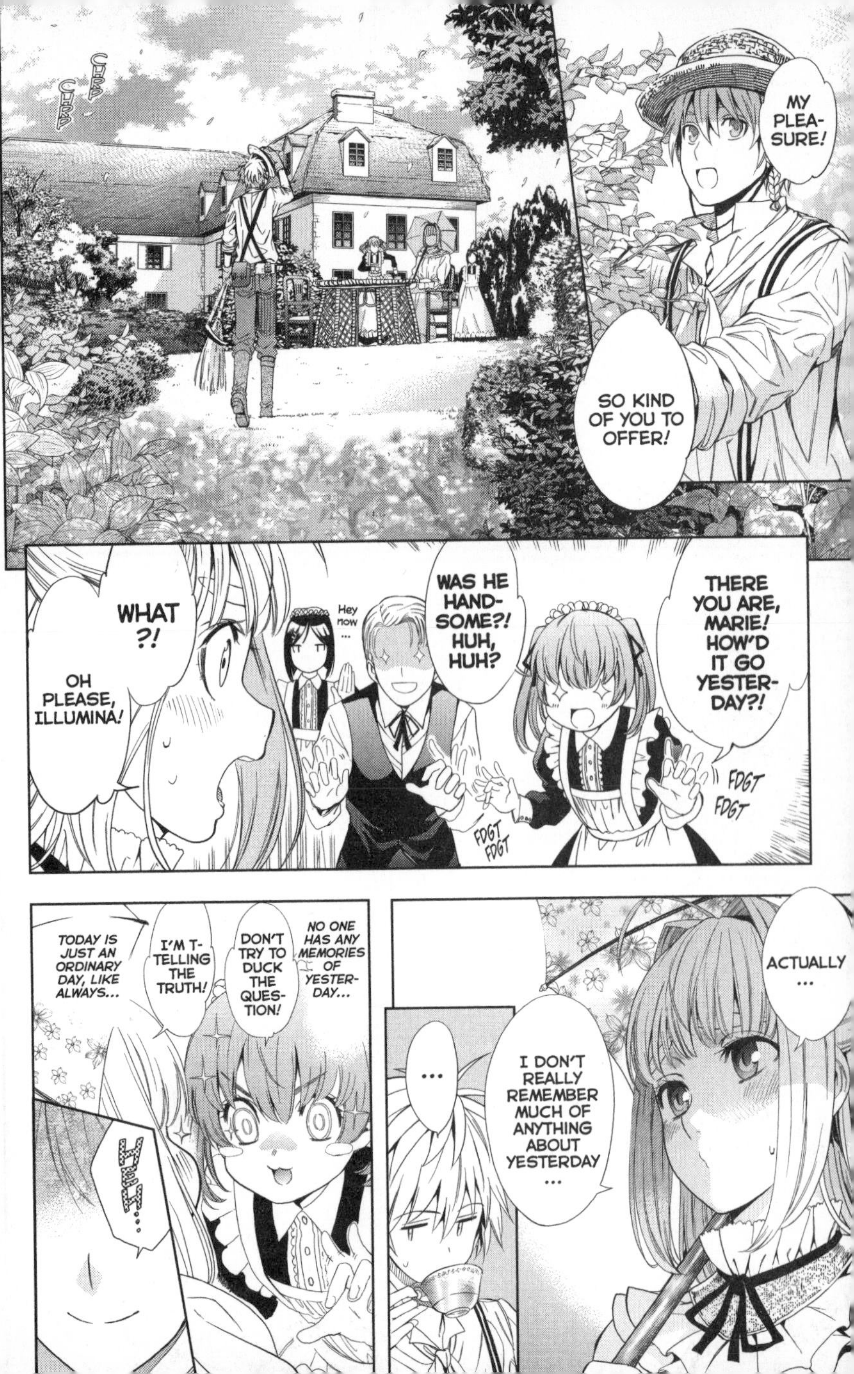
MY PLEASURE!
SO KIND OF YOU TO OFFER!
CHIRP
CHIRP
THERE YOU ARE, MARIE! HOW'D IT GO YESTERDAY?!
FDGT FDGT
WAS HE HANDSOME?! HUH, HUH?
Hey now...
FDGT FDGT
WHAT?!
OH PLEASE, ILLUMINA!
ACTUALLY...
I DON'T REALLY REMEMBER MUCH OF ANYTHING ABOUT YESTERDAY...
...
NO ONE HAS ANY MEMORIES OF YESTERDAY...
DON'T TRY TO DUCK THE QUESTION!
I'M T-TELLING THE TRUTH!
TODAY IS JUST AN ORDINARY DAY, LIKE ALWAYS...
HEH...

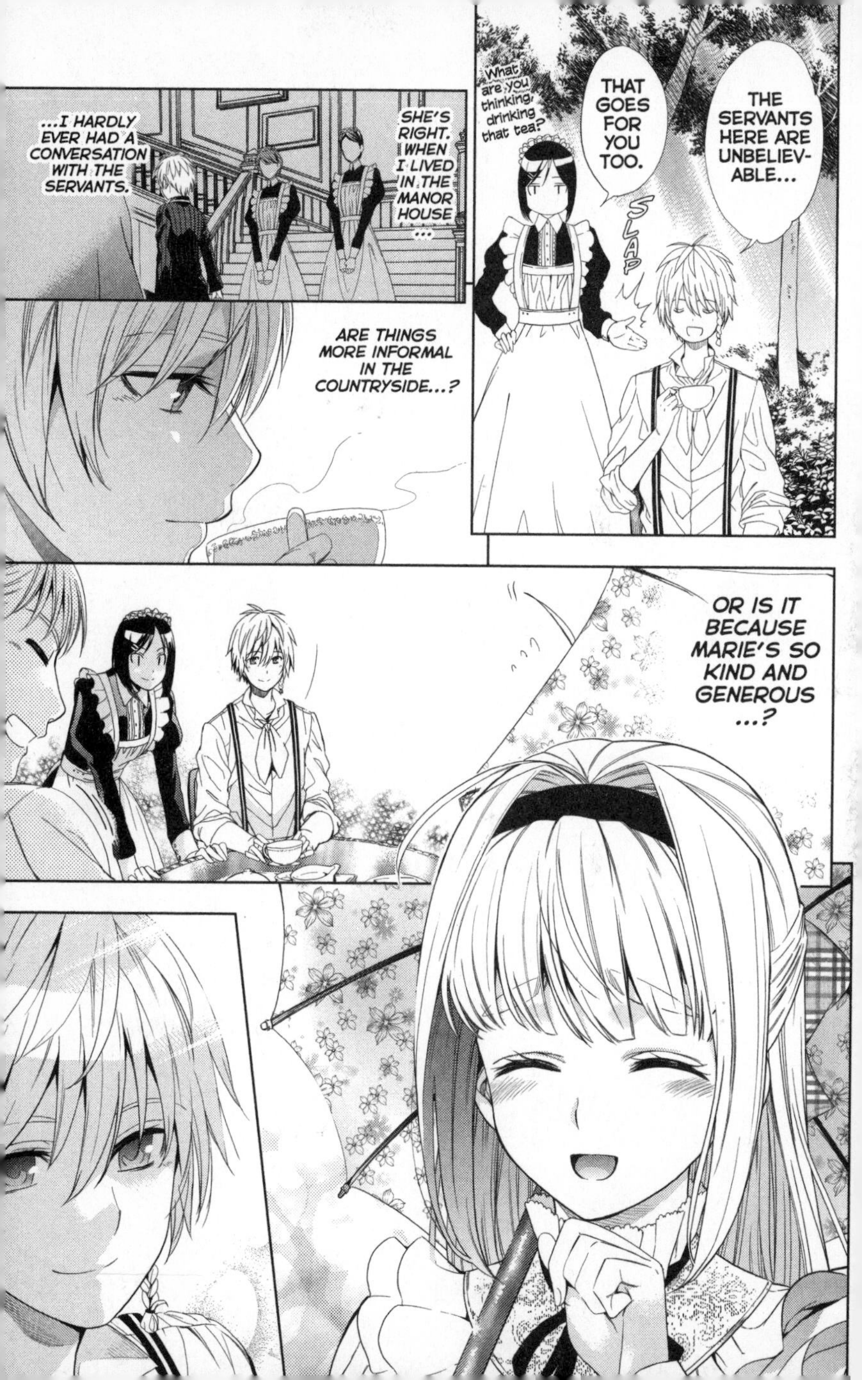
THE SERVANTS HERE ARE UNBELIEV-ABLE...
THAT GOES FOR YOU TOO.
What are you thinking, drinking that tea?
SLAP
SHE'S RIGHT. WHEN I LIVED IN THE MANOR HOUSE...
...I HARDLY EVER HAD A CONVERSATION WITH THE SERVANTS.
ARE THINGS MORE INFORMAL IN THE COUNTRYSIDE...?
OR IS IT BECAUSE MARIE'S SO KIND AND GENEROUS...?

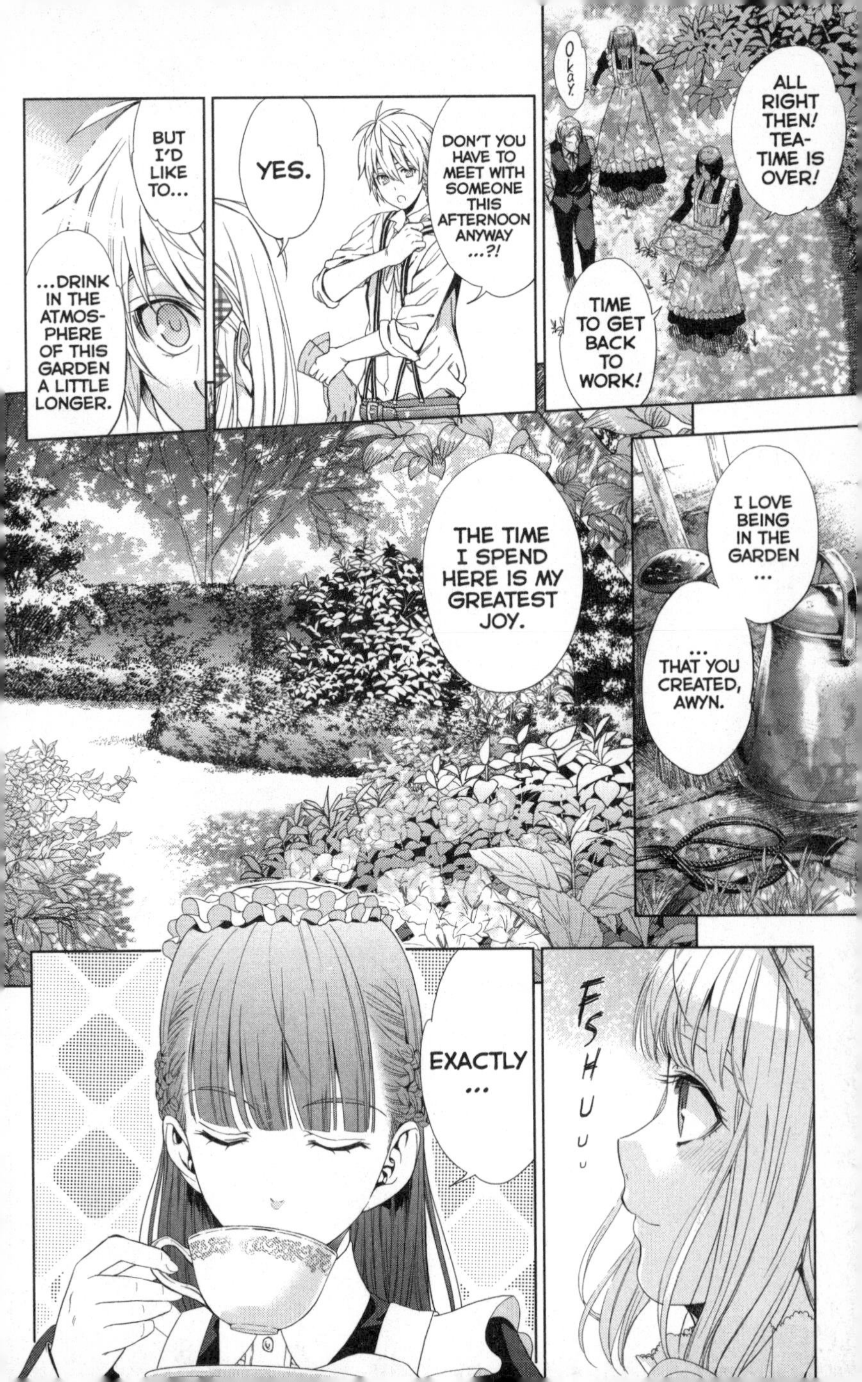
ALL RIGHT THEN! TEA-TIME IS OVER!
Okay.
TIME TO GET BACK TO WORK!
DON'T YOU HAVE TO MEET WITH SOMEONE THIS AFTERNOON ANYWAY ...?!
YES.
BUT I'D LIKE TO...
...DRINK IN THE ATMOS-PHERE OF THIS GARDEN A LITTLE LONGER.
I LOVE BEING IN THE GARDEN ...
... THAT YOU CREATED, AWYN.
THE TIME I SPEND HERE IS MY GREATEST JOY.
FSHUUU
EXACTLY ...

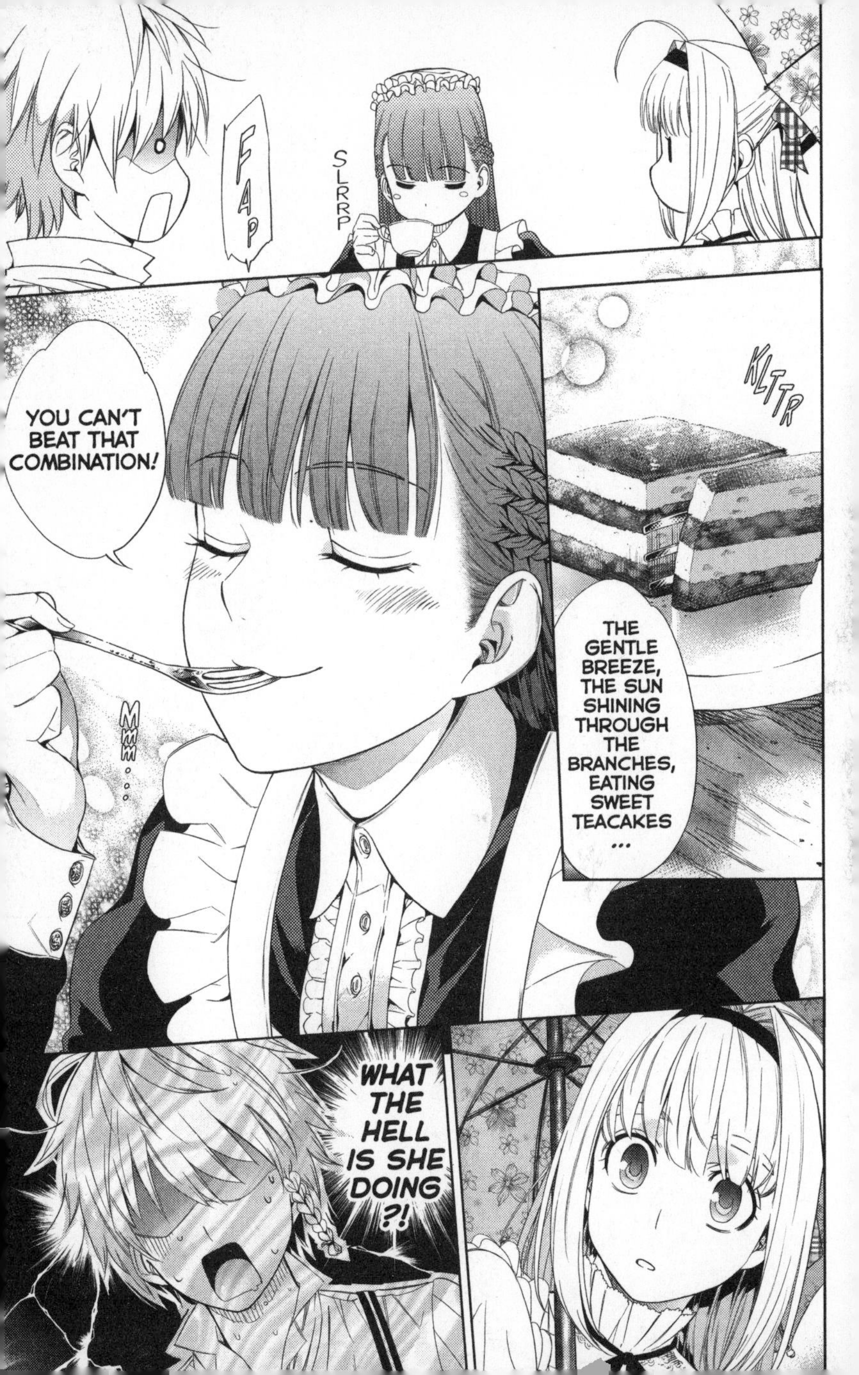
SLRRP
FAP
KLTTR
THE GENTLE BREEZE, THE SUN SHINING THROUGH THE BRANCHES, EATING SWEET TEACAKES...
YOU CAN'T BEAT THAT COMBINATION!
Mmm...
WHAT THE HELL IS SHE DOING?!

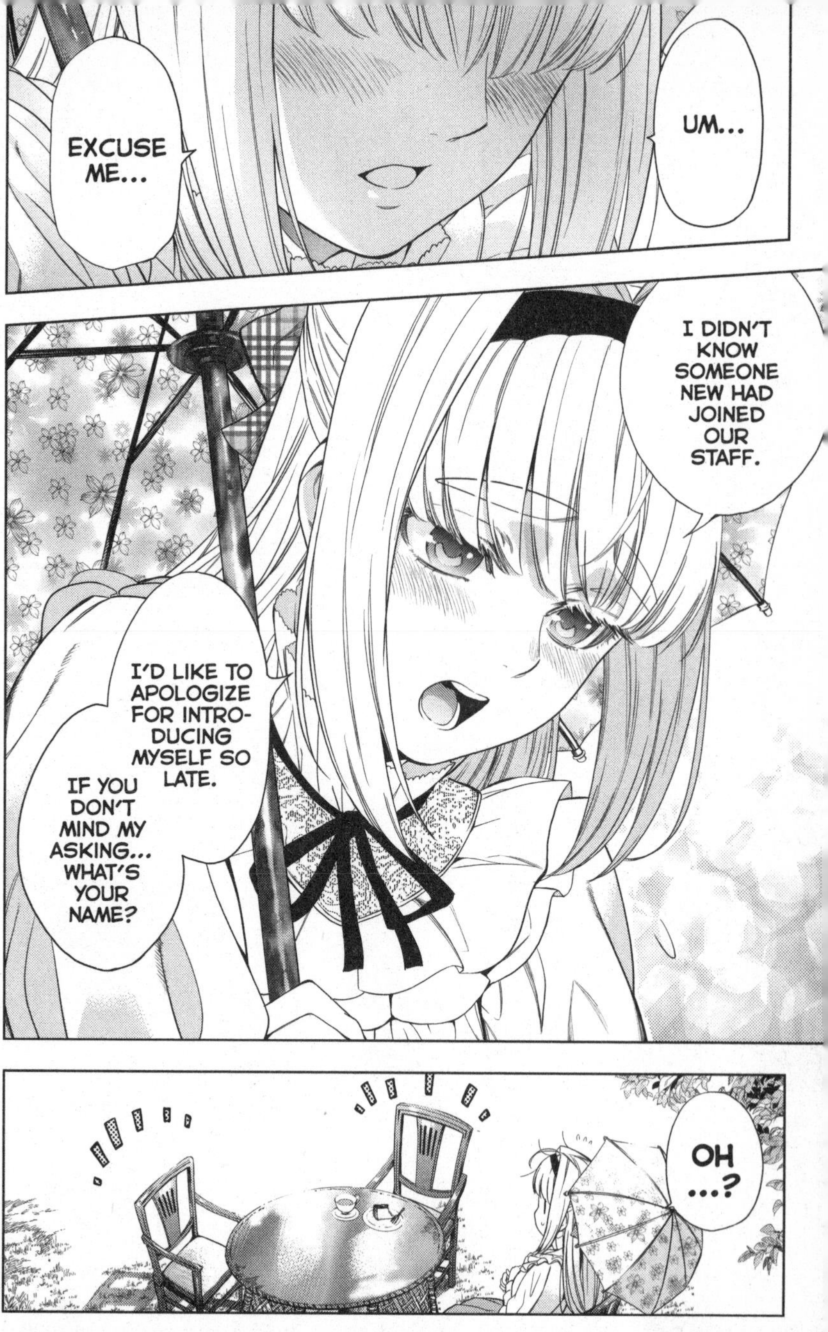
UM...
EXCUSE ME...
I DIDN'T KNOW SOMEONE NEW HAD JOINED OUR STAFF.
I'D LIKE TO APOLOGIZE FOR INTRO-DUCING MYSELF SO LATE.
IF YOU DON'T MIND MY ASKING... WHAT'S YOUR NAME?
OH ...?

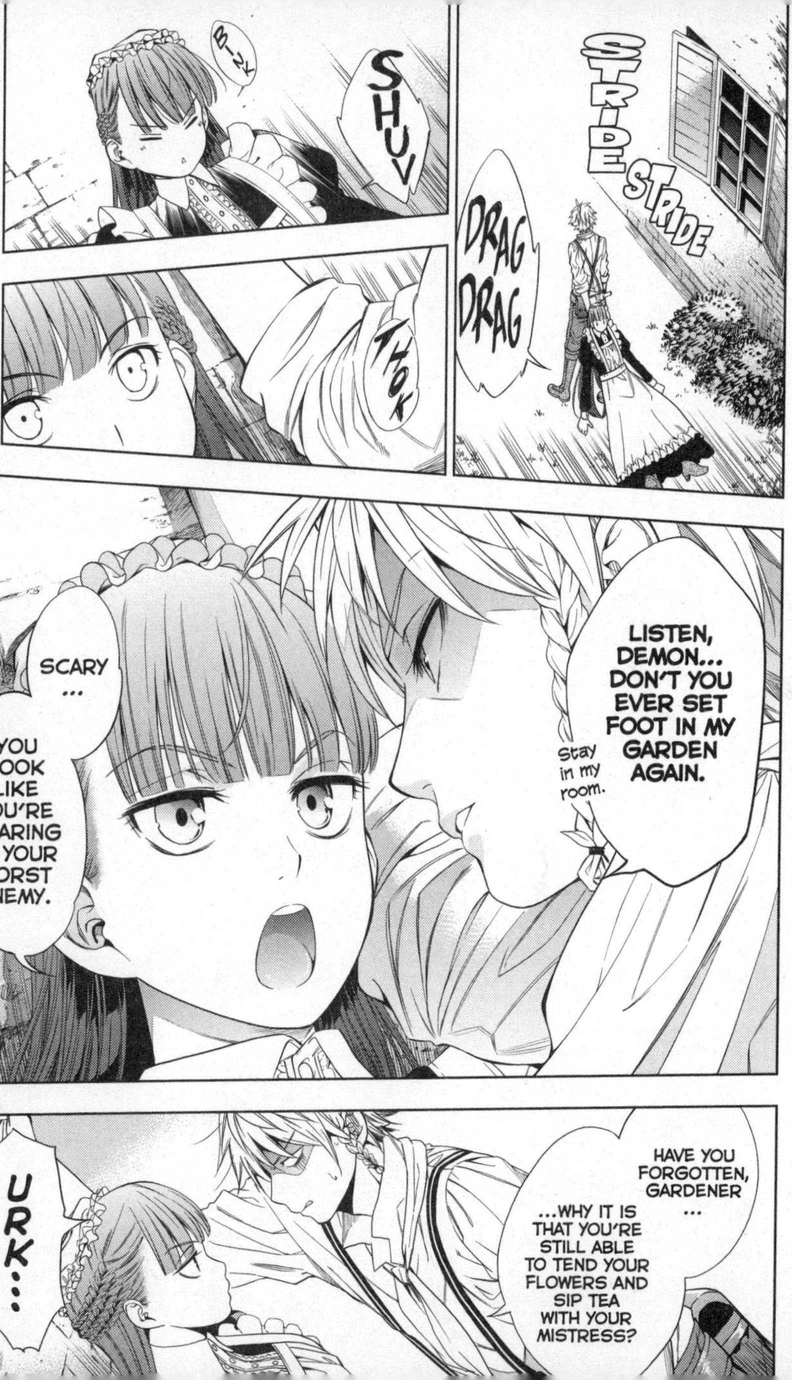
STRIDE STRIDE
DRAG DRAG
SHUV
B-ZK
THOK
LISTEN, DEMON... DON'T YOU EVER SET FOOT IN MY GARDEN AGAIN.
Stay in my room.
SCARY ...
YOU LOOK LIKE YOU'RE GLARING AT YOUR WORST ENEMY.
HAVE YOU FORGOTTEN, GARDENER ...
...WHY IT IS THAT YOU'RE STILL ABLE TO TEND YOUR FLOWERS AND SIP TEA WITH YOUR MISTRESS?
URK...

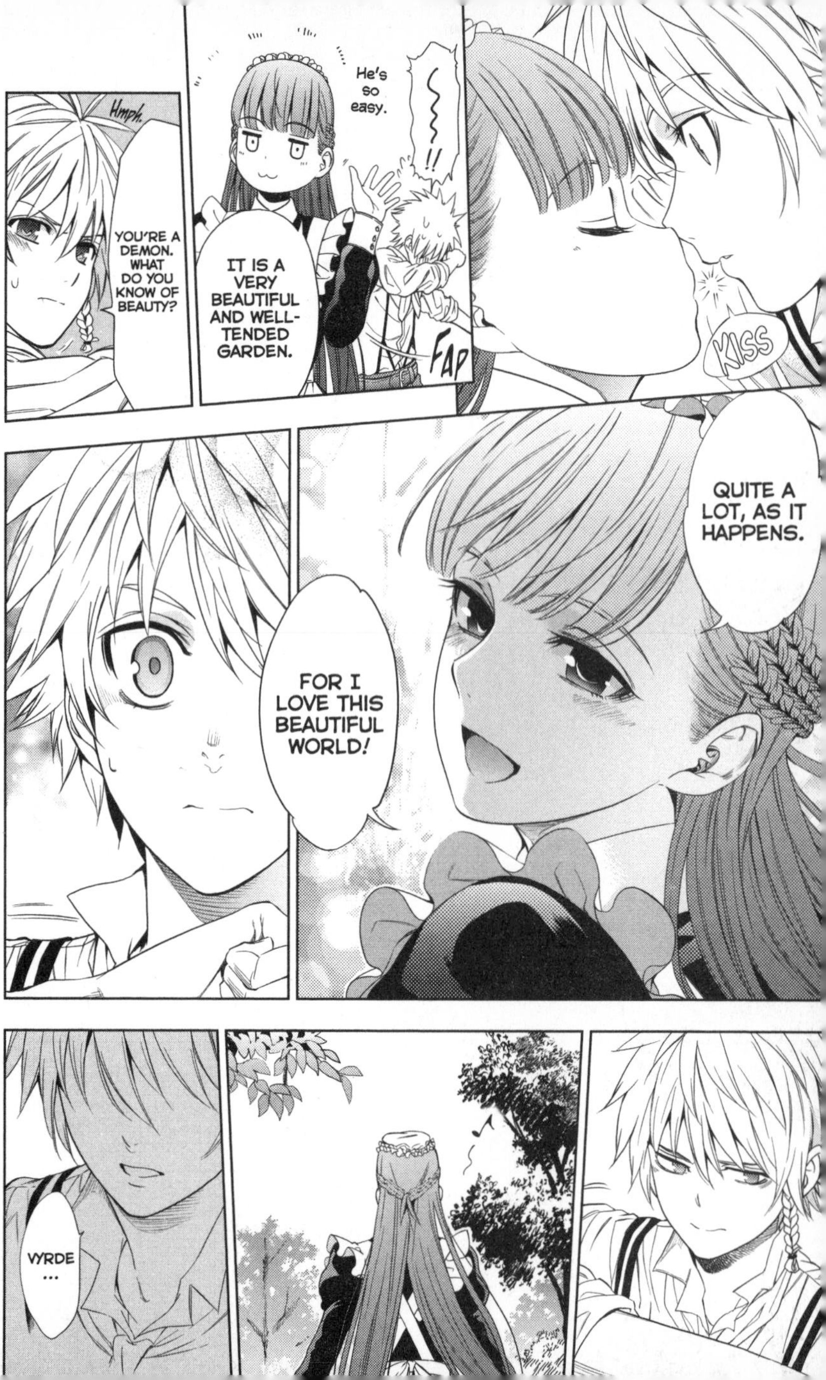
KISS
!!
He's so easy.
IT IS A VERY BEAUTIFUL AND WELL-TENDED GARDEN.
FAP
Hmph.
YOU'RE A DEMON. WHAT DO YOU KNOW OF BEAUTY?
QUITE A LOT, AS IT HAPPENS.
FOR I LOVE THIS BEAUTIFUL WORLD!
VYRDE ...

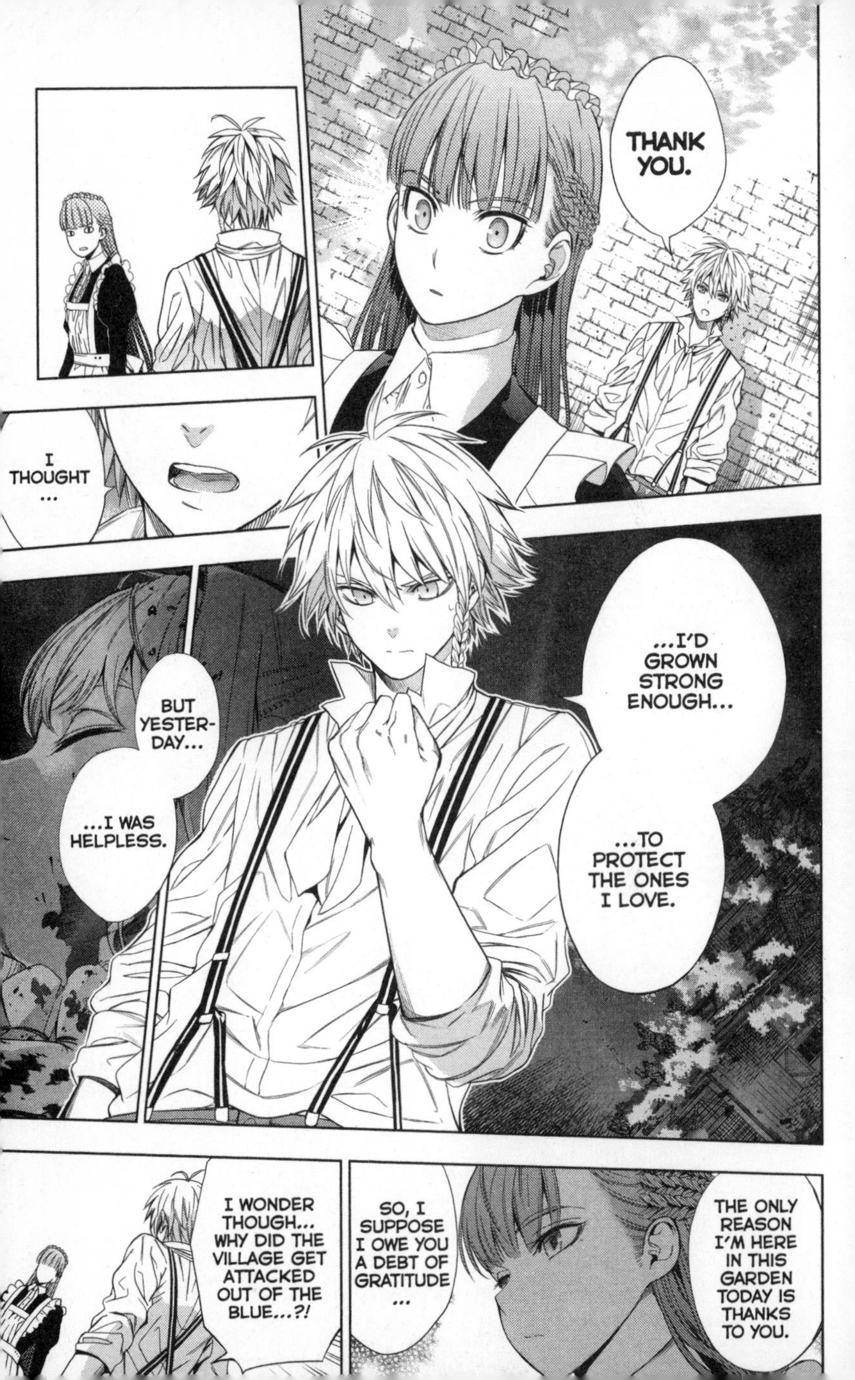
THANK YOU.
I THOUGHT ...
...I'D GROWN STRONG ENOUGH...
...TO PROTECT THE ONES I LOVE.
BUT YESTER-DAY...
...I WAS HELPLESS.
THE ONLY REASON I'M HERE IN THIS GARDEN TODAY IS THANKS TO YOU.
SO, I SUPPOSE I OWE YOU A DEBT OF GRATITUDE ...
I WONDER THOUGH... WHY DID THE VILLAGE GET ATTACKED OUT OF THE BLUE...?!

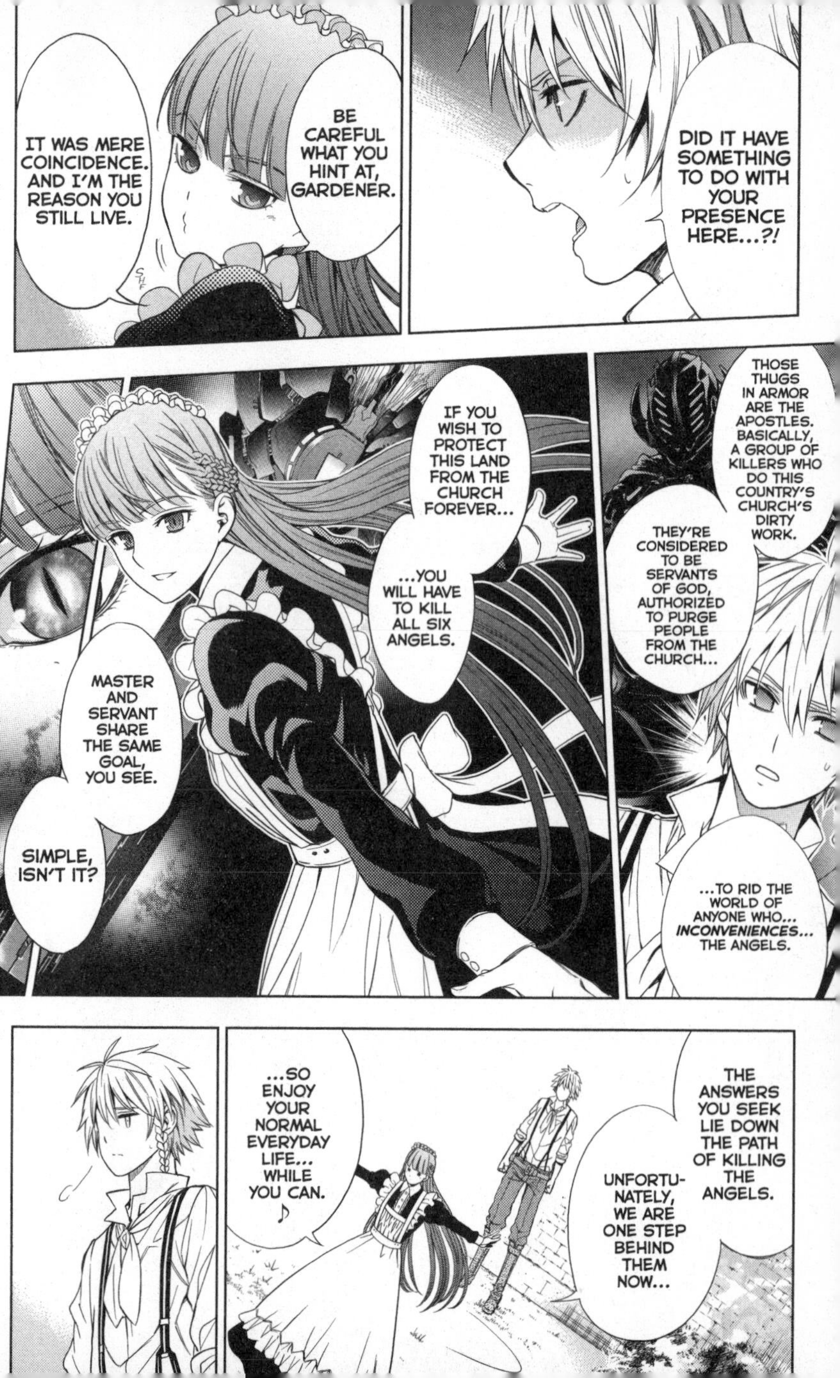
DID IT HAVE SOMETHING TO DO WITH YOUR PRESENCE HERE...?!
BE CAREFUL WHAT YOU HINT AT, GARDENER.
IT WAS MERE COINCIDENCE. AND I'M THE REASON YOU STILL LIVE.
SHF
THOSE THUGS IN ARMOR ARE THE APOSTLES. BASICALLY, A GROUP OF KILLERS WHO DO THIS COUNTRY'S CHURCH'S DIRTY WORK.
THEY'RE CONSIDERED TO BE SERVANTS OF GOD, AUTHORIZED TO PURGE PEOPLE FROM THE CHURCH...
...TO RID THE WORLD OF ANYONE WHO... *INCONVENIENCES*... THE ANGELS.
IF YOU WISH TO PROTECT THIS LAND FROM THE CHURCH FOREVER...
...YOU WILL HAVE TO KILL ALL SIX ANGELS.
MASTER AND SERVANT SHARE THE SAME GOAL, YOU SEE.
SIMPLE, ISN'T IT?
THE ANSWERS YOU SEEK LIE DOWN THE PATH OF KILLING THE ANGELS.
UNFORTU-NATELY, WE ARE ONE STEP BEHIND THEM NOW...
...SO ENJOY YOUR NORMAL EVERYDAY LIFE... WHILE YOU CAN. ♪

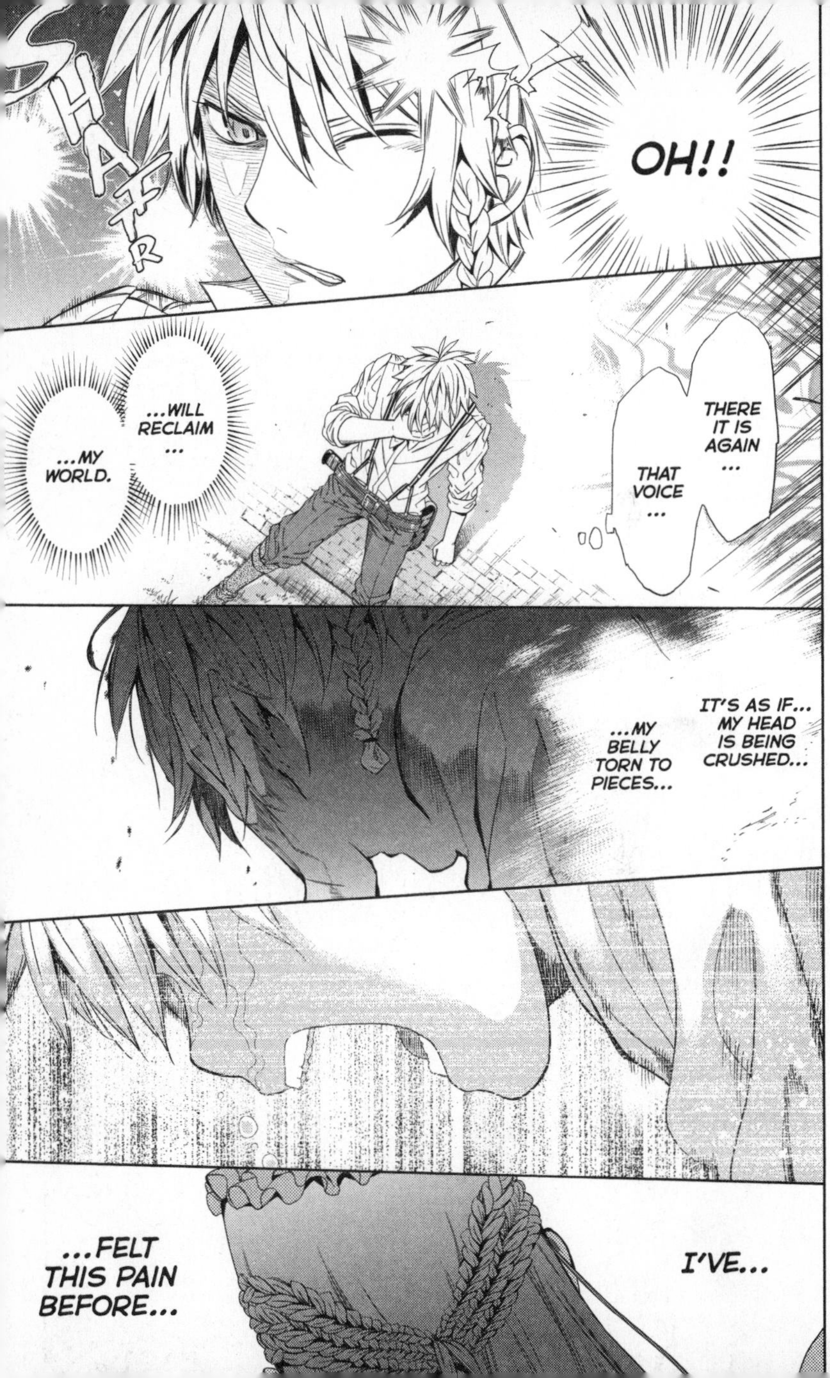
OH!!
SHAFFR
THERE IT IS AGAIN...
THAT VOICE...
...WILL RECLAIM...
...MY WORLD.
IT'S AS IF... MY HEAD IS BEING CRUSHED...
...MY BELLY TORN TO PIECES...
I'VE...
...FELT THIS PAIN BEFORE...

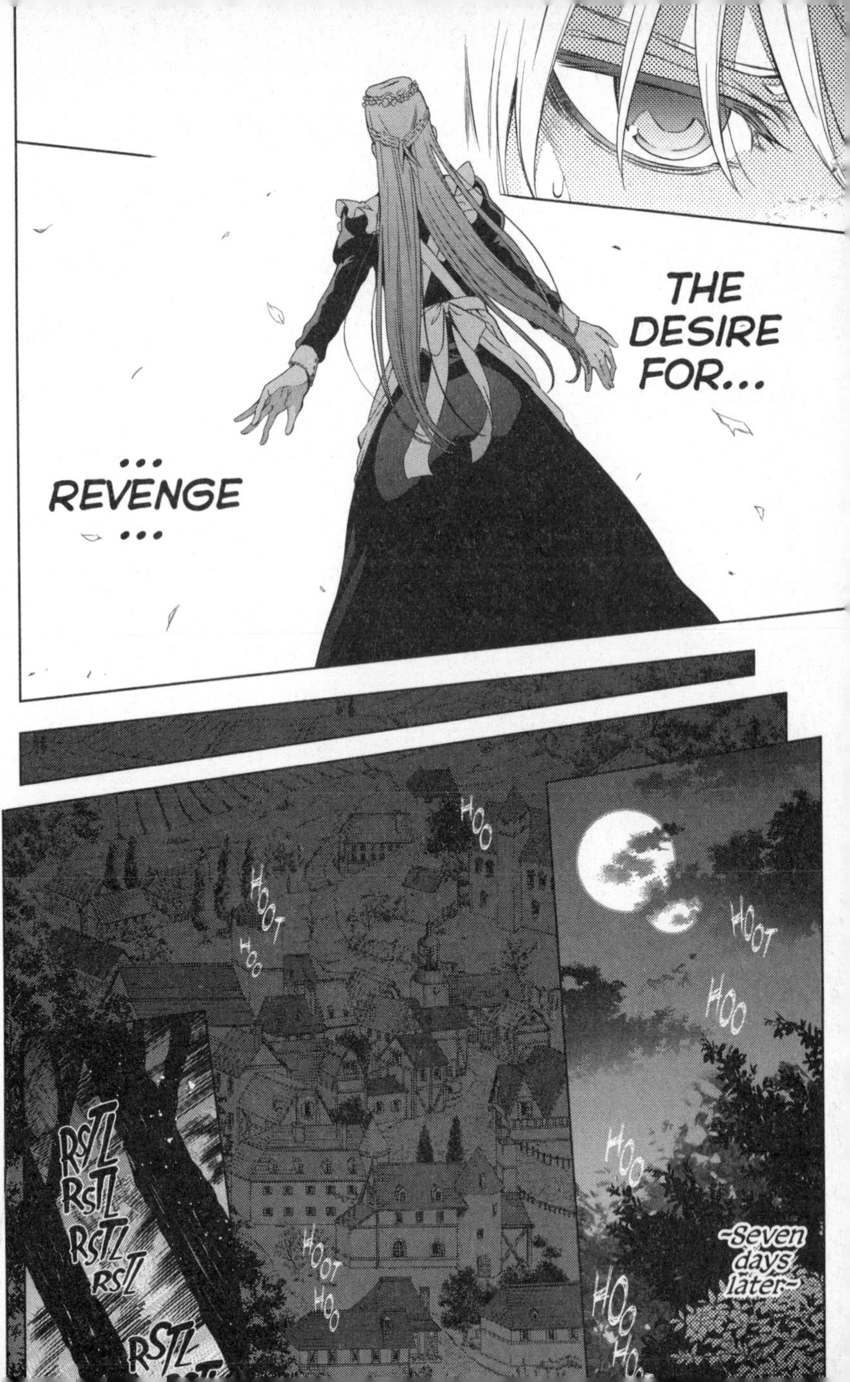
THE DESIRE FOR...
...REVENGE...
HOO
HOOT
HOO
HOOT
HOO
HOO
HOOT
HOO
HOO
-Seven days later-
RSTL
RSTL
RSTL
RSTL
RSTL

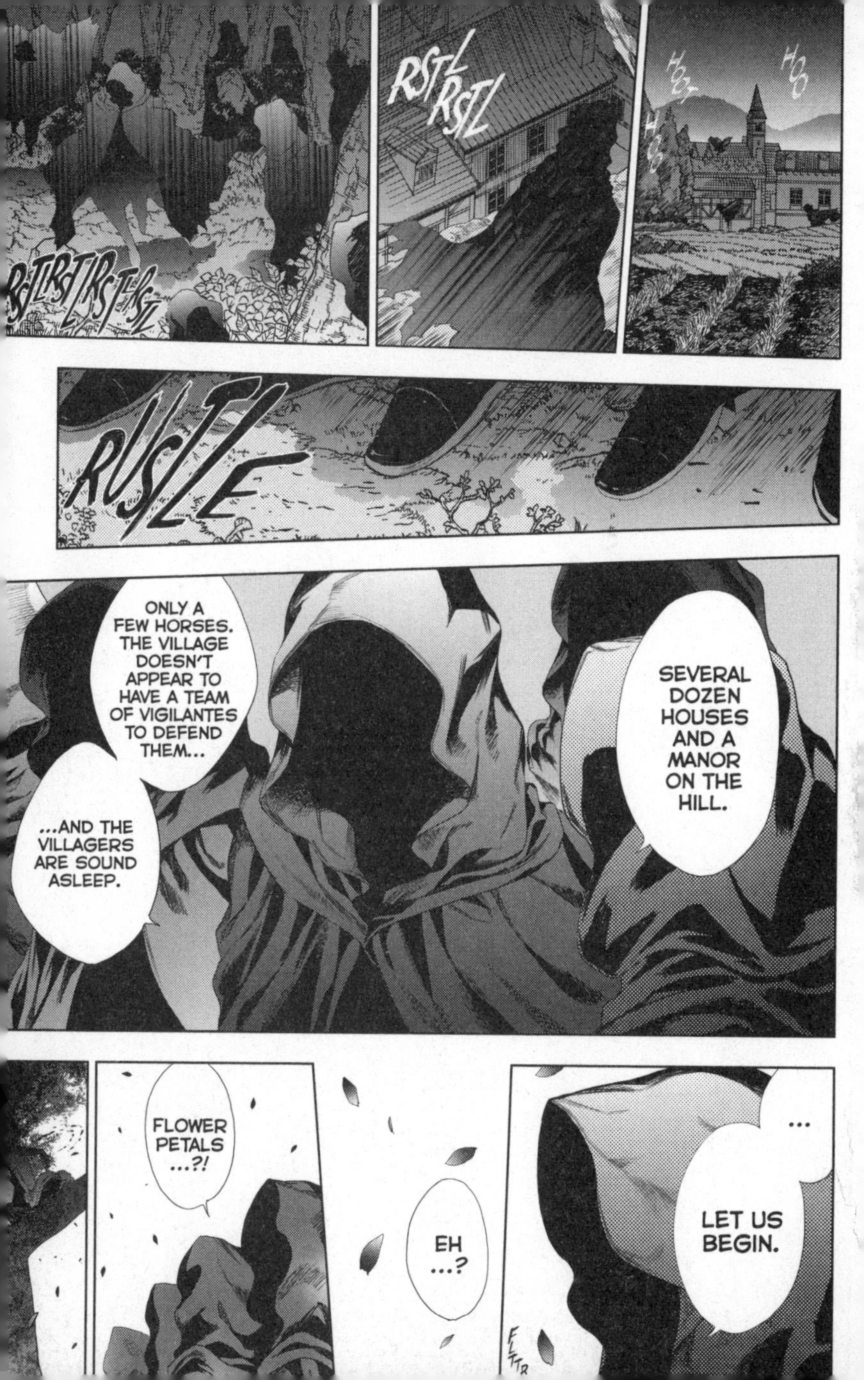
RSTL RSTL
RSTL RSTL RSTL RSTL
RUSTLE
SEVERAL DOZEN HOUSES AND A MANOR ON THE HILL.
ONLY A FEW HORSES. THE VILLAGE DOESN'T APPEAR TO HAVE A TEAM OF VIGILANTES TO DEFEND THEM...
...AND THE VILLAGERS ARE SOUND ASLEEP.
...
LET US BEGIN.
FLTTR
EH ...?
FLOWER PETALS ...?!

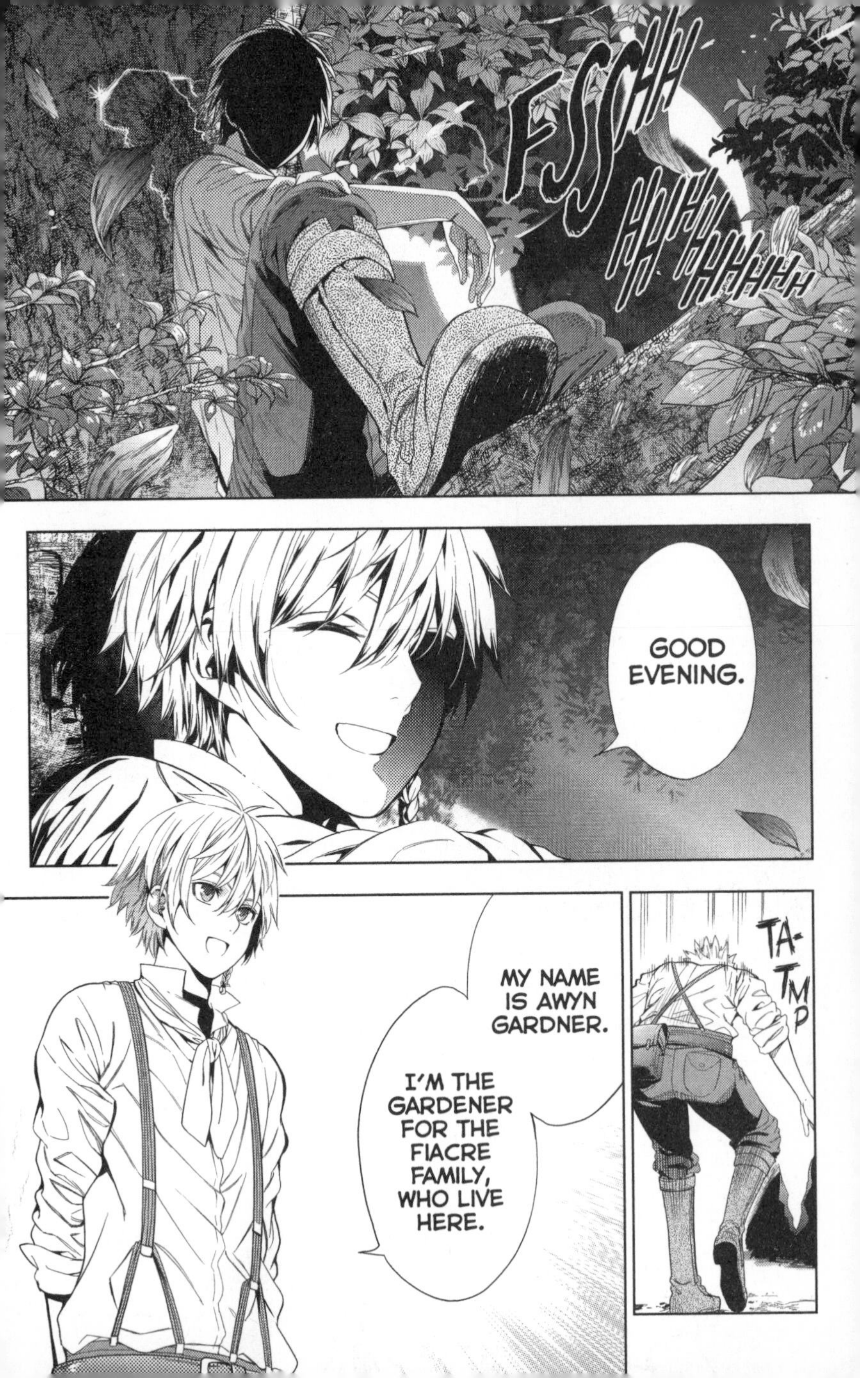
FSSCHH
HHHHHHHHHHHHH
GOOD EVENING.
TA-TMP
MY NAME IS AWYN GARDNER.
I'M THE GARDENER FOR THE FIACRE FAMILY, WHO LIVE HERE.

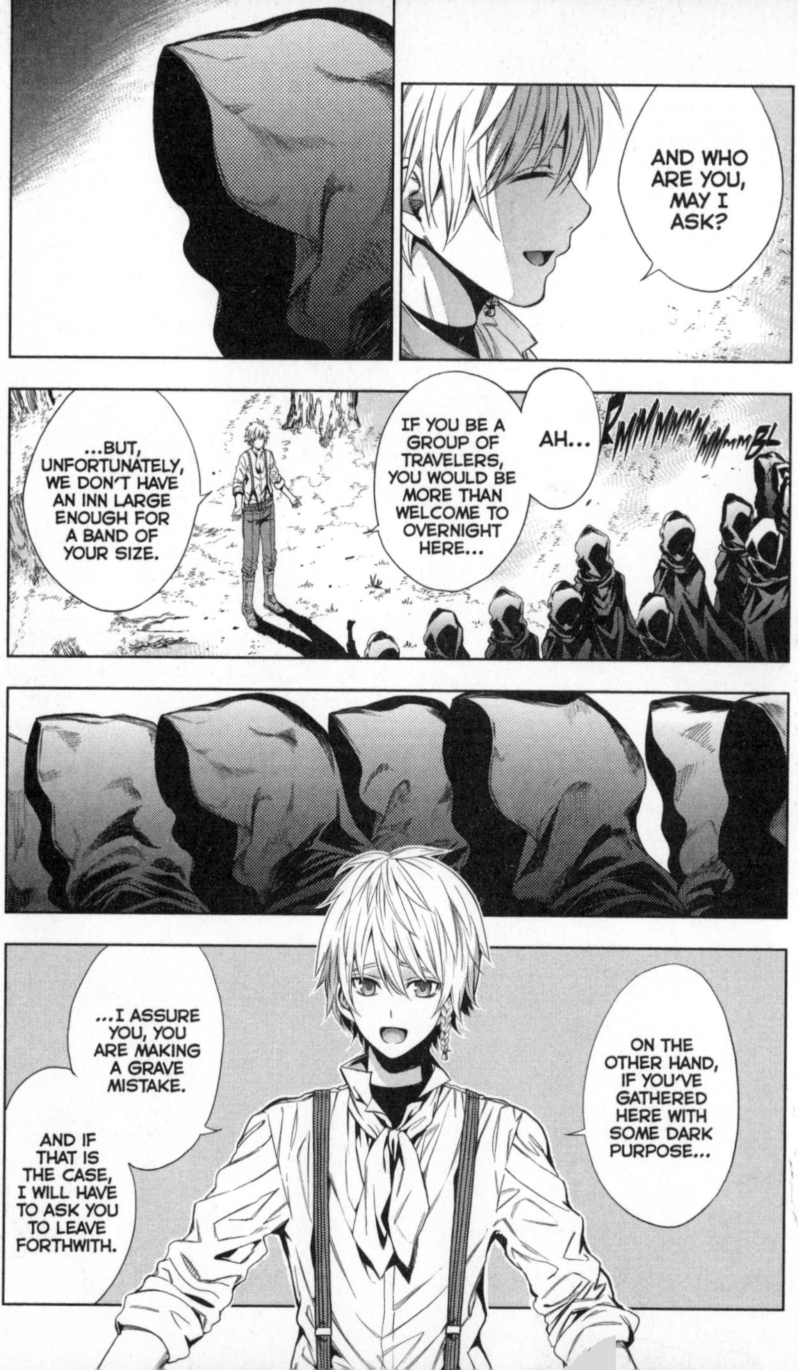
AND WHO ARE YOU, MAY I ASK?
RMMMMMMMMMMMMBL
AH...
IF YOU BE A GROUP OF TRAVELERS, YOU WOULD BE MORE THAN WELCOME TO OVERNIGHT HERE...
...BUT, UNFORTUNATELY, WE DON'T HAVE AN INN LARGE ENOUGH FOR A BAND OF YOUR SIZE.
ON THE OTHER HAND, IF YOU'VE GATHERED HERE WITH SOME DARK PURPOSE...
...I ASSURE YOU, YOU ARE MAKING A GRAVE MISTAKE.
AND IF THAT IS THE CASE, I WILL HAVE TO ASK YOU TO LEAVE FORTHWITH.

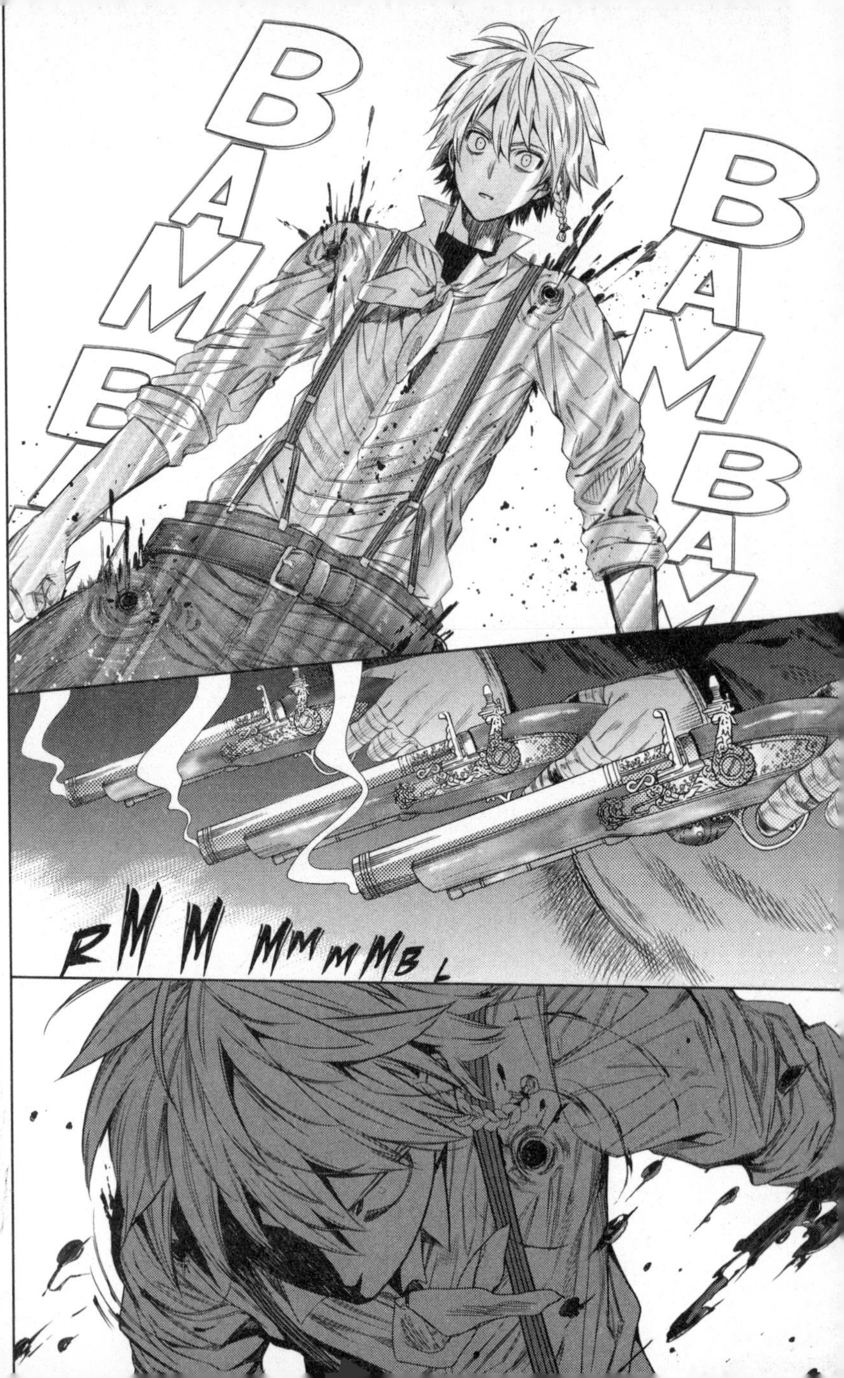
BAMBAM
BAMB
RMM MMMMMB

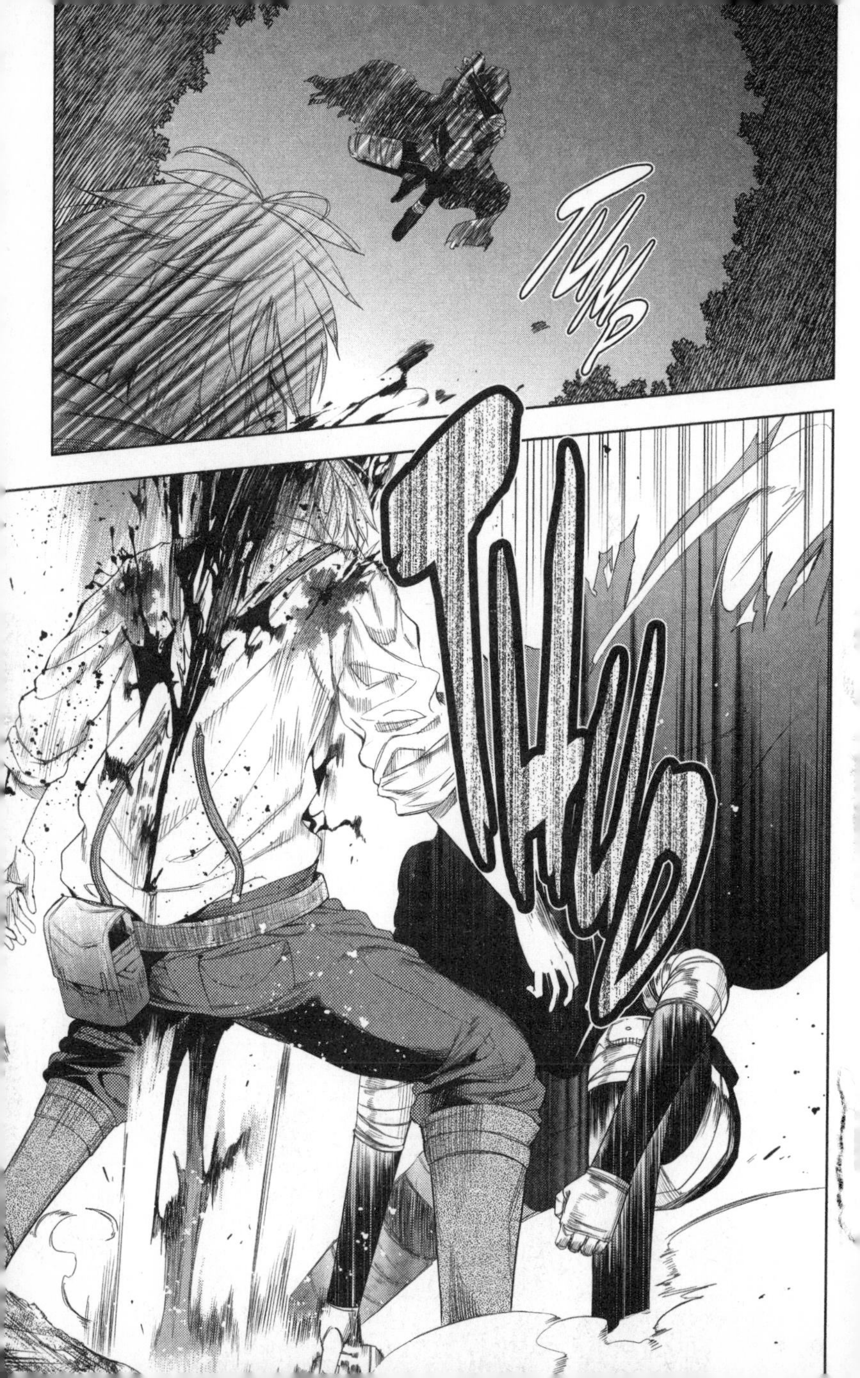
TUMP
THUD

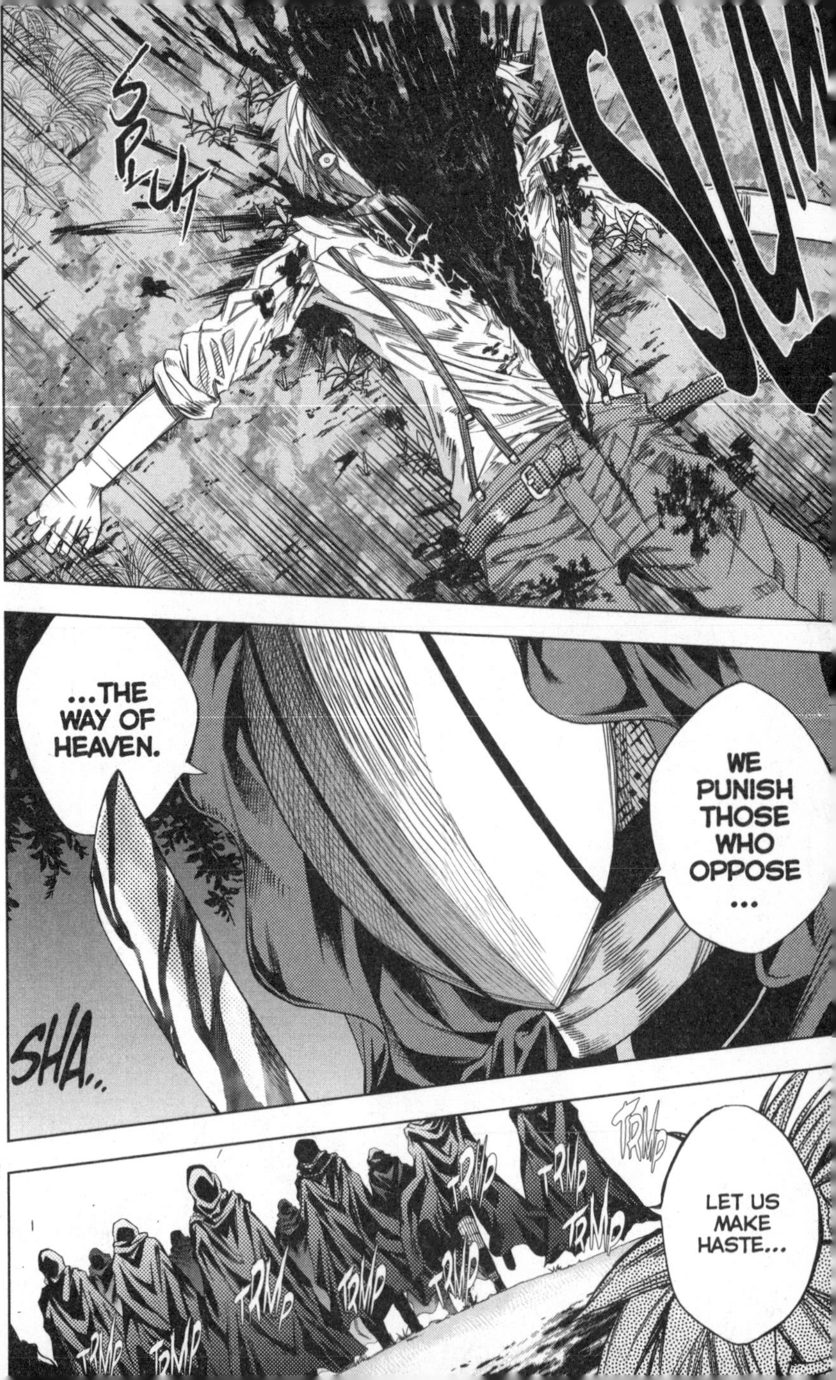
SPLUT
WE PUNISH THOSE WHO OPPOSE...
...THE WAY OF HEAVEN.
SHA...
LET US MAKE HASTE...
TRMP
TRMP
TRMP
TRMP
TRMP
TRMP
TRMP
TRMP
TRMP

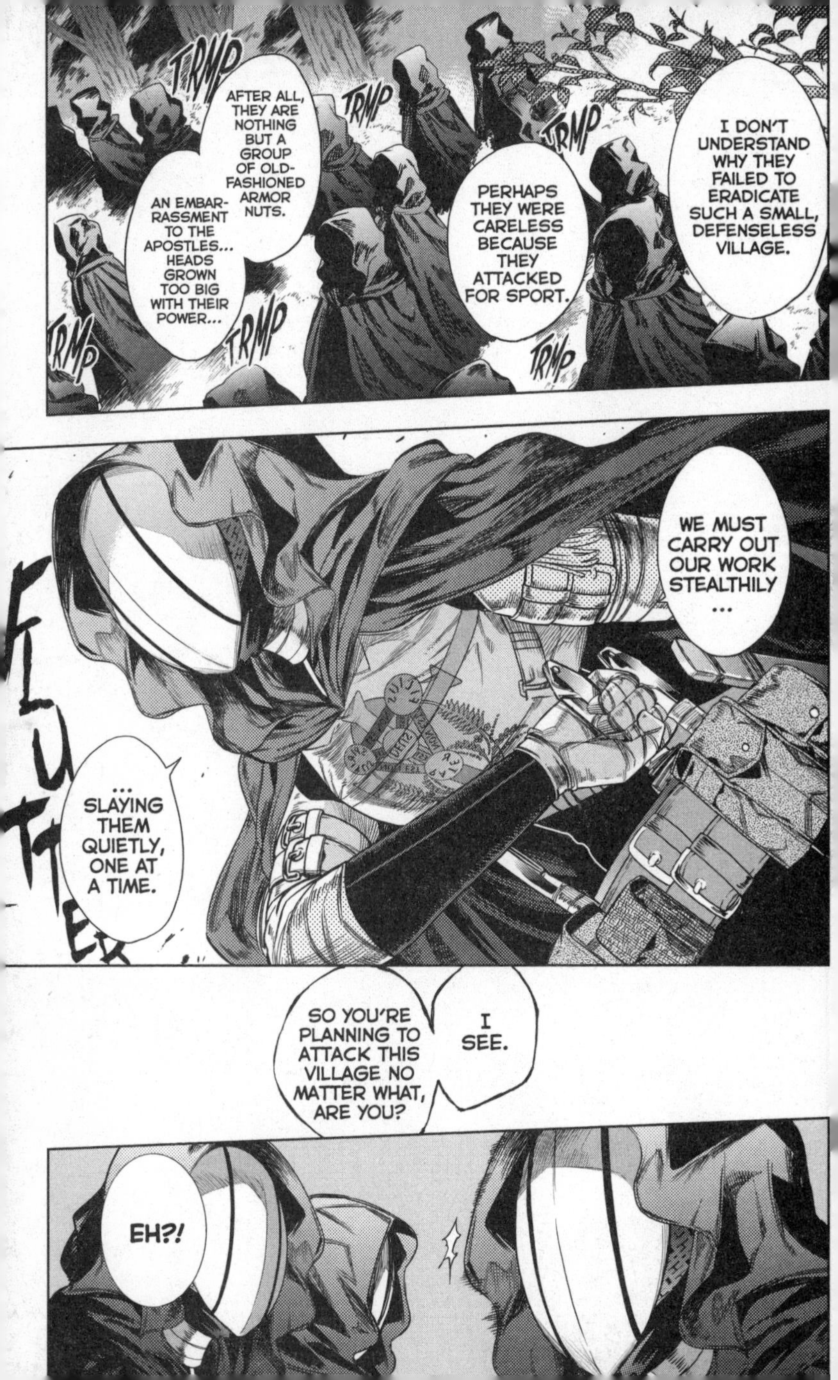
TRMP
TRMP
TRMP
TRMP
TRMP
TRMP
I DON'T UNDERSTAND WHY THEY FAILED TO ERADICATE SUCH A SMALL, DEFENSELESS VILLAGE.
PERHAPS THEY WERE CARELESS BECAUSE THEY ATTACKED FOR SPORT.
AFTER ALL, THEY ARE NOTHING BUT A GROUP OF OLD-FASHIONED ARMOR NUTS.
AN EMBARRASSMENT TO THE APOSTLES... HEADS GROWN TOO BIG WITH THEIR POWER...
WE MUST CARRY OUT OUR WORK STEALTHILY...
...SLAYING THEM QUIETLY, ONE AT A TIME.
FLUTTER
I SEE.
SO YOU'RE PLANNING TO ATTACK THIS VILLAGE NO MATTER WHAT, ARE YOU?
EH?!

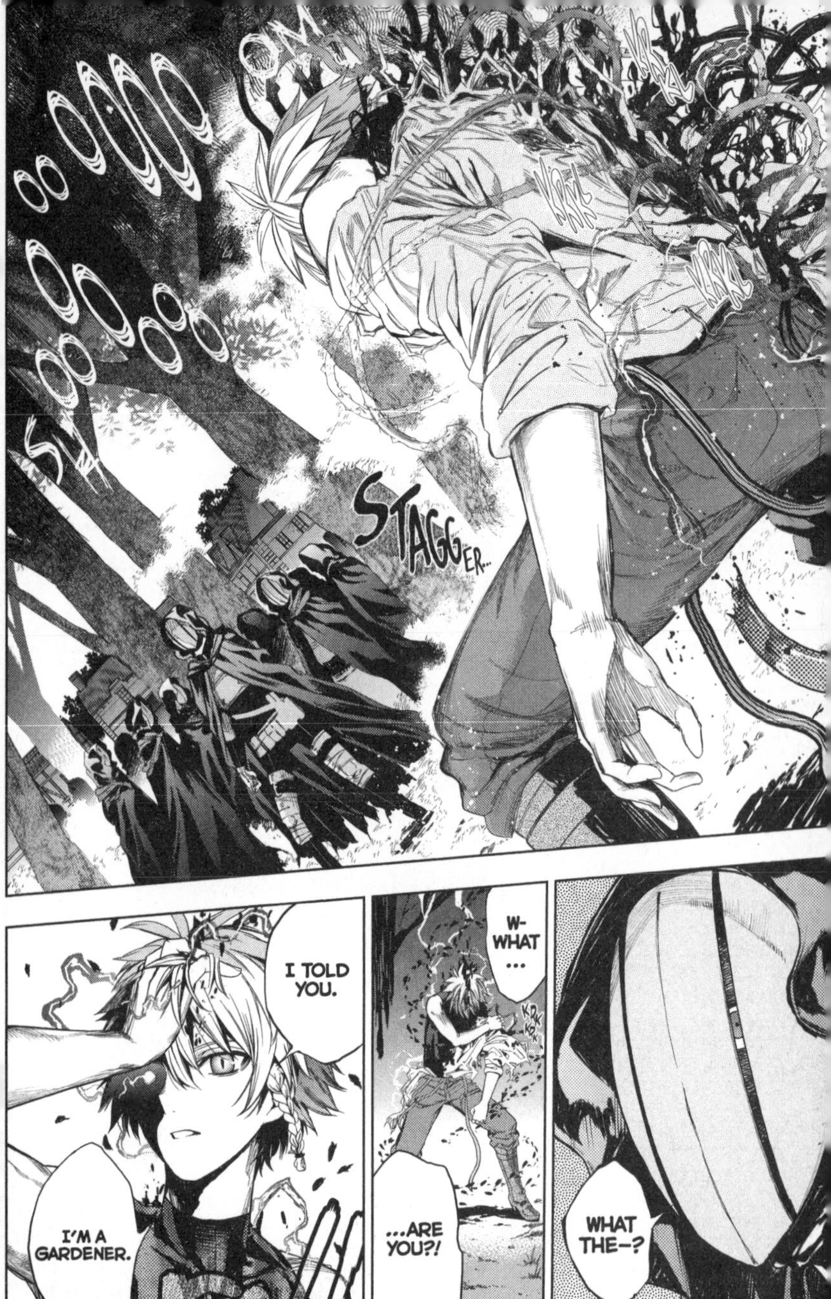
STAGGER...
WHAT THE–?
W-WHAT...
...ARE YOU?!
I TOLD YOU.
I'M A GARDENER.

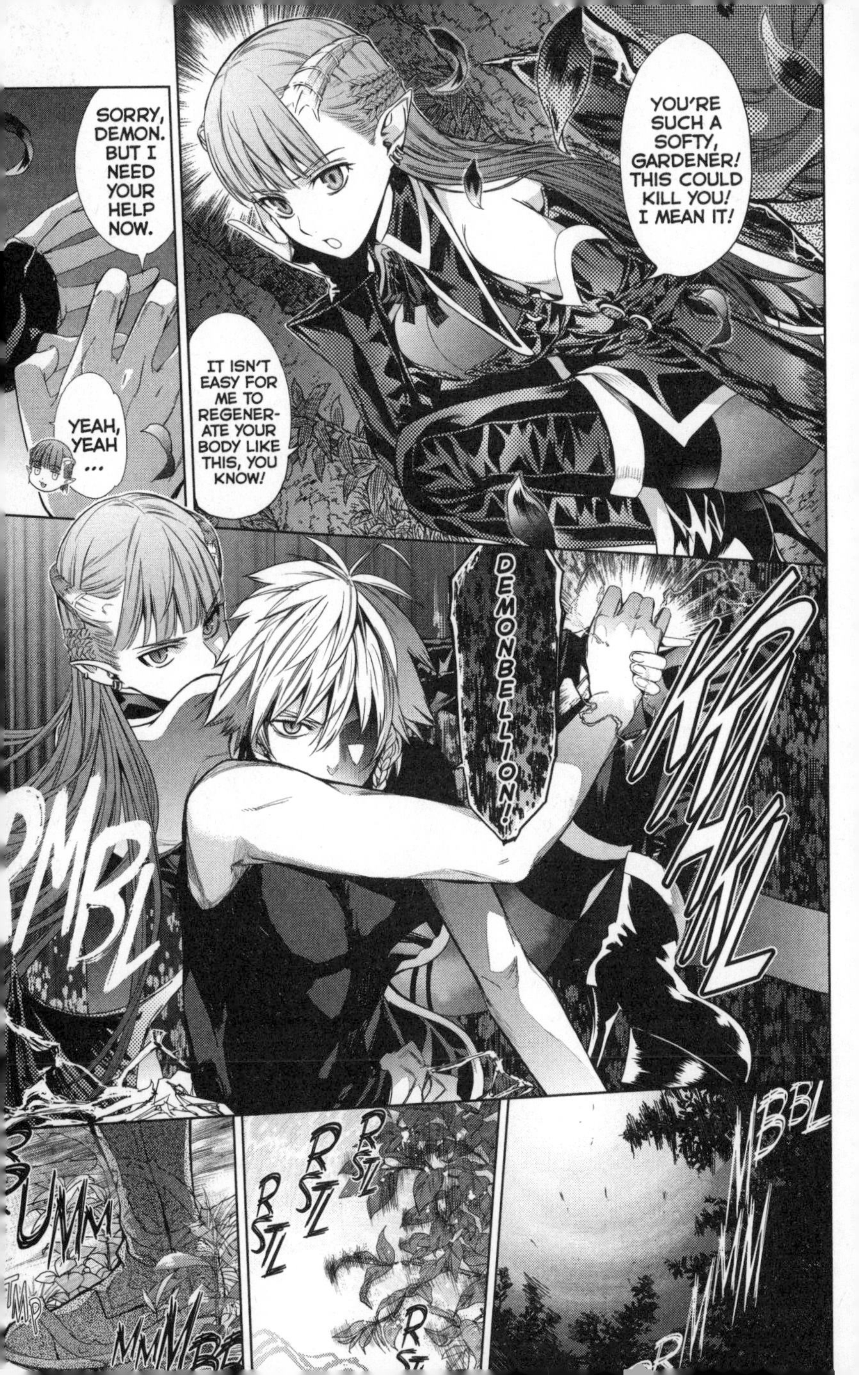

YOU'RE SUCH A SOFTY, GARDENER! THIS COULD KILL YOU! I MEAN IT!
IT ISN'T EASY FOR ME TO REGENERATE YOUR BODY LIKE THIS, YOU KNOW!
SORRY, DEMON. BUT I NEED YOUR HELP NOW.
YEAH, YEAH ...
DEMONBELLION!
RSTL
RSTL
RSTL

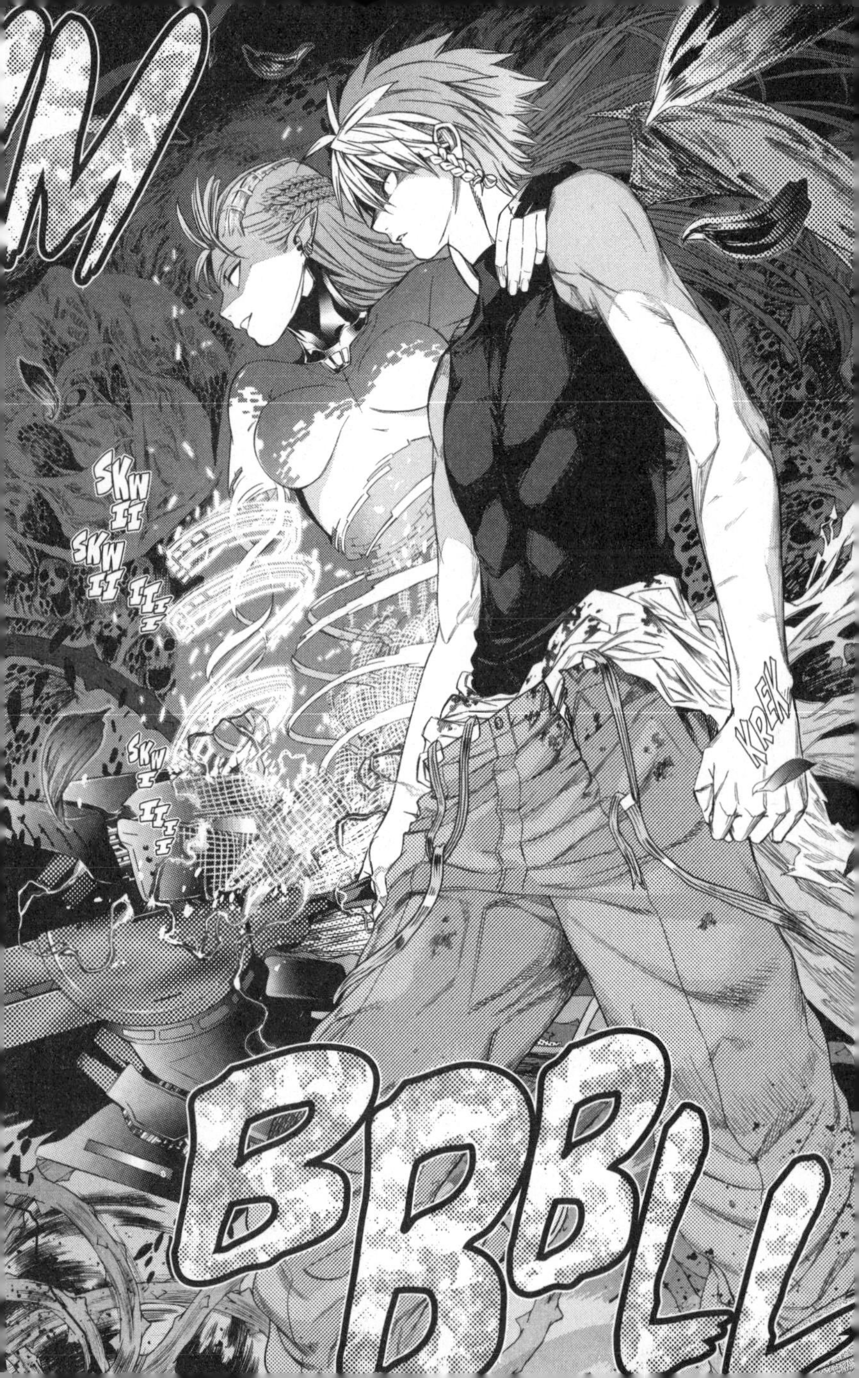
M
SKWII
SKWII IIII
SKWI IIII
KREK
BBBLL

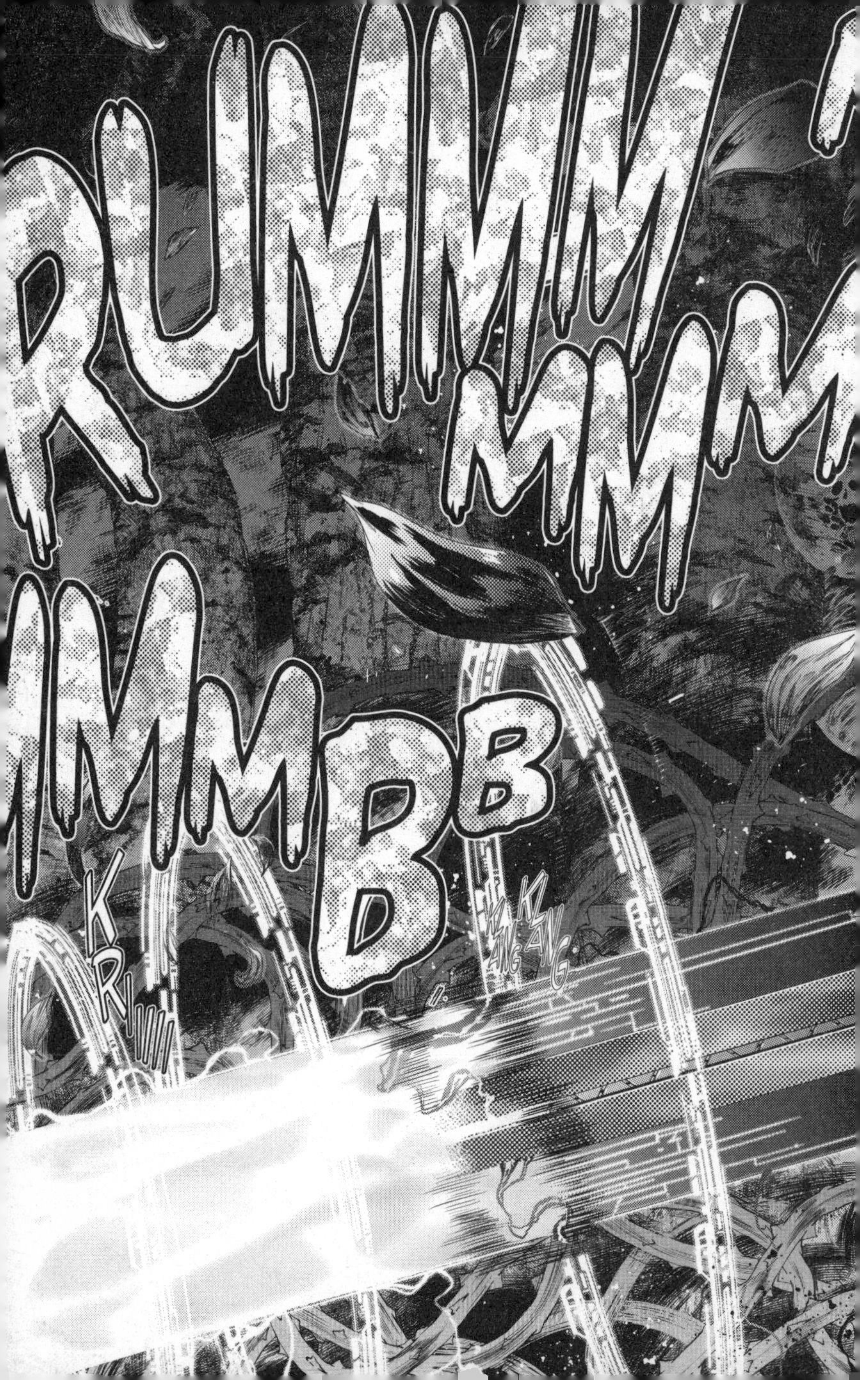
RUMMMMMMMMMBB
KRIIIII
KLANG
KLANG

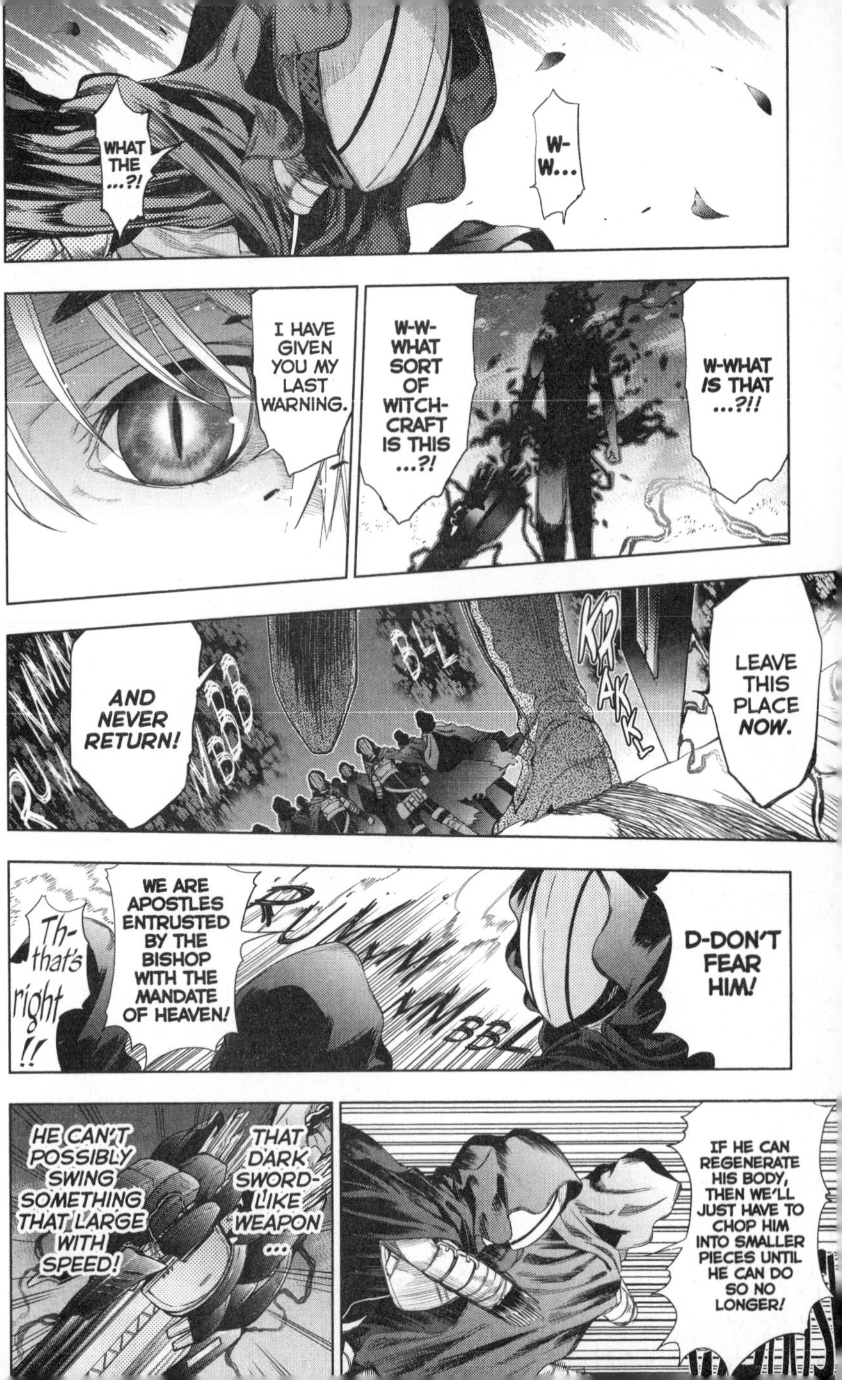
W- W...
WHAT THE ...?!
W-WHAT IS THAT ...?!!
W-W-WHAT SORT OF WITCH-CRAFT IS THIS ...?!
I HAVE GIVEN YOU MY LAST WARNING.
LEAVE THIS PLACE NOW.
BLL
AND NEVER RETURN!
D-DON'T FEAR HIM!
WE ARE APOSTLES ENTRUSTED BY THE BISHOP WITH THE MANDATE OF HEAVEN!
Th-that's right!!
IF HE CAN REGENERATE HIS BODY, THEN WE'LL JUST HAVE TO CHOP HIM INTO SMALLER PIECES UNTIL HE CAN DO SO NO LONGER!
THAT DARK SWORD-LIKE WEAPON ...
HE CAN'T POSSIBLY SWING SOMETHING THAT LARGE WITH SPEED!

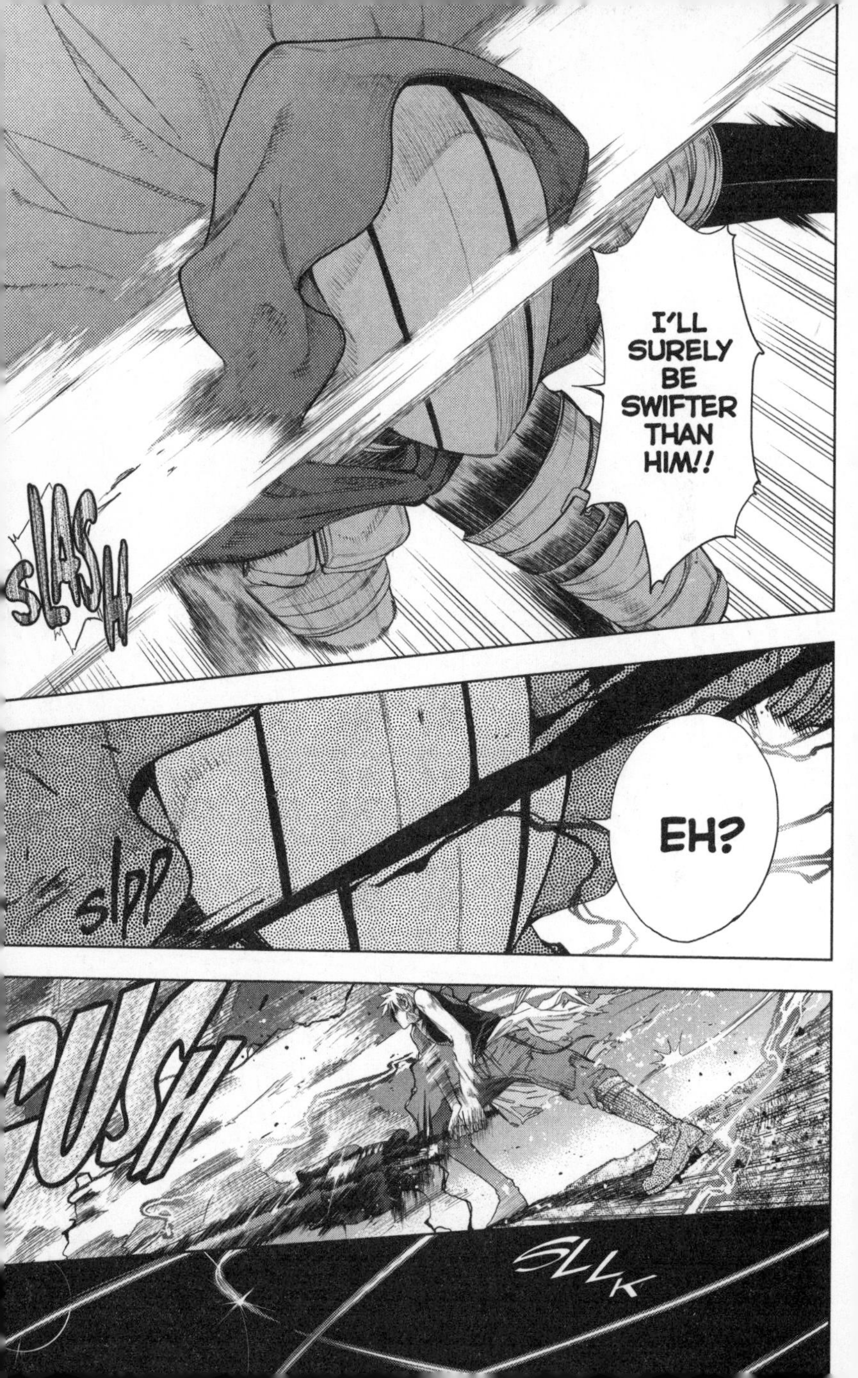
I'LL SURELY BE SWIFTER THAN HIM!!
SLASH
EH?
SLIP
GUSH
SLLK

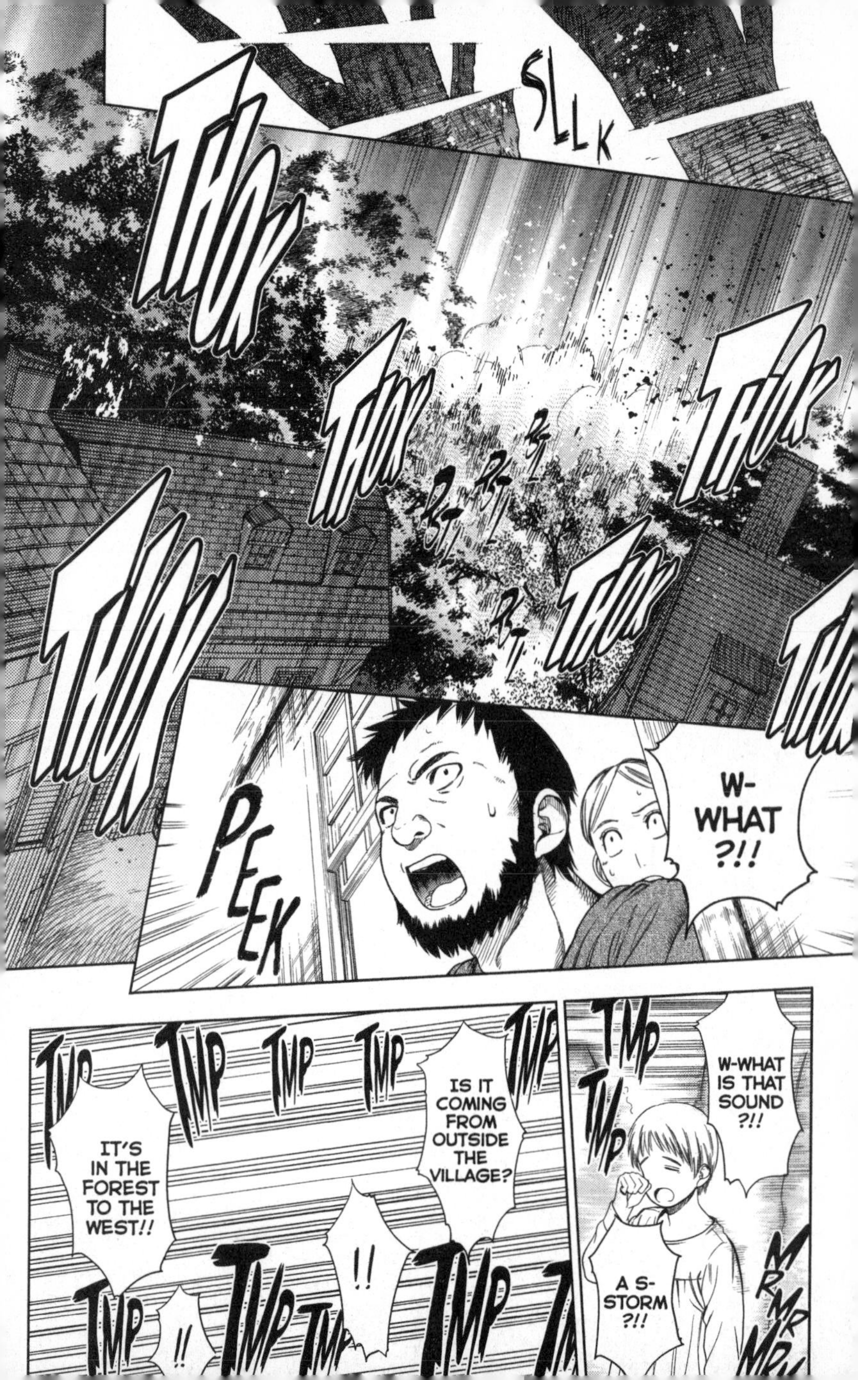
SLLK
THOK
THOK
THOK
THOK
THOK
PEEK
W-WHAT?!!
TMP TMP
W-WHAT IS THAT SOUND?!!
A S-STORM?!!
IS IT COMING FROM OUTSIDE THE VILLAGE?
IT'S IN THE FOREST TO THE WEST!!
!!
!!
TMP TMP TMP TMP TMP
TMP TMP TMP TMP

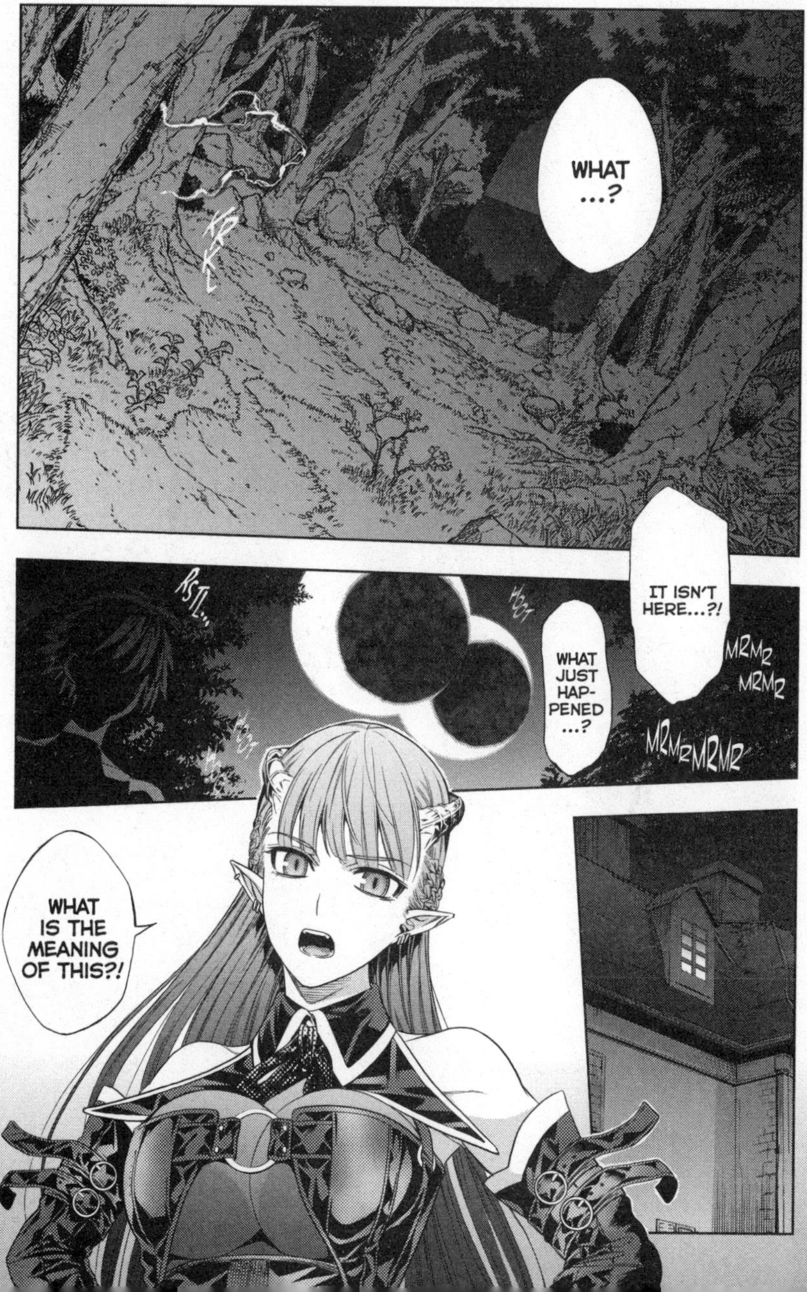
WHAT ...?
IT ISN'T HERE...?!
MRMR MRMR
WHAT JUST HAP-PENED ...?
MRMRMRMR
RSTL...
WHAT IS THE MEANING OF THIS?!

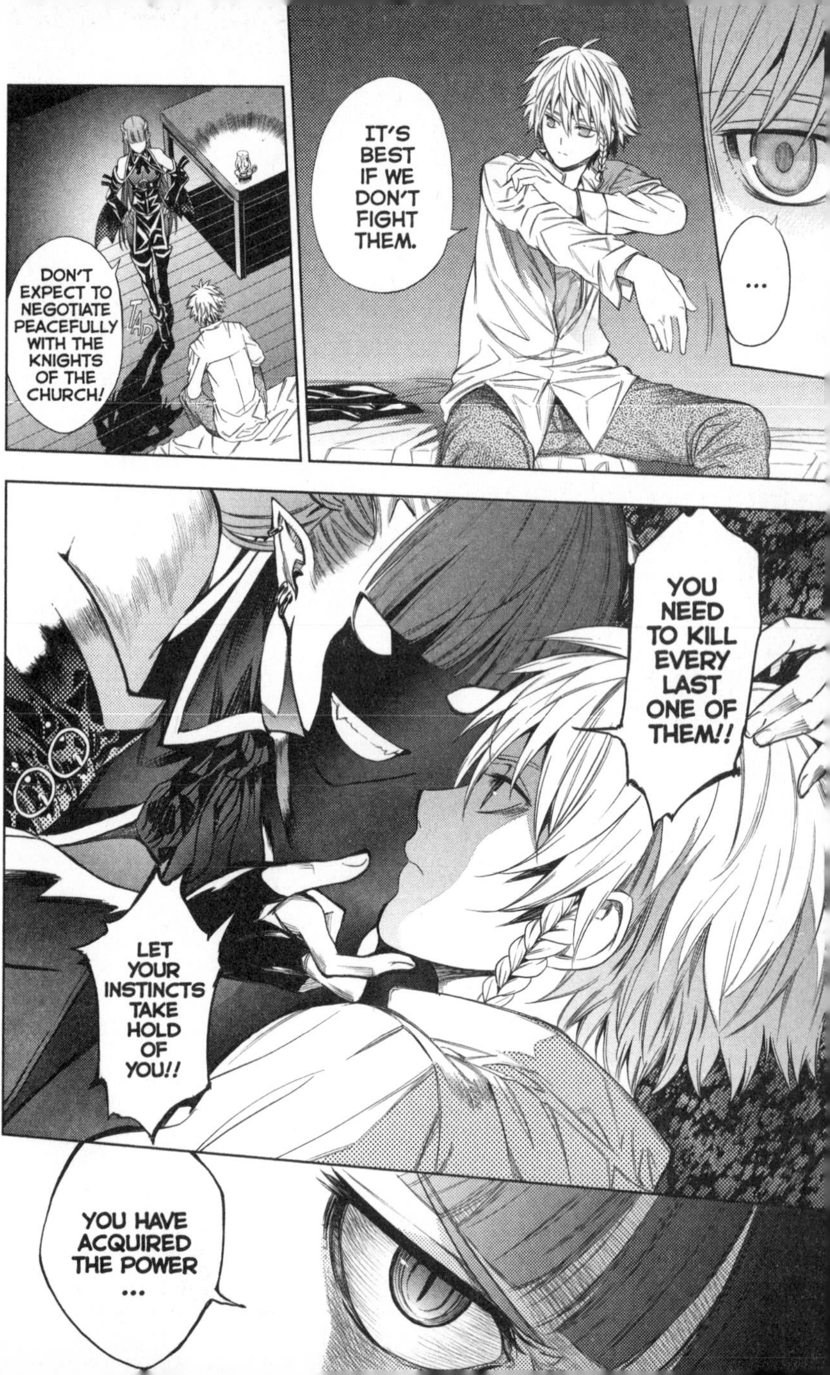
...
IT'S BEST IF WE DON'T FIGHT THEM.
DON'T EXPECT TO NEGOTIATE PEACEFULLY WITH THE KNIGHTS OF THE CHURCH!
TAP
YOU NEED TO KILL EVERY LAST ONE OF THEM!!
LET YOUR INSTINCTS TAKE HOLD OF YOU!!
YOU HAVE ACQUIRED THE POWER ...

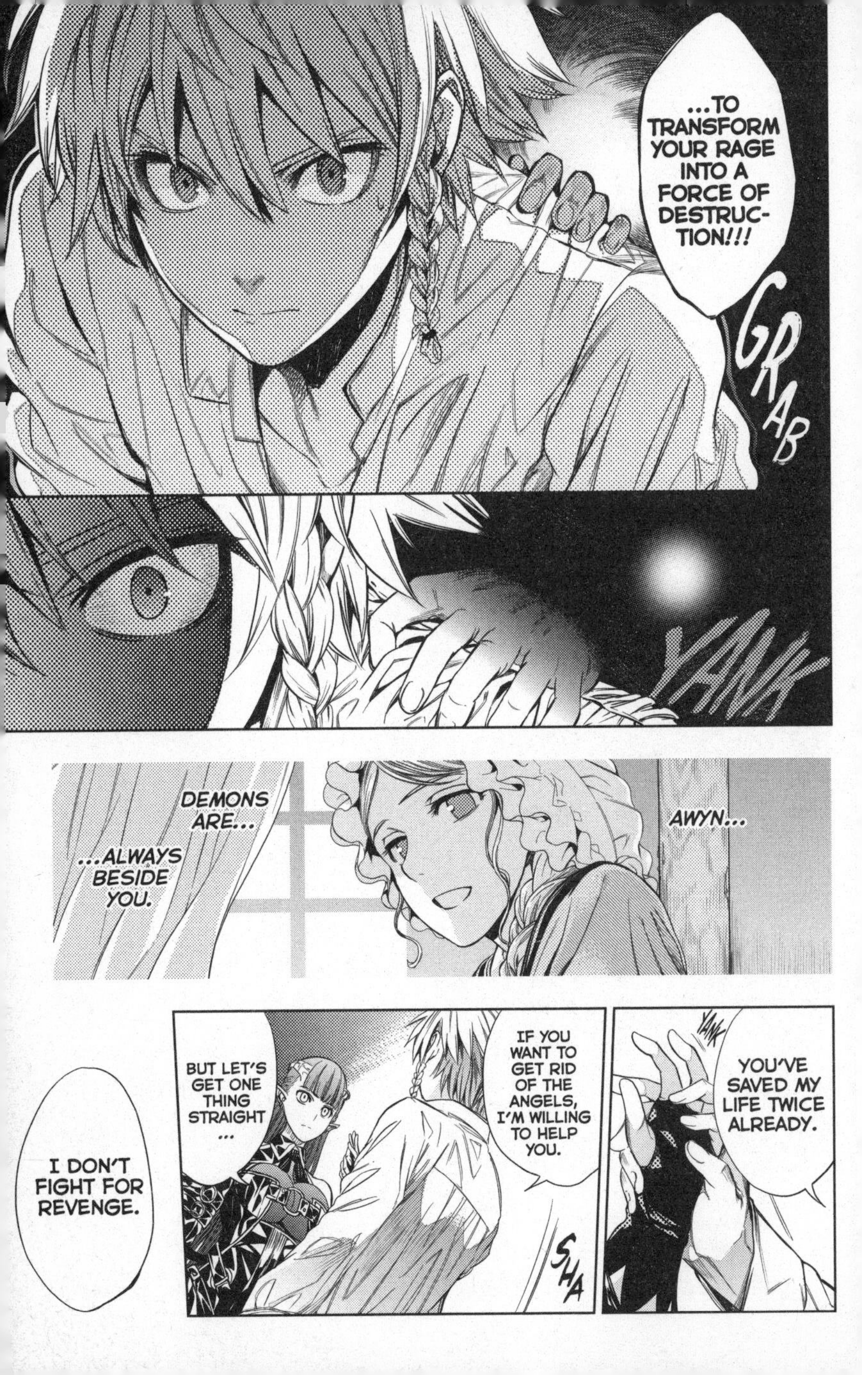
...TO TRANSFORM YOUR RAGE INTO A FORCE OF DESTRUCTION!!!
GRAB
YANK
AWYN...
DEMONS ARE...
...ALWAYS BESIDE YOU.
YANK
YOU'VE SAVED MY LIFE TWICE ALREADY.
IF YOU WANT TO GET RID OF THE ANGELS, I'M WILLING TO HELP YOU.
BUT LET'S GET ONE THING STRAIGHT...
SHA
I DON'T FIGHT FOR REVENGE.

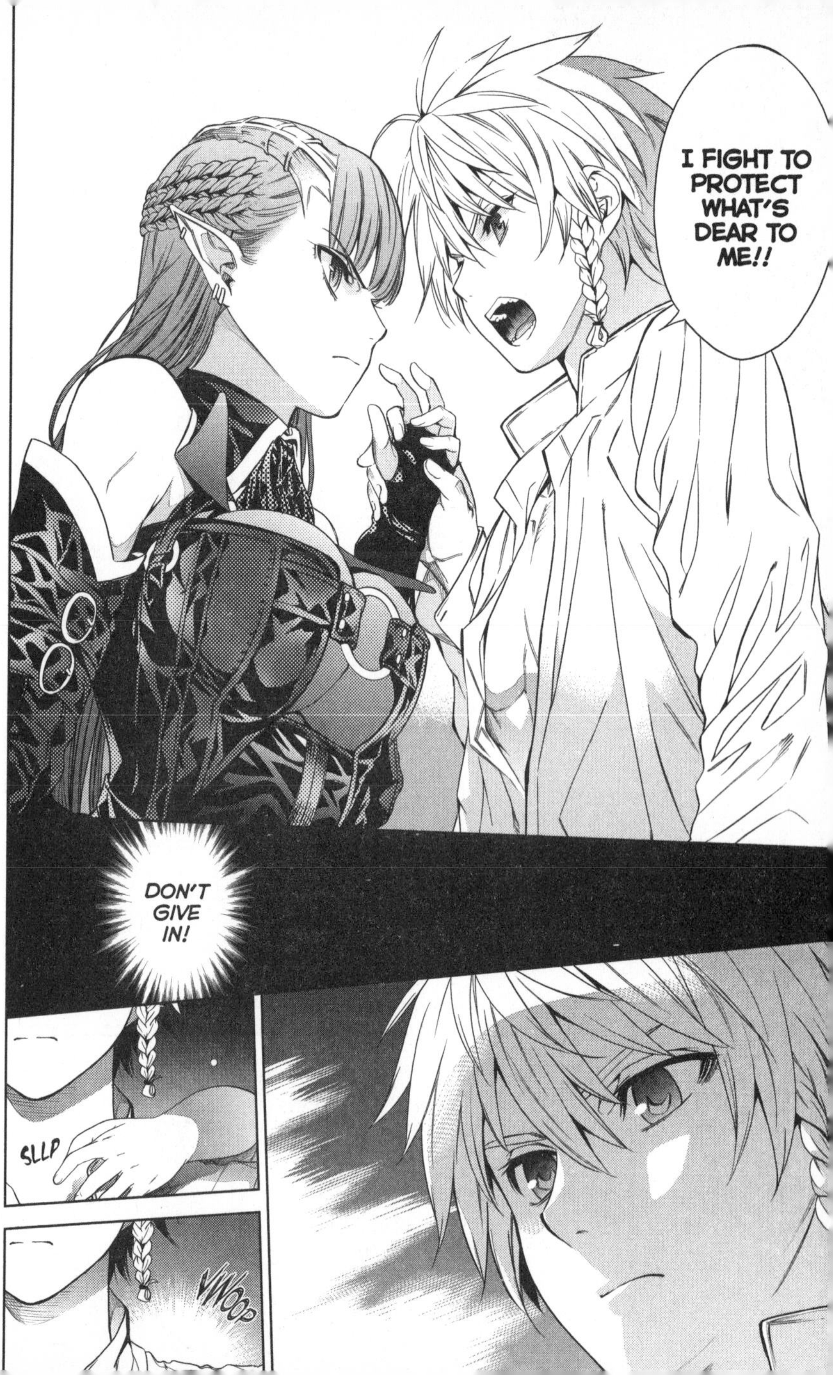
I FIGHT TO PROTECT WHAT'S DEAR TO ME!!
DON'T GIVE IN!
SLLP
VWOOP

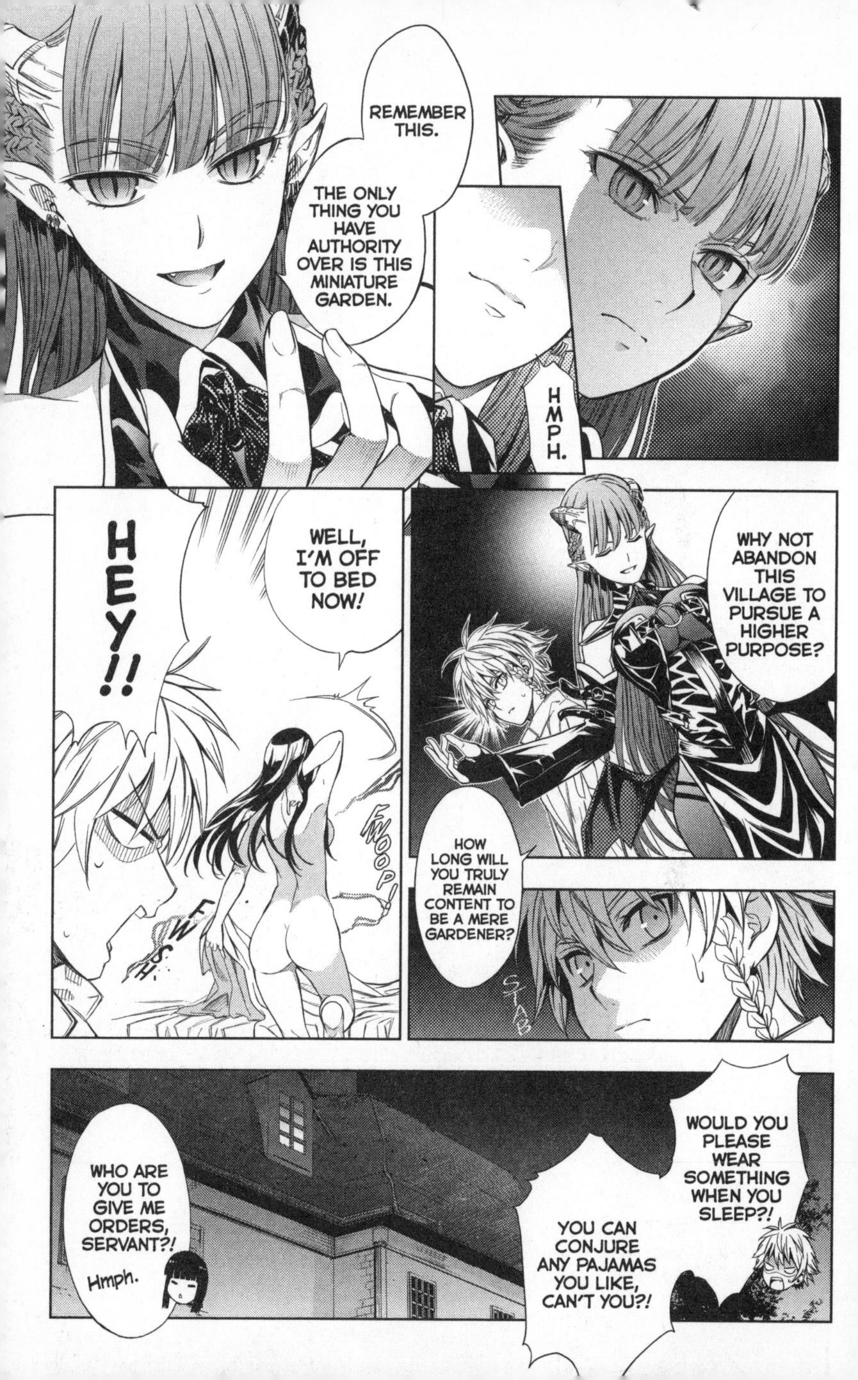

HMPH.
REMEMBER THIS.
THE ONLY THING YOU HAVE AUTHORITY OVER IS THIS MINIATURE GARDEN.
WHY NOT ABANDON THIS VILLAGE TO PURSUE A HIGHER PURPOSE?
HOW LONG WILL YOU TRULY REMAIN CONTENT TO BE A MERE GARDENER?
STAB
WELL, I'M OFF TO BED NOW!
HEY!!
FWOOP!
FWSH
WOULD YOU PLEASE WEAR SOMETHING WHEN YOU SLEEP?!
YOU CAN CONJURE ANY PAJAMAS YOU LIKE, CAN'T YOU?!
WHO ARE YOU TO GIVE ME ORDERS, SERVANT?!
Hmph.

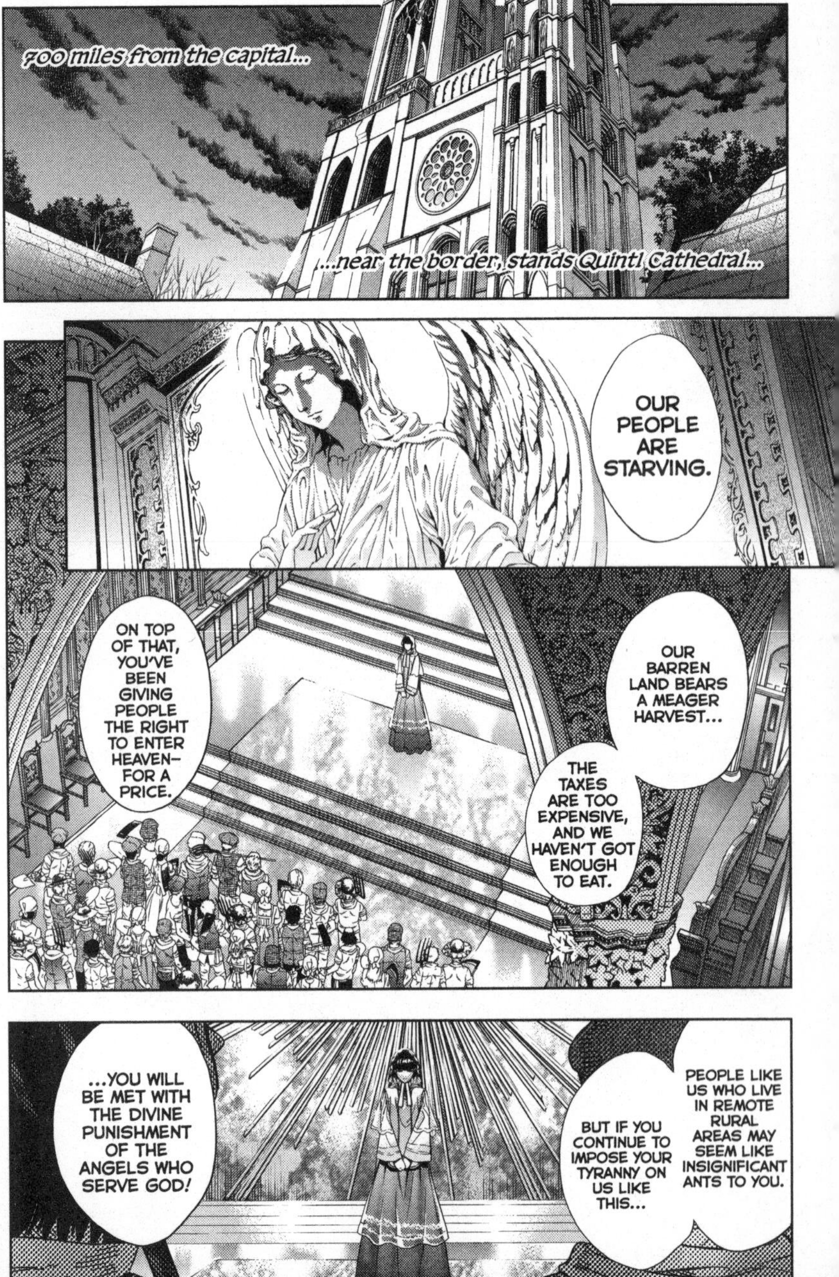

700 miles from the capital...
...near the border, stands Quintl Cathedral...
OUR PEOPLE ARE STARVING.
OUR BARREN LAND BEARS A MEAGER HARVEST...
THE TAXES ARE TOO EXPENSIVE, AND WE HAVEN'T GOT ENOUGH TO EAT.
ON TOP OF THAT, YOU'VE BEEN GIVING PEOPLE THE RIGHT TO ENTER HEAVEN—FOR A PRICE.
PEOPLE LIKE US WHO LIVE IN REMOTE RURAL AREAS MAY SEEM LIKE INSIGNIFICANT ANTS TO YOU.
BUT IF YOU CONTINUE TO IMPOSE YOUR TYRANNY ON US LIKE THIS...
...YOU WILL BE MET WITH THE DIVINE PUNISHMENT OF THE ANGELS WHO SERVE GOD!

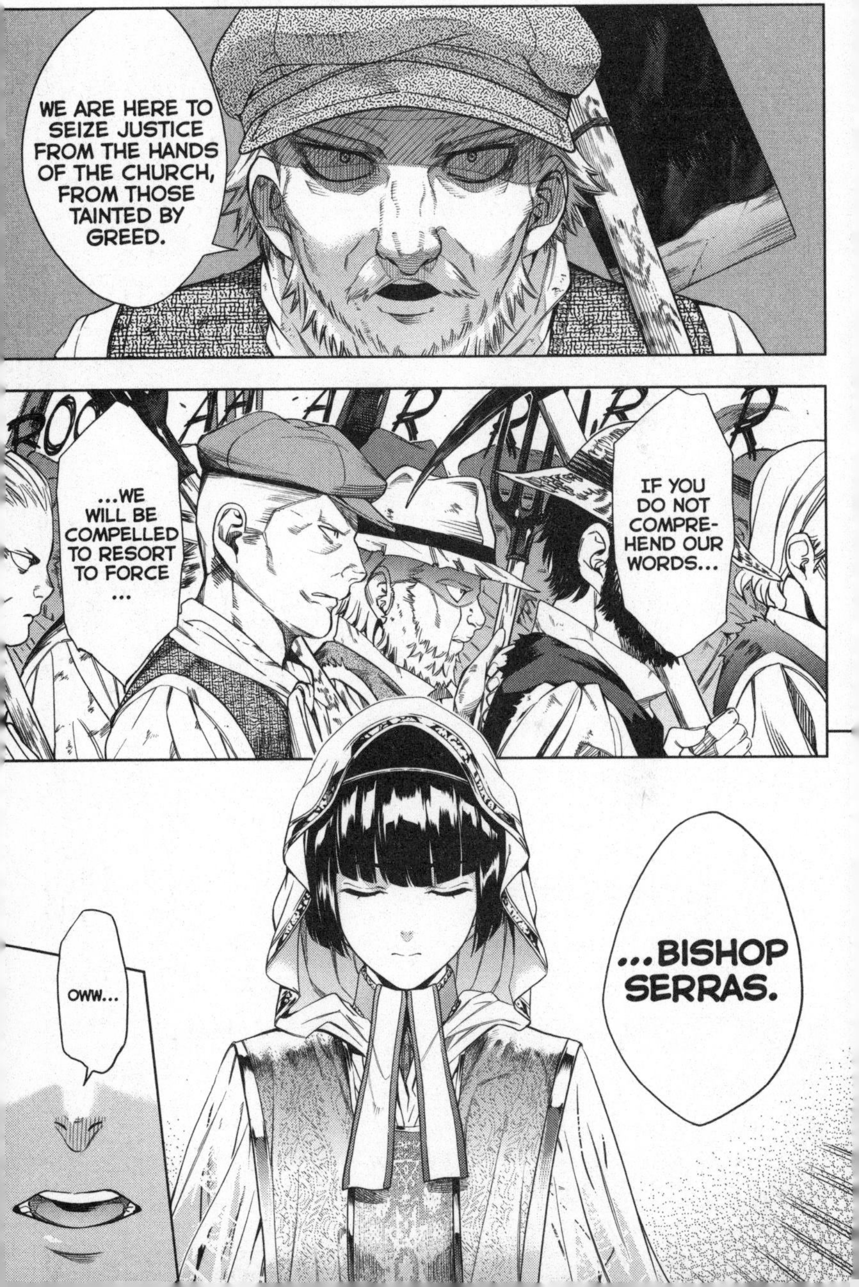
WE ARE HERE TO SEIZE JUSTICE FROM THE HANDS OF THE CHURCH, FROM THOSE TAINTED BY GREED.
IF YOU DO NOT COMPRE-HEND OUR WORDS...
...WE WILL BE COMPELLED TO RESORT TO FORCE...
...BISHOP SERRAS.
OWW...

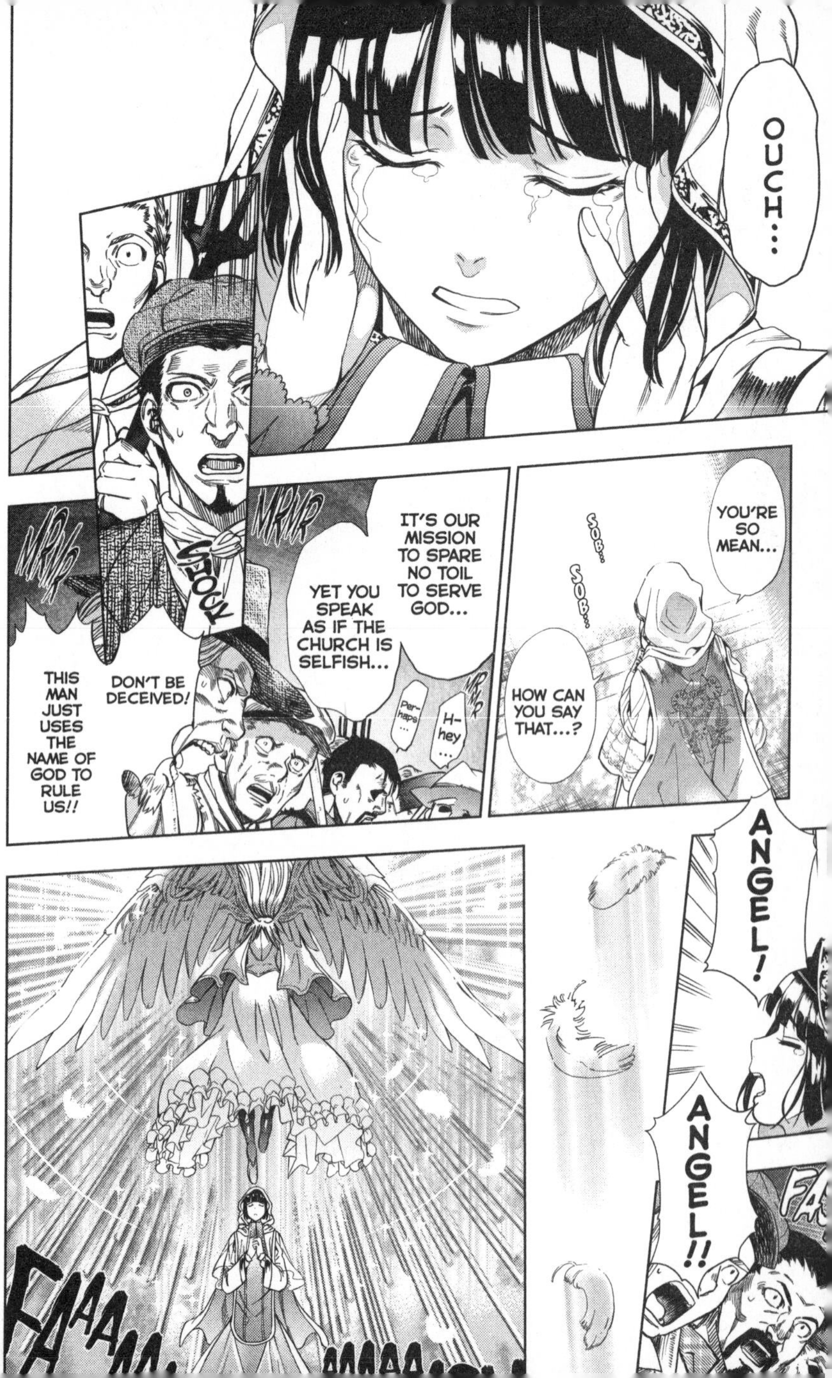
OUCH...
SHOCK
YOU'RE SO MEAN...
SOB... SOB...
HOW CAN YOU SAY THAT...?
MRMR
IT'S OUR MISSION TO SPARE NO TOIL TO SERVE GOD...
YET YOU SPEAK AS IF THE CHURCH IS SELFISH...
H-hey...
Per-haps...
DON'T BE DECEIVED!
THIS MAN JUST USES THE NAME OF GOD TO RULE US!!
ANGEL!
ANGEL!!

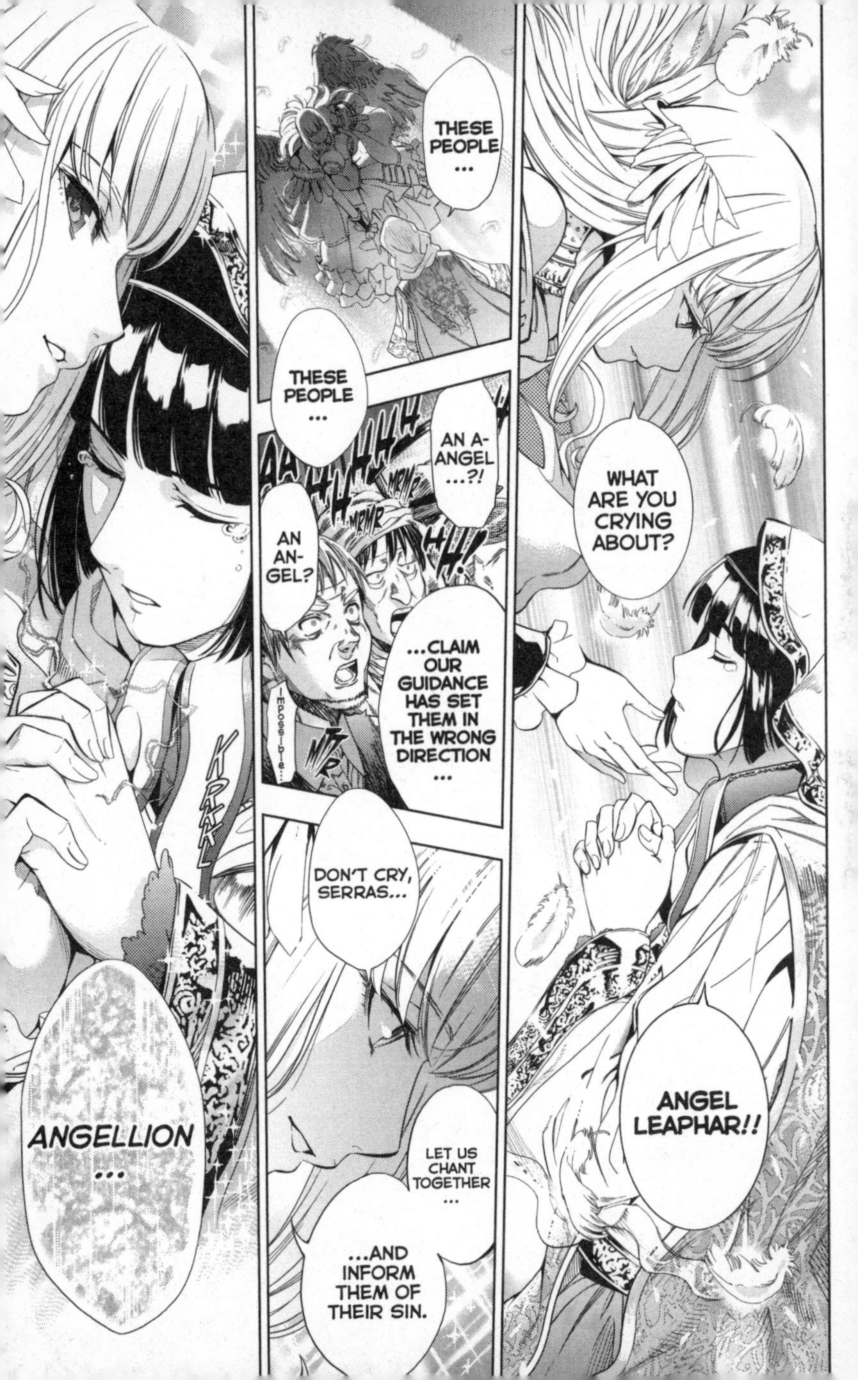
WHAT ARE YOU CRYING ABOUT?
ANGEL LEAPHAR!!
THESE PEOPLE...
THESE PEOPLE...
AN A-ANGEL...?!
AN ANGEL?
...CLAIM OUR GUIDANCE HAS SET THEM IN THE WRONG DIRECTION...
Impossible...
DON'T CRY, SERRAS...
LET US CHANT TOGETHER...
...AND INFORM THEM OF THEIR SIN.
KRAKL
ANGELLION...

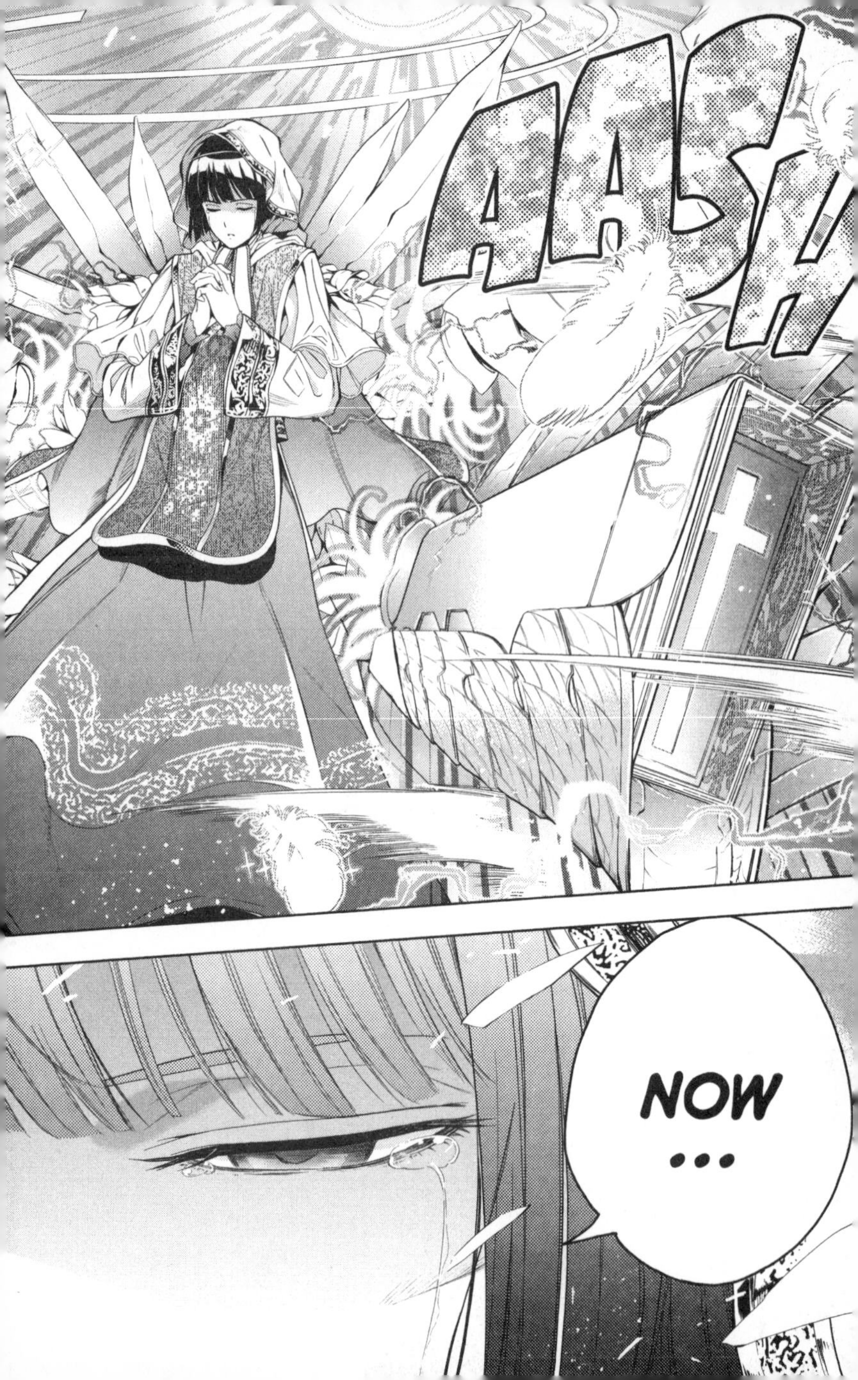
AASH
NOW ...

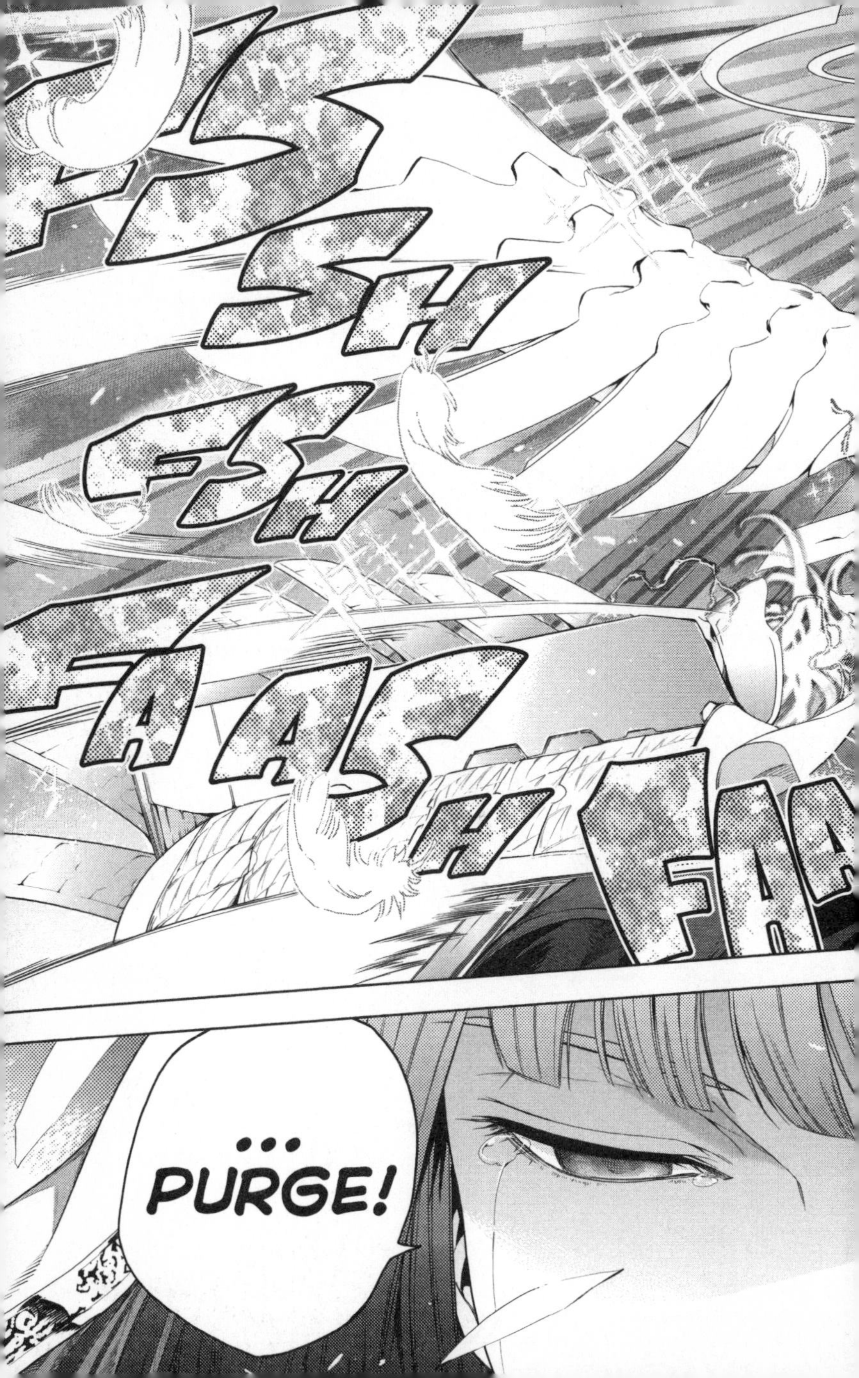
FASH
FSH
FAASH
FAA
...PURGE!

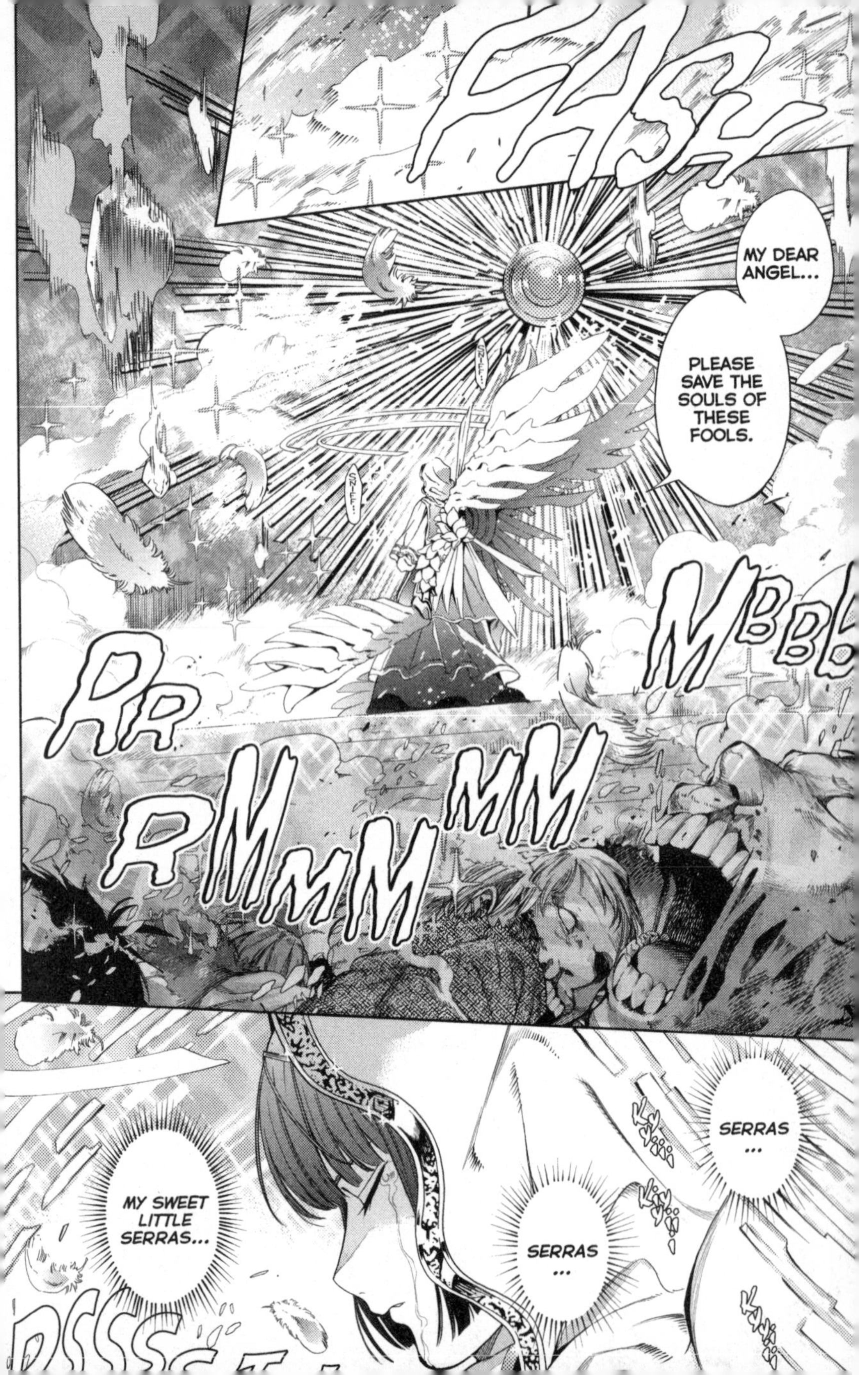
FASH
MY DEAR ANGEL...
PLEASE SAVE THE SOULS OF THESE FOOLS.
SNIFF...
SNIFF...
RRRMMMMM
SERRAS...
SERRAS...
MY SWEET LITTLE SERRAS...

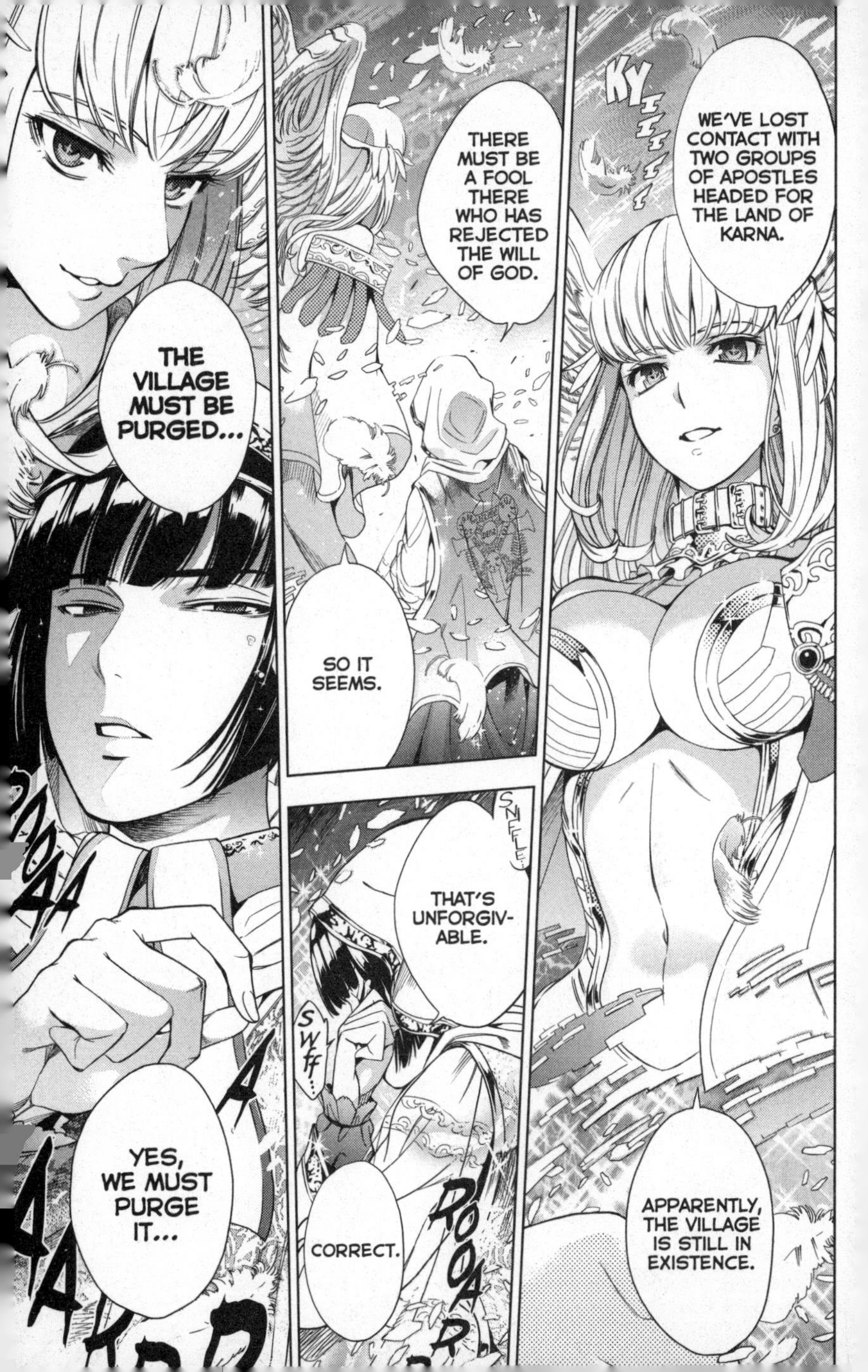
WE'VE LOST CONTACT WITH TWO GROUPS OF APOSTLES HEADED FOR THE LAND OF KARNA.
APPARENTLY, THE VILLAGE IS STILL IN EXISTENCE.
THERE MUST BE A FOOL THERE WHO HAS REJECTED THE WILL OF GOD.
SO IT SEEMS.
SNIFFLE...
THAT'S UNFORGIV-ABLE.
SWFF...
CORRECT.
THE VILLAGE MUST BE PURGED...
YES, WE MUST PURGE IT...

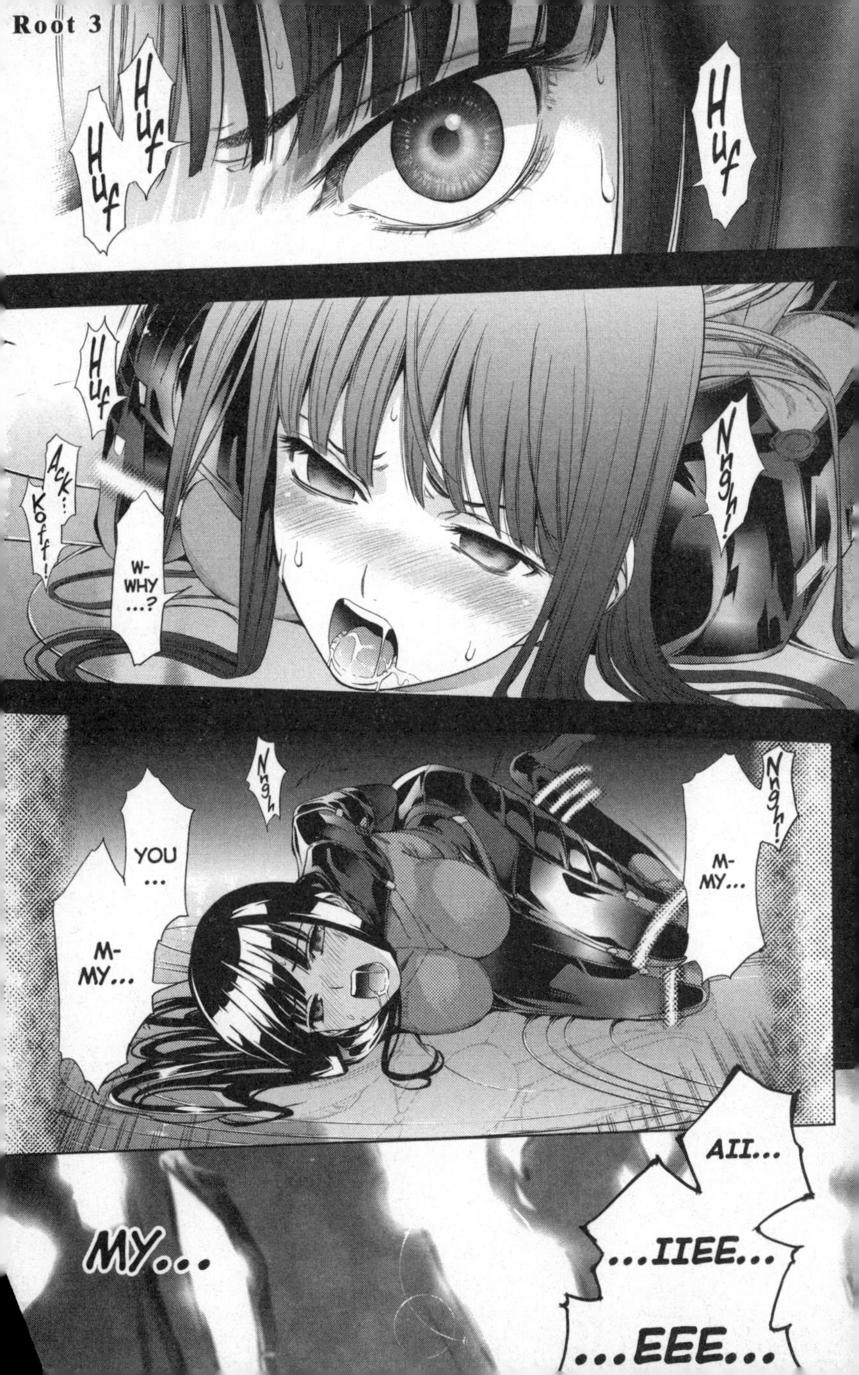
Huf
Huf
Huf
Nngh!
Huf
Ack... Koff!
W-WHY ...?
Nngh!
M-MY...
Nngh
YOU ...
M-MY...
AII...
...IIEE...
...EEE...
MY...

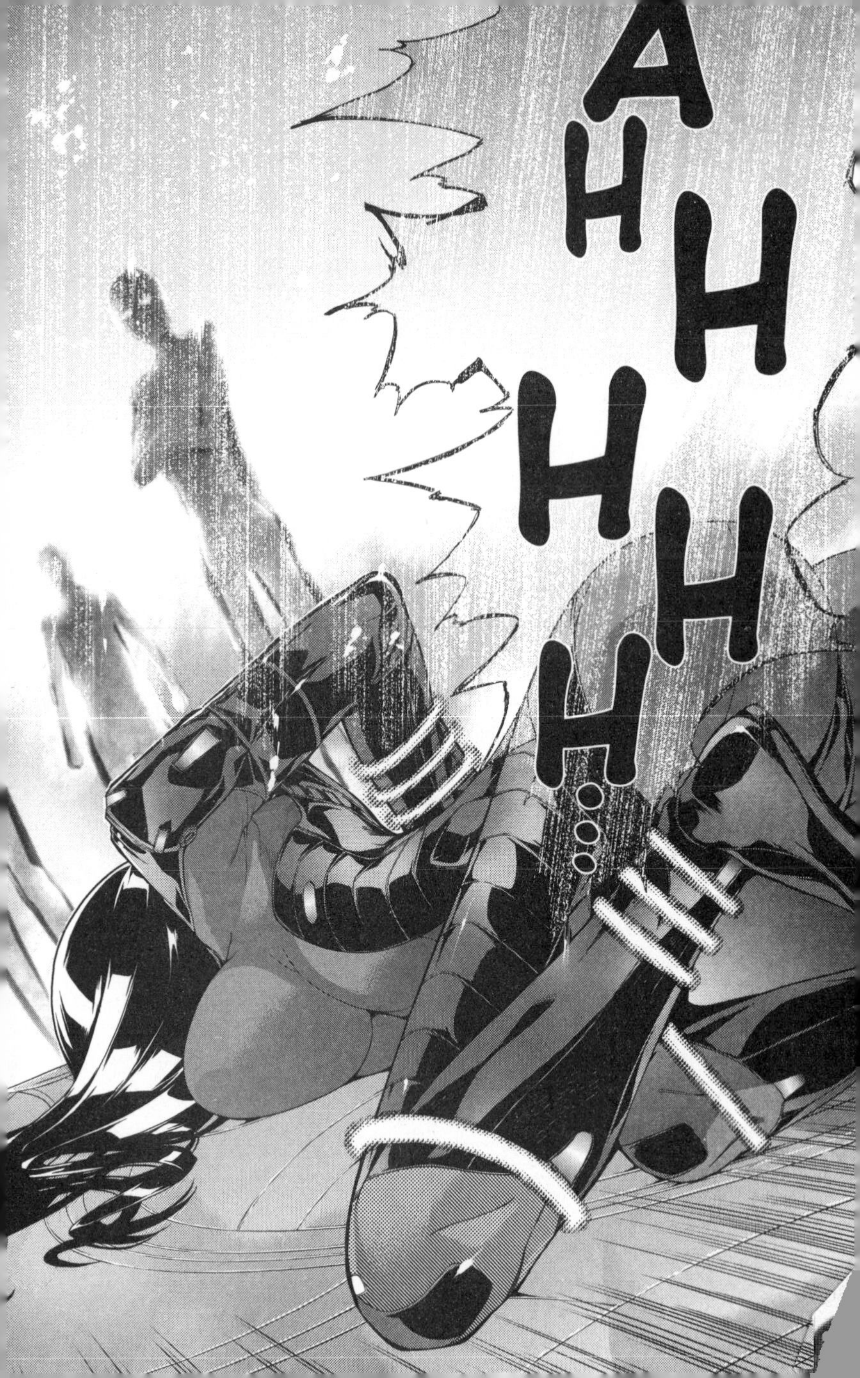
AHHHHHHH...

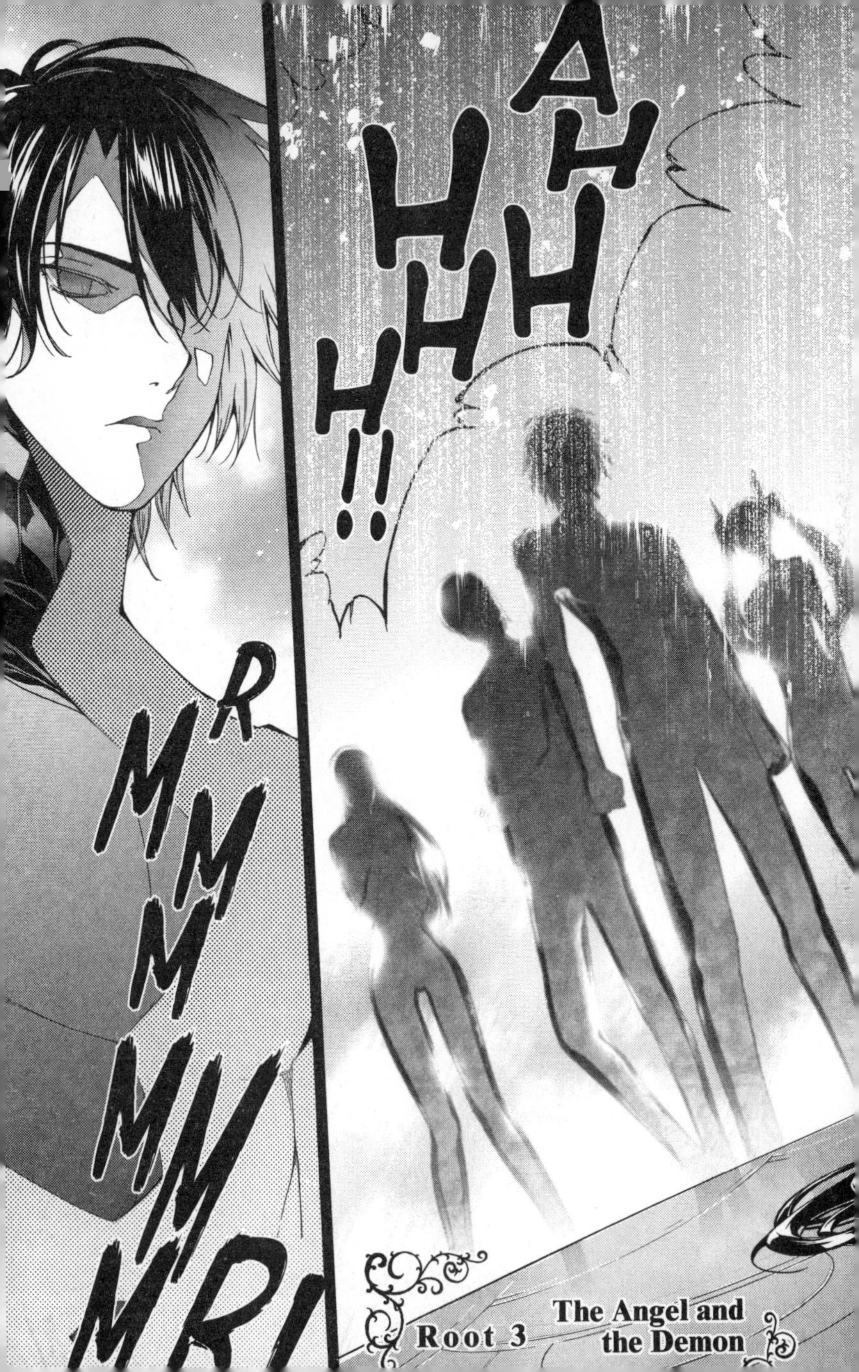
AHHHHHH!!
MRMMMMMMMRI

Root 3 The Angel and the Demon

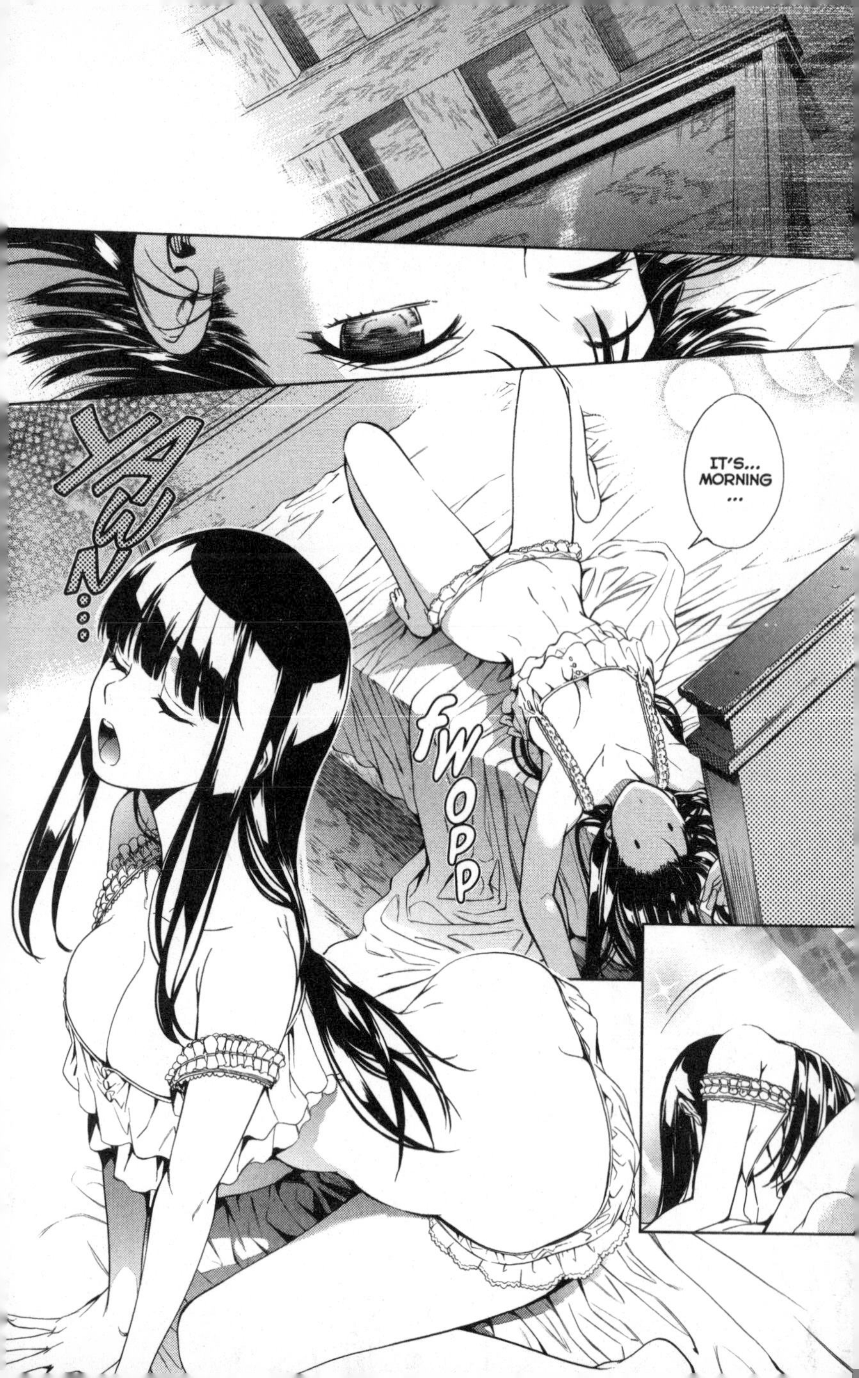
IT'S... MORNING ...
fWOPP
YAWN...

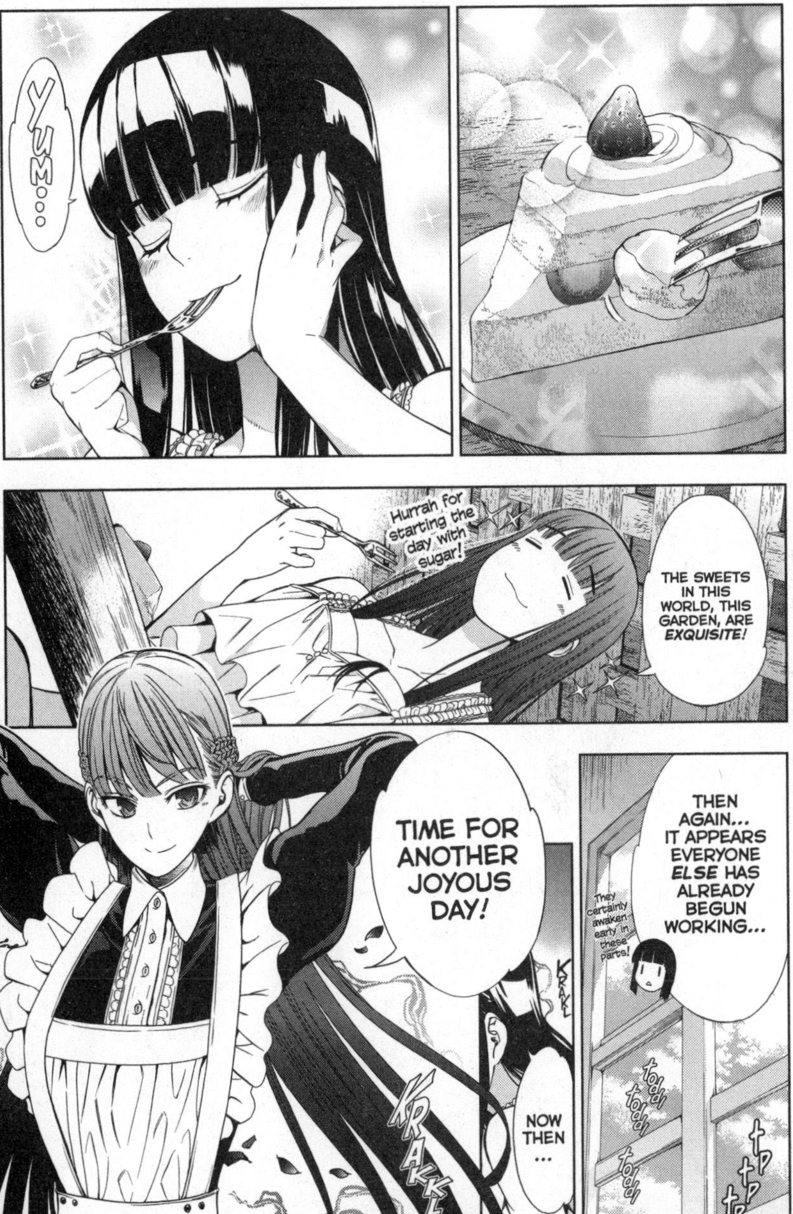
YUM...
THE SWEETS IN THIS WORLD, THIS GARDEN, ARE EXQUISITE!
Hurrah for starting the day with sugar!
THEN AGAIN... IT APPEARS EVERYONE ELSE HAS ALREADY BEGUN WORKING...
They certainly awaken early in these parts!
toddl toddl toddl
tp tp tp
KRAKL
NOW THEN ...
TIME FOR ANOTHER JOYOUS DAY!
KRAKKL

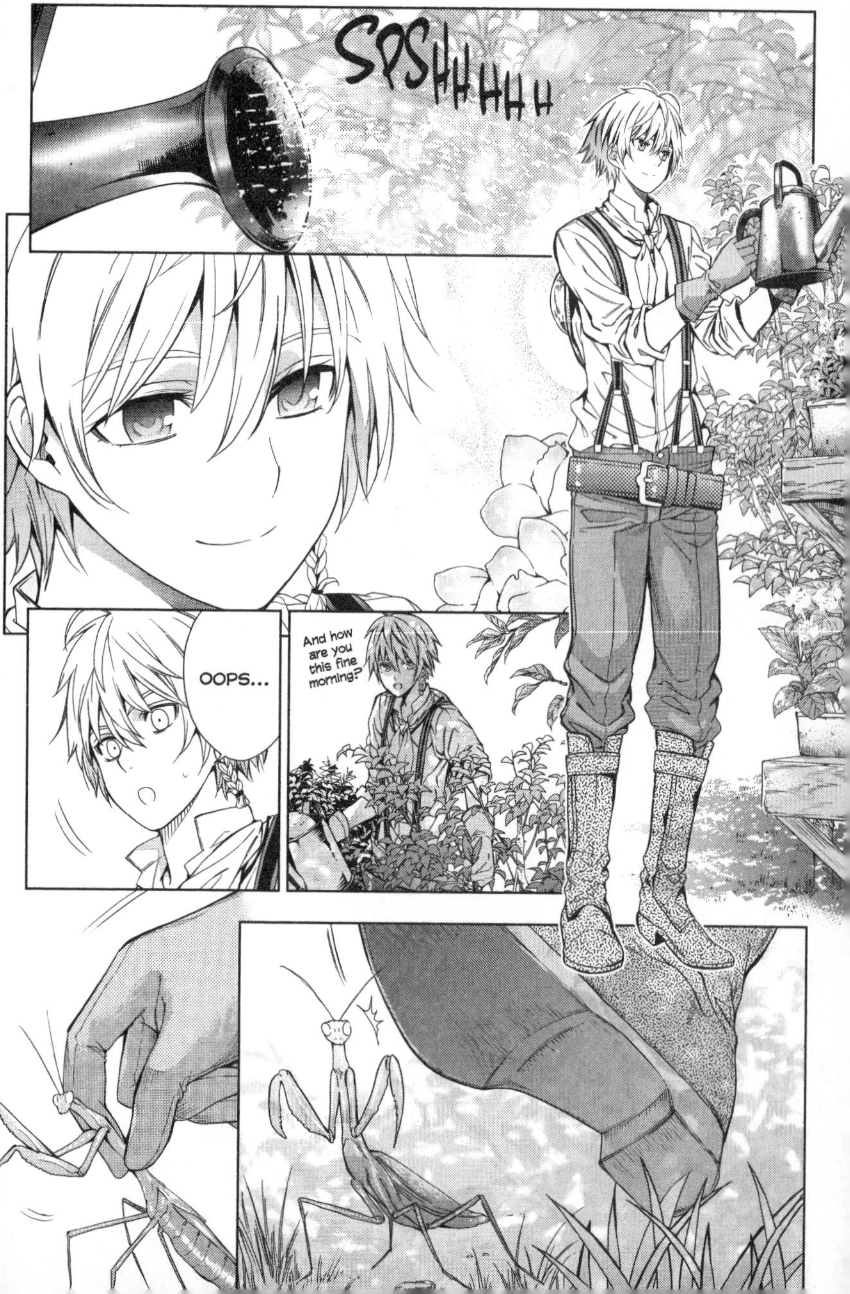
SPSHHHHH
And how are you this fine morning?
OOPS...

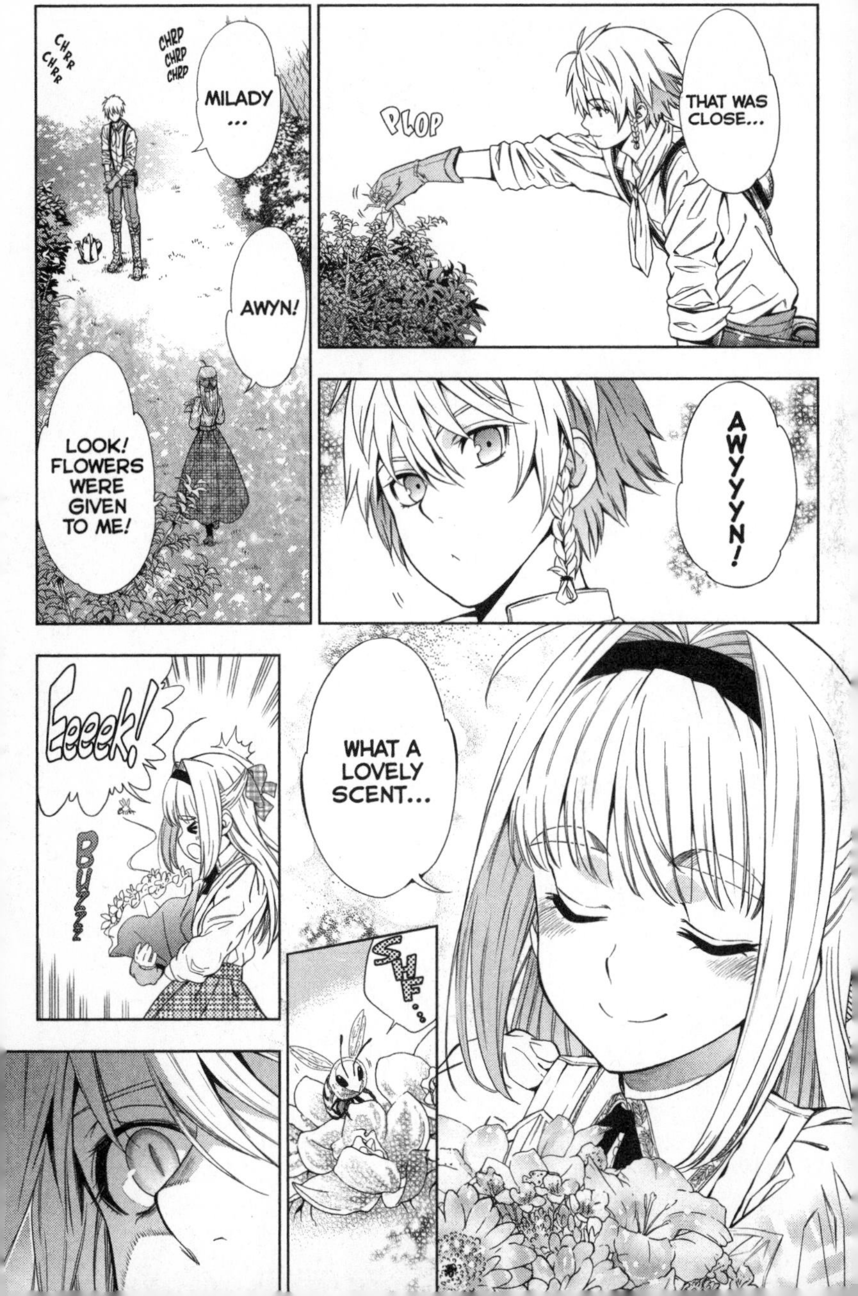
PLOP
THAT WAS CLOSE...
AWYYYN!
CHRR CHRR
CHRP CHRP CHRP
MILADY...
AWYN!
LOOK! FLOWERS WERE GIVEN TO ME!
WHAT A LOVELY SCENT...
Eeeek!
BUZZZ
SNFF..

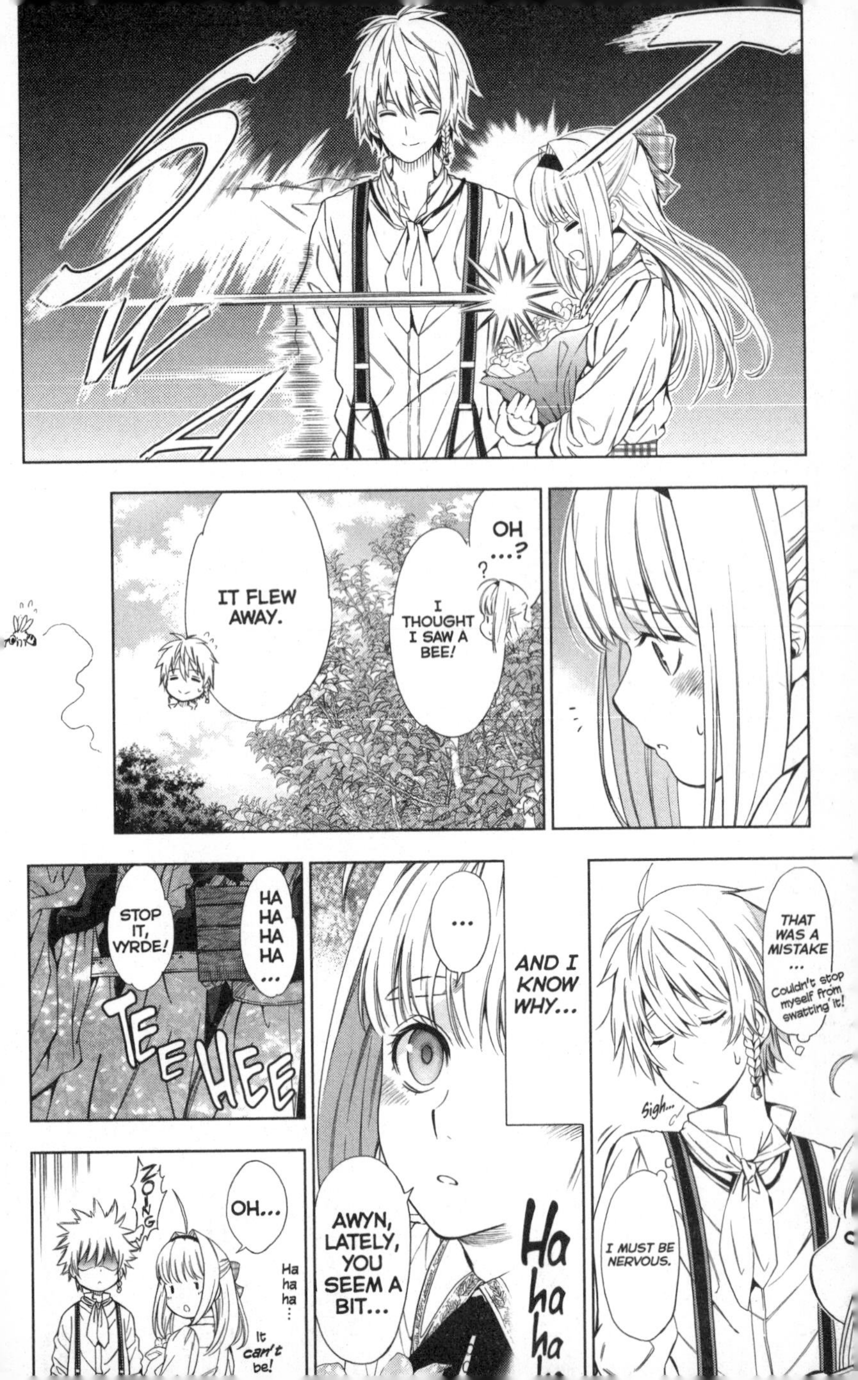
SWAT
OH ...?
I THOUGHT I SAW A BEE!
IT FLEW AWAY.
THAT WAS A MISTAKE...
Couldn't stop myself from swatting it!
Sigh...
I MUST BE NERVOUS.
...
AND I KNOW WHY...
AWYN, LATELY, YOU SEEM A BIT...
Ha ha ha...
HA HA HA HA...
STOP IT, VYRDE!
TEE HEE
ZOING
OH...
Ha ha ha...
It can't be!

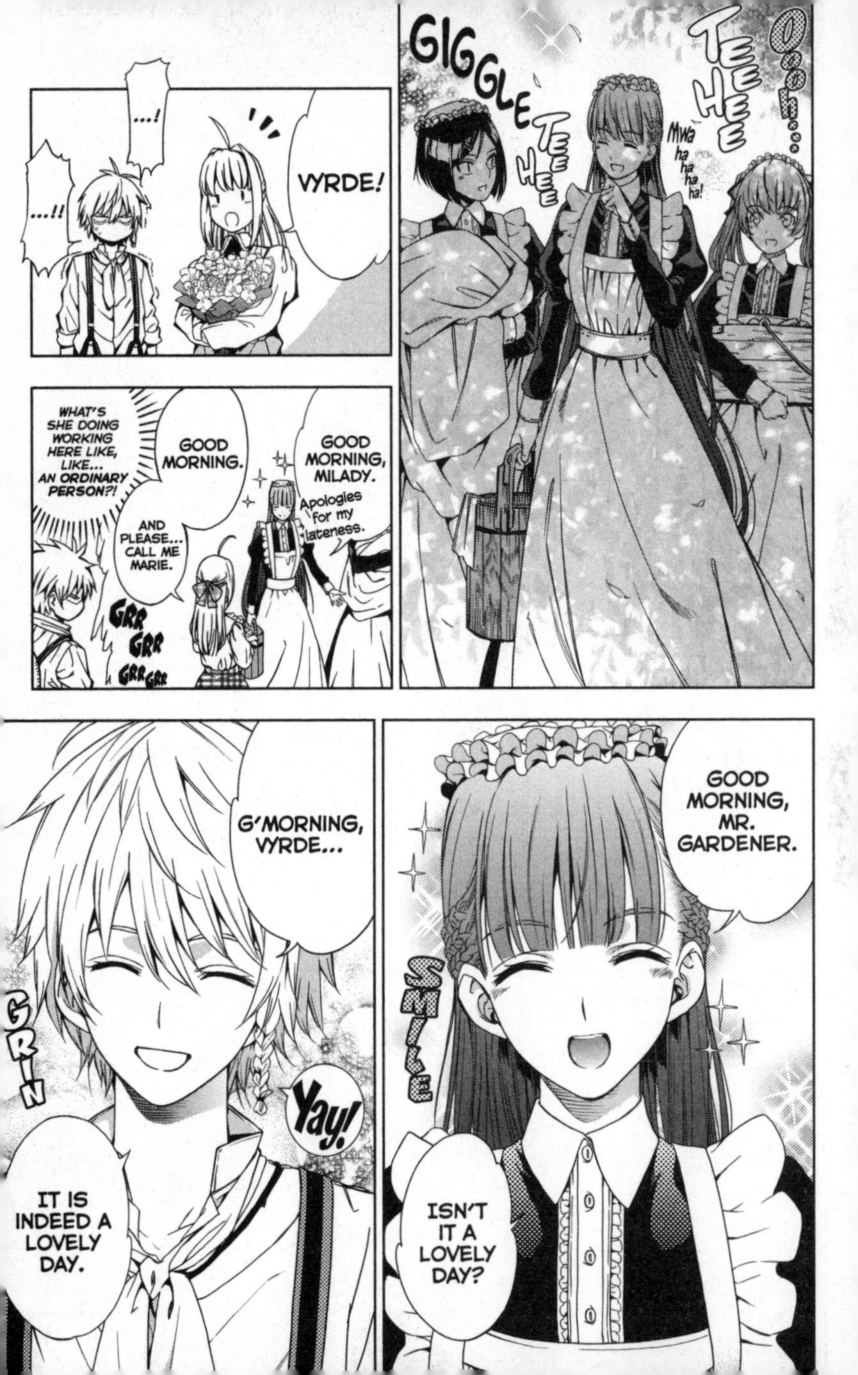
Oooh...
TEE HEE HEE
Mwa ha ha ha ha!
GIGGLE
TEE HEE
VYRDE!
...!
...!!
GOOD MORNING, MILADY.
Apologies for my lateness.
GOOD MORNING.
AND PLEASE... CALL ME MARIE.
WHAT'S SHE DOING WORKING HERE LIKE, LIKE... AN ORDINARY PERSON?!
GRR GRR GRR GRR
GOOD MORNING, MR. GARDENER.
SMILE
ISN'T IT A LOVELY DAY?
G'MORNING, VYRDE...
Yay!
GRIN
IT IS INDEED A LOVELY DAY.

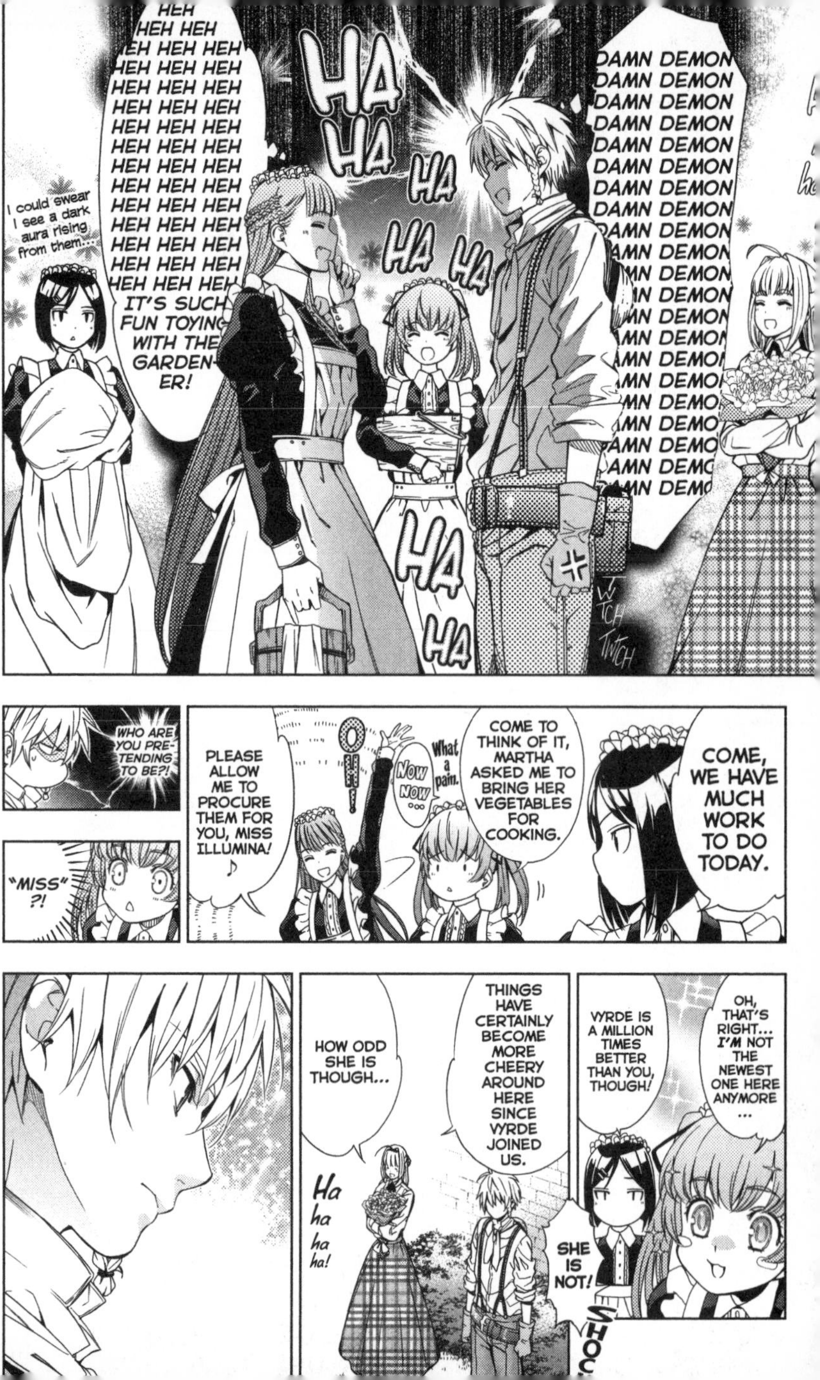
DAMN DEMON DAMN DEMON
HA HA HA HA HA HA HA HA
HEH HEH HEH HEH HEH HEH HEH HEH HEH HEH HEH HEH HEH HEH HEH HEH HEH HEH HEH HEH HEH HEH HEH HEH HEH HEH HEH HEH HEH HEH HEH HEH HEH HEH HEH HEH HEH HEH HEH HEH HEH HEH IT'S SUCH FUN TOYING WITH THE GARDENER!
I could swear I see a dark aura rising from them...
TWITCH TWITCH
COME, WE HAVE MUCH WORK TO DO TODAY.
COME TO THINK OF IT, MARTHA ASKED ME TO BRING HER VEGETABLES FOR COOKING.
What a pain.
Now now...
PLEASE ALLOW ME TO PROCURE THEM FOR YOU, MISS ILLUMINA! ♪
WHO ARE YOU PRETENDING TO BE?!
"MISS" ?!
OH, THAT'S RIGHT... I'M NOT THE NEWEST ONE HERE ANYMORE...
VYRDE IS A MILLION TIMES BETTER THAN YOU, THOUGH!
SHE IS NOT!
THINGS HAVE CERTAINLY BECOME MORE CHEERY AROUND HERE SINCE VYRDE JOINED US.
HOW ODD SHE IS THOUGH...
Ha ha ha ha!

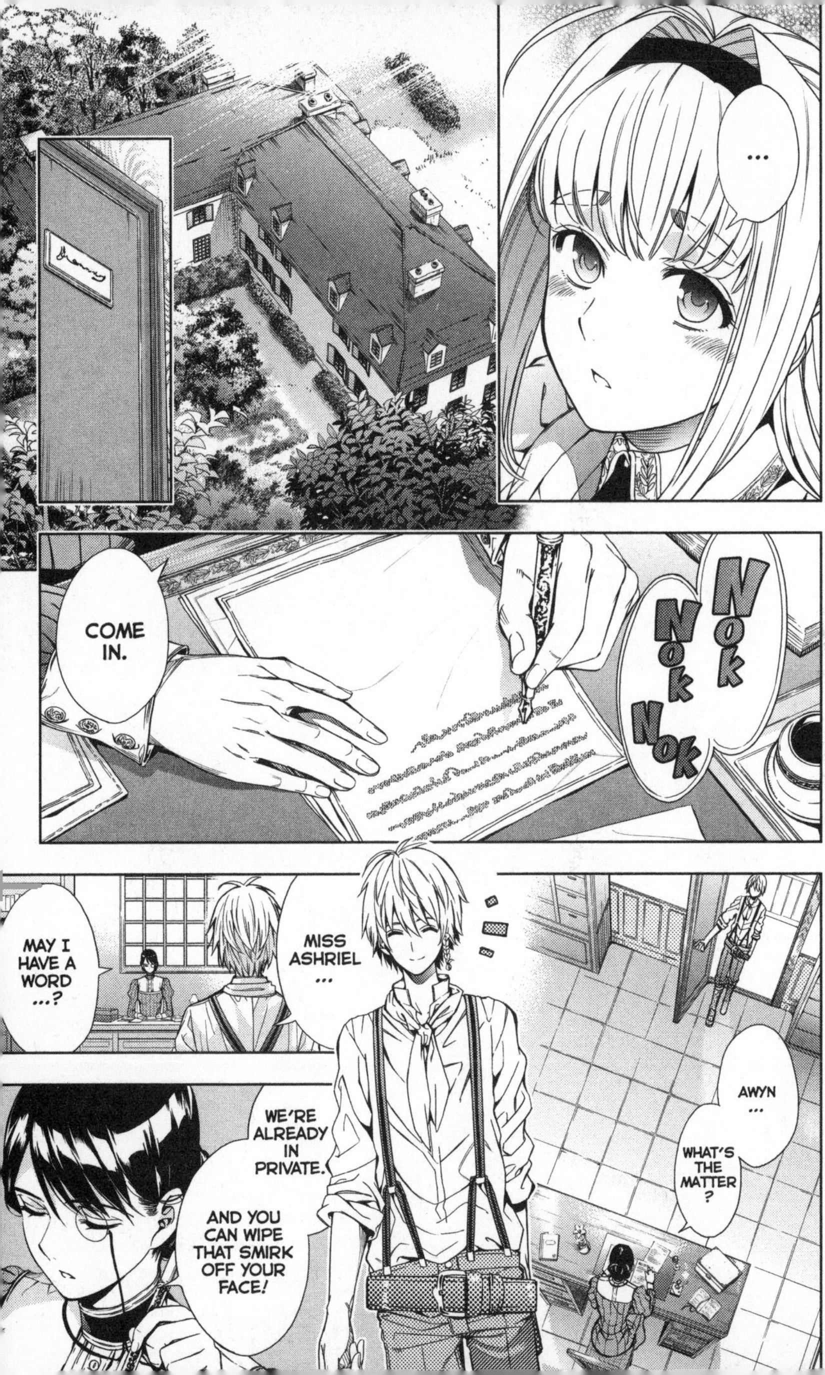
...
NOK NOK NOK
COME IN.
AWYN ...
WHAT'S THE MATTER ?
MISS ASHRIEL ...
MAY I HAVE A WORD ...?
WE'RE ALREADY IN PRIVATE.
AND YOU CAN WIPE THAT SMIRK OFF YOUR FACE!

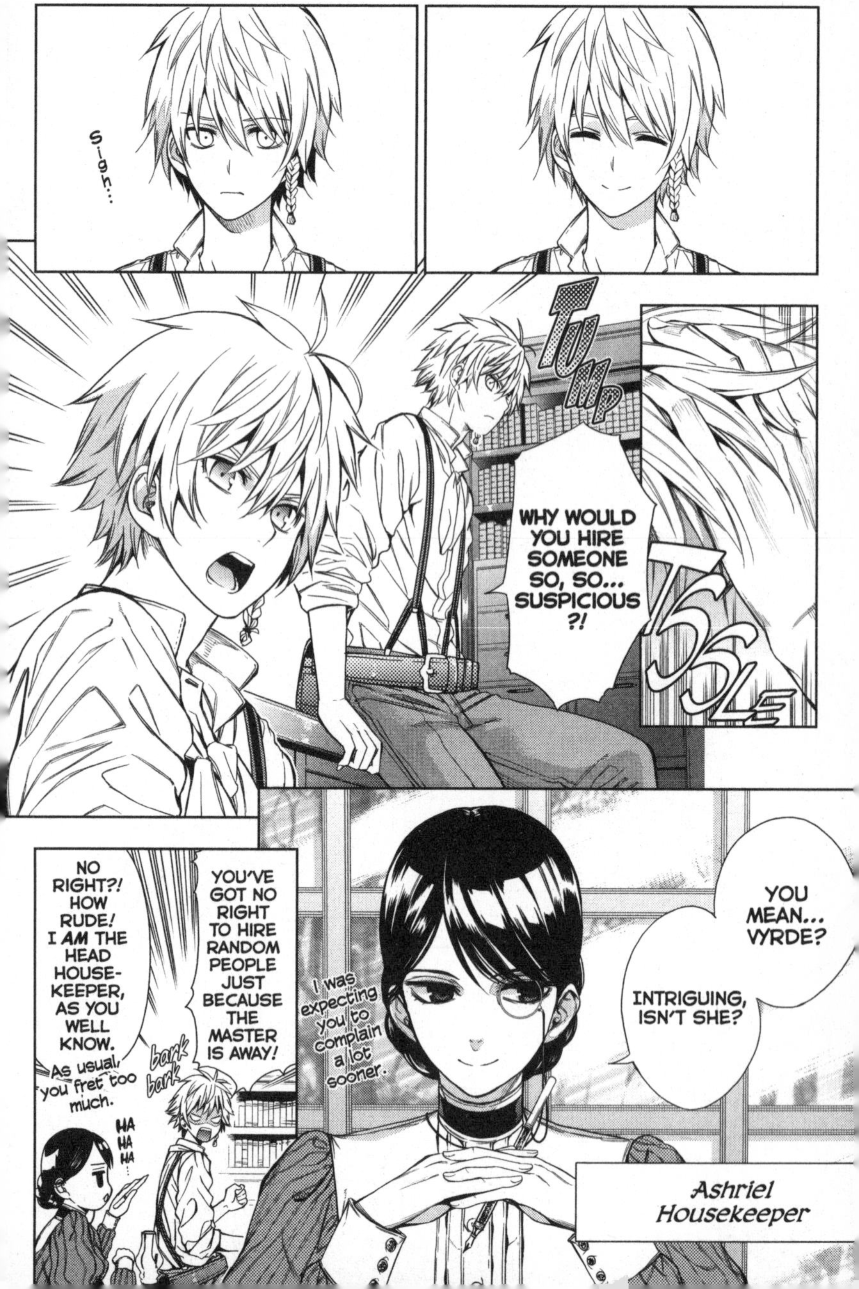
Sigh...
TUSSLE
TUMP
WHY WOULD YOU HIRE SOMEONE SO, SO... SUSPICIOUS?!
YOU MEAN... VYRDE?
INTRIGUING, ISN'T SHE?
Ashriel Housekeeper
I was expecting you to complain a lot sooner.
YOU'VE GOT NO RIGHT TO HIRE RANDOM PEOPLE JUST BECAUSE THE MASTER IS AWAY!
NO RIGHT?! HOW RUDE! I *AM* THE HEAD HOUSE-KEEPER, AS YOU WELL KNOW.
bark bark
As usual, you fret too much.
HA HA HA...

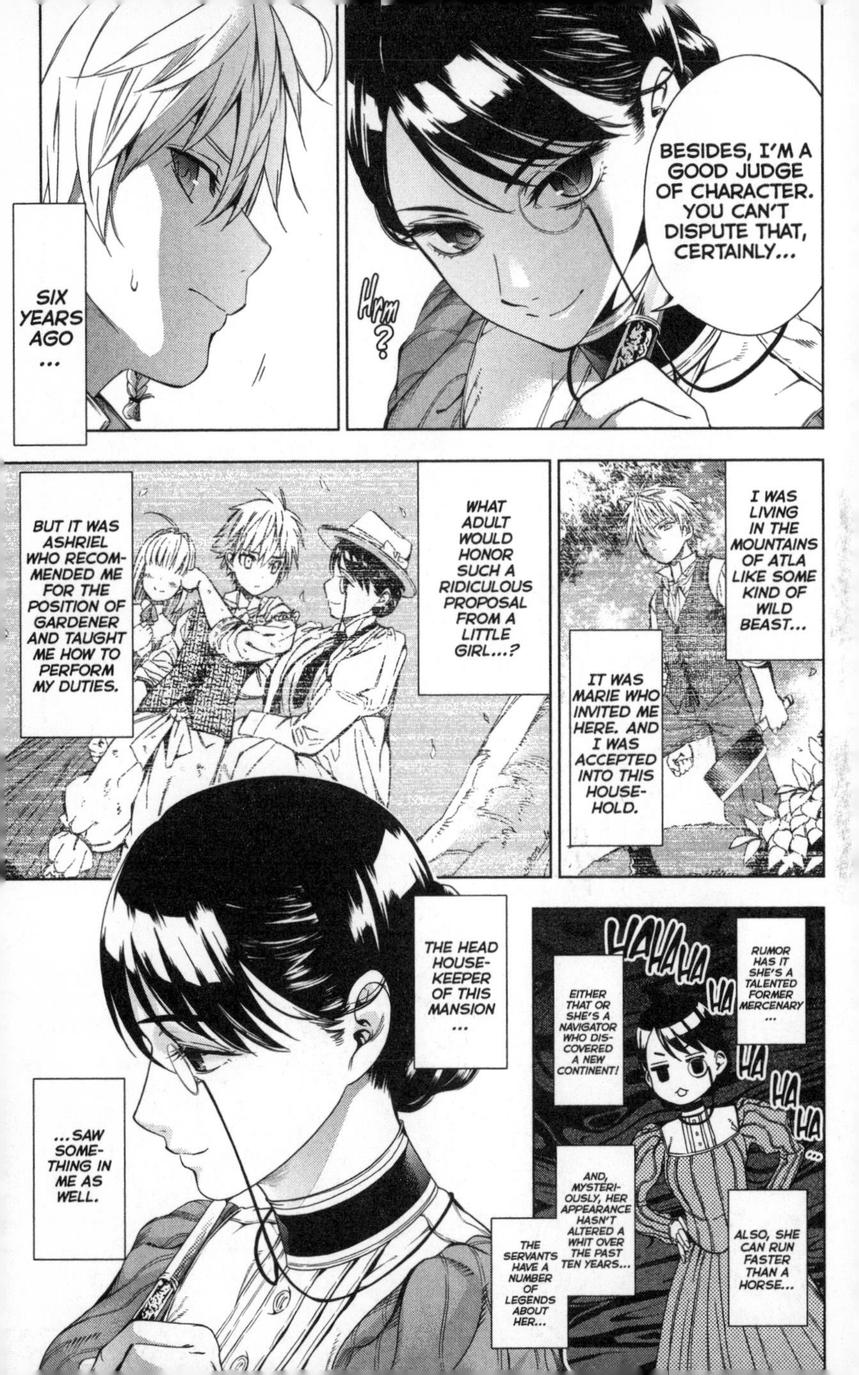
BESIDES, I'M A GOOD JUDGE OF CHARACTER. YOU CAN'T DISPUTE THAT, CERTAINLY...
Hrm?
SIX YEARS AGO...
I WAS LIVING IN THE MOUNTAINS OF ATLA LIKE SOME KIND OF WILD BEAST...
IT WAS MARIE WHO INVITED ME HERE. AND I WAS ACCEPTED INTO THIS HOUSEHOLD.
WHAT ADULT WOULD HONOR SUCH A RIDICULOUS PROPOSAL FROM A LITTLE GIRL...?
BUT IT WAS ASHRIEL WHO RECOMMENDED ME FOR THE POSITION OF GARDENER AND TAUGHT ME HOW TO PERFORM MY DUTIES.
HAHAHA HA
RUMOR HAS IT SHE'S A TALENTED FORMER MERCENARY...
EITHER THAT OR SHE'S A NAVIGATOR WHO DISCOVERED A NEW CONTINENT!
HA HA HA HA...
ALSO, SHE CAN RUN FASTER THAN A HORSE...
AND, MYSTERIOUSLY, HER APPEARANCE HASN'T ALTERED A WHIT OVER THE PAST TEN YEARS...
THE SERVANTS HAVE A NUMBER OF LEGENDS ABOUT HER...
THE HEAD HOUSEKEEPER OF THIS MANSION...
...SAW SOMETHING IN ME AS WELL.

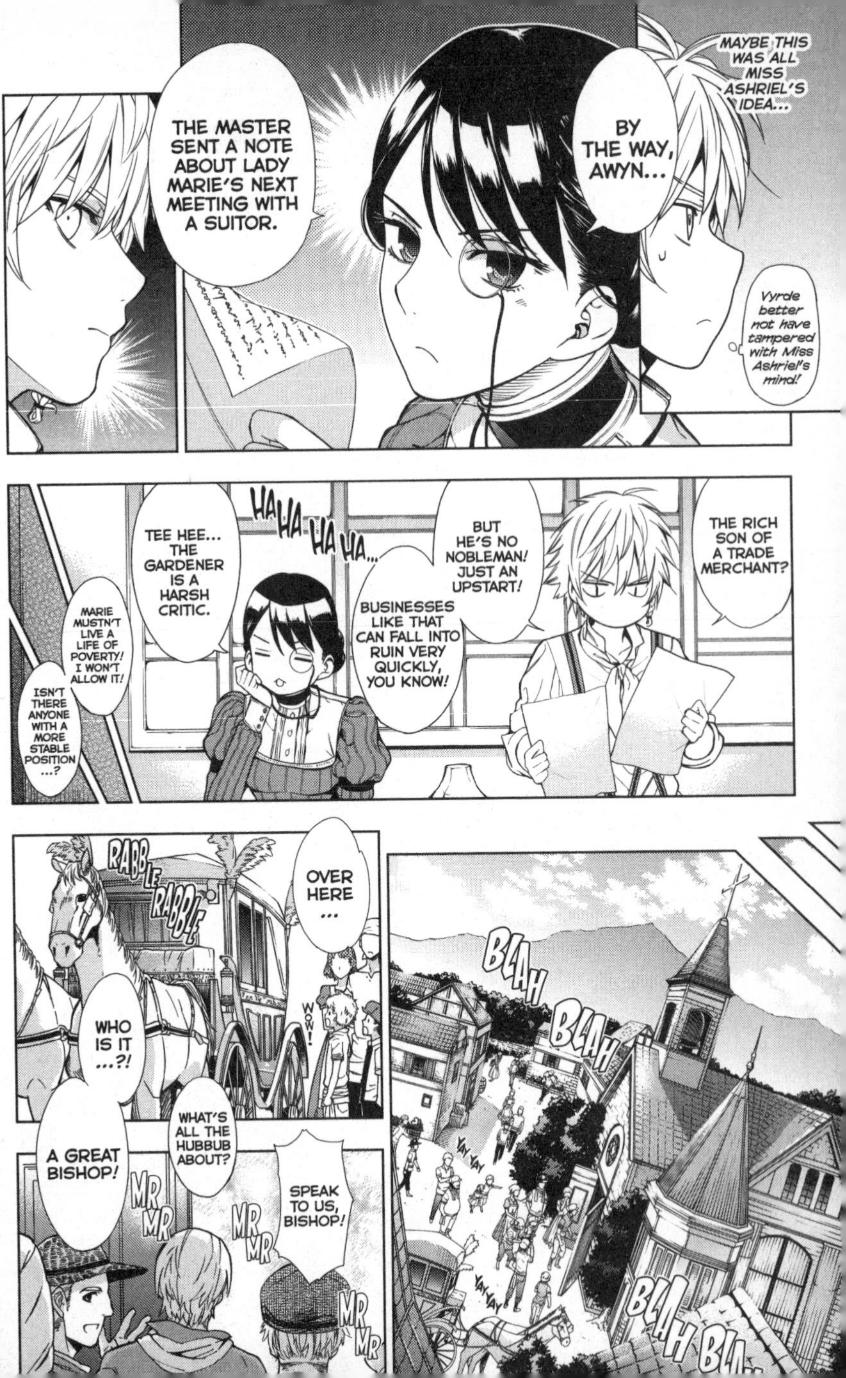
MAYBE THIS WAS ALL MISS ASHRIEL'S IDEA...
Vyrde better not have tampered with Miss Ashriel's mind!
BY THE WAY, AWYN...
THE MASTER SENT A NOTE ABOUT LADY MARIE'S NEXT MEETING WITH A SUITOR.
THE RICH SON OF A TRADE MERCHANT?
BUT HE'S NO NOBLEMAN! JUST AN UPSTART!
BUSINESSES LIKE THAT CAN FALL INTO RUIN VERY QUICKLY, YOU KNOW!
HA HA HA HA...
TEE HEE... THE GARDENER IS A HARSH CRITIC.
MARIE MUSTN'T LIVE A LIFE OF POVERTY! I WON'T ALLOW IT!
ISN'T THERE ANYONE WITH A MORE STABLE POSITION...?
BLAH BLAH
YAY YAY
YAY YAY
BLAH BLAH
OVER HERE...
WOW!
RABBLE RABBLE
WHO IS IT...?!
WHAT'S ALL THE HUBBUB ABOUT?
SPEAK TO US, BISHOP!
A GREAT BISHOP!
MR MR
MR MR
MR MR

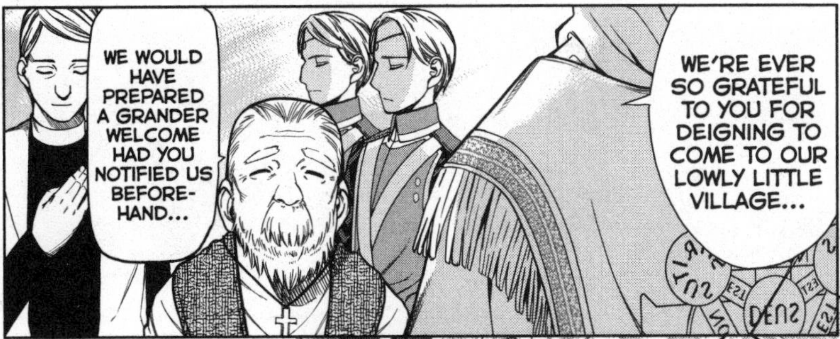
WE'RE EVER SO GRATEFUL TO YOU FOR DEIGNING TO COME TO OUR LOWLY LITTLE VILLAGE...
WE WOULD HAVE PREPARED A GRANDER WELCOME HAD YOU NOTIFIED US BEFORE-HAND...
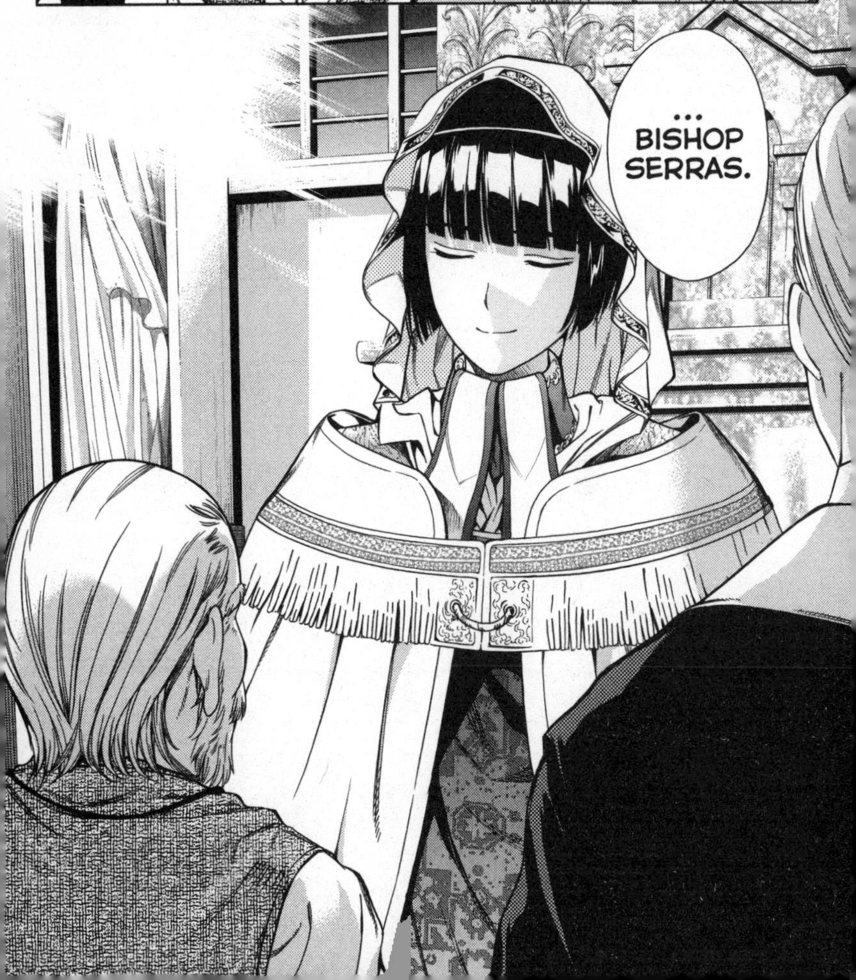
... BISHOP SERRAS.

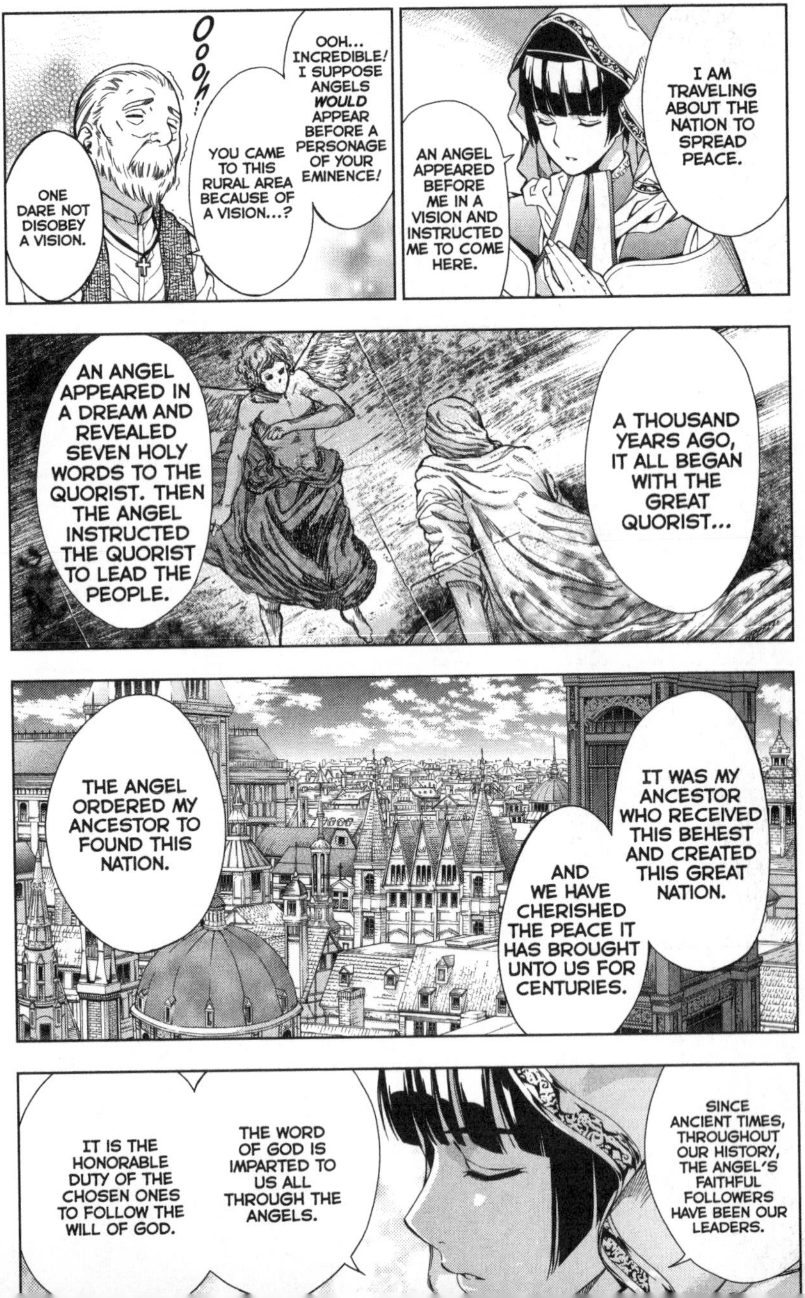

I AM TRAVELING ABOUT THE NATION TO SPREAD PEACE.
AN ANGEL APPEARED BEFORE ME IN A VISION AND INSTRUCTED ME TO COME HERE.
OOH... INCREDIBLE! I SUPPOSE ANGELS *WOULD* APPEAR BEFORE A PERSONAGE OF YOUR EMINENCE!
Oooh...!
YOU CAME TO THIS RURAL AREA BECAUSE OF A VISION...?
ONE DARE NOT DISOBEY A VISION.
A THOUSAND YEARS AGO, IT ALL BEGAN WITH THE GREAT QUORIST...
AN ANGEL APPEARED IN A DREAM AND REVEALED SEVEN HOLY WORDS TO THE QUORIST. THEN THE ANGEL INSTRUCTED THE QUORIST TO LEAD THE PEOPLE.
IT WAS MY ANCESTOR WHO RECEIVED THIS BEHEST AND CREATED THIS GREAT NATION.
AND WE HAVE CHERISHED THE PEACE IT HAS BROUGHT UNTO US FOR CENTURIES.
THE ANGEL ORDERED MY ANCESTOR TO FOUND THIS NATION.
SINCE ANCIENT TIMES, THROUGHOUT OUR HISTORY, THE ANGEL'S FAITHFUL FOLLOWERS HAVE BEEN OUR LEADERS.
THE WORD OF GOD IS IMPARTED TO US ALL THROUGH THE ANGELS.
IT IS THE HONORABLE DUTY OF THE CHOSEN ONES TO FOLLOW THE WILL OF GOD.

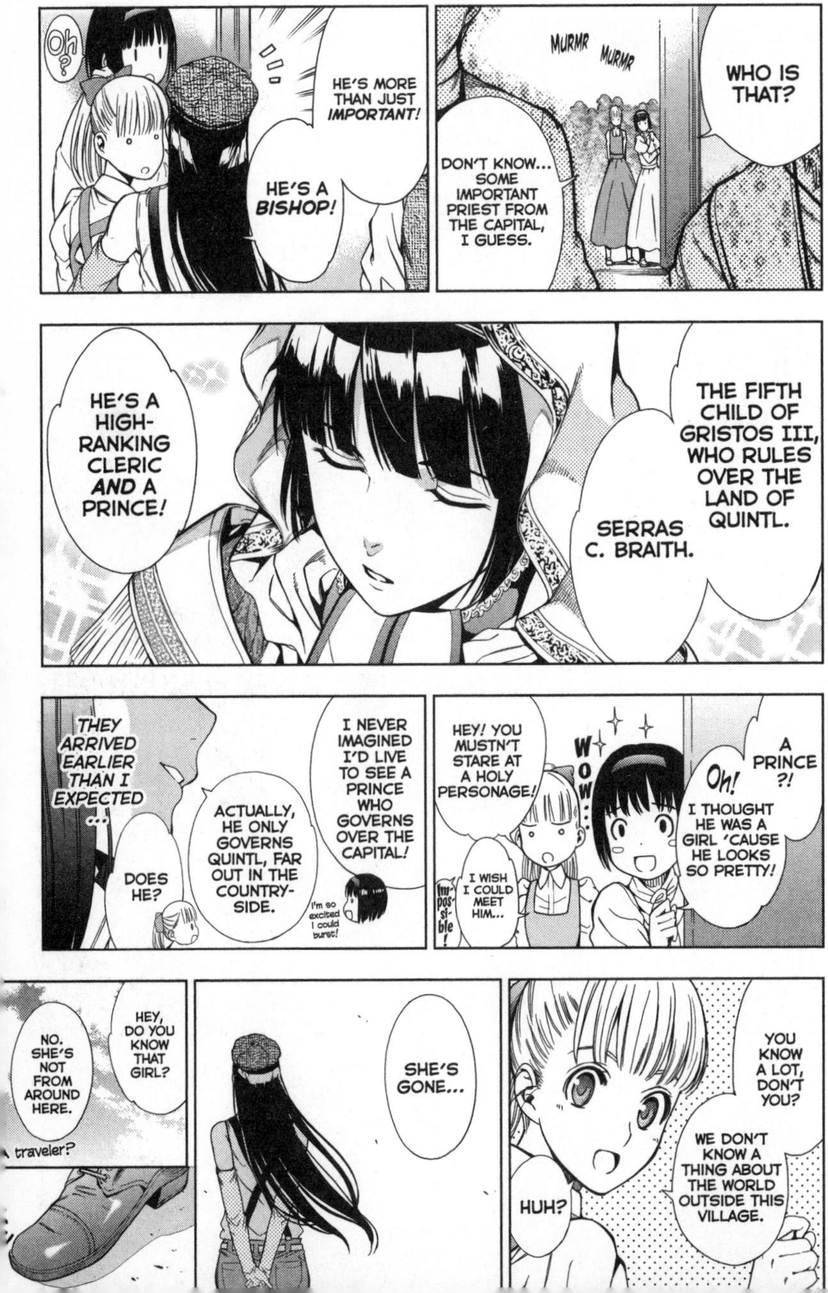
MURMR MURMR
WHO IS THAT?
DON'T KNOW... SOME IMPORTANT PRIEST FROM THE CAPITAL, I GUESS.
HE'S MORE THAN JUST *IMPORTANT*!
HE'S A *BISHOP*!
Oh?
THE FIFTH CHILD OF GRISTOS III, WHO RULES OVER THE LAND OF QUINTL.
SERRAS C. BRAITH.
HE'S A HIGH-RANKING CLERIC *AND* A PRINCE!
A PRINCE?!
Oh!
I THOUGHT HE WAS A GIRL 'CAUSE HE LOOKS SO PRETTY!
WOW...
HEY! YOU MUSTN'T STARE AT A HOLY PERSONAGE!
I WISH I COULD MEET HIM...
Impossible!
I NEVER IMAGINED I'D LIVE TO SEE A PRINCE WHO GOVERNS OVER THE CAPITAL!
I'm so excited I could burst!
ACTUALLY, HE ONLY GOVERNS QUINTL, FAR OUT IN THE COUNTRYSIDE.
THEY ARRIVED EARLIER THAN I EXPECTED...
DOES HE?
YOU KNOW A LOT, DON'T YOU?
WE DON'T KNOW A THING ABOUT THE WORLD OUTSIDE THIS VILLAGE.
HUH?
SHE'S GONE...
HEY, DO YOU KNOW THAT GIRL?
NO. SHE'S NOT FROM AROUND HERE.
traveler?

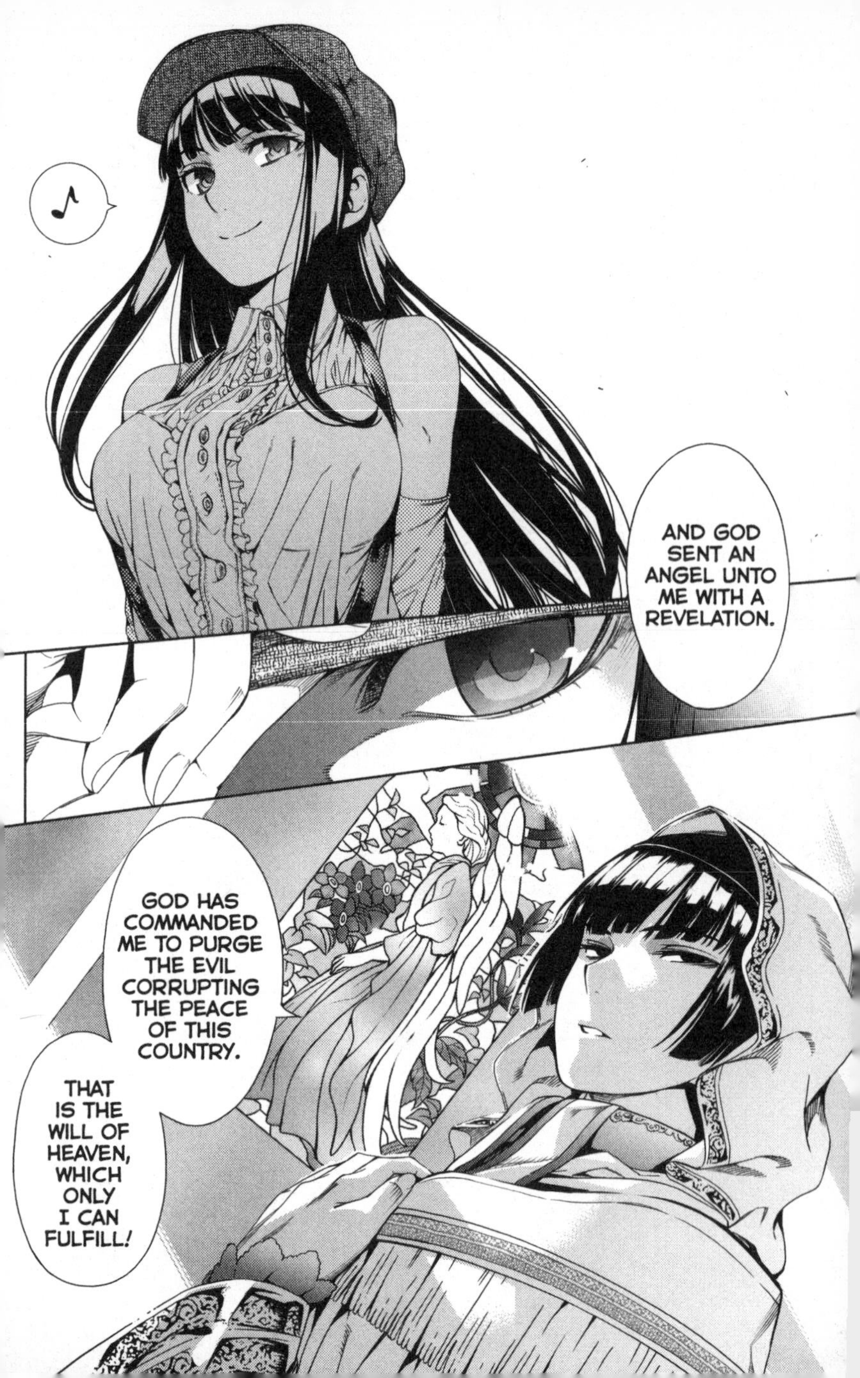
♪
AND GOD SENT AN ANGEL UNTO ME WITH A REVELATION.
GOD HAS COMMANDED ME TO PURGE THE EVIL CORRUPTING THE PEACE OF THIS COUNTRY.
THAT IS THE WILL OF HEAVEN, WHICH ONLY I CAN FULFILL!

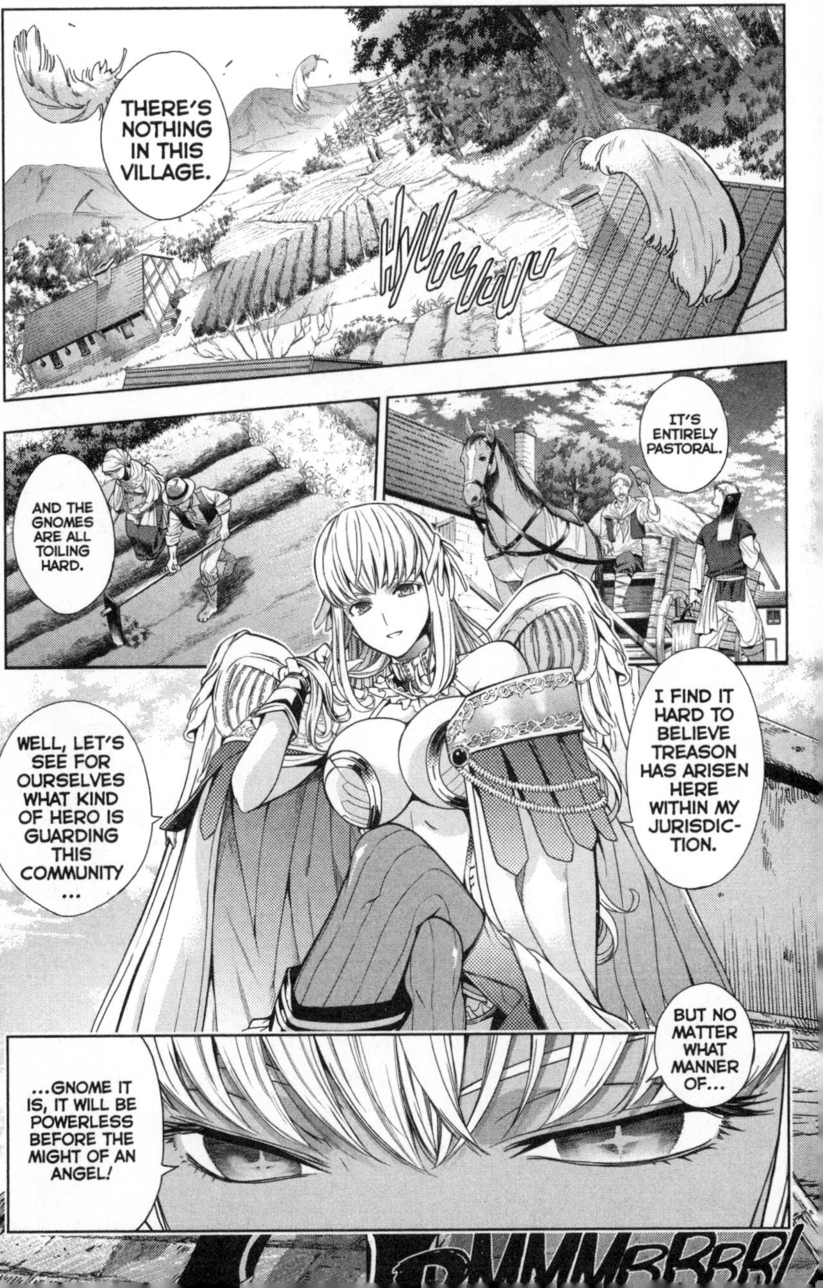
THERE'S NOTHING IN THIS VILLAGE.
HYUUUUUU
IT'S ENTIRELY PASTORAL.
AND THE GNOMES ARE ALL TOILING HARD.
I FIND IT HARD TO BELIEVE TREASON HAS ARISEN HERE WITHIN MY JURISDICTION.
WELL, LET'S SEE FOR OURSELVES WHAT KIND OF HERO IS GUARDING THIS COMMUNITY...
BUT NO MATTER WHAT MANNER OF...
...GNOME IT IS, IT WILL BE POWERLESS BEFORE THE MIGHT OF AN ANGEL!

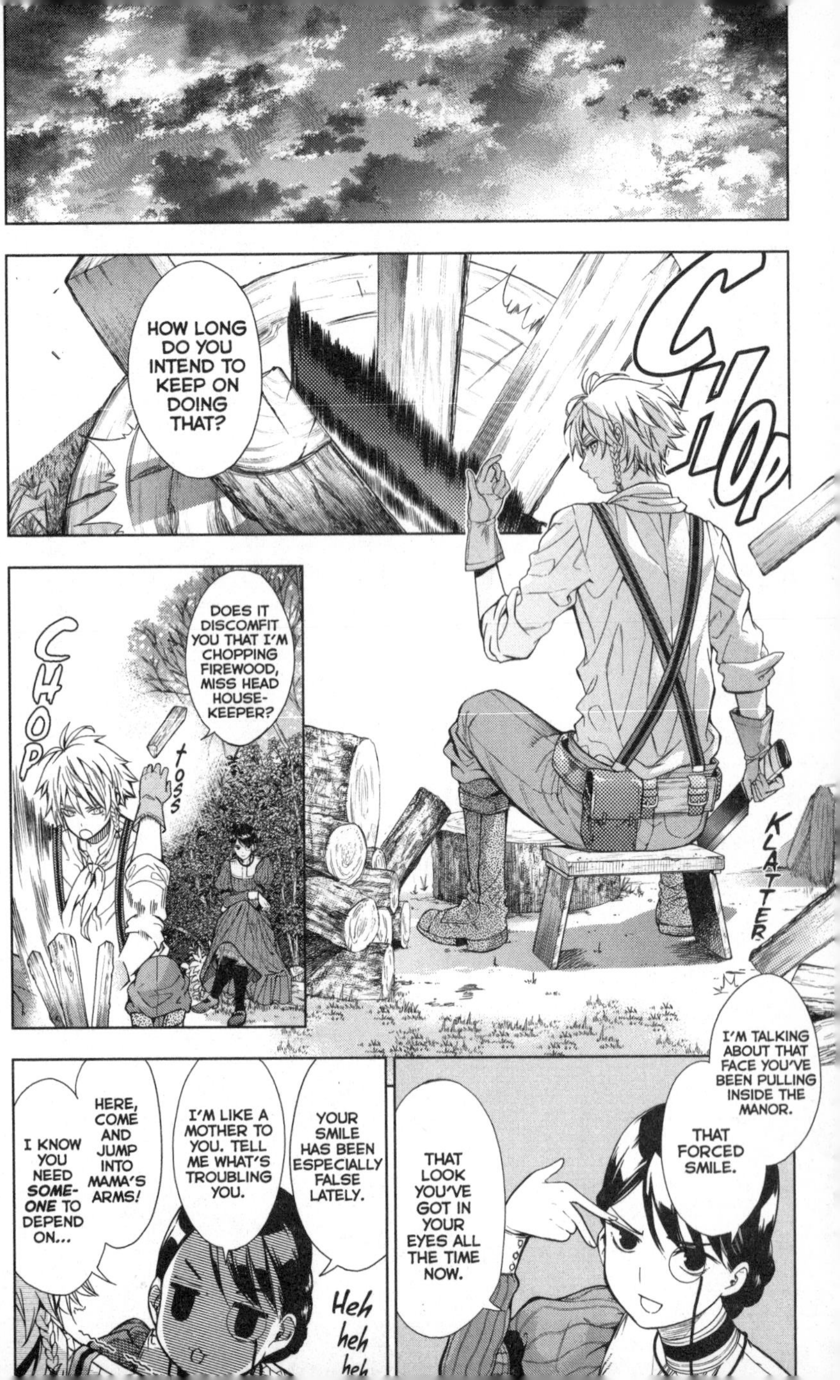
CHOP
HOW LONG DO YOU INTEND TO KEEP ON DOING THAT?
KLATTER
DOES IT DISCOMFIT YOU THAT I'M CHOPPING FIREWOOD, MISS HEAD HOUSE-KEEPER?
TOSS
CHOP
I'M TALKING ABOUT THAT FACE YOU'VE BEEN PULLING INSIDE THE MANOR.
THAT FORCED SMILE.
THAT LOOK YOU'VE GOT IN YOUR EYES ALL THE TIME NOW.
YOUR SMILE HAS BEEN ESPECIALLY FALSE LATELY.
I'M LIKE A MOTHER TO YOU. TELL ME WHAT'S TROUBLING YOU.
HERE, COME AND JUMP INTO MAMA'S ARMS!
I KNOW YOU NEED SOMEONE TO DEPEND ON...
Heh heh heh

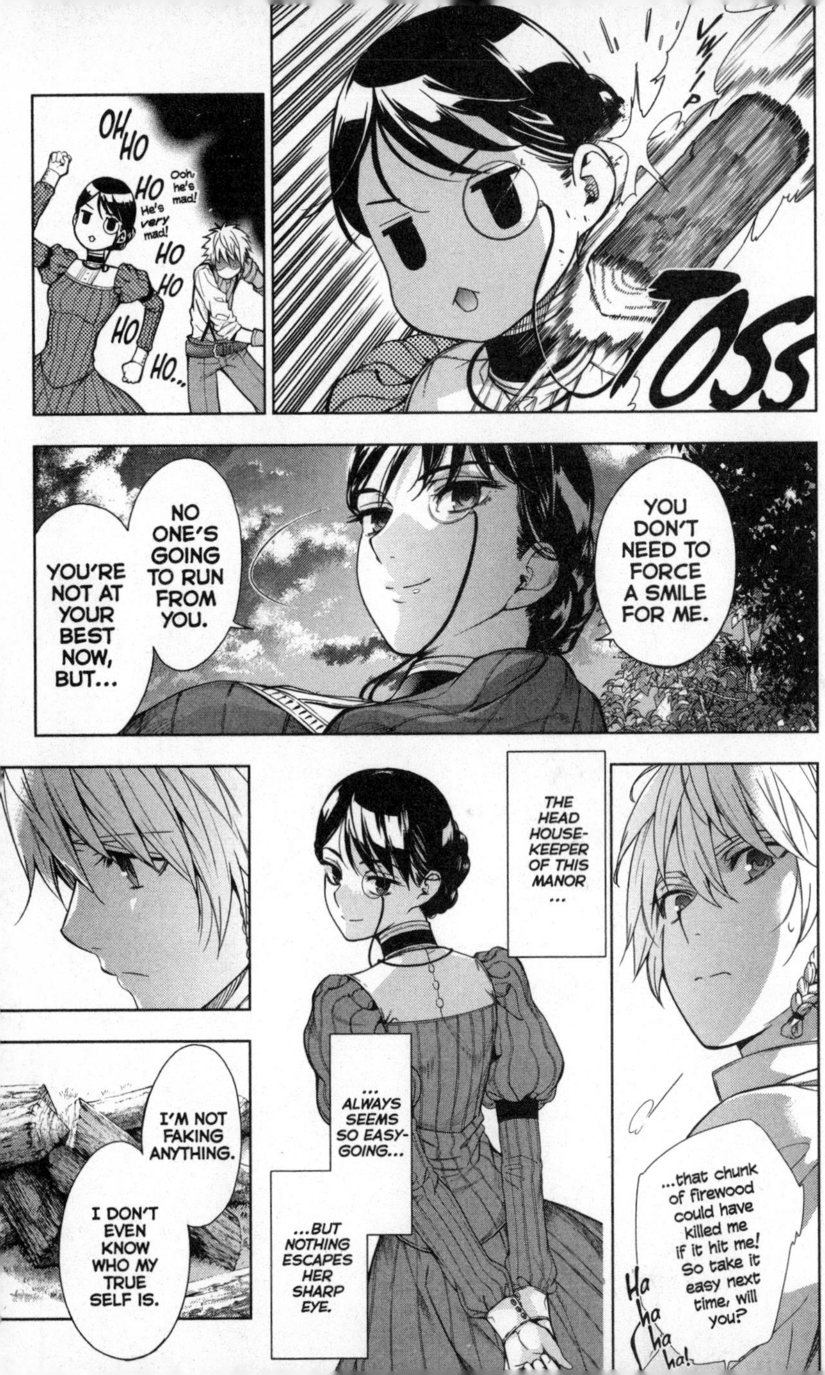
WHIP
TOSS
OH HO HO HO HO HO HO...
Ooh, he's mad!
He's very mad!
YOU DON'T NEED TO FORCE A SMILE FOR ME.
NO ONE'S GOING TO RUN FROM YOU.
YOU'RE NOT AT YOUR BEST NOW, BUT...
...that chunk of firewood could have killed me if it hit me! So take it easy next time, will you?
Ha ha ha ha!
THE HEAD HOUSE-KEEPER OF THIS MANOR...
...ALWAYS SEEMS SO EASY-GOING...
...BUT NOTHING ESCAPES HER SHARP EYE.
I'M NOT FAKING ANYTHING.
I DON'T EVEN KNOW WHO MY TRUE SELF IS.

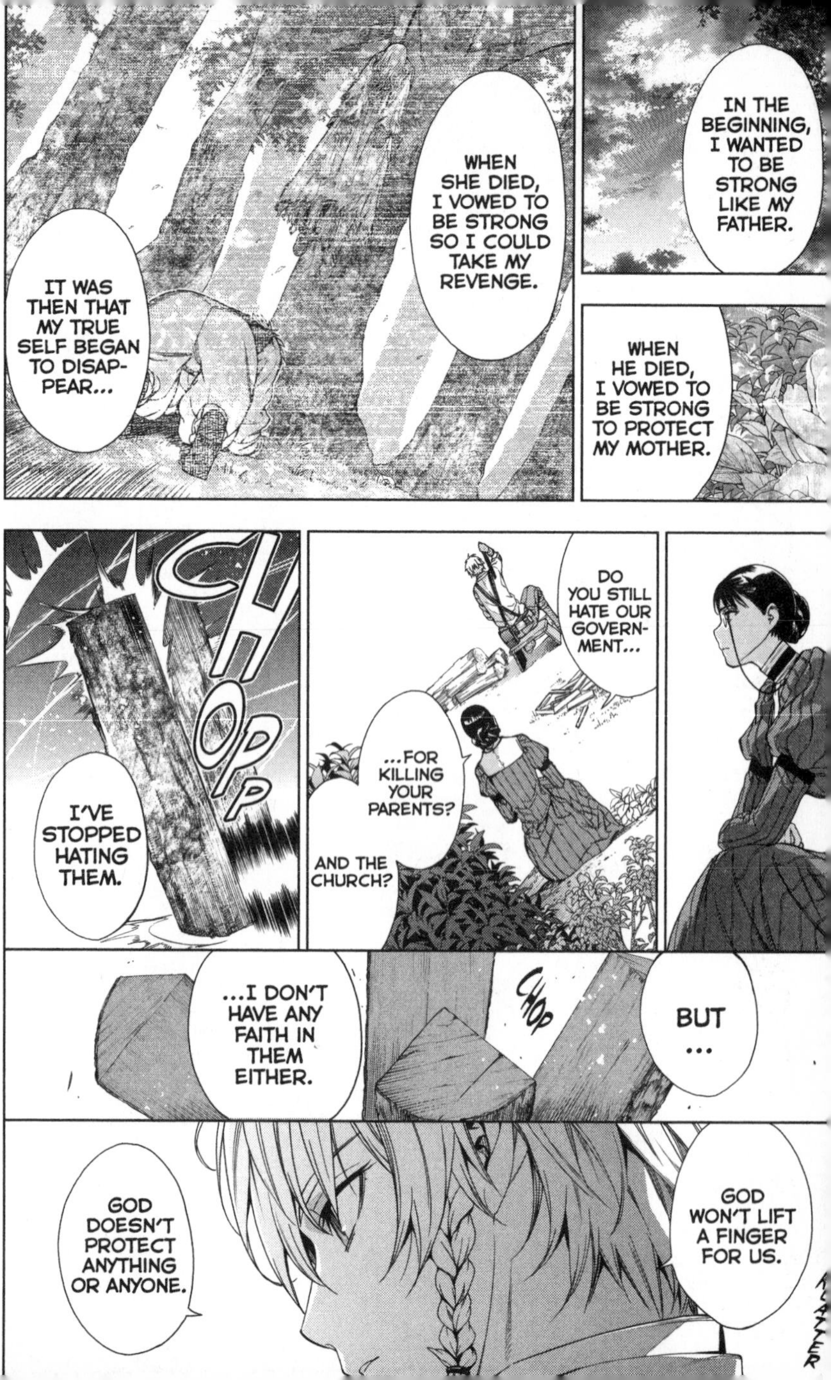
IN THE BEGINNING, I WANTED TO BE STRONG LIKE MY FATHER.
WHEN HE DIED, I VOWED TO BE STRONG TO PROTECT MY MOTHER.
WHEN SHE DIED, I VOWED TO BE STRONG SO I COULD TAKE MY REVENGE.
IT WAS THEN THAT MY TRUE SELF BEGAN TO DISAP-PEAR...
DO YOU STILL HATE OUR GOVERN-MENT...
...FOR KILLING YOUR PARENTS?
AND THE CHURCH?
CHOP
I'VE STOPPED HATING THEM.
BUT...
CHOP
...I DON'T HAVE ANY FAITH IN THEM EITHER.
GOD WON'T LIFT A FINGER FOR US.
GOD DOESN'T PROTECT ANYTHING OR ANYONE.

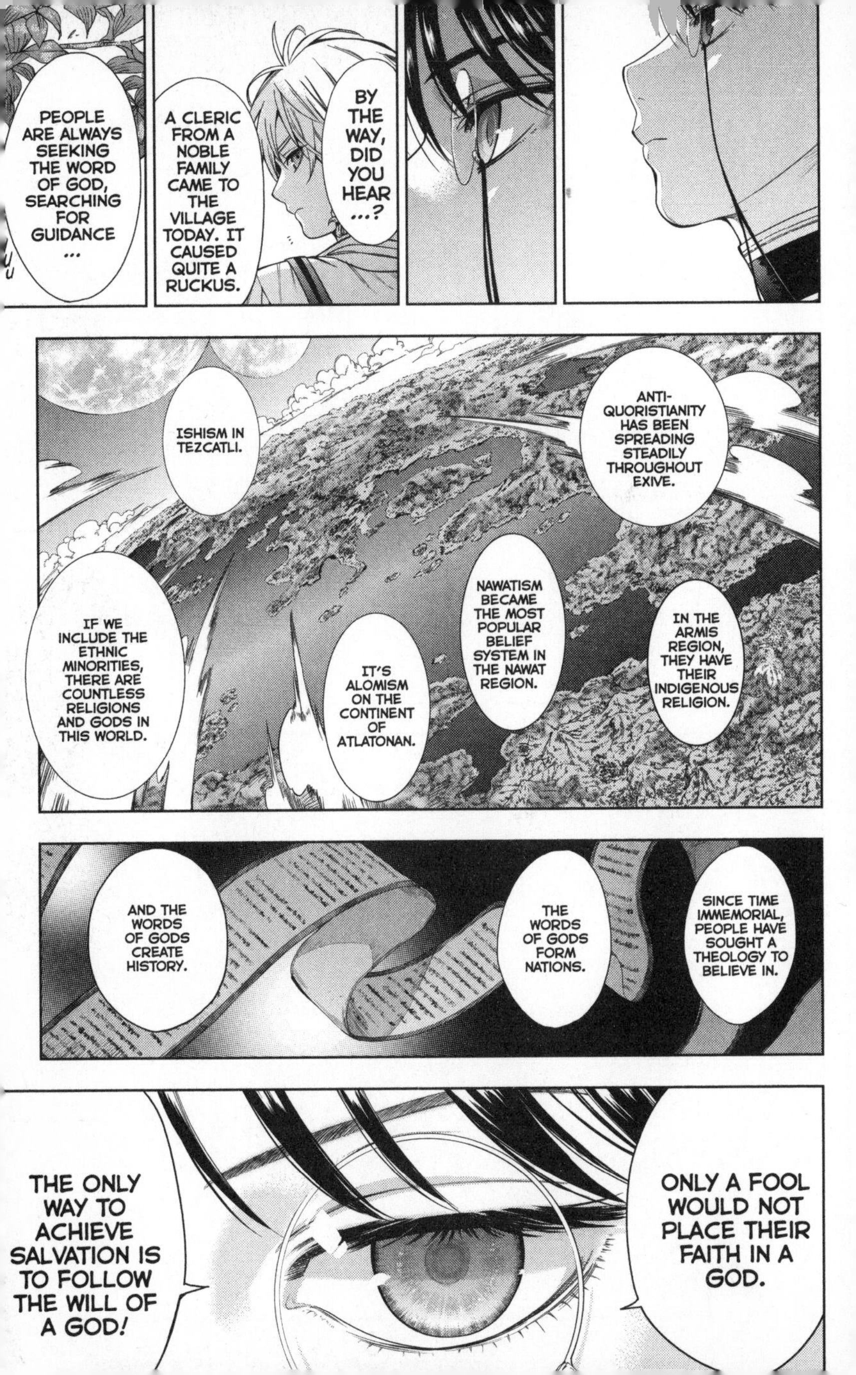
BY THE WAY, DID YOU HEAR...?
A CLERIC FROM A NOBLE FAMILY CAME TO THE VILLAGE TODAY. IT CAUSED QUITE A RUCKUS.
PEOPLE ARE ALWAYS SEEKING THE WORD OF GOD, SEARCHING FOR GUIDANCE...
ANTI-QUORISTIANITY HAS BEEN SPREADING STEADILY THROUGHOUT EXIVE.
ISHISM IN TEZCATLI.
IN THE ARMIS REGION, THEY HAVE THEIR INDIGENOUS RELIGION.
NAWATISM BECAME THE MOST POPULAR BELIEF SYSTEM IN THE NAWAT REGION.
IT'S ALOMISM ON THE CONTINENT OF ATLATONAN.
IF WE INCLUDE THE ETHNIC MINORITIES, THERE ARE COUNTLESS RELIGIONS AND GODS IN THIS WORLD.
SINCE TIME IMMEMORIAL, PEOPLE HAVE SOUGHT A THEOLOGY TO BELIEVE IN.
THE WORDS OF GODS FORM NATIONS.
AND THE WORDS OF GODS CREATE HISTORY.
ONLY A FOOL WOULD NOT PLACE THEIR FAITH IN A GOD.
THE ONLY WAY TO ACHIEVE SALVATION IS TO FOLLOW THE WILL OF A GOD!

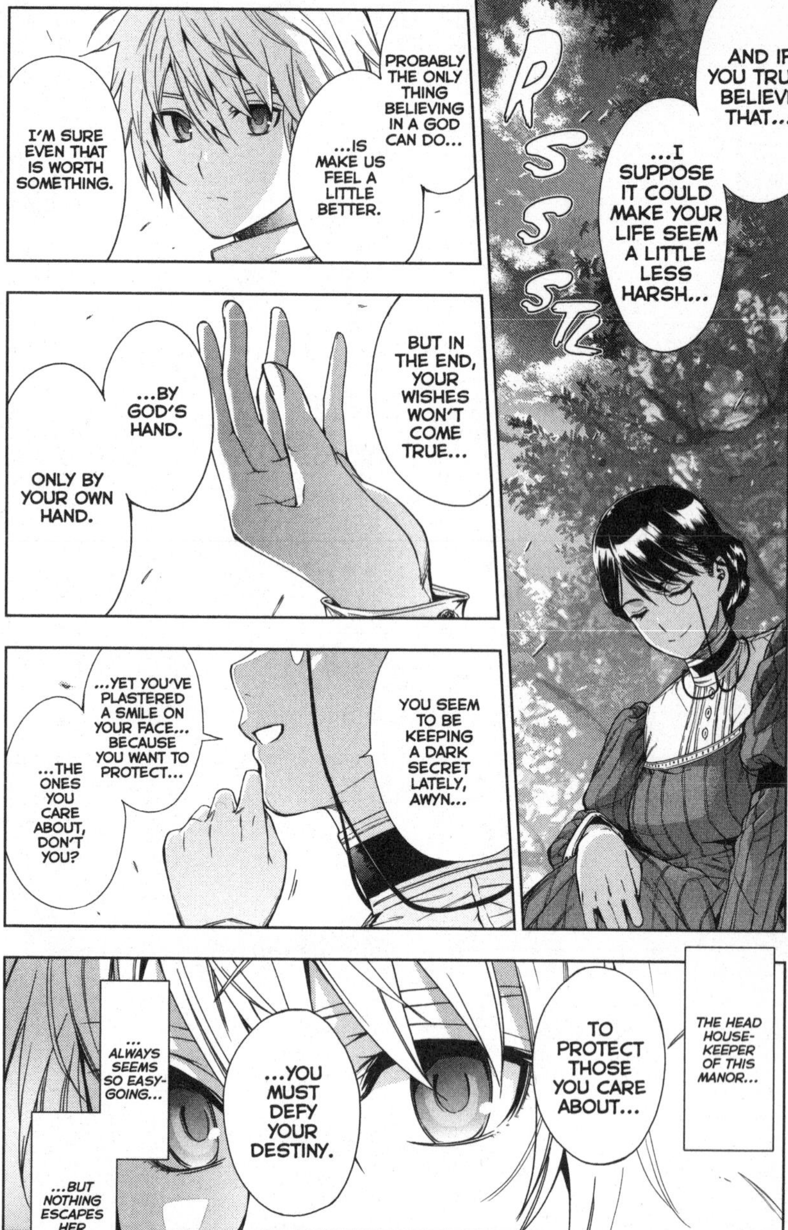
AND IF YOU TRULY BELIEVE THAT...
...I SUPPOSE IT COULD MAKE YOUR LIFE SEEM A LITTLE LESS HARSH...
RSSSTL
PROBABLY THE ONLY THING BELIEVING IN A GOD CAN DO...
...IS MAKE US FEEL A LITTLE BETTER.
I'M SURE EVEN THAT IS WORTH SOMETHING.
BUT IN THE END, YOUR WISHES WON'T COME TRUE...
...BY GOD'S HAND.
ONLY BY YOUR OWN HAND.
YOU SEEM TO BE KEEPING A DARK SECRET LATELY, AWYN...
...YET YOU'VE PLASTERED A SMILE ON YOUR FACE... BECAUSE YOU WANT TO PROTECT...
...THE ONES YOU CARE ABOUT, DON'T YOU?
THE HEAD HOUSE-KEEPER OF THIS MANOR...
TO PROTECT THOSE YOU CARE ABOUT...
...YOU MUST DEFY YOUR DESTINY.
...ALWAYS SEEMS SO EASY-GOING...
...BUT NOTHING ESCAPES HER SHARP EYE.

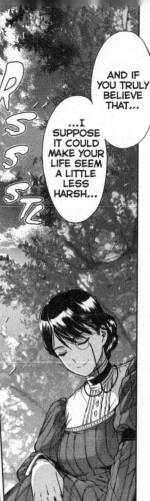

DO YOUR BEST...

...GARDENER.

THE HEAD HOUSE-KEEPER OF THIS MANOR...

...AL-WAYS SEEMS SO—

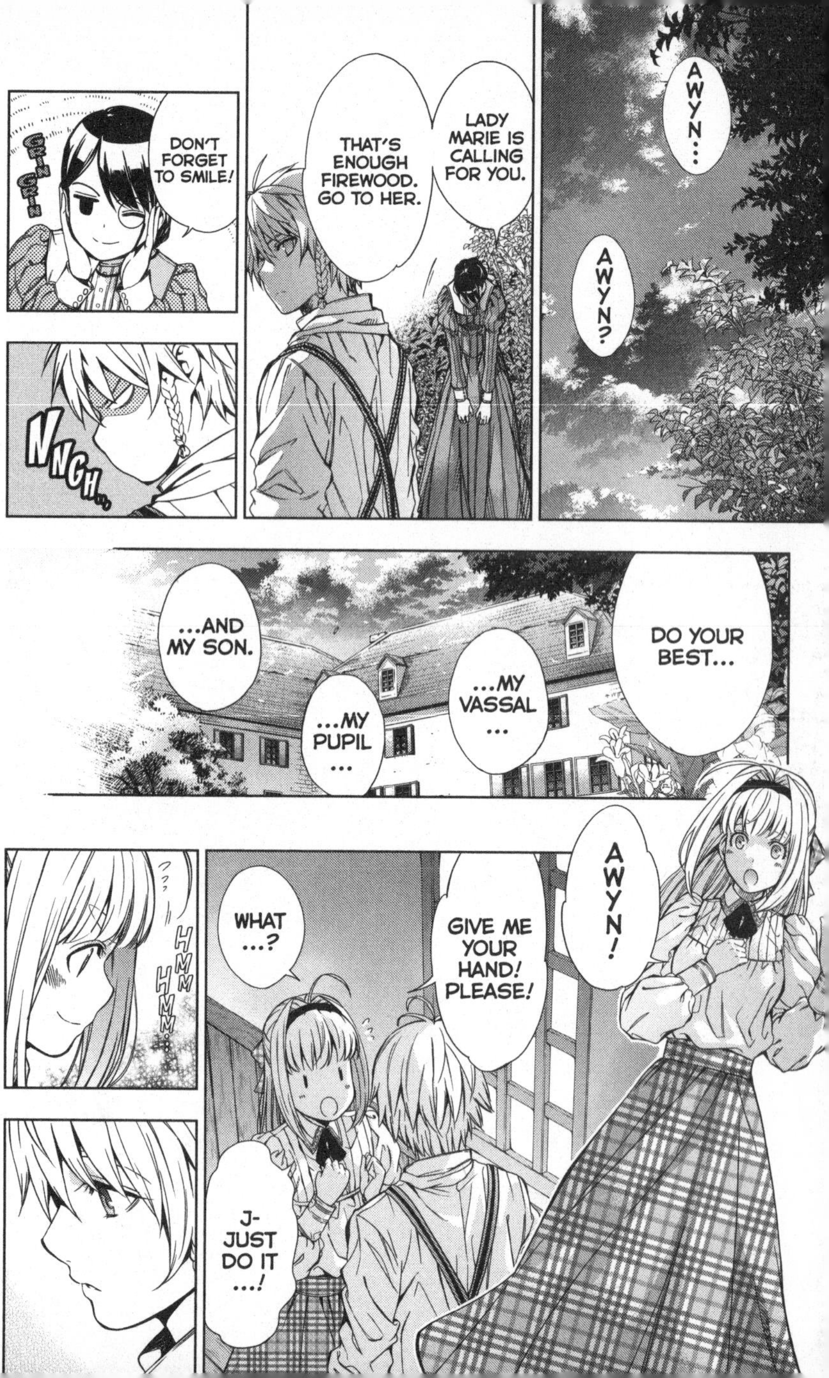
AWYN...
AWYN?
LADY MARIE IS CALLING FOR YOU.
THAT'S ENOUGH FIREWOOD. GO TO HER.
DON'T FORGET TO SMILE!
GRIN GRIN
NNGH...
DO YOUR BEST...
...MY VASSAL ...
...MY PUPIL ...
...AND MY SON.
AWYN!
GIVE ME YOUR HAND! PLEASE!
WHAT ...?
J- JUST DO IT ...!
HMM HMM...

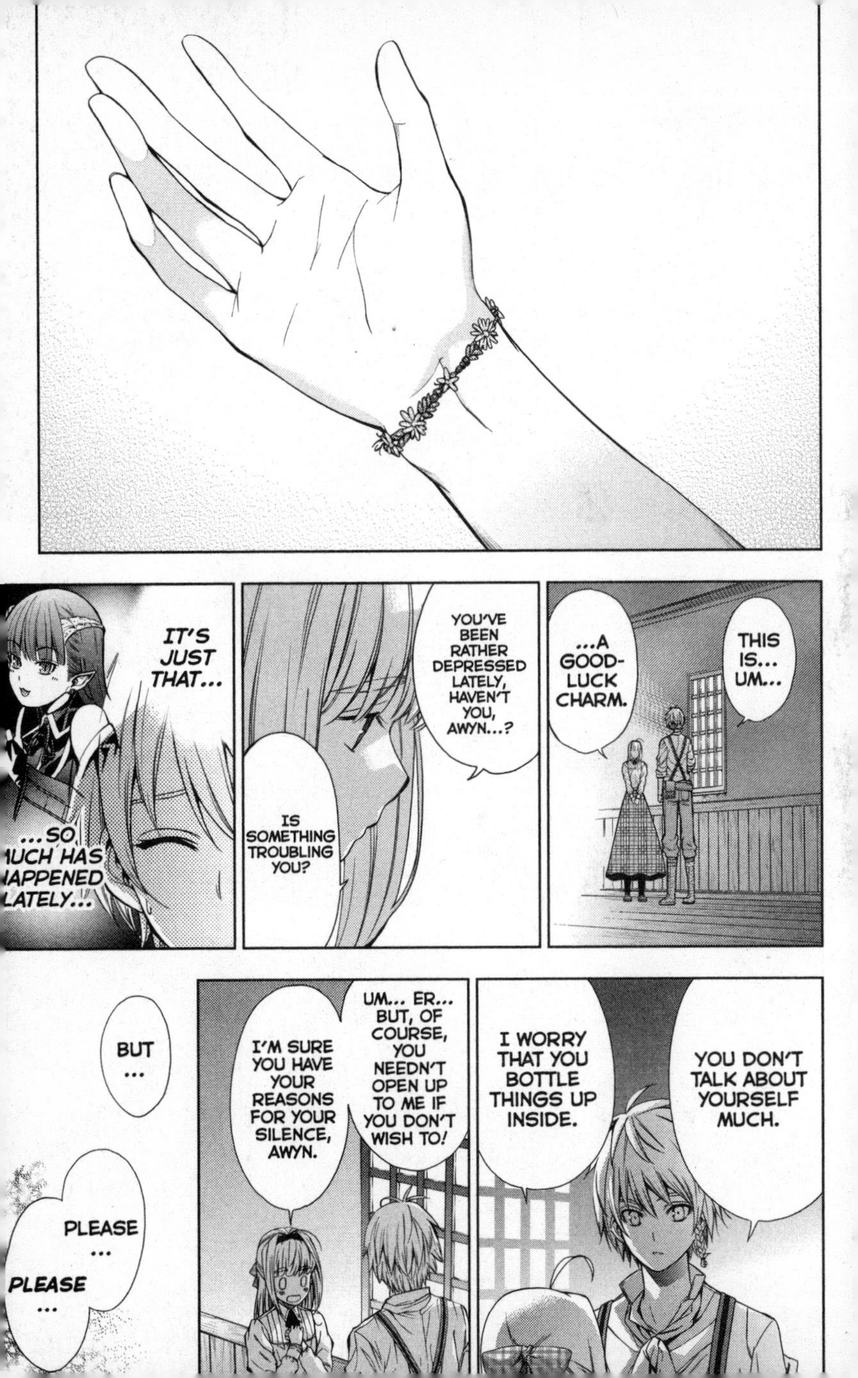
THIS IS... UM...
...A GOOD-LUCK CHARM.
YOU'VE BEEN RATHER DEPRESSED LATELY, HAVEN'T YOU, AWYN...?
IS SOMETHING TROUBLING YOU?
IT'S JUST THAT...
...SO UCH HAS APPENED LATELY...
YOU DON'T TALK ABOUT YOURSELF MUCH.
I WORRY THAT YOU BOTTLE THINGS UP INSIDE.
UM... ER... BUT, OF COURSE, YOU NEEDN'T OPEN UP TO ME IF YOU DON'T WISH TO!
I'M SURE YOU HAVE YOUR REASONS FOR YOUR SILENCE, AWYN.
BUT ...
PLEASE ...
PLEASE ...

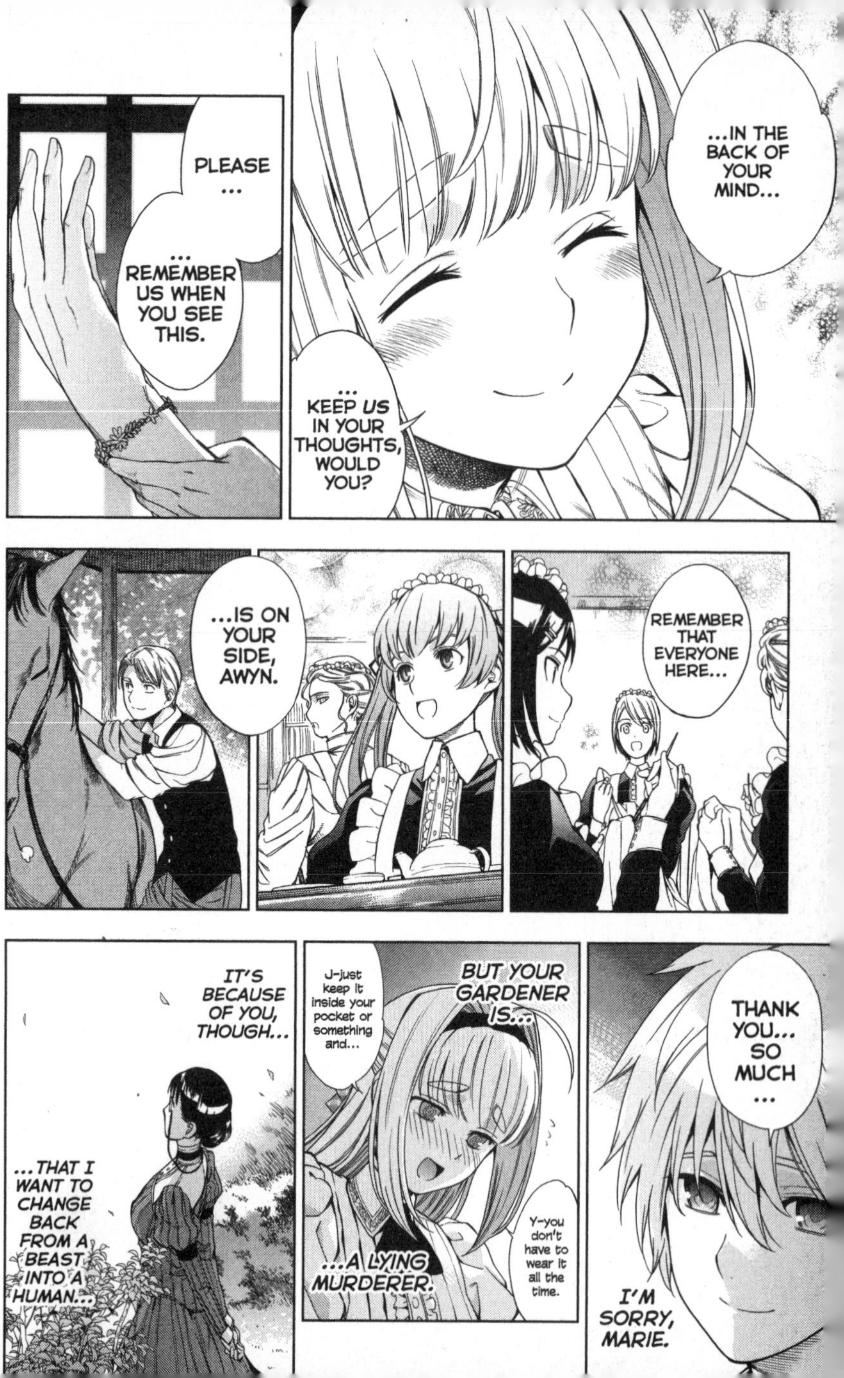
...IN THE BACK OF YOUR MIND...
... KEEP *US* IN YOUR THOUGHTS, WOULD YOU?
PLEASE ...
... REMEMBER US WHEN YOU SEE THIS.
REMEMBER THAT EVERYONE HERE...
...IS ON YOUR SIDE, AWYN.
THANK YOU... SO MUCH ...
I'M SORRY, MARIE.
BUT YOUR GARDENER IS...
J-just keep it inside your pocket or something and...
Y-you don't have to wear it all the time.
...A LYING MURDERER.
IT'S BECAUSE OF YOU, THOUGH...
...THAT I WANT TO CHANGE BACK FROM A BEAST INTO A HUMAN...

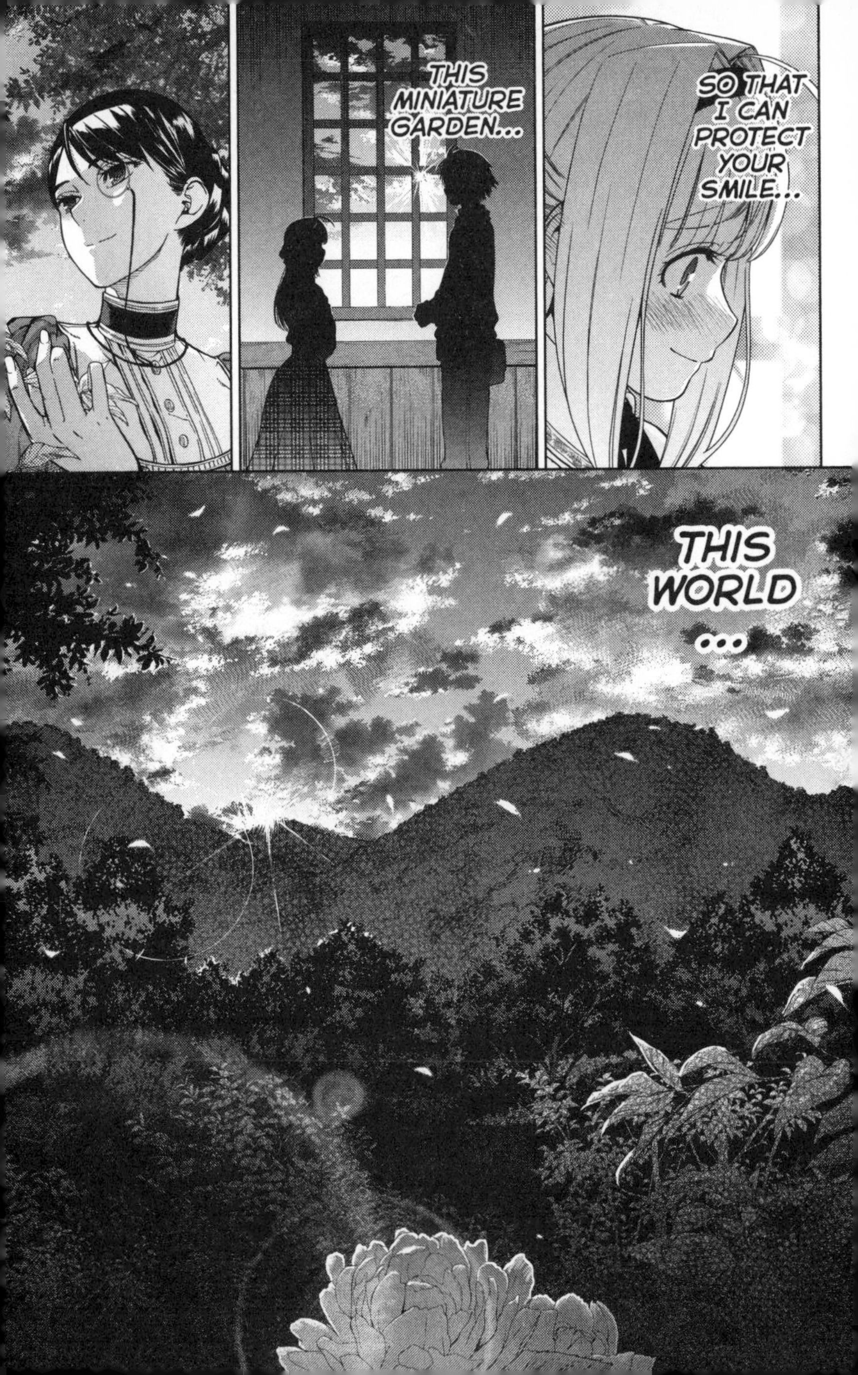
SO THAT I CAN PROTECT YOUR SMILE...
THIS MINIATURE GARDEN...
THIS WORLD ...

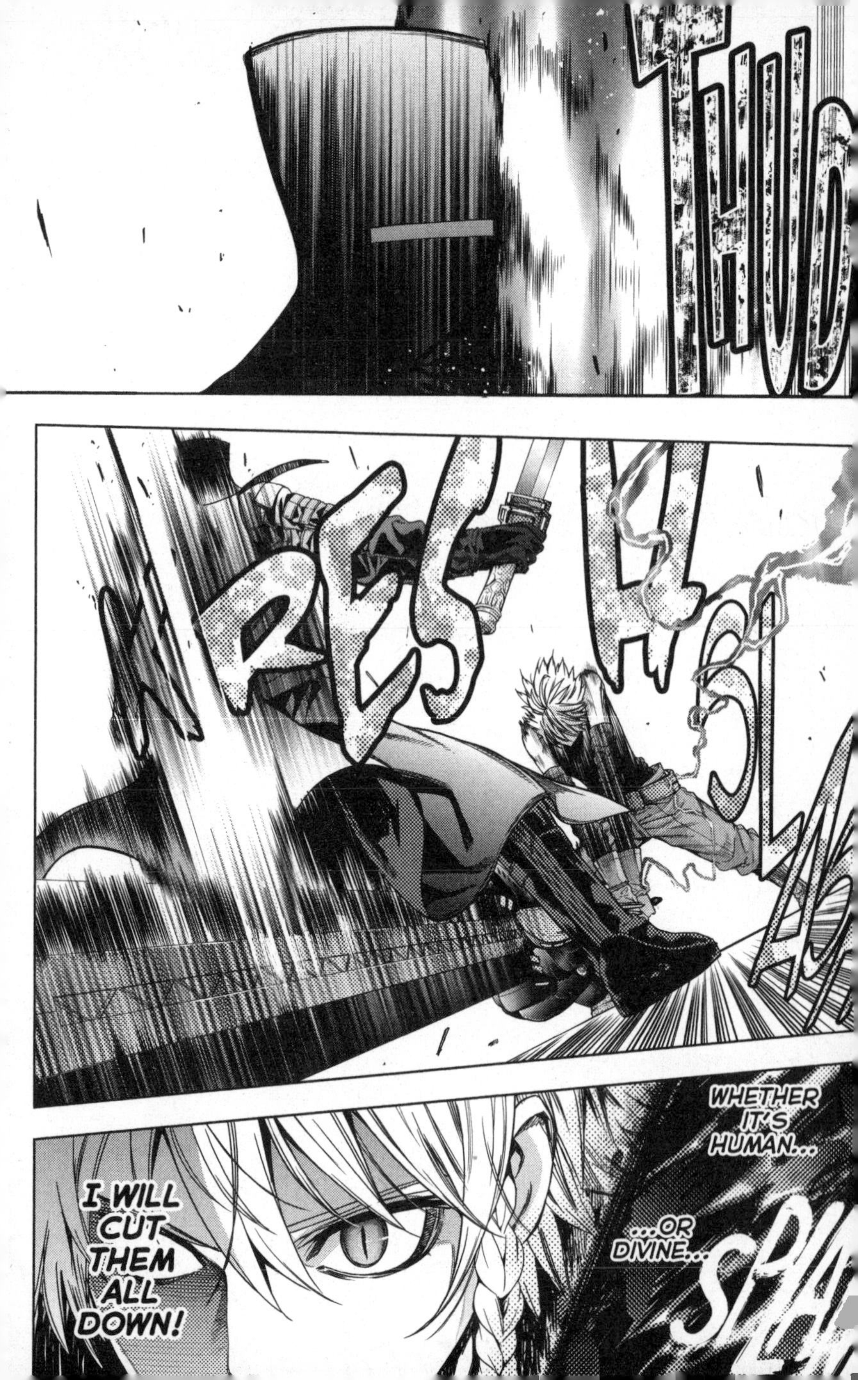
THUD
WHETHER IT'S HUMAN...
...OR DIVINE...
I WILL CUT THEM ALL DOWN!

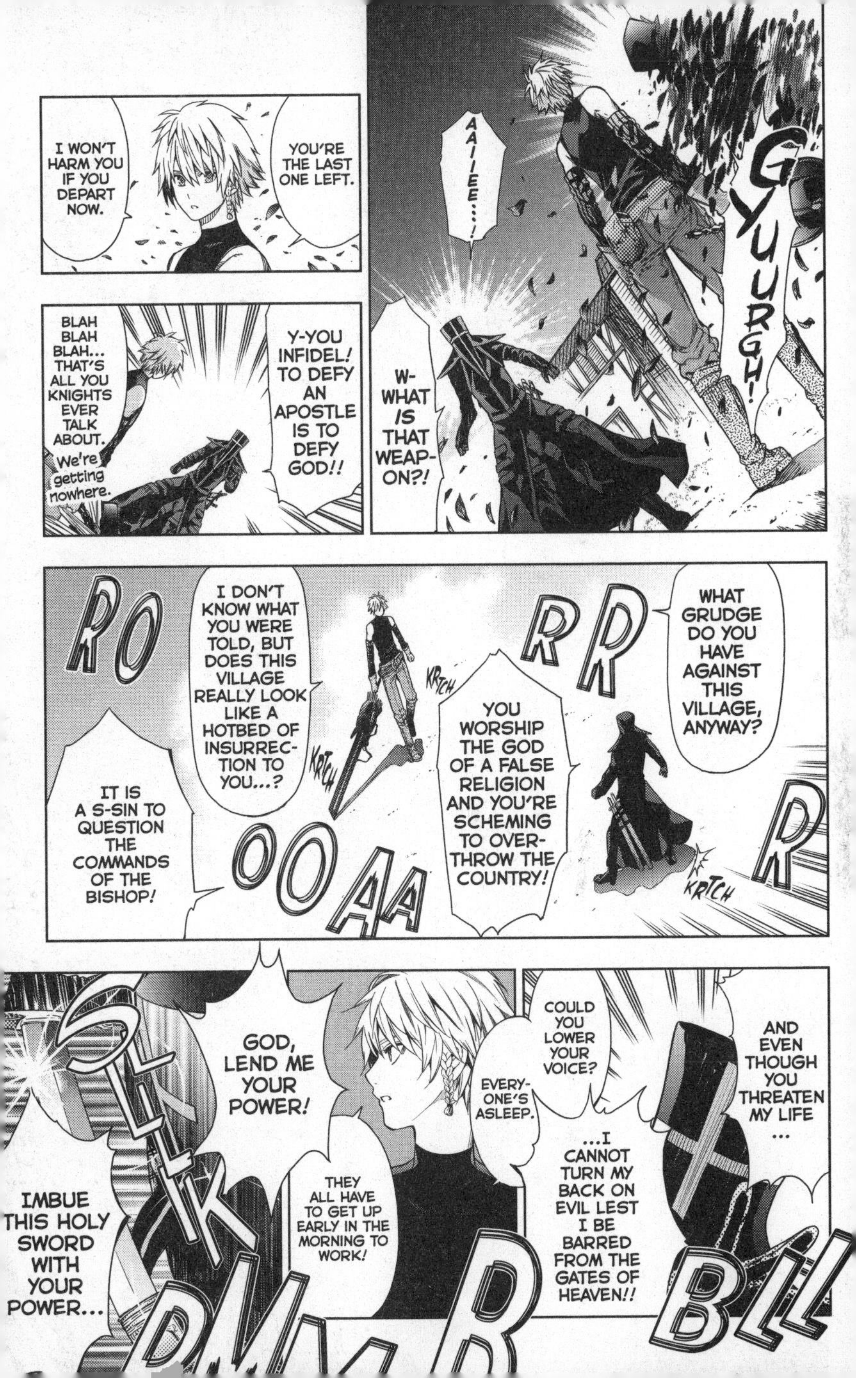

AAIIEE...!
GYUURGH!
W-WHAT IS THAT WEAPON?!
YOU'RE THE LAST ONE LEFT.
I WON'T HARM YOU IF YOU DEPART NOW.
Y-YOU INFIDEL! TO DEFY AN APOSTLE IS TO DEFY GOD!!
BLAH BLAH BLAH... THAT'S ALL YOU KNIGHTS EVER TALK ABOUT.
We're getting nowhere.
WHAT GRUDGE DO YOU HAVE AGAINST THIS VILLAGE, ANYWAY?
RRR
KRTCH
YOU WORSHIP THE GOD OF A FALSE RELIGION AND YOU'RE SCHEMING TO OVERTHROW THE COUNTRY!
KRTCH
I DON'T KNOW WHAT YOU WERE TOLD, BUT DOES THIS VILLAGE REALLY LOOK LIKE A HOTBED OF INSURRECTION TO YOU...?
KRTCH
ROOOAA
IT IS A S-SIN TO QUESTION THE COMMANDS OF THE BISHOP!
AND EVEN THOUGH YOU THREATEN MY LIFE...
...I CANNOT TURN MY BACK ON EVIL LEST I BE BARRED FROM THE GATES OF HEAVEN!!
COULD YOU LOWER YOUR VOICE?
EVERYONE'S ASLEEP.
THEY ALL HAVE TO GET UP EARLY IN THE MORNING TO WORK!
GOD, LEND ME YOUR POWER!
IMBUE THIS HOLY SWORD WITH YOUR POWER...

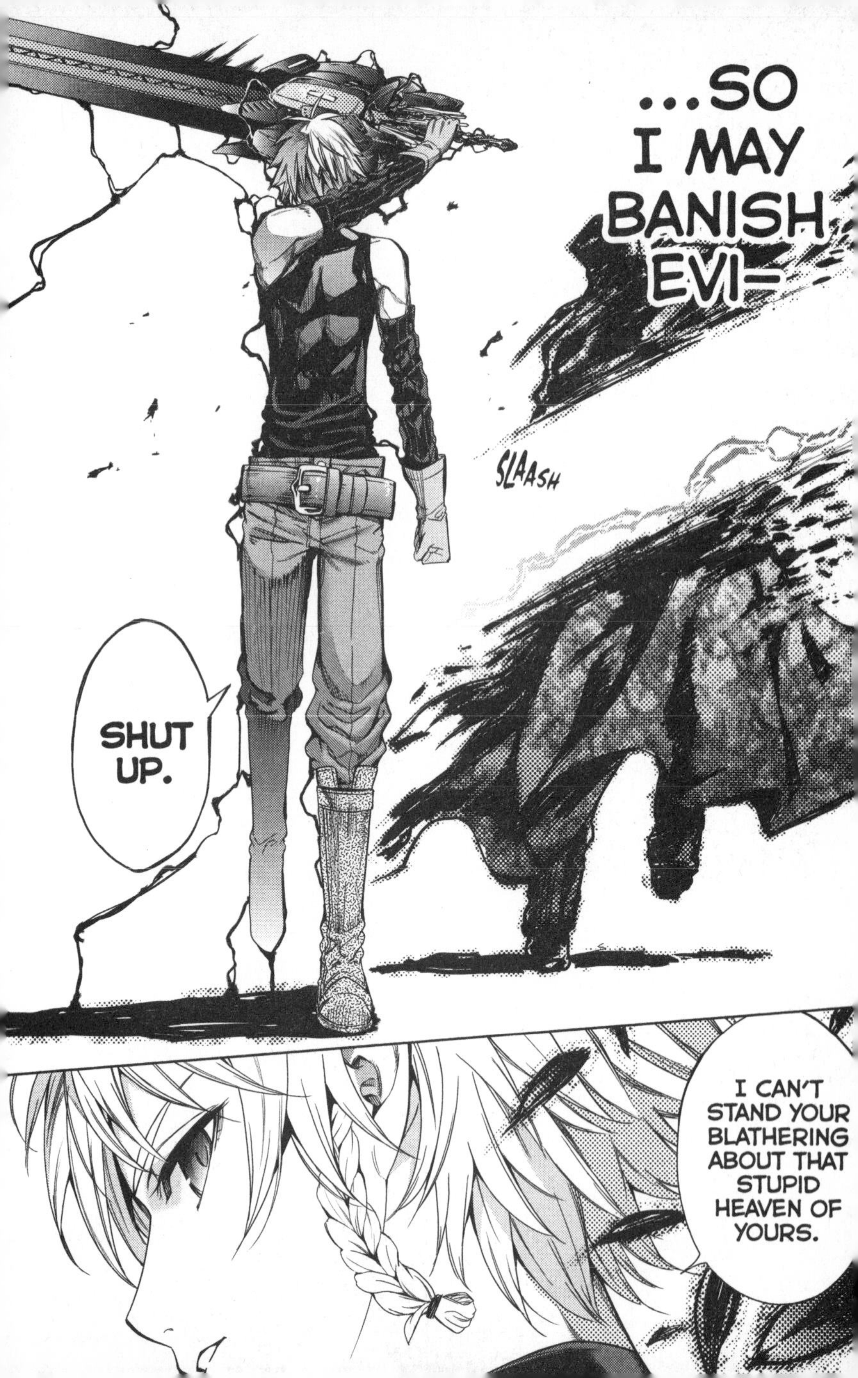
...SO I MAY BANISH EVI–
SLAASH
SHUT UP.
I CAN'T STAND YOUR BLATHERING ABOUT THAT STUPID HEAVEN OF YOURS.

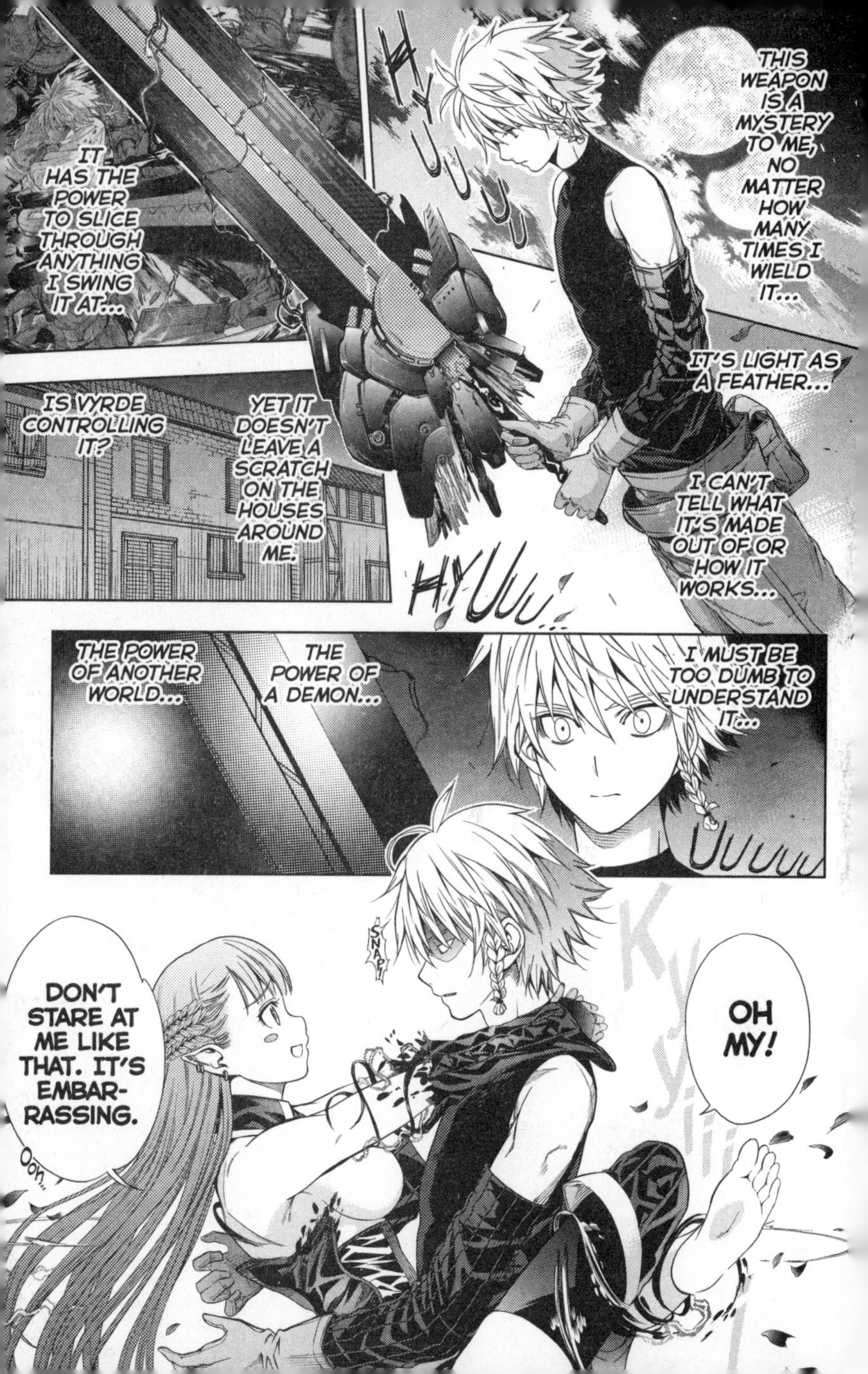
HYUUUU
THIS WEAPON IS A MYSTERY TO ME, NO MATTER HOW MANY TIMES I WIELD IT...
IT'S LIGHT AS A FEATHER...
I CAN'T TELL WHAT IT'S MADE OUT OF OR HOW IT WORKS...
HYUUU...
IT HAS THE POWER TO SLICE THROUGH ANYTHING I SWING IT AT...
YET IT DOESN'T LEAVE A SCRATCH ON THE HOUSES AROUND ME.
IS VYRDE CONTROLLING IT?
I MUST BE TOO DUMB TO UNDERSTAND IT...
THE POWER OF A DEMON...
THE POWER OF ANOTHER WORLD...
UUUUU
OH MY!
Kyliii
SNAP!
DON'T STARE AT ME LIKE THAT. IT'S EMBARRASSING.
Ooh..

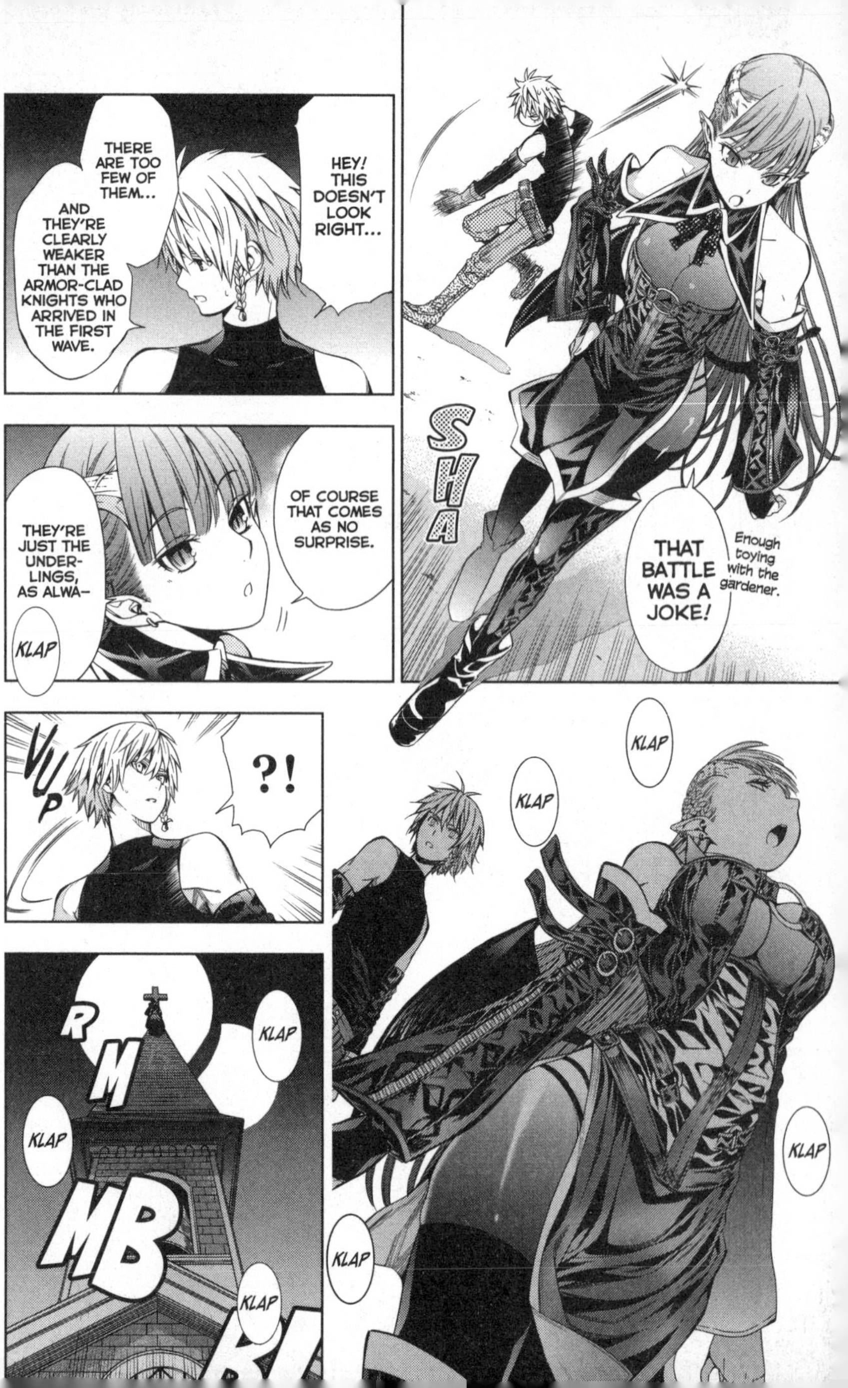
SHA
Enough toying with the gardener.
THAT BATTLE WAS A JOKE!
HEY! THIS DOESN'T LOOK RIGHT...
THERE ARE TOO FEW OF THEM...
AND THEY'RE CLEARLY WEAKER THAN THE ARMOR-CLAD KNIGHTS WHO ARRIVED IN THE FIRST WAVE.
OF COURSE THAT COMES AS NO SURPRISE.
THEY'RE JUST THE UNDERLINGS, AS ALWA—
KLAP
KLAP
KLAP
KLAP
KLAP
?!
VUP
KLAP
KLAP
KLAP
RMMB

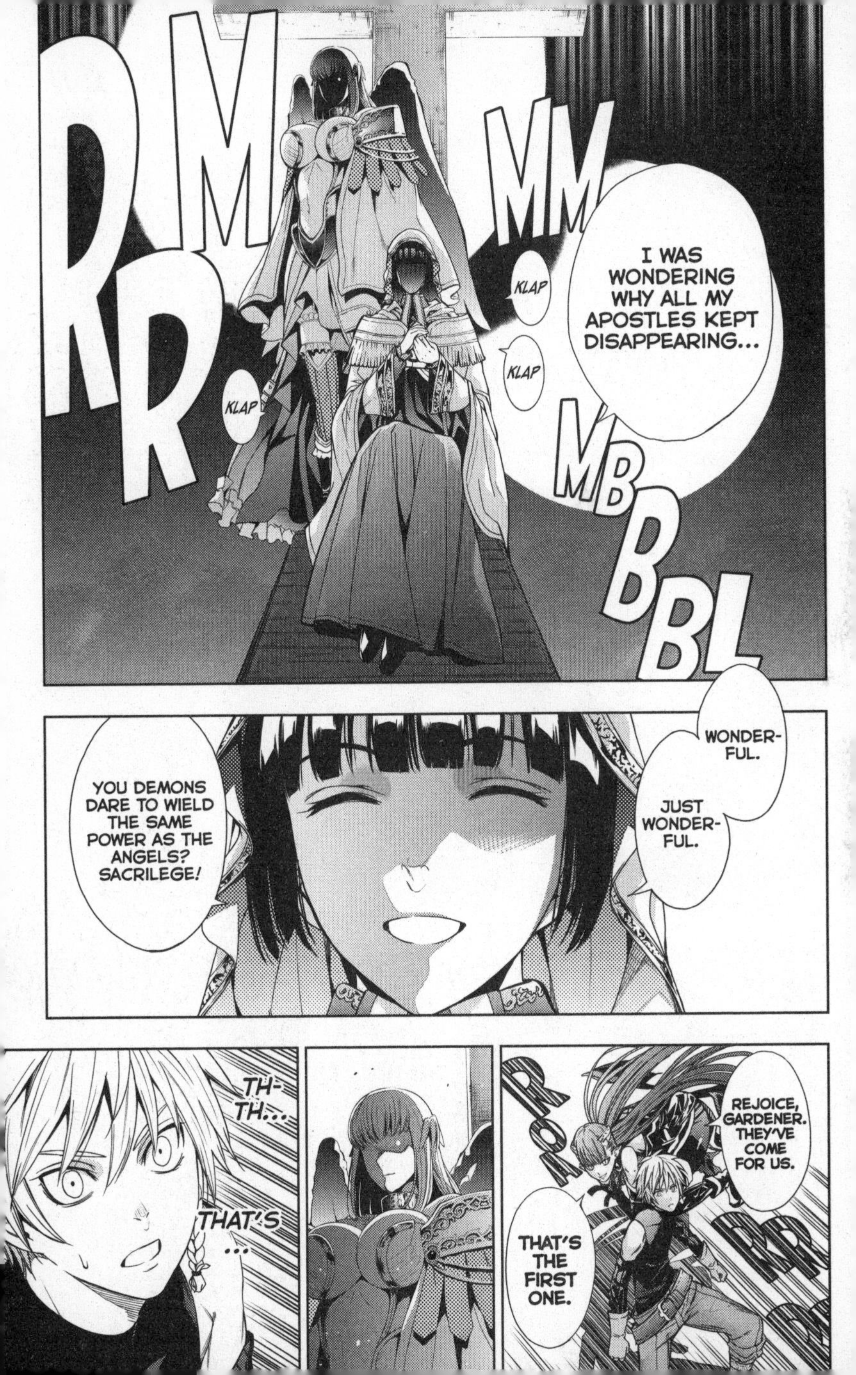
I WAS WONDERING WHY ALL MY APOSTLES KEPT DISAPPEARING...
KLAP
KLAP
KLAP
RRMMMMBBBL
WONDER-FUL.
JUST WONDER-FUL.
YOU DEMONS DARE TO WIELD THE SAME POWER AS THE ANGELS? SACRILEGE!
ROAR
REJOICE, GARDENER. THEY'VE COME FOR US.
THAT'S THE FIRST ONE.
TH-TH...
THAT'S...

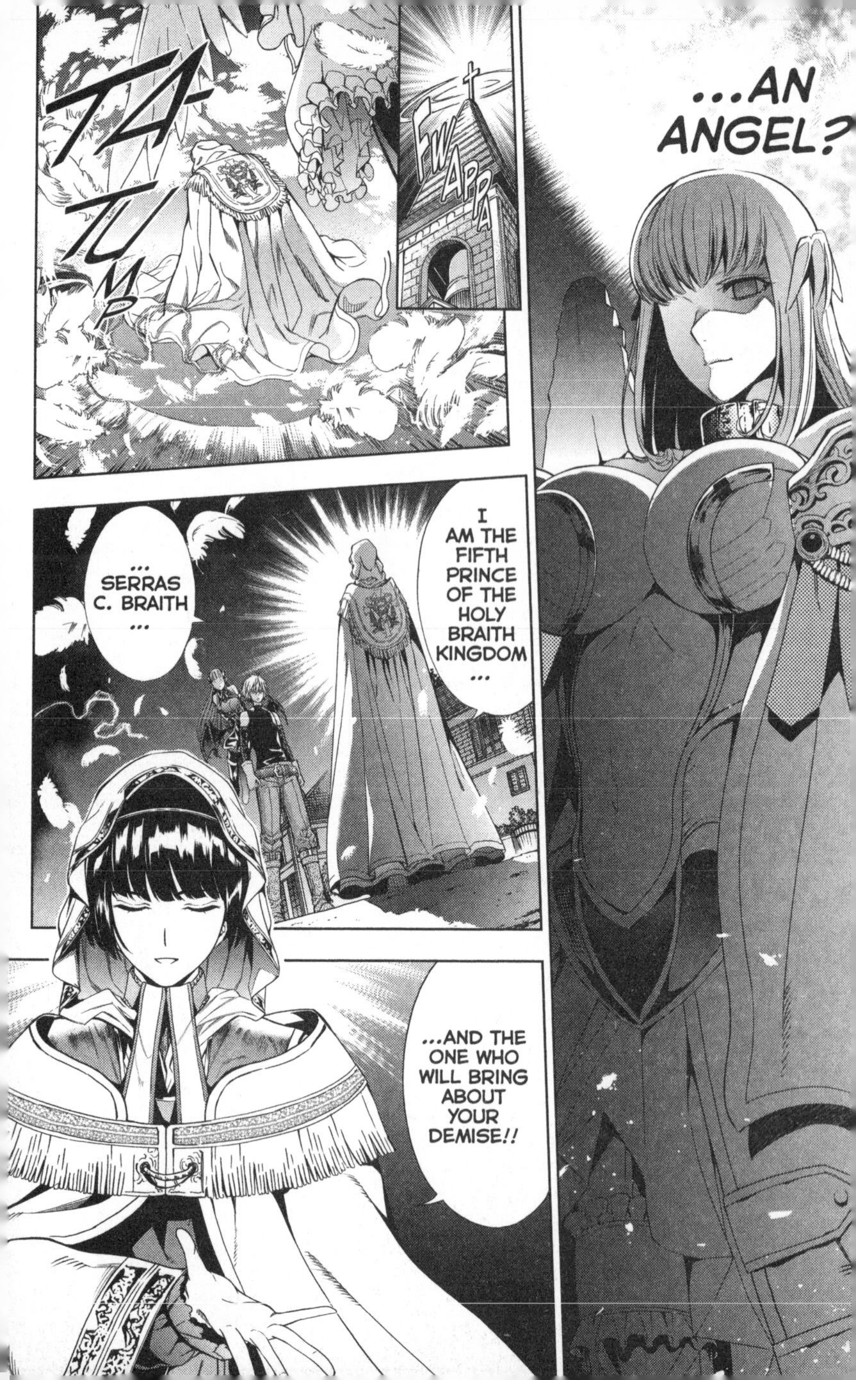
...AN ANGEL?
FWAPPA
TA-TUMP
I AM THE FIFTH PRINCE OF THE HOLY BRAITH KINGDOM...
...SERRAS C. BRAITH...
...AND THE ONE WHO WILL BRING ABOUT YOUR DEMISE!!

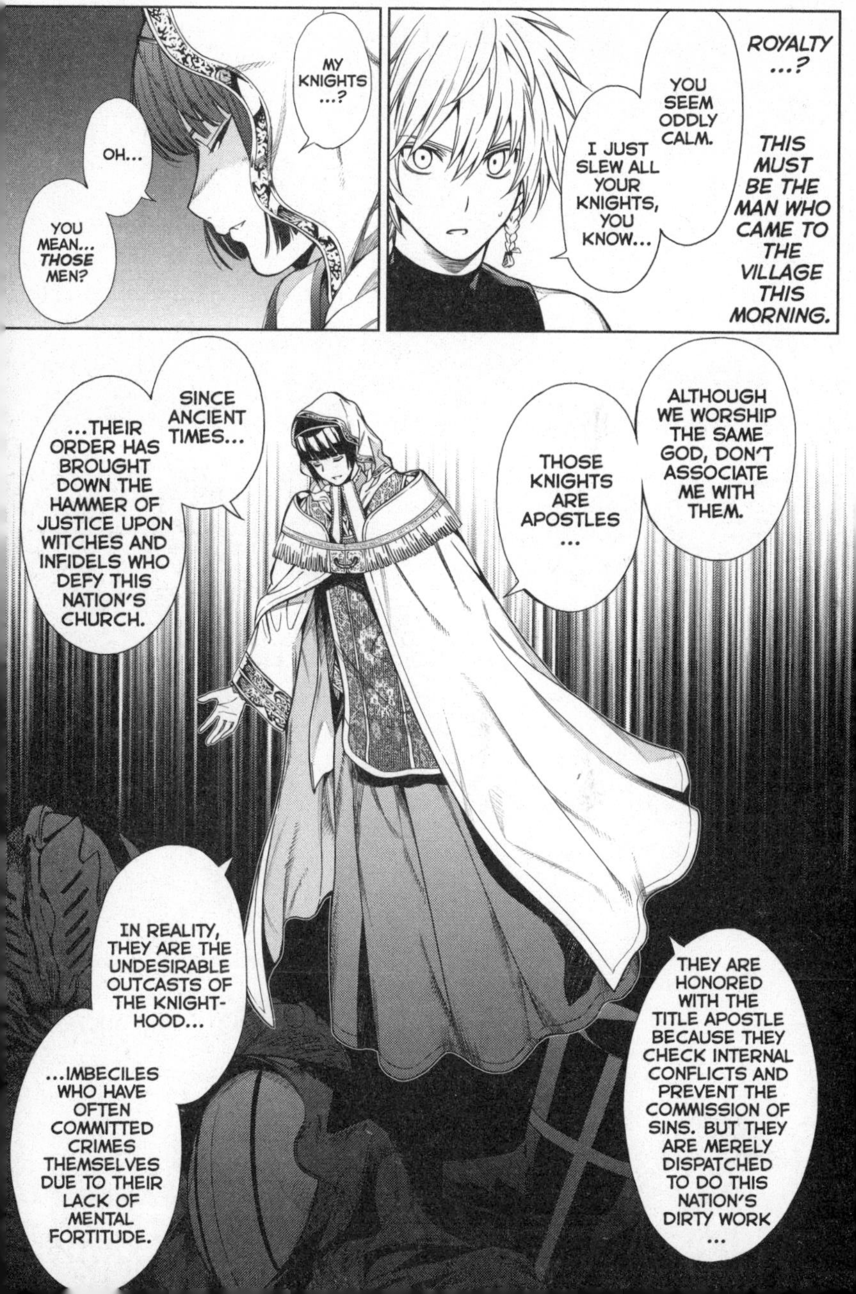
ROYALTY ...?
THIS MUST BE THE MAN WHO CAME TO THE VILLAGE THIS MORNING.
YOU SEEM ODDLY CALM.
I JUST SLEW ALL YOUR KNIGHTS, YOU KNOW...
MY KNIGHTS ...?
OH...
YOU MEAN... *THOSE* MEN?
ALTHOUGH WE WORSHIP THE SAME GOD, DON'T ASSOCIATE ME WITH THEM.
THOSE KNIGHTS ARE APOSTLES ...
SINCE ANCIENT TIMES...
...THEIR ORDER HAS BROUGHT DOWN THE HAMMER OF JUSTICE UPON WITCHES AND INFIDELS WHO DEFY THIS NATION'S CHURCH.
THEY ARE HONORED WITH THE TITLE APOSTLE BECAUSE THEY CHECK INTERNAL CONFLICTS AND PREVENT THE COMMISSION OF SINS. BUT THEY ARE MERELY DISPATCHED TO DO THIS NATION'S DIRTY WORK ...
IN REALITY, THEY ARE THE UNDESIRABLE OUTCASTS OF THE KNIGHT-HOOD...
...IMBECILES WHO HAVE OFTEN COMMITTED CRIMES THEMSELVES DUE TO THEIR LACK OF MENTAL FORTITUDE.

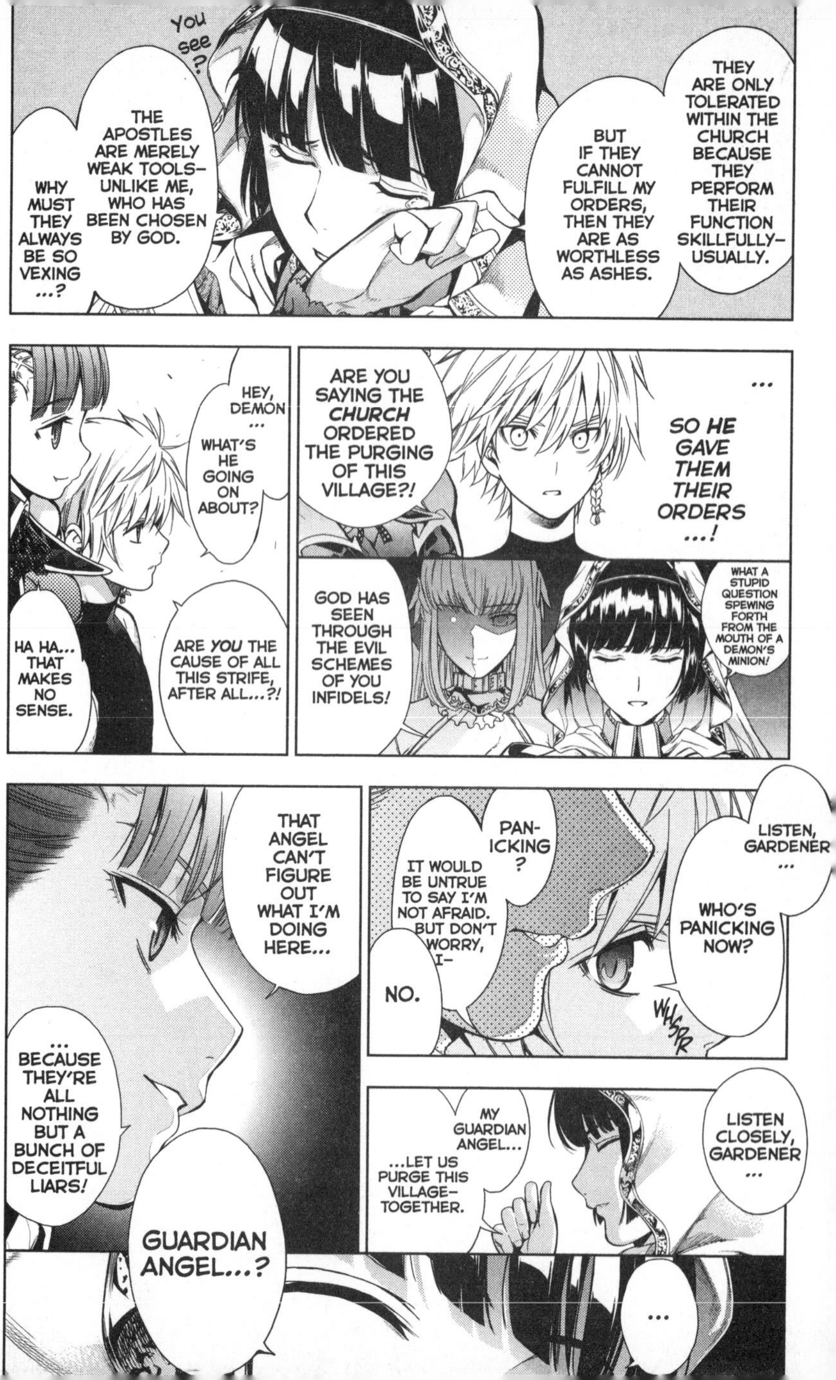
THEY ARE ONLY TOLERATED WITHIN THE CHURCH BECAUSE THEY PERFORM THEIR FUNCTION SKILLFULLY—USUALLY.
BUT IF THEY CANNOT FULFILL MY ORDERS, THEN THEY ARE AS WORTHLESS AS ASHES.
You see?
THE APOSTLES ARE MERELY WEAK TOOLS—UNLIKE ME, WHO HAS BEEN CHOSEN BY GOD.
WHY MUST THEY ALWAYS BE SO VEXING...?
...
SO HE GAVE THEM THEIR ORDERS...!
ARE YOU SAYING THE CHURCH ORDERED THE PURGING OF THIS VILLAGE?!
WHAT A STUPID QUESTION SPEWING FORTH FROM THE MOUTH OF A DEMON'S MINION!
GOD HAS SEEN THROUGH THE EVIL SCHEMES OF YOU INFIDELS!
HEY, DEMON... WHAT'S HE GOING ON ABOUT?
ARE YOU THE CAUSE OF ALL THIS STRIFE, AFTER ALL...?!
HA HA... THAT MAKES NO SENSE.
LISTEN, GARDENER...
WHO'S PANICKING NOW?
WHSPR
PAN-ICKING?
IT WOULD BE UNTRUE TO SAY I'M NOT AFRAID. BUT DON'T WORRY, I—
NO.
LISTEN CLOSELY, GARDENER...
MY GUARDIAN ANGEL...
...LET US PURGE THIS VILLAGE—TOGETHER.
THAT ANGEL CAN'T FIGURE OUT WHAT I'M DOING HERE...
...BECAUSE THEY'RE ALL NOTHING BUT A BUNCH OF DECEITFUL LIARS!
...
GUARDIAN ANGEL...?

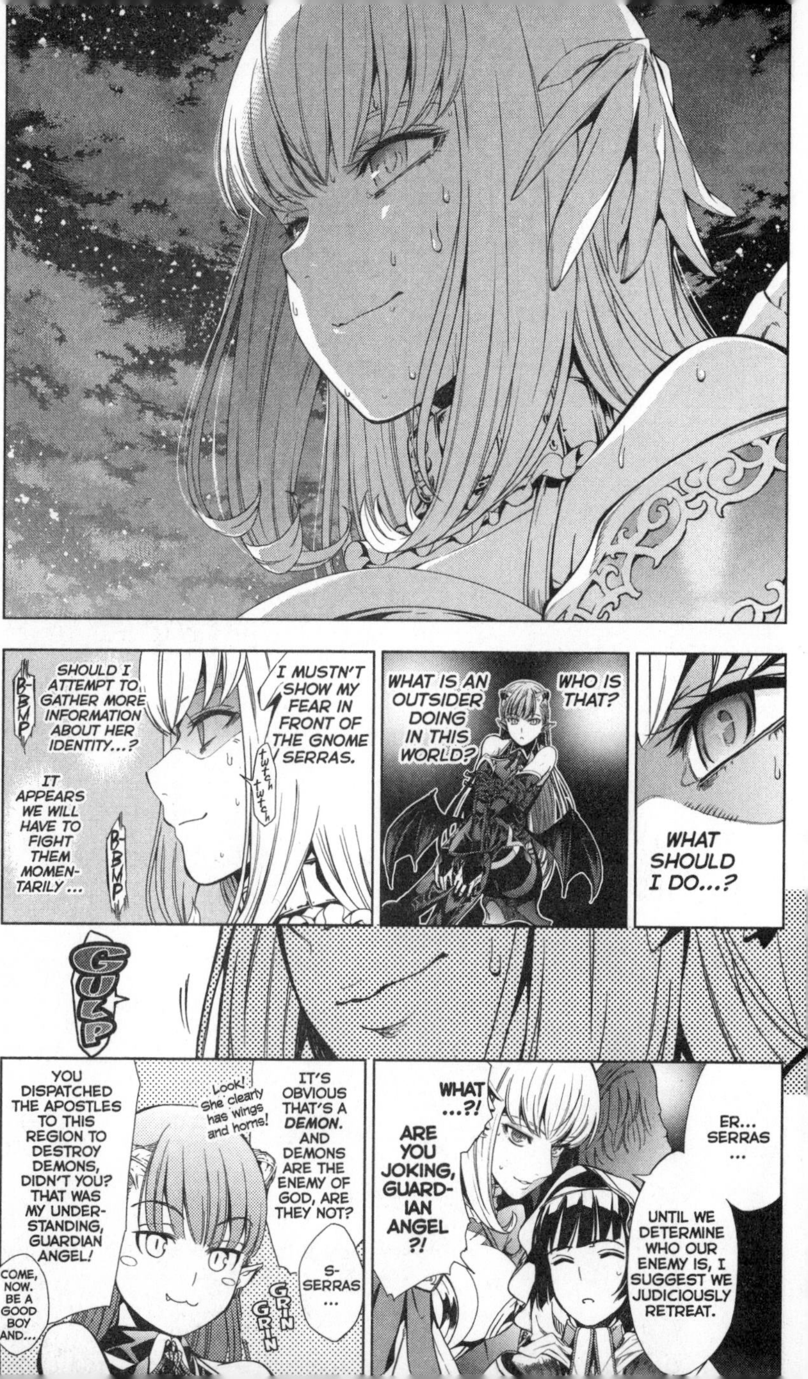
WHAT SHOULD I DO...?
WHO IS THAT?
WHAT IS AN OUTSIDER DOING IN THIS WORLD?
I MUSTN'T SHOW MY FEAR IN FRONT OF THE GNOME SERRAS.
twitch twitch
SHOULD I ATTEMPT TO GATHER MORE INFORMATION ABOUT HER IDENTITY...?
B-BMP
IT APPEARS WE WILL HAVE TO FIGHT THEM MOMENTARILY...
B-BMP
GULP
ER... SERRAS ...
WHAT ...?!
ARE YOU JOKING, GUARDIAN ANGEL ?!
UNTIL WE DETERMINE WHO OUR ENEMY IS, I SUGGEST WE JUDICIOUSLY RETREAT.
IT'S OBVIOUS THAT'S A *DEMON*. AND DEMONS ARE THE ENEMY OF GOD, ARE THEY NOT?
Look! She clearly has wings and horns!
YOU DISPATCHED THE APOSTLES TO THIS REGION TO DESTROY DEMONS, DIDN'T YOU? THAT WAS MY UNDERSTANDING, GUARDIAN ANGEL!
S-SERRAS ...
GRIN GRIN
COME, NOW. BE A GOOD BOY AND...

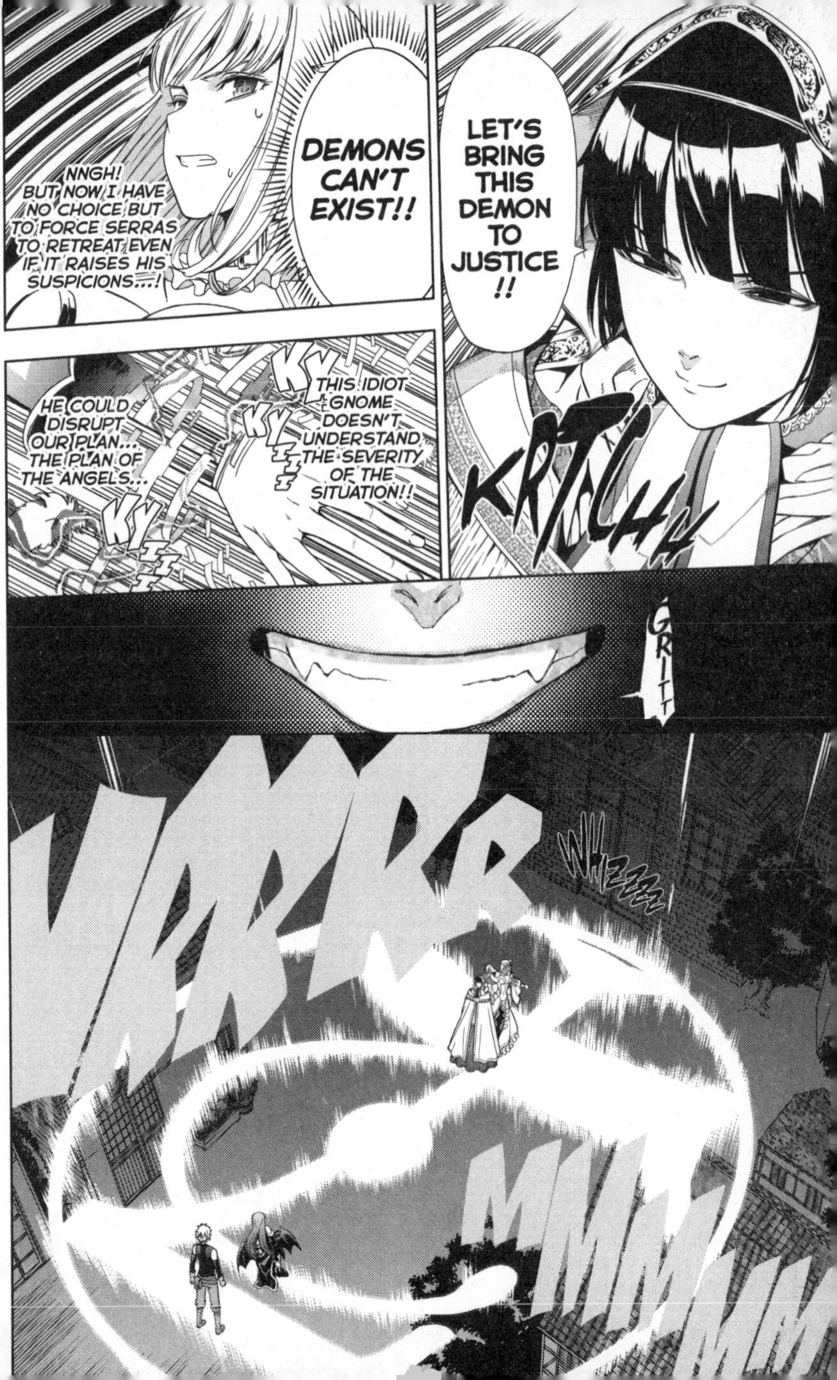
LET'S BRING THIS DEMON TO JUSTICE!!
KRTCHH
DEMONS CAN'T EXIST!!
NNGH! BUT NOW I HAVE NO CHOICE BUT TO FORCE SERRAS TO RETREAT EVEN IF IT RAISES HIS SUSPICIONS...!
KYIII
THIS IDIOT GNOME DOESN'T UNDERSTAND THE SEVERITY OF THE SITUATION!!
HE COULD DISRUPT OUR PLAN... THE PLAN OF THE ANGELS...
KYIII
GRITT
VRRR
WHIZZZZ
MMMM

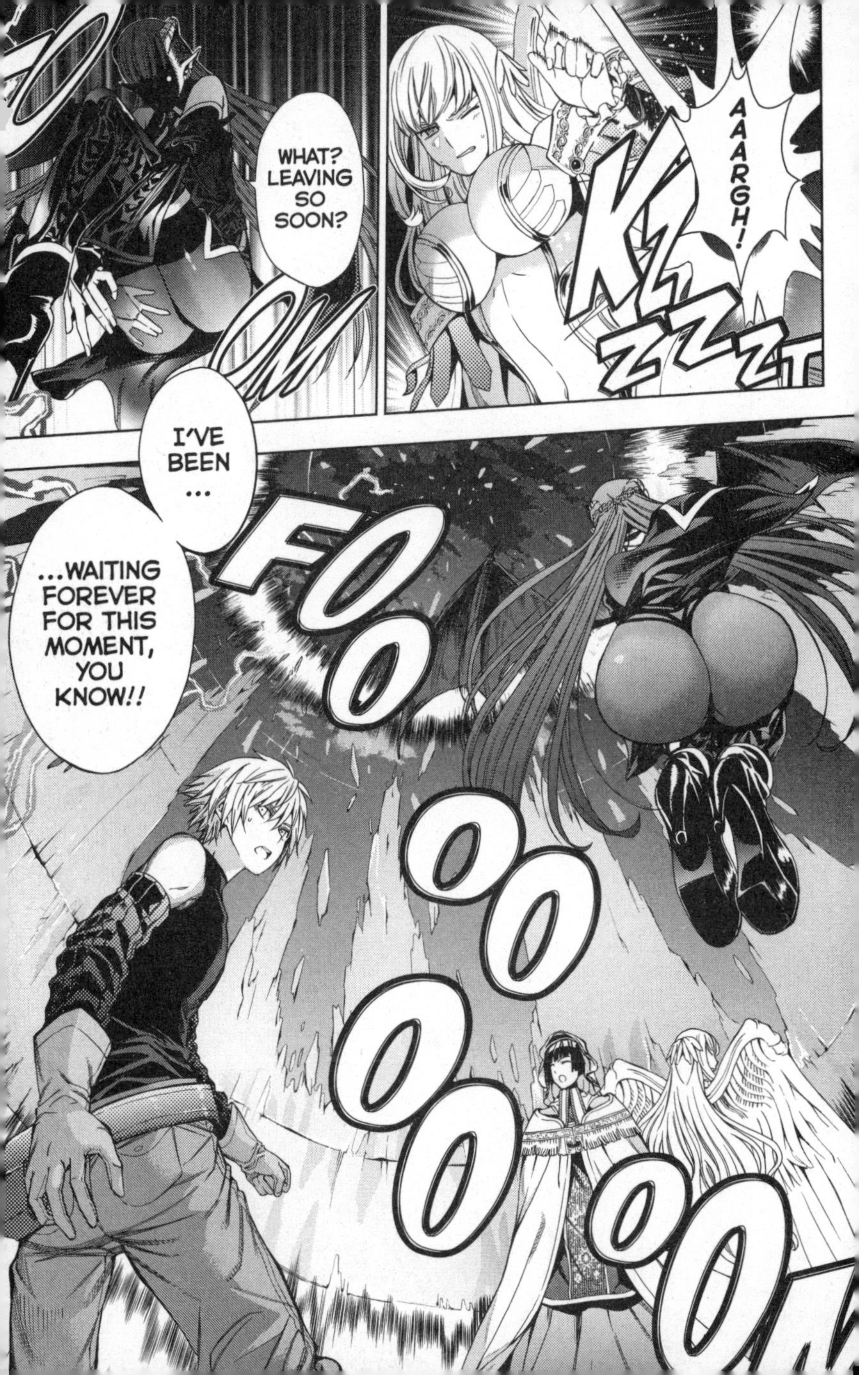
AAAARGH!
KZZZZT
WHAT? LEAVING SO SOON?
OM
I'VE BEEN ...
...WAITING FOREVER FOR THIS MOMENT, YOU KNOW!!
FOOOOOOOOOM

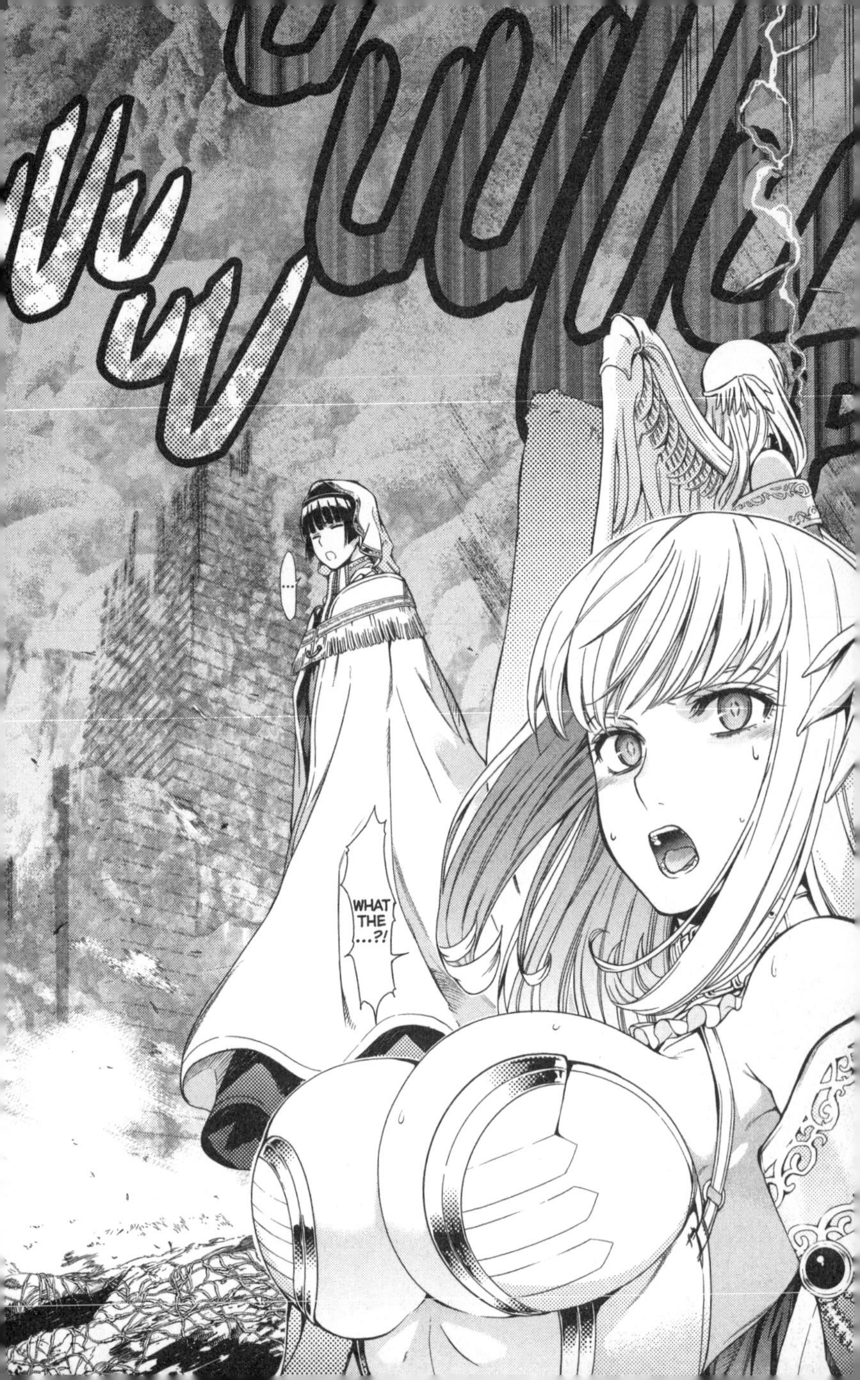
...!
WHAT THE ...?!

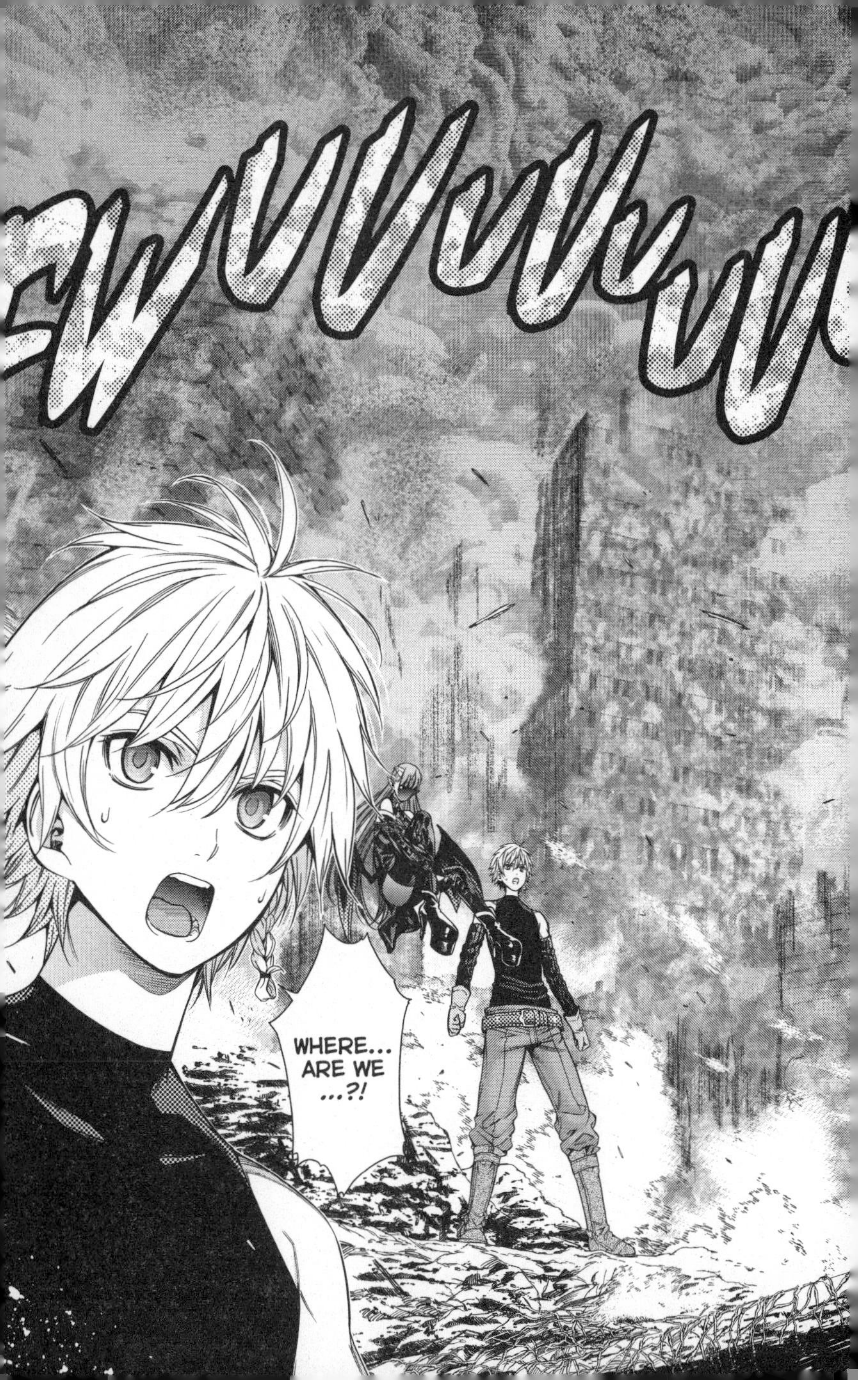
WHERE... ARE WE ...?!

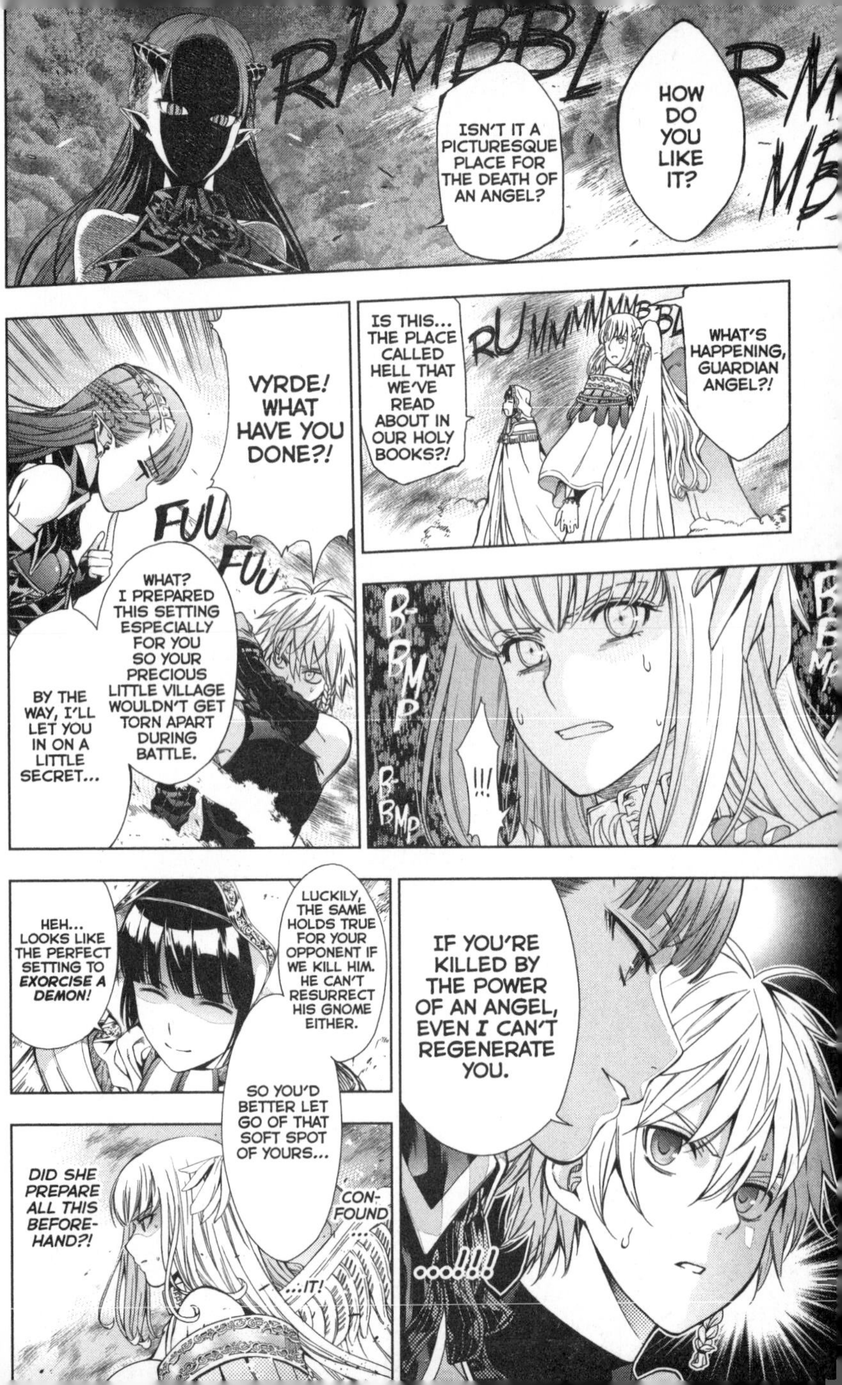
RKMBBL
HOW DO YOU LIKE IT?
ISN'T IT A PICTURESQUE PLACE FOR THE DEATH OF AN ANGEL?
WHAT'S HAPPENING, GUARDIAN ANGEL?!
RUMMMMMBBL
IS THIS... THE PLACE CALLED HELL THAT WE'VE READ ABOUT IN OUR HOLY BOOKS?!
B-BMP
B-BMP
!!!
VYRDE! WHAT HAVE YOU DONE?!
FUU
FUU
WHAT? I PREPARED THIS SETTING ESPECIALLY FOR YOU SO YOUR PRECIOUS LITTLE VILLAGE WOULDN'T GET TORN APART DURING BATTLE.
BY THE WAY, I'LL LET YOU IN ON A LITTLE SECRET...
IF YOU'RE KILLED BY THE POWER OF AN ANGEL, EVEN *I* CAN'T REGENERATE YOU.
...!!!
LUCKILY, THE SAME HOLDS TRUE FOR YOUR OPPONENT IF WE KILL HIM. HE CAN'T RESURRECT HIS GNOME EITHER.
SO YOU'D BETTER LET GO OF THAT SOFT SPOT OF YOURS...
HEH... LOOKS LIKE THE PERFECT SETTING TO *EXORCISE A DEMON!*
CON-FOUND...
...IT!
DID SHE PREPARE ALL THIS BEFORE-HAND?!

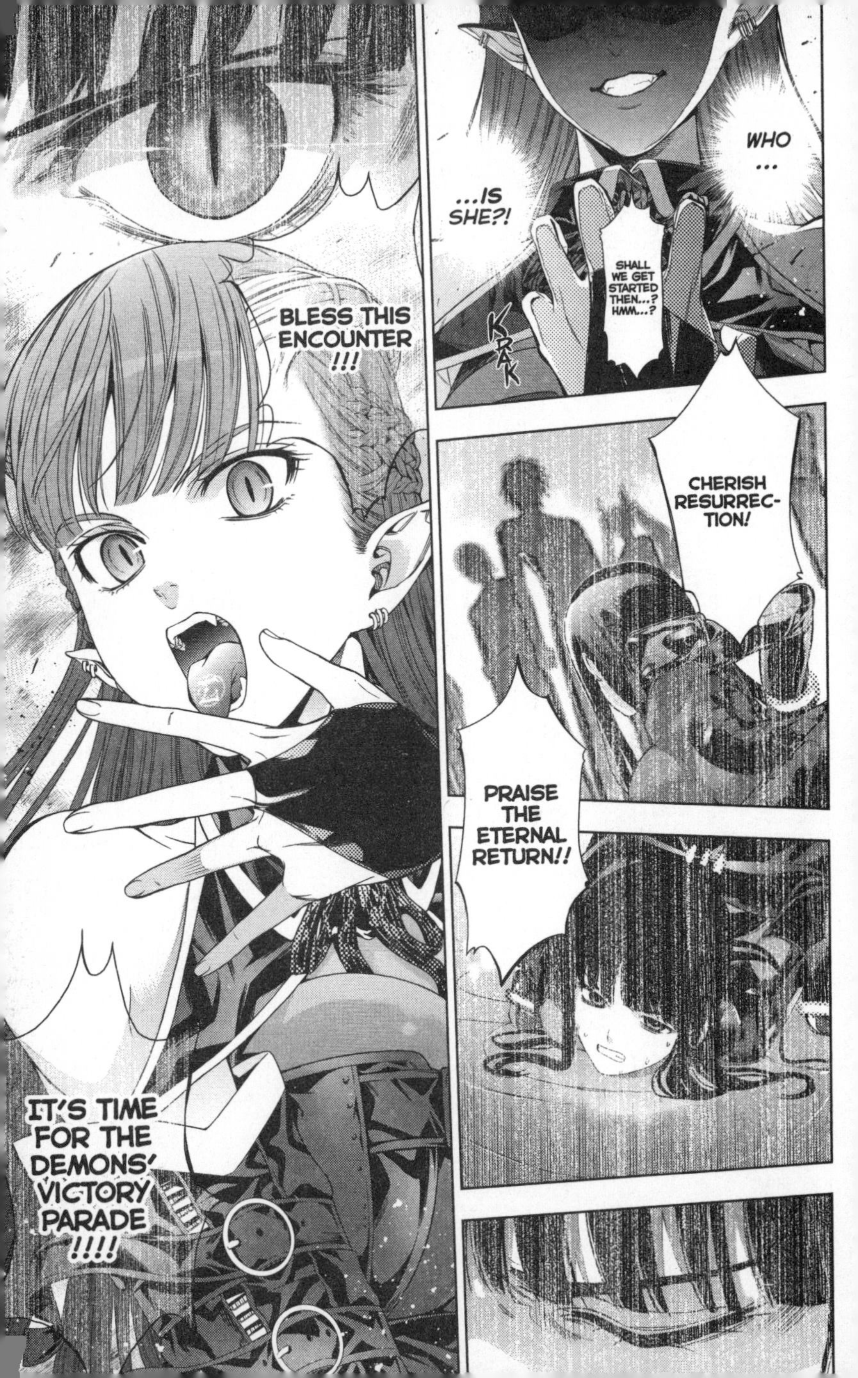
WHO ...
...IS SHE?!
SHALL WE GET STARTED THEN...? HMM...?
KRAK
CHERISH RESURRECTION!
PRAISE THE ETERNAL RETURN!!
BLESS THIS ENCOUNTER !!!
IT'S TIME FOR THE DEMONS' VICTORY PARADE !!!!

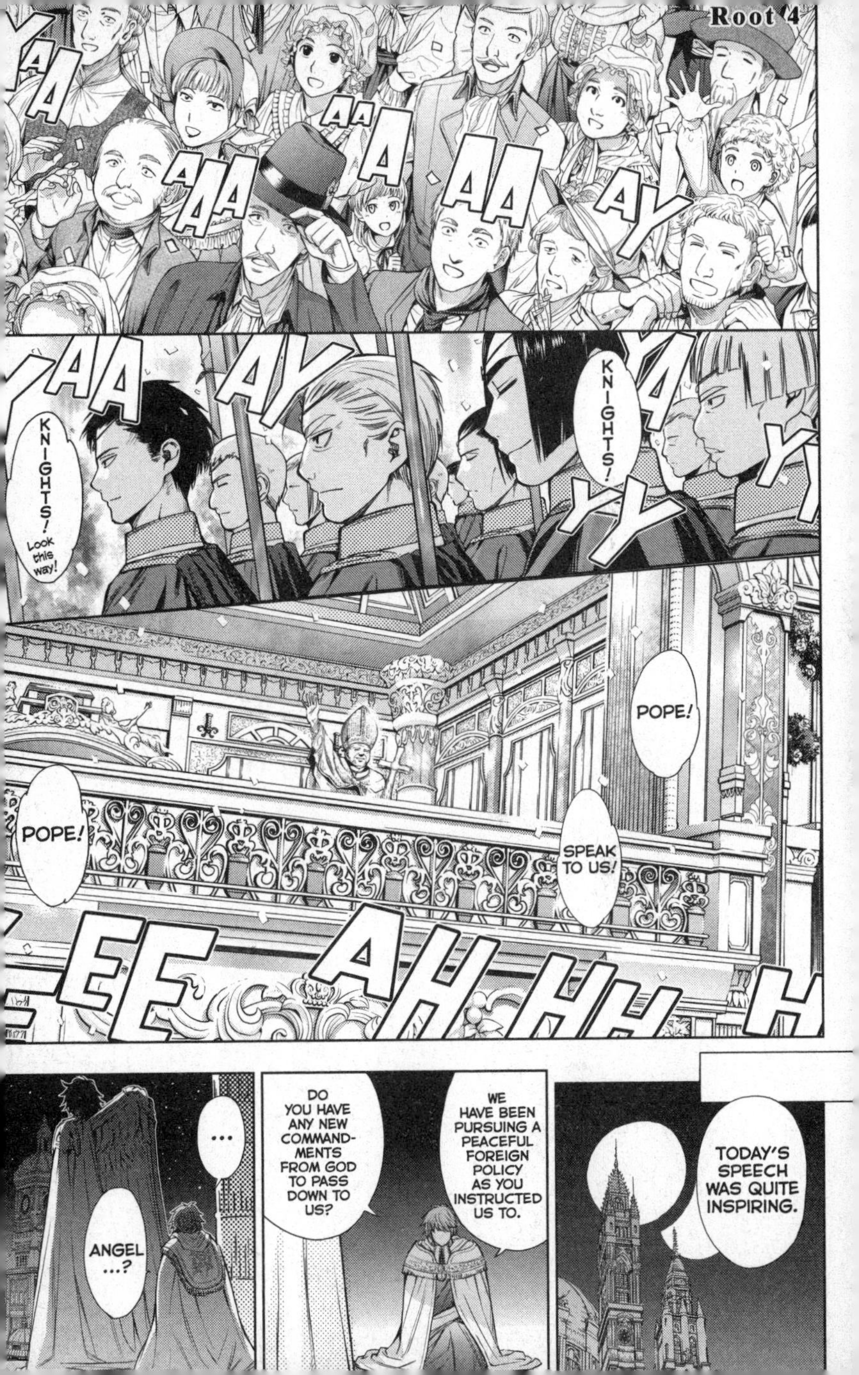
YAAAAAAAAAAAY
YAAAAY
YYY
KNIGHTS!
KNIGHTS! Look this way!
POPE!
SPEAK TO US!
POPE!
EEEAHHHH
TODAY'S SPEECH WAS QUITE INSPIRING.
WE HAVE BEEN PURSUING A PEACEFUL FOREIGN POLICY AS YOU INSTRUCTED US TO.
DO YOU HAVE ANY NEW COMMAND-MENTS FROM GOD TO PASS DOWN TO US?
...
ANGEL ...?

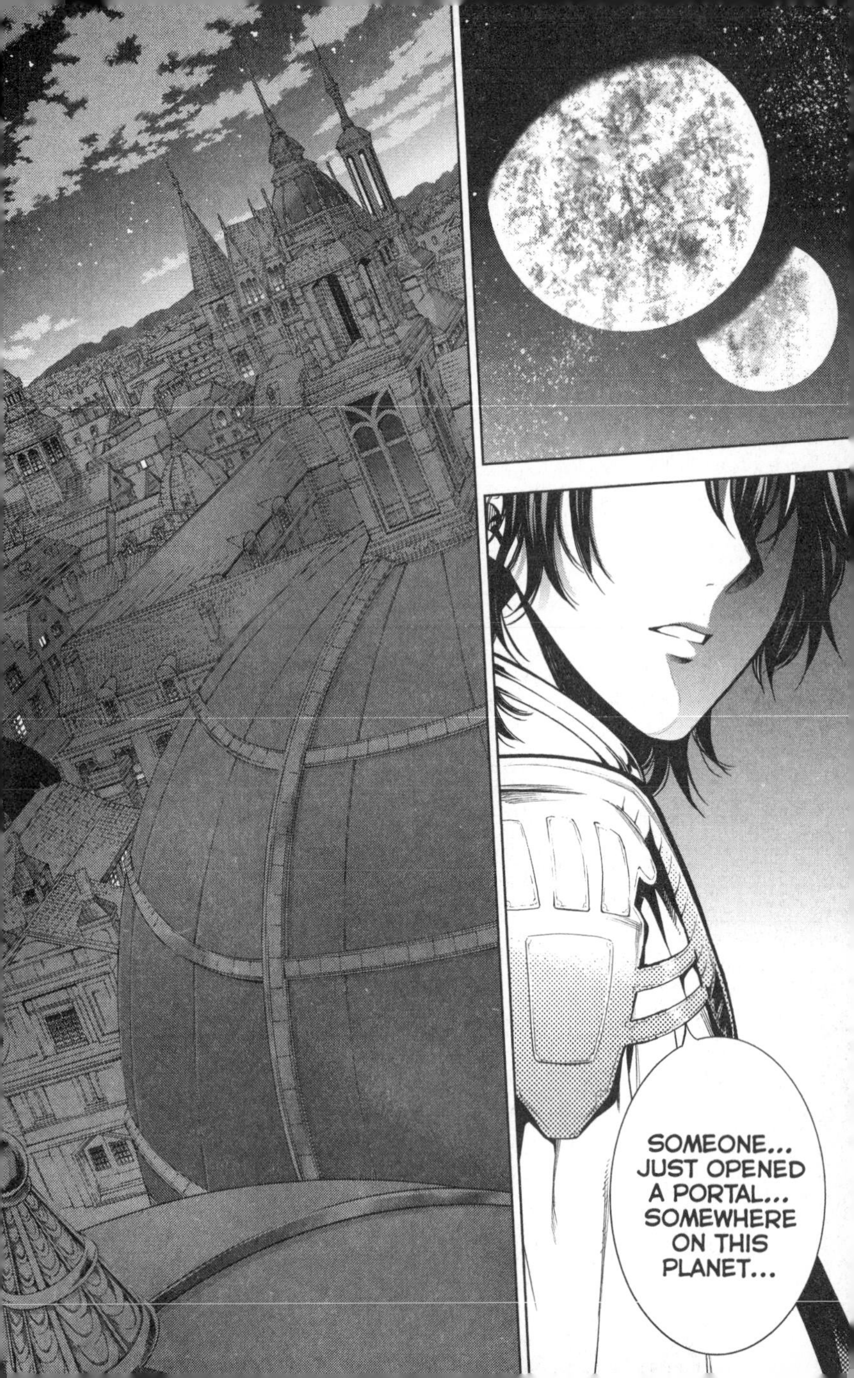
SOMEONE... JUST OPENED A PORTAL... SOMEWHERE ON THIS PLANET...

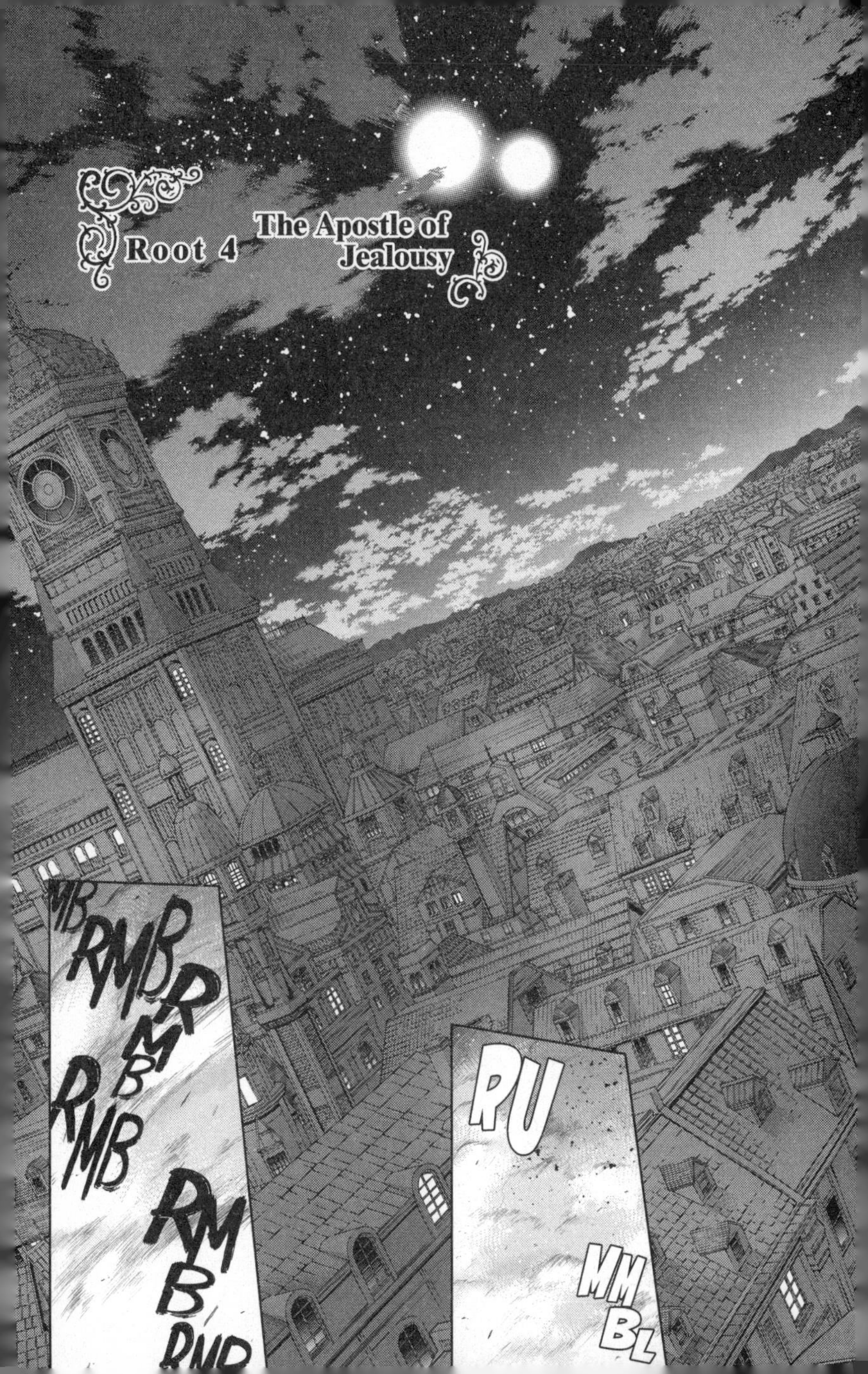
Root 4
The Apostle of Jealousy
RU
MMBL
MB
RMB
RMB
RMB
RMB

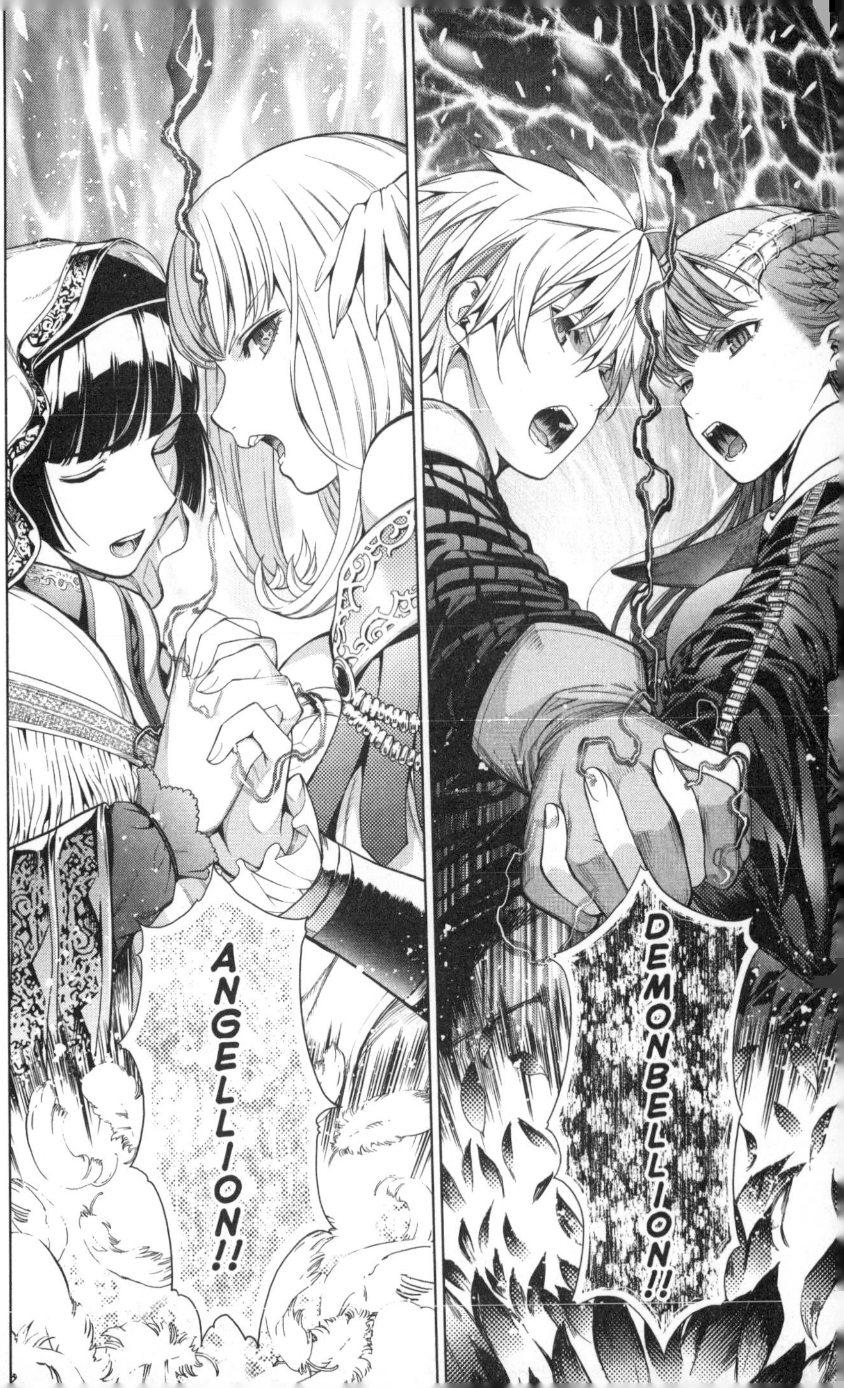
DEMONBELLION!!
ANGELLION!!

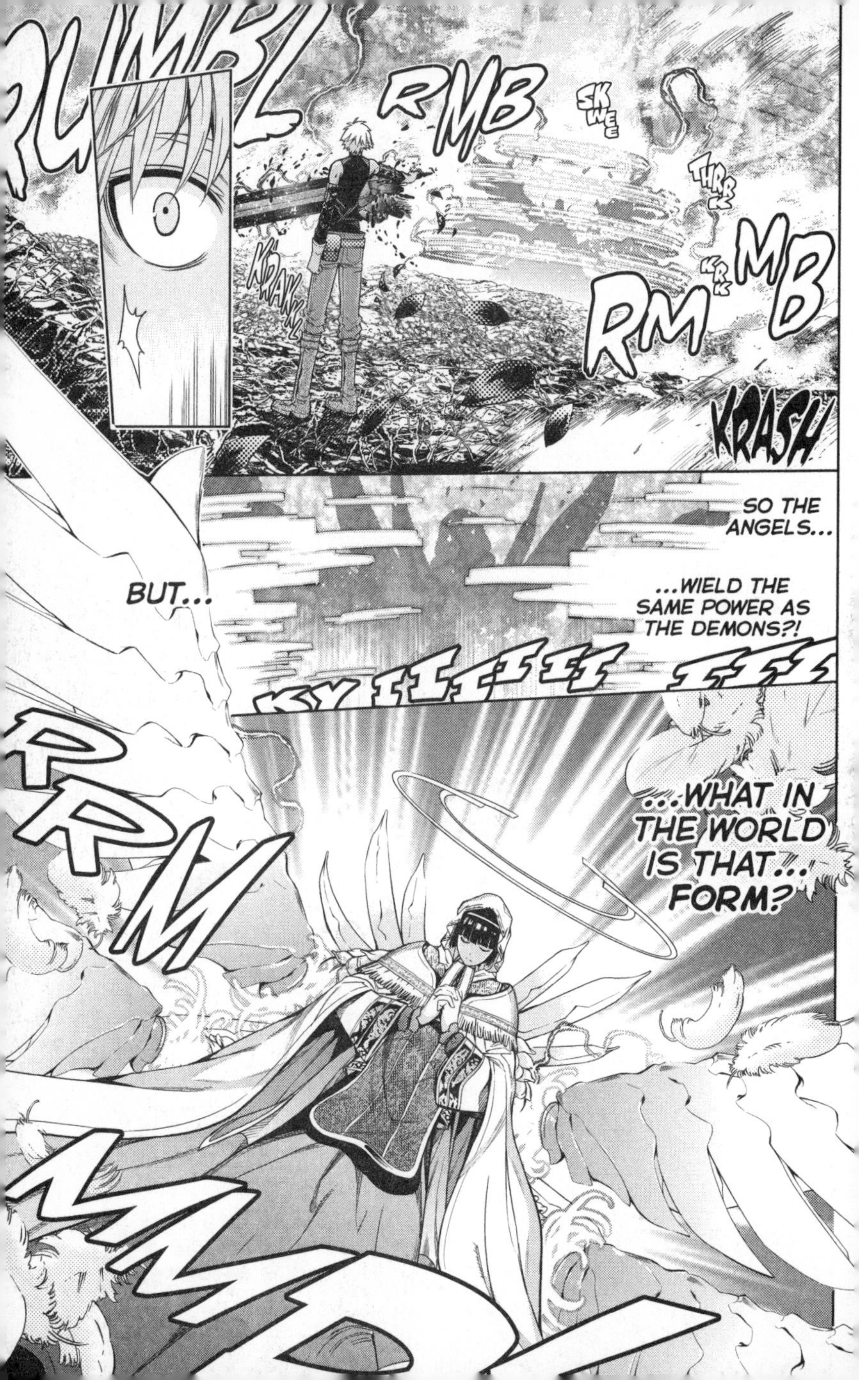
RMB
SKWEE
THRRK
RM MB
KRK
KRAKKL
RUMBL
KRASH
SO THE ANGELS...
...WIELD THE SAME POWER AS THE DEMONS?!
BUT...
KYIIIIII III
...WHAT IN THE WORLD IS THAT... FORM?
PRVM

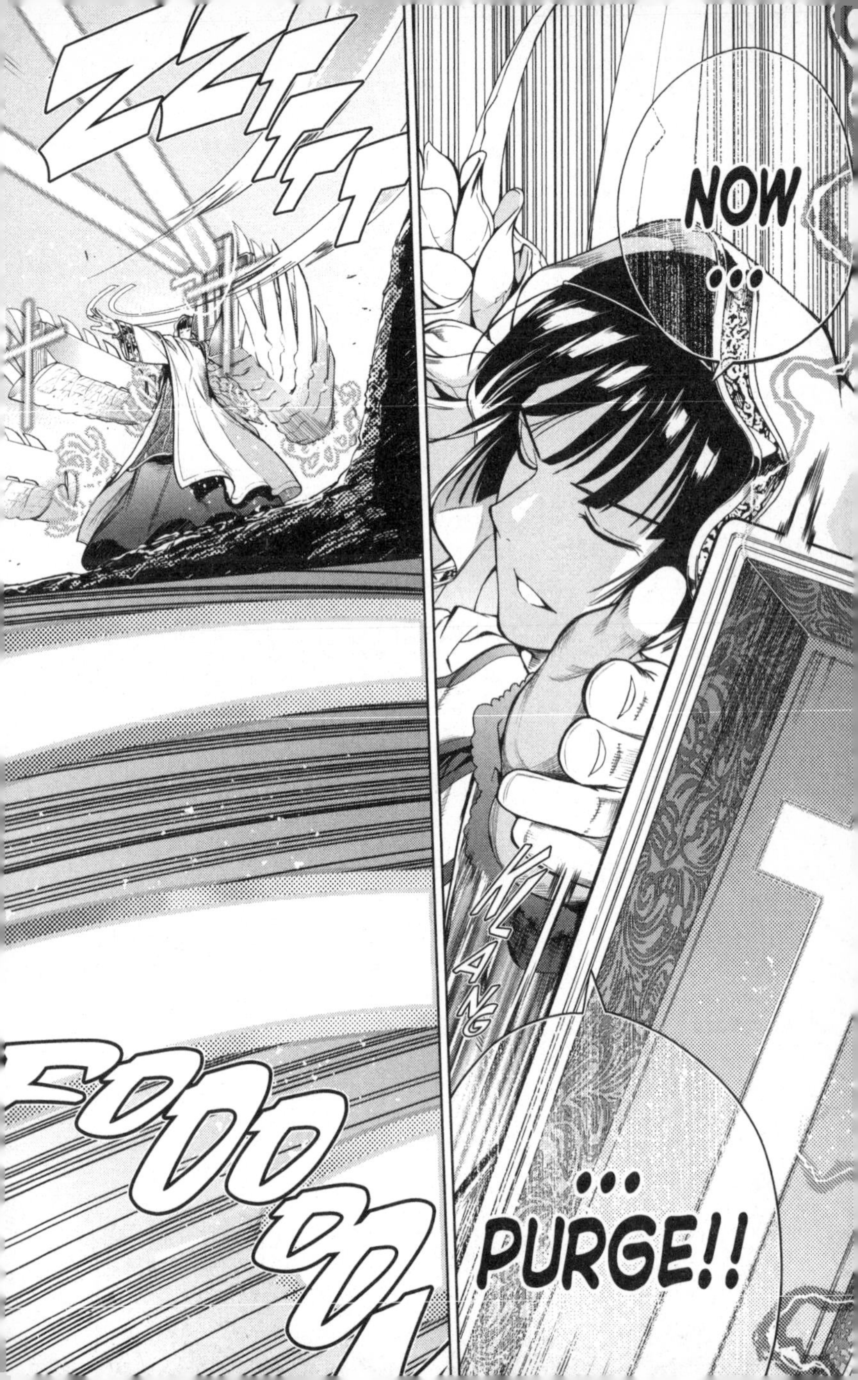
NOW…
KLANG
…PURGE!!

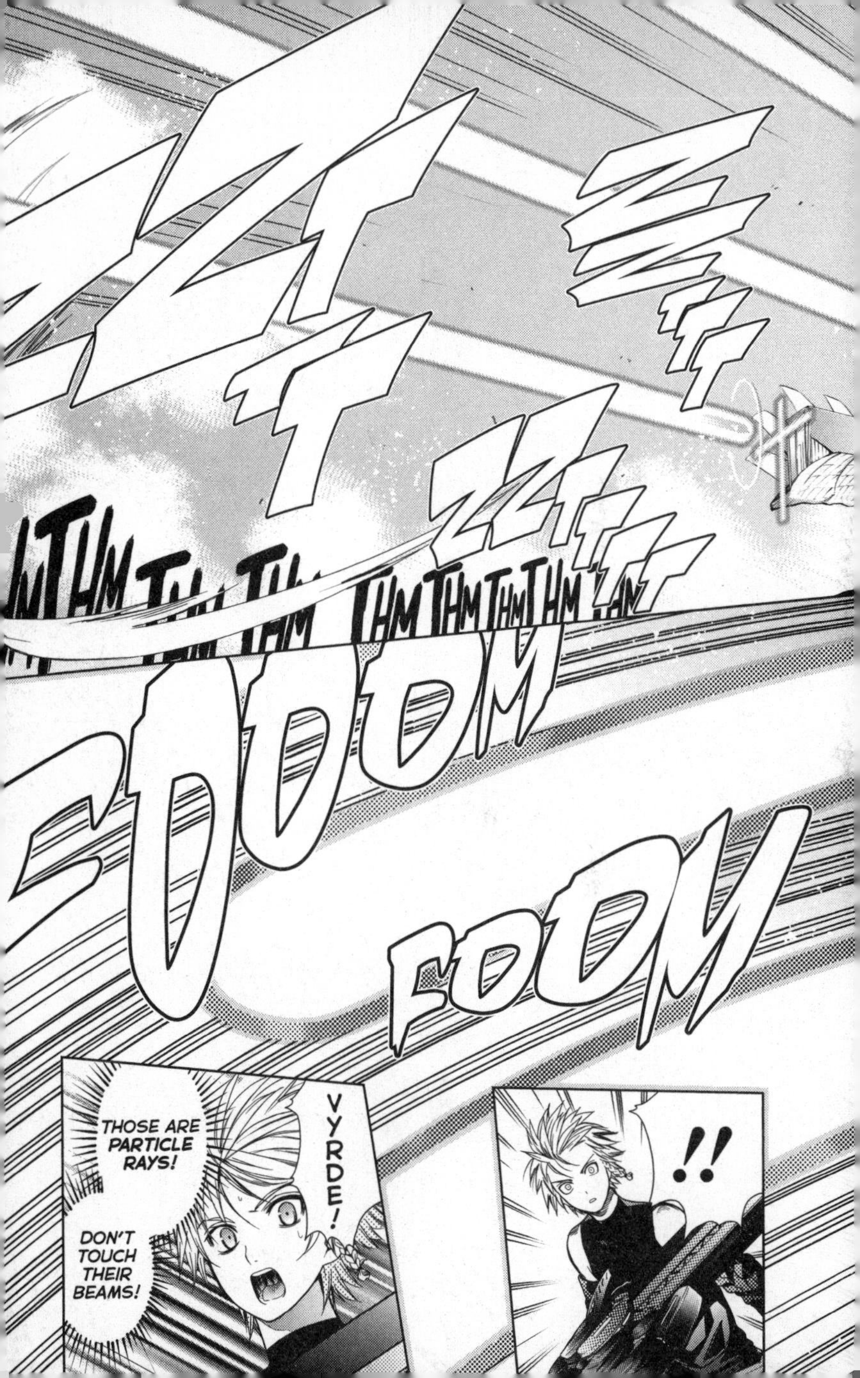
THM THM THM THM THM THM THM THM
DOOM
DOOM
!!
VYRDE!
THOSE ARE PARTICLE RAYS!
DON'T TOUCH THEIR BEAMS!

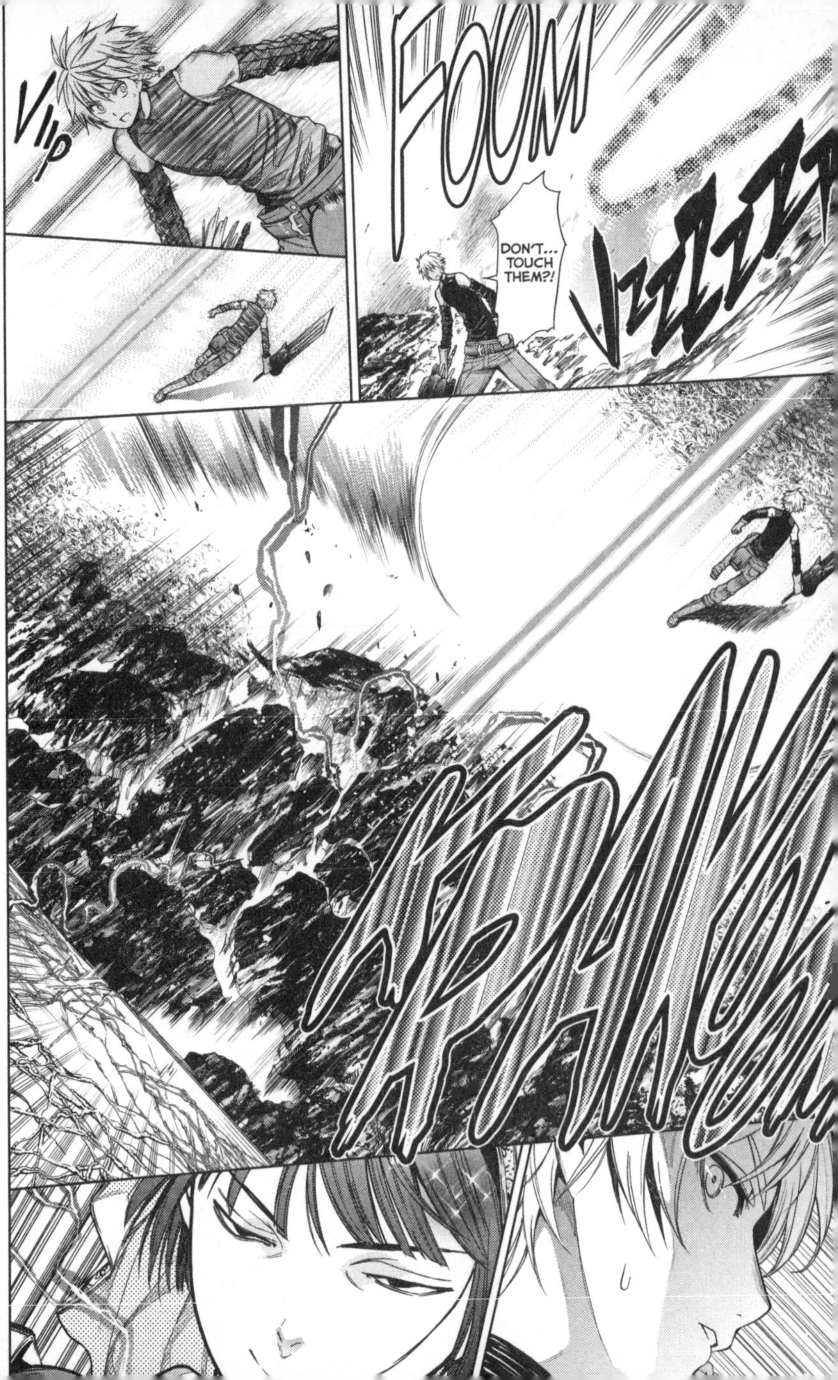
FOOM
DON'T... TOUCH THEM?!
Vlip

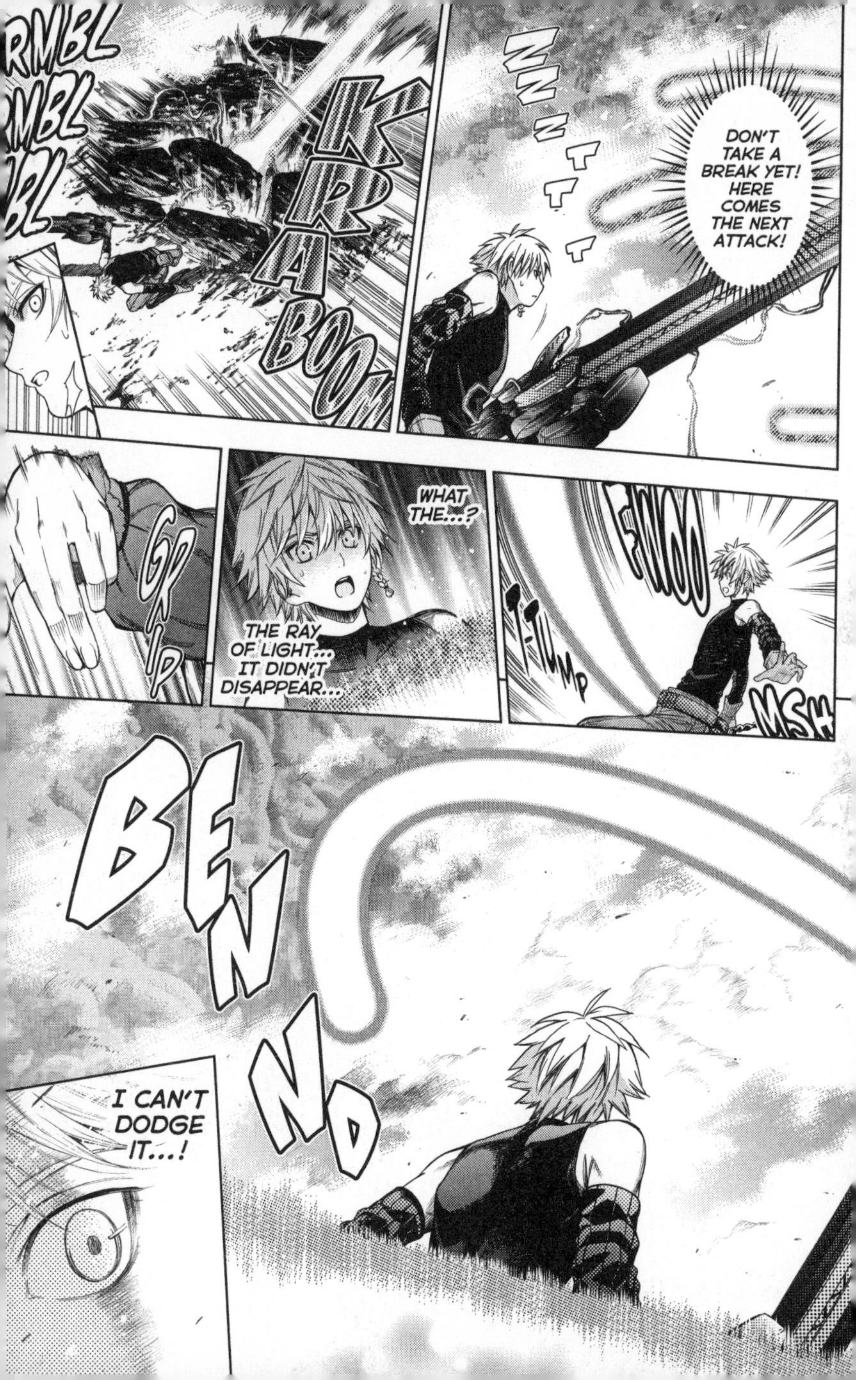
ZZZTTTT
DON'T TAKE A BREAK YET! HERE COMES THE NEXT ATTACK!
KRRABOOM
RMBL
RMBL
FWOO
T-TUMP
MSH
WHAT THE...?
THE RAY OF LIGHT... IT DIDN'T DISAPPEAR...
GRIP
BENNND
I CAN'T DODGE IT...!

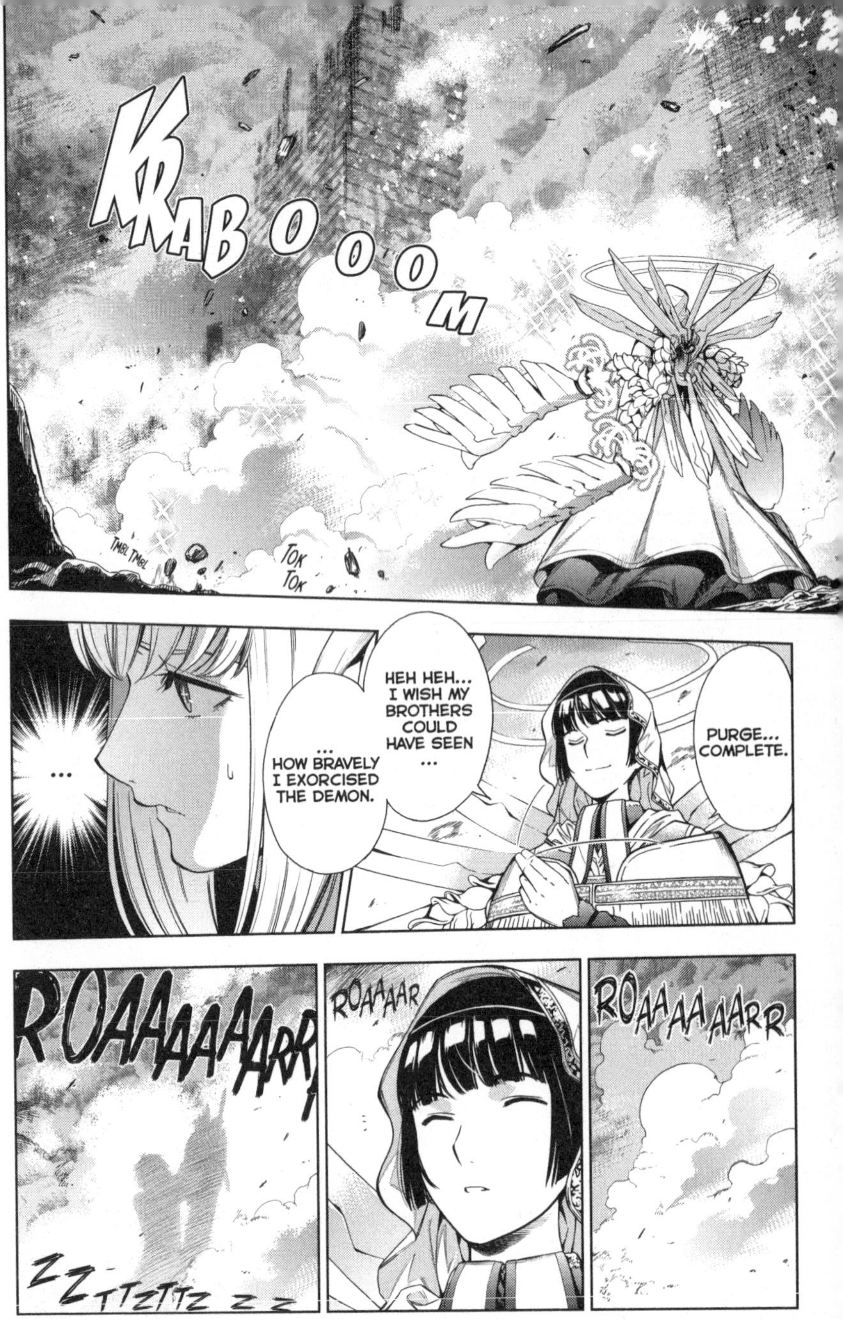
KRABOOOM
TMBL TMBL
TOK TOK
PURGE... COMPLETE.
HEH HEH... I WISH MY BROTHERS COULD HAVE SEEN...
...HOW BRAVELY I EXORCISED THE DEMON.
...
ROAAAAAARR
ROAAAAR
ROAAAAAARR
ZZTTZTTZ ZZ

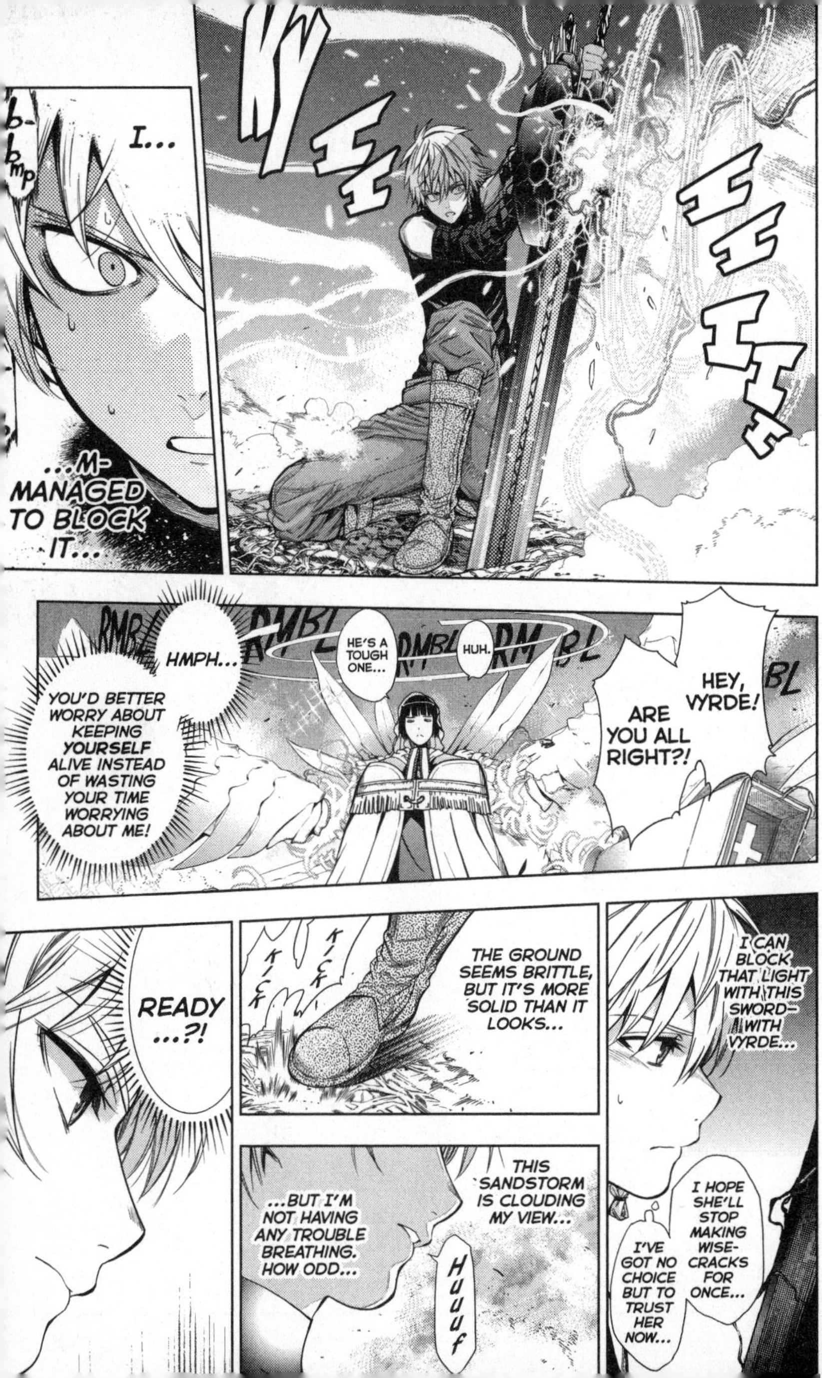
b-bmp
I...
...M-MANAGED TO BLOCK IT...
HEY, VYRDE!
ARE YOU ALL RIGHT?!
RMBL RMBL RMBL
HUH.
HE'S A TOUGH ONE...
HMPH...
YOU'D BETTER WORRY ABOUT KEEPING YOURSELF ALIVE INSTEAD OF WASTING YOUR TIME WORRYING ABOUT ME!
I CAN BLOCK THAT LIGHT WITH THIS SWORD—WITH VYRDE...
I HOPE SHE'LL STOP MAKING WISE-CRACKS FOR ONCE...
I'VE GOT NO CHOICE BUT TO TRUST HER NOW...
THE GROUND SEEMS BRITTLE, BUT IT'S MORE SOLID THAN IT LOOKS...
KICK
KICK
THIS SANDSTORM IS CLOUDING MY VIEW...
...BUT I'M NOT HAVING ANY TROUBLE BREATHING. HOW ODD...
Huuuf
READY...?!

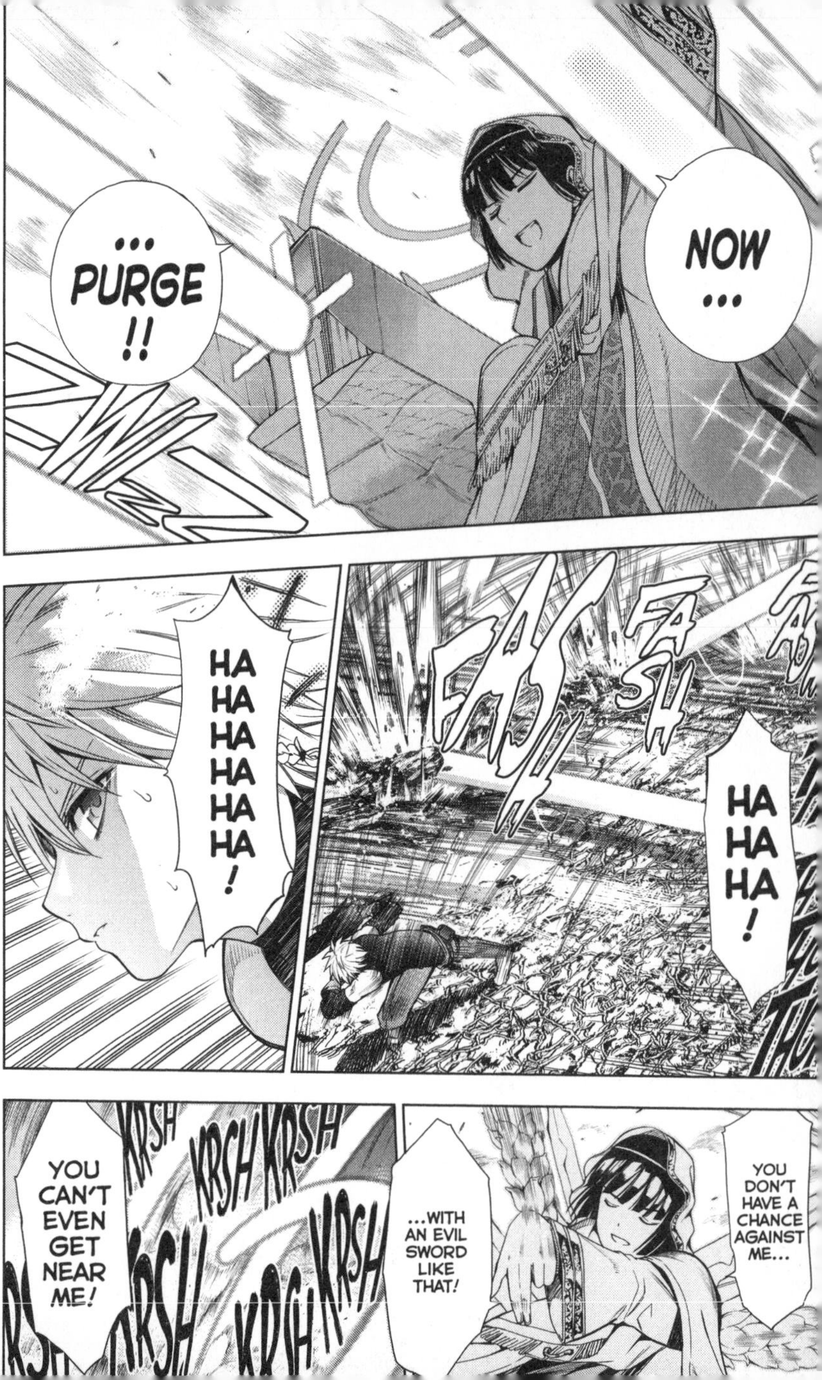
NOW...
...PURGE!!
FASH
FASH
HA HA HA!
HA HA HA HA HA HA!
YOU DON'T HAVE A CHANCE AGAINST ME...
...WITH AN EVIL SWORD LIKE THAT!
KRSH KRSH KRSH KRSH
YOU CAN'T EVEN GET NEAR ME!

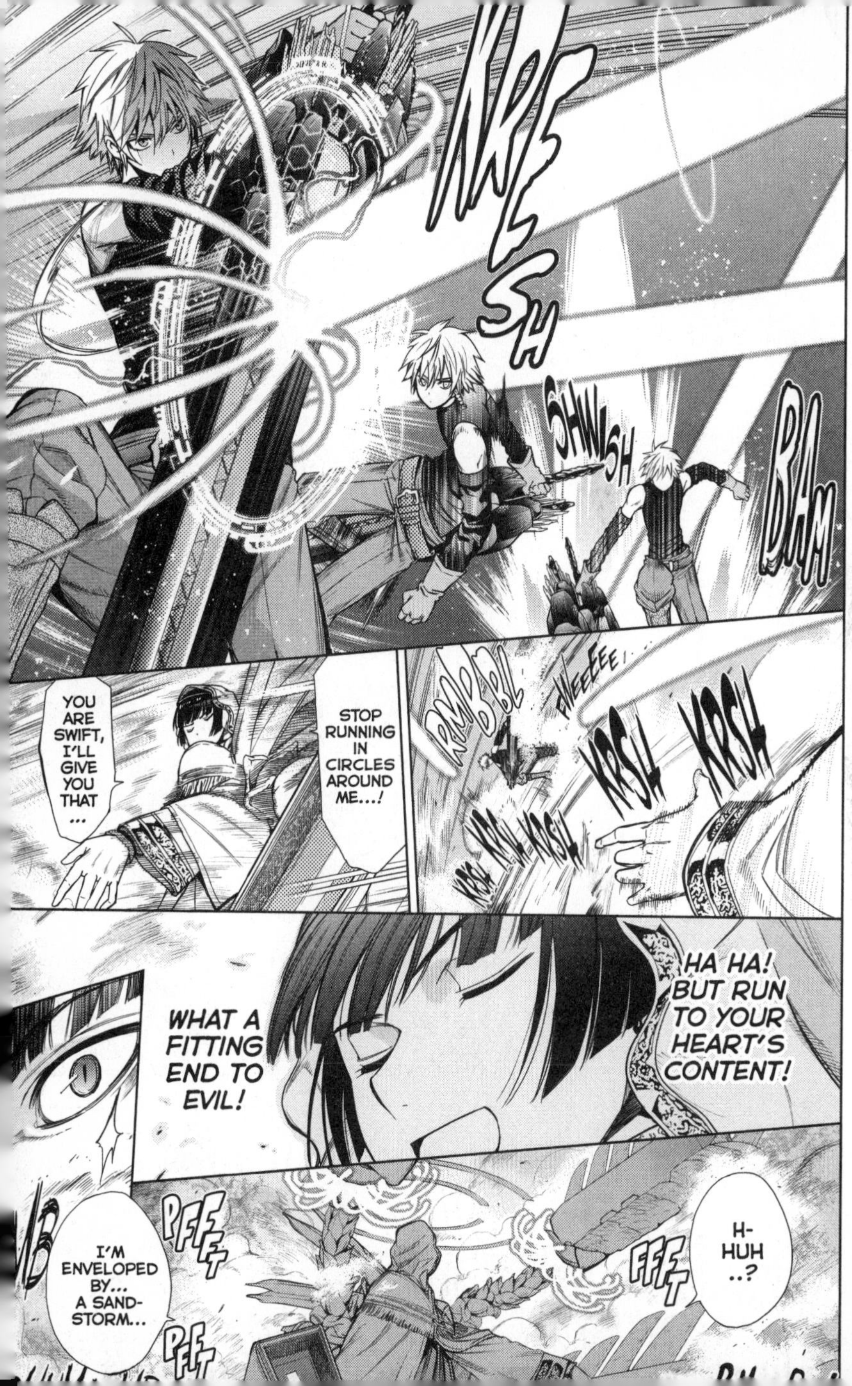
SHWISH
BAM
RMBBL
WEEEE
KRSH KRSH
KRSH KRSH KRSH KRSH
STOP RUNNING IN CIRCLES AROUND ME...!
YOU ARE SWIFT, I'LL GIVE YOU THAT...
HA HA! BUT RUN TO YOUR HEART'S CONTENT!
WHAT A FITTING END TO EVIL!
H-HUH..?
FFFT
PFFFT
I'M ENVELOPED BY... A SAND-STORM...
PFFT

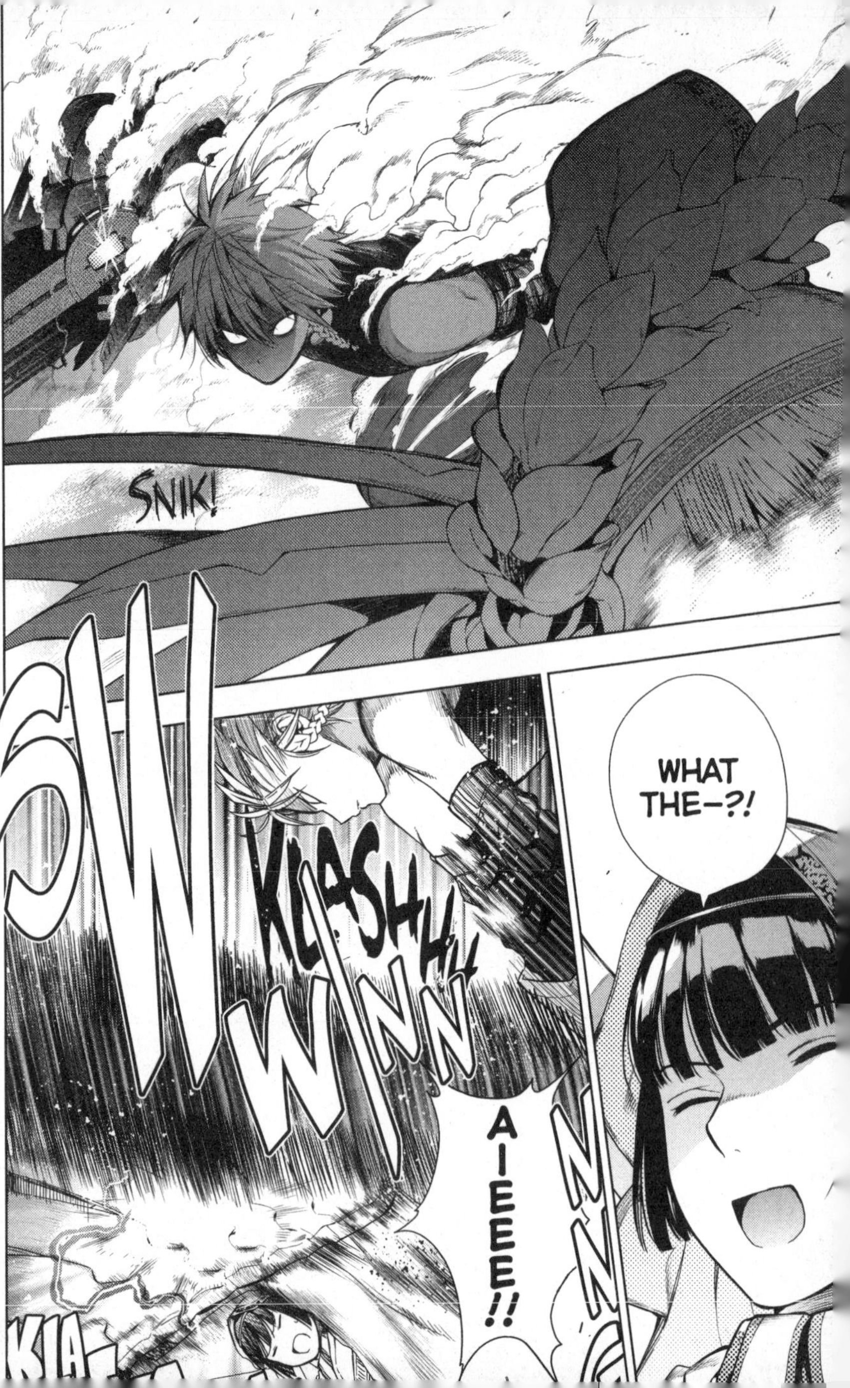
SNIK!
WHAT THE–?!
SWWINNN
KLASHHH
AIEEEE!!

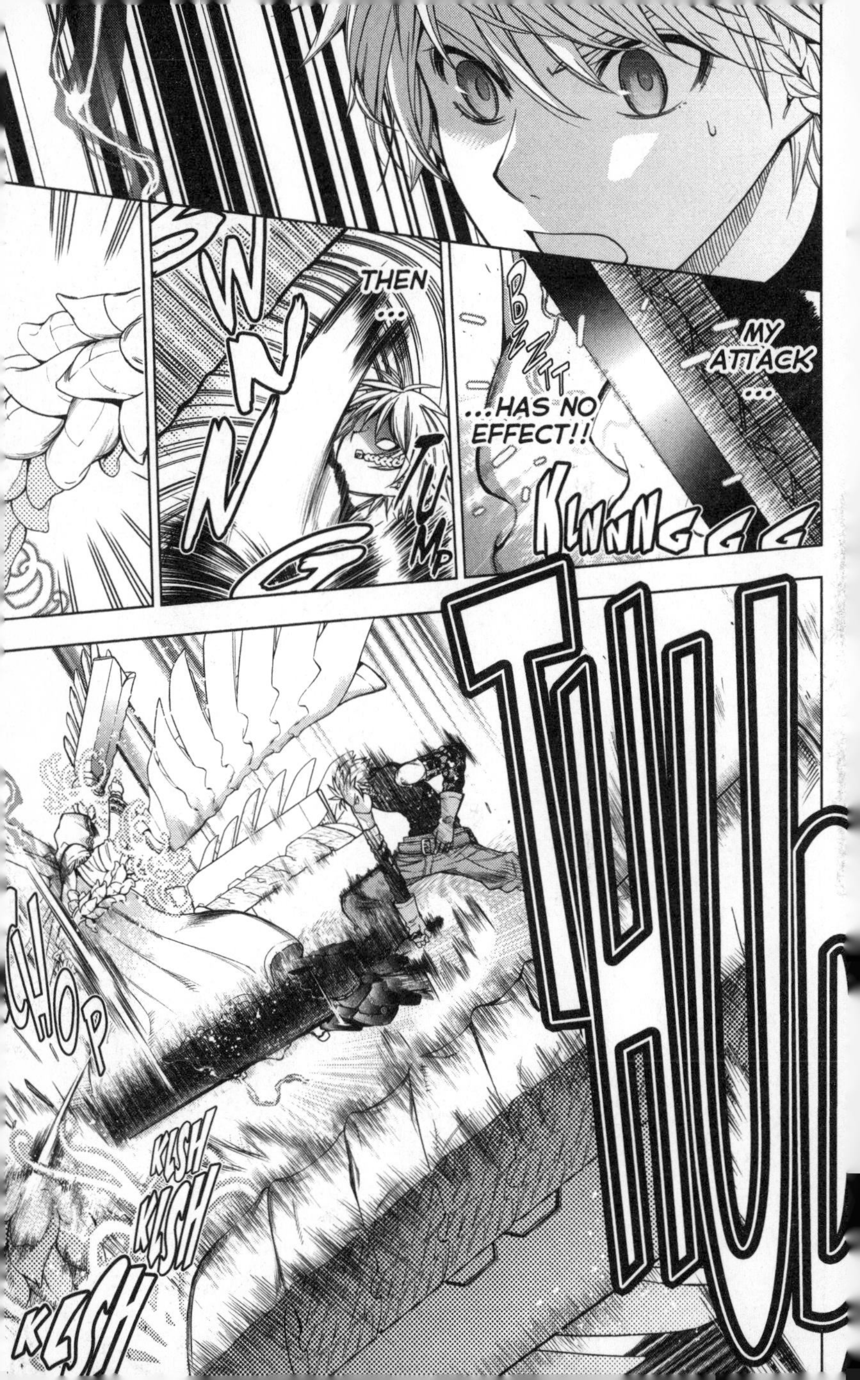

MY ATTACK...
...HAS NO EFFECT!!
BZZTT
KLNNNGGG
THEN...
SWNNG
JUMP
THUD
CHOP
KLSH
KLSH
KLCH

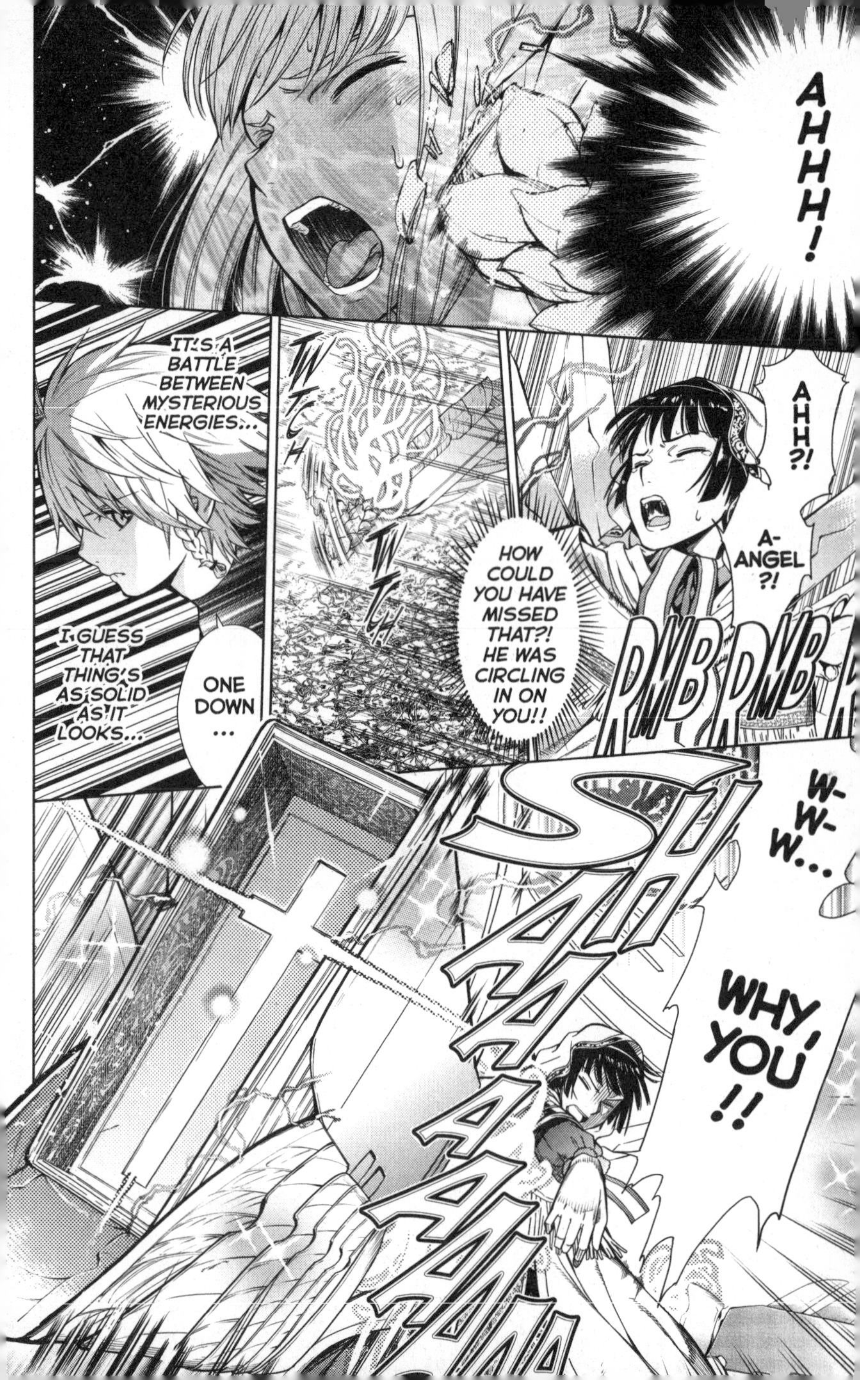
AHHH!
AHH?!
A-ANGEL?!
HOW COULD YOU HAVE MISSED THAT?! HE WAS CIRCLING IN ON YOU!!
RMB RMB
IT'S A BATTLE BETWEEN MYSTERIOUS ENERGIES...
ONE DOWN...
I GUESS THAT THING'S AS SOLID AS IT LOOKS...
W-W-W...
WHY, YOU!!
SHAAAAAA

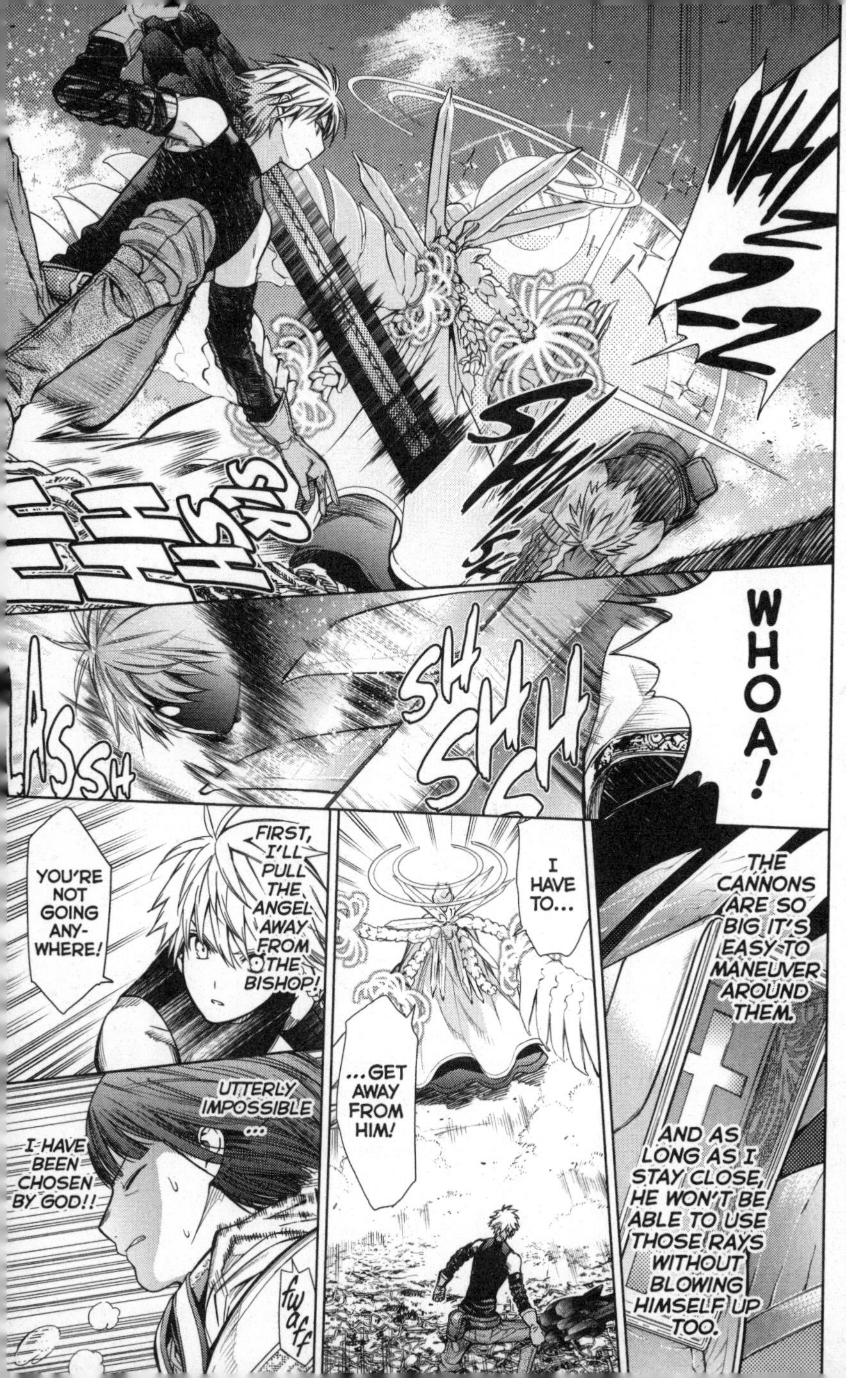
WHIZZZ
WHOA!
THE CANNONS ARE SO BIG IT'S EASY TO MANEUVER AROUND THEM.
AND AS LONG AS I STAY CLOSE, HE WON'T BE ABLE TO USE THOSE RAYS WITHOUT BLOWING HIMSELF UP TOO.
I HAVE TO...
...GET AWAY FROM HIM!
FIRST, I'LL PULL THE ANGEL AWAY FROM THE BISHOP!
YOU'RE NOT GOING ANYWHERE!
UTTERLY IMPOSSIBLE...
I HAVE BEEN CHOSEN BY GOD!!
fwaff

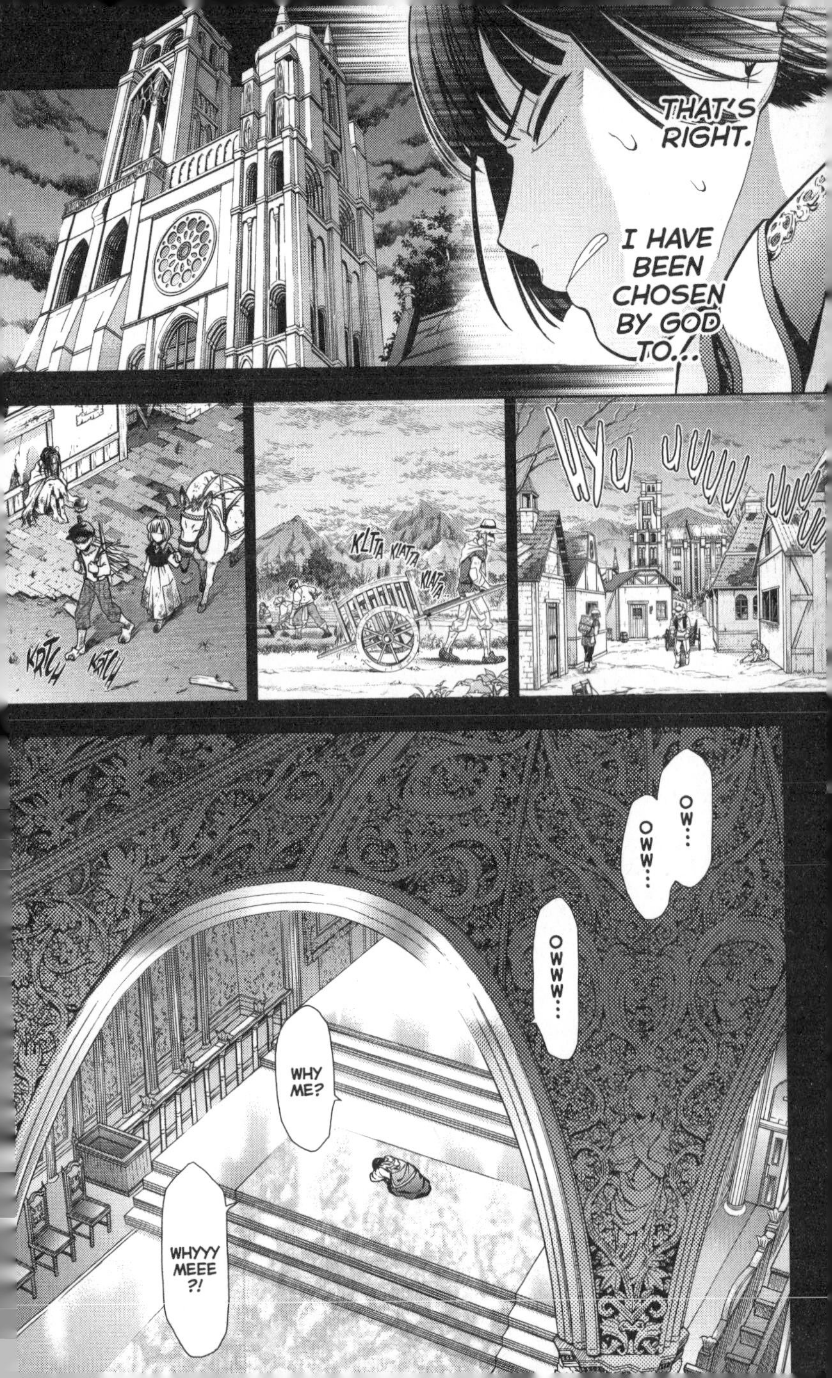
THAT'S RIGHT.
I HAVE BEEN CHOSEN BY GOD TO...
HYU UUUU UUU
KLTTA KLATTA KLATTA
KRTCH KRTCH
OW...
OWW...
OWWW...
WHY ME?
WHYYY MEEE?!

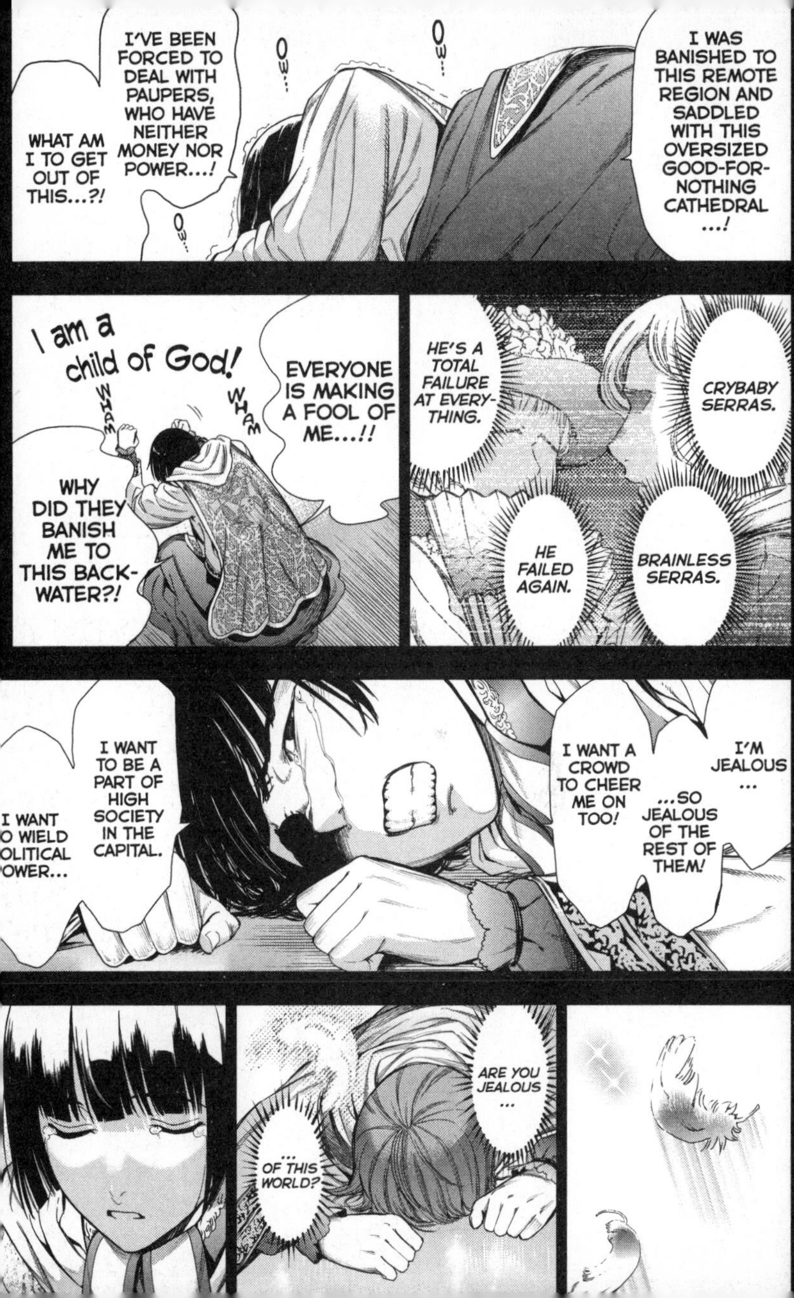
I WAS BANISHED TO THIS REMOTE REGION AND SADDLED WITH THIS OVERSIZED GOOD-FOR-NOTHING CATHEDRAL...!
OW...
OW...
I'VE BEEN FORCED TO DEAL WITH PAUPERS, WHO HAVE NEITHER MONEY NOR POWER...!
OW...
WHAT AM I TO GET OUT OF THIS...?!
CRYBABY SERRAS.
HE'S A TOTAL FAILURE AT EVERYTHING.
BRAINLESS SERRAS.
HE FAILED AGAIN.
EVERYONE IS MAKING A FOOL OF ME...!!
WHAM
WHAM
I am a child of God!
WHY DID THEY BANISH ME TO THIS BACKWATER?!
I'M JEALOUS...
...SO JEALOUS OF THE REST OF THEM!
I WANT A CROWD TO CHEER ME ON TOO!
I WANT TO BE A PART OF HIGH SOCIETY IN THE CAPITAL.
I WANT O WIELD OLITICAL OWER...
ARE YOU JEALOUS...
...OF THIS WORLD?

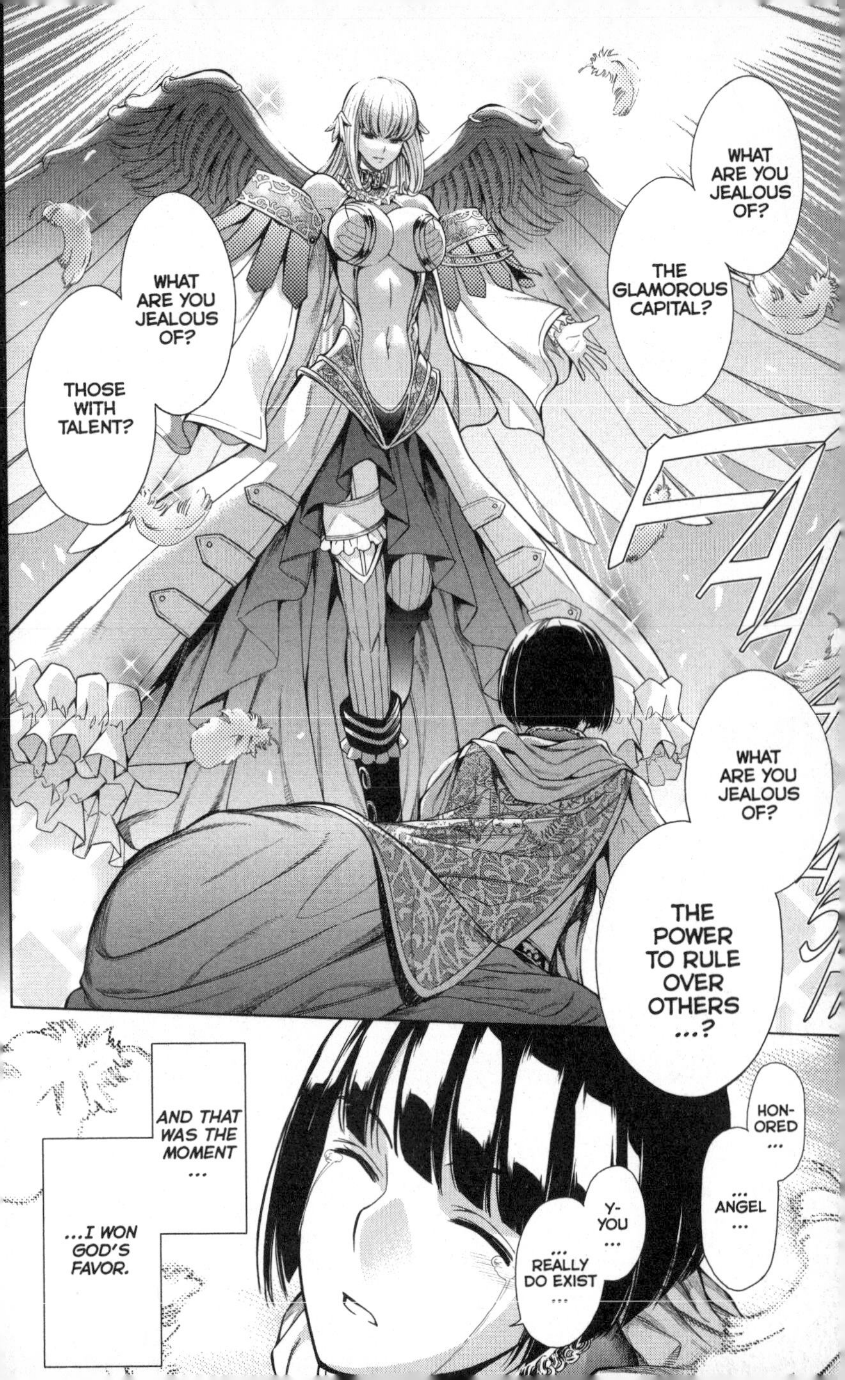
WHAT ARE YOU JEALOUS OF?
THE GLAMOROUS CAPITAL?
WHAT ARE YOU JEALOUS OF?
THOSE WITH TALENT?
WHAT ARE YOU JEALOUS OF?
THE POWER TO RULE OVER OTHERS ...?
HON-ORED ...
... ANGEL ...
Y-YOU ...
... REALLY DO EXIST ...
AND THAT WAS THE MOMENT ...
...I WON GOD'S FAVOR.

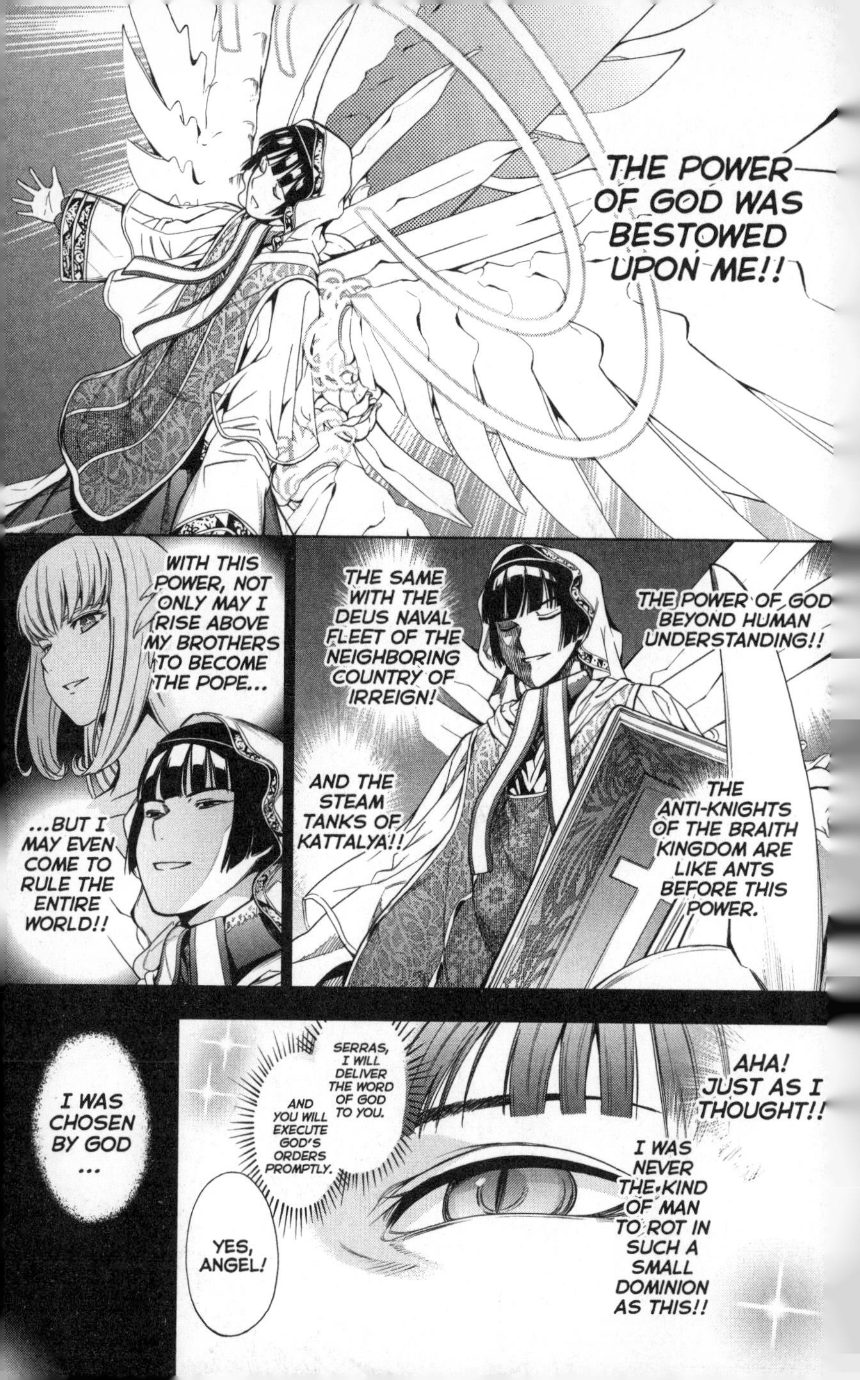
THE POWER OF GOD WAS BESTOWED UPON ME!!
THE POWER OF GOD BEYOND HUMAN UNDERSTANDING!!
THE ANTI-KNIGHTS OF THE BRAITH KINGDOM ARE LIKE ANTS BEFORE THIS POWER.
THE SAME WITH THE DEUS NAVAL FLEET OF THE NEIGHBORING COUNTRY OF IRREIGN!
AND THE STEAM TANKS OF KATTALYA!!
WITH THIS POWER, NOT ONLY MAY I RISE ABOVE MY BROTHERS TO BECOME THE POPE...
...BUT I MAY EVEN COME TO RULE THE ENTIRE WORLD!!
AHA! JUST AS I THOUGHT!!
I WAS NEVER THE KIND OF MAN TO ROT IN SUCH A SMALL DOMINION AS THIS!!
SERRAS, I WILL DELIVER THE WORD OF GOD TO YOU.
AND YOU WILL EXECUTE GOD'S ORDERS PROMPTLY.
YES, ANGEL!
I WAS CHOSEN BY GOD ...

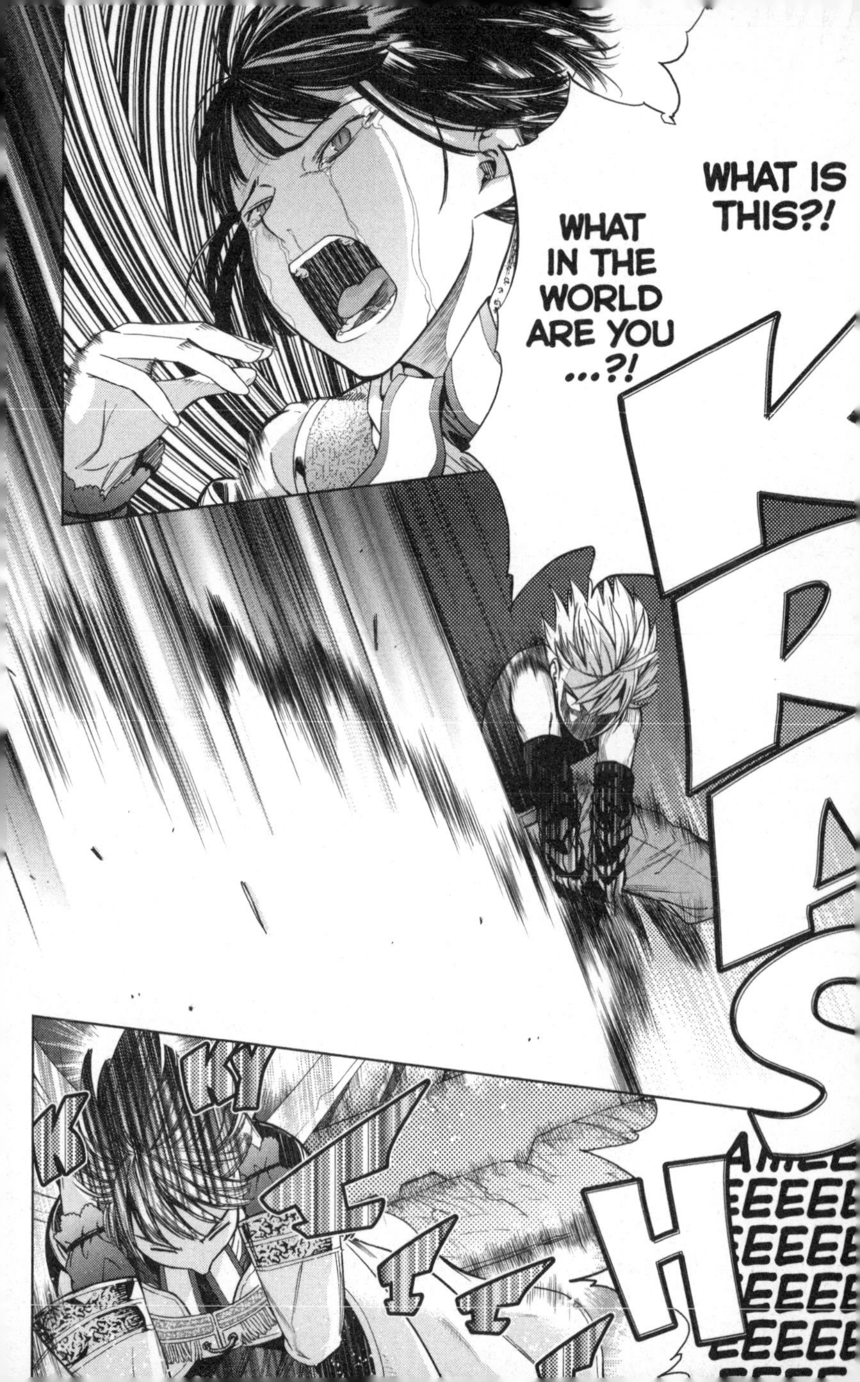
WHAT IS THIS?!
WHAT IN THE WORLD ARE YOU ...?!
KRASH
AHEEEEEEEEEEEEEEEEEEEEEEEEE
HIIIEEEE
KYAAAAAAAAH

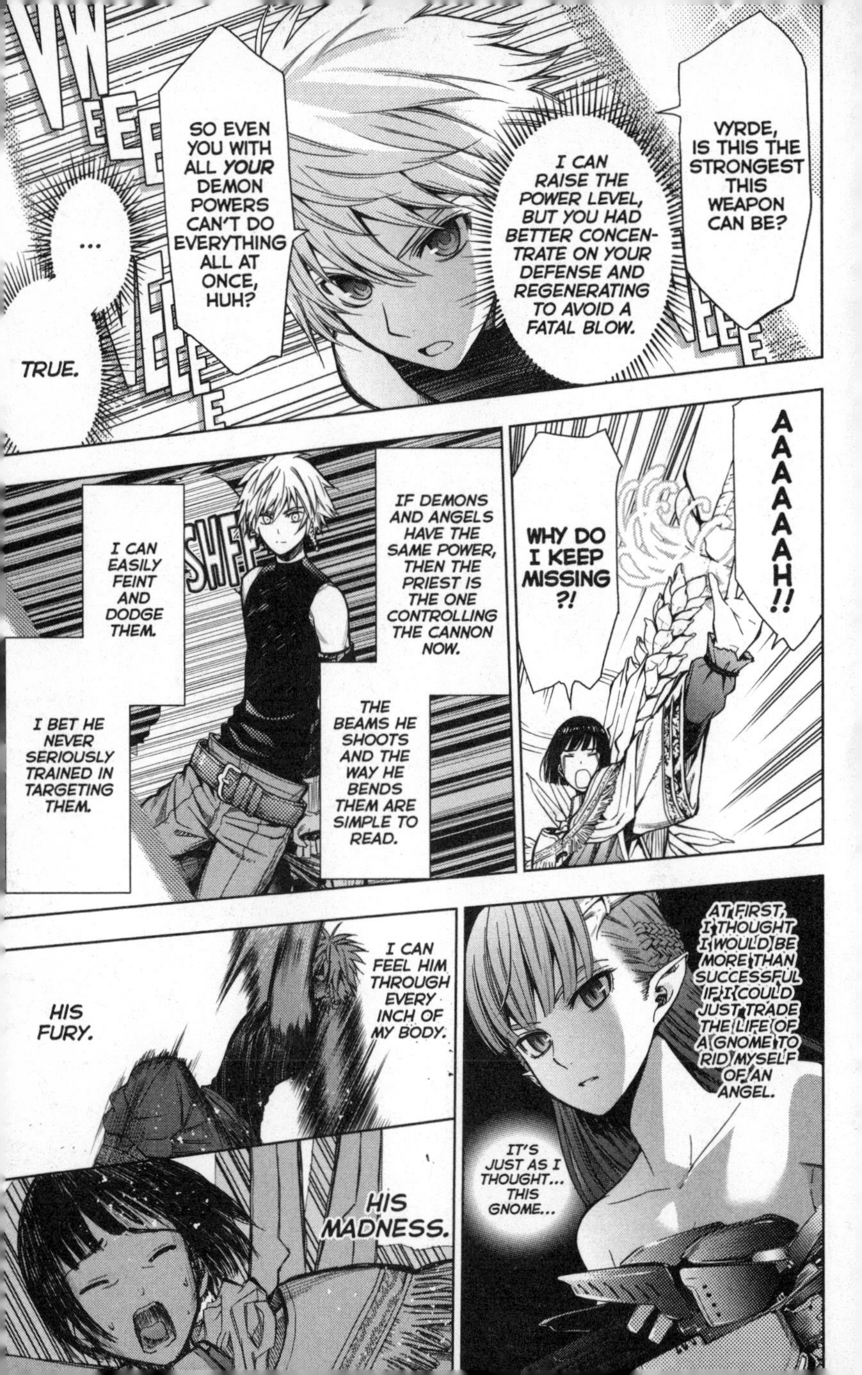
VYRDE, IS THIS THE STRONGEST THIS WEAPON CAN BE?
I CAN RAISE THE POWER LEVEL, BUT YOU HAD BETTER CONCENTRATE ON YOUR DEFENSE AND REGENERATING TO AVOID A FATAL BLOW.
SO EVEN YOU WITH ALL *YOUR* DEMON POWERS CAN'T DO EVERYTHING ALL AT ONCE, HUH?
VWEEE
...
TRUE.
AAAAAAAH!!
WHY DO I KEEP MISSING?!
IF DEMONS AND ANGELS HAVE THE SAME POWER, THEN THE PRIEST IS THE ONE CONTROLLING THE CANNON NOW.
THE BEAMS HE SHOOTS AND THE WAY HE BENDS THEM ARE SIMPLE TO READ.
SHFF
I CAN EASILY FEINT AND DODGE THEM.
I BET HE NEVER SERIOUSLY TRAINED IN TARGETING THEM.
AT FIRST, I THOUGHT I WOULD BE MORE THAN SUCCESSFUL IF I COULD JUST TRADE THE LIFE OF A GNOME TO RID MYSELF OF AN ANGEL.
IT'S JUST AS I THOUGHT... THIS GNOME...
I CAN FEEL HIM THROUGH EVERY INCH OF MY BODY.
HIS FURY.
HIS MADNESS.

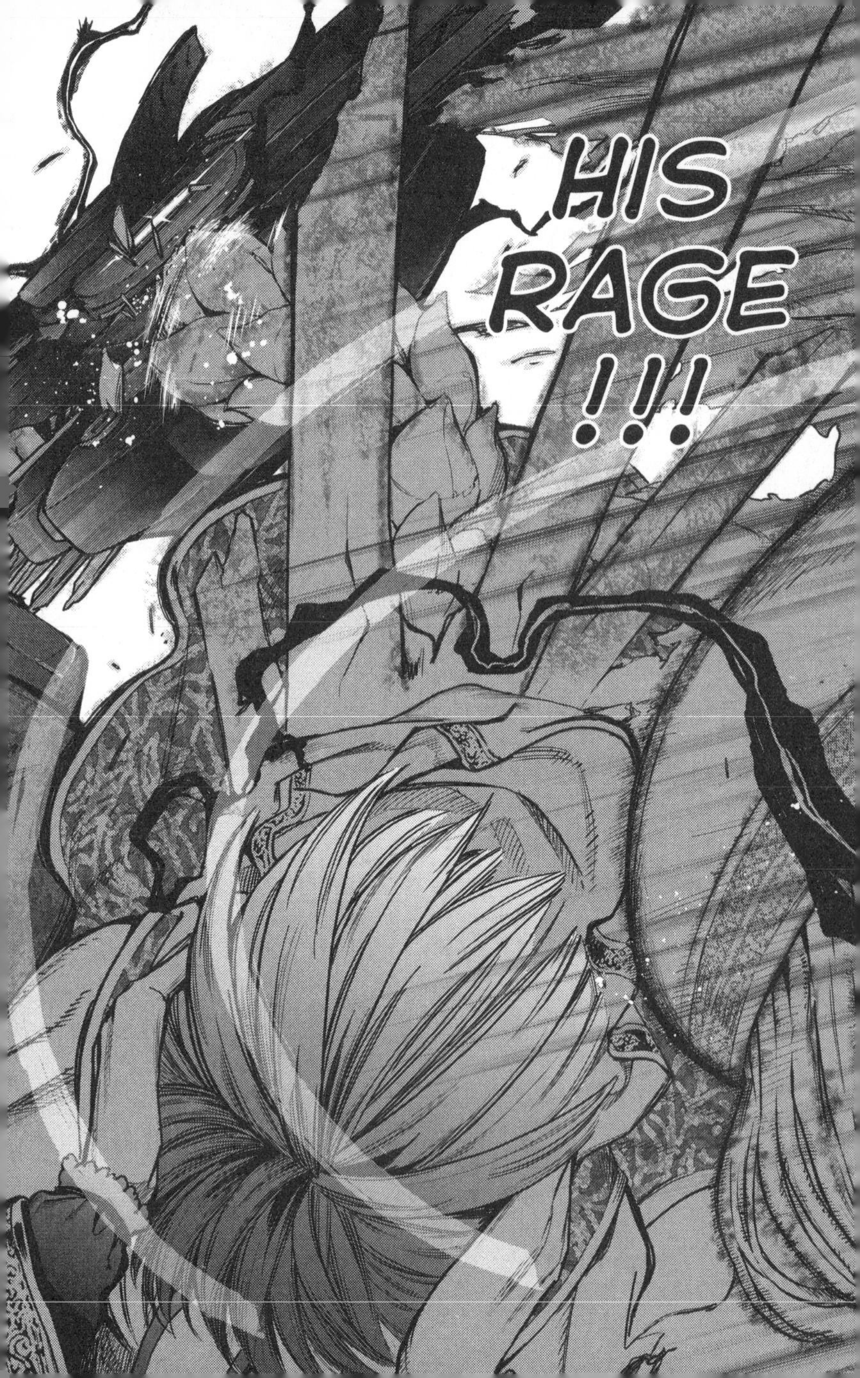
HIS RAGE !!!

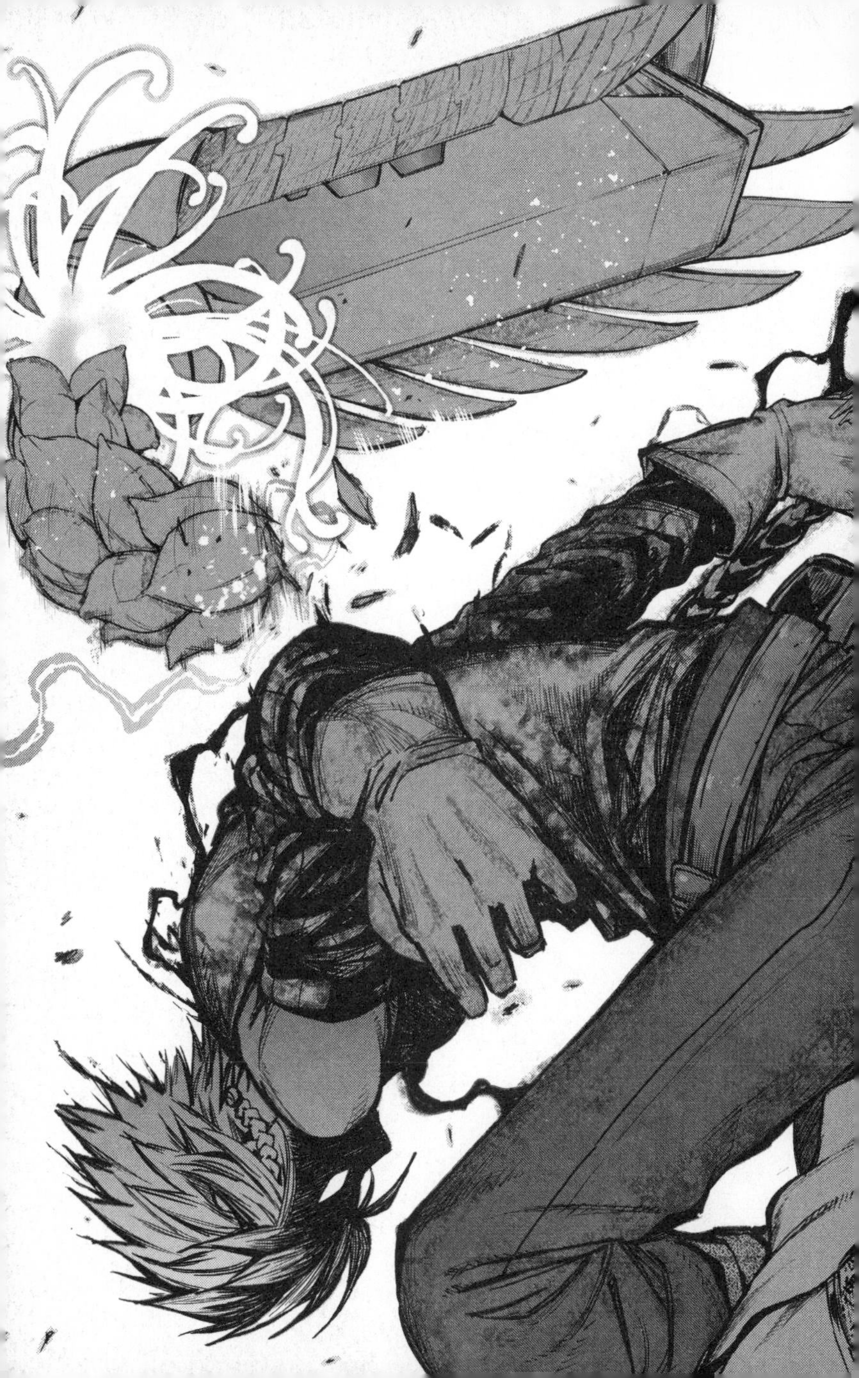

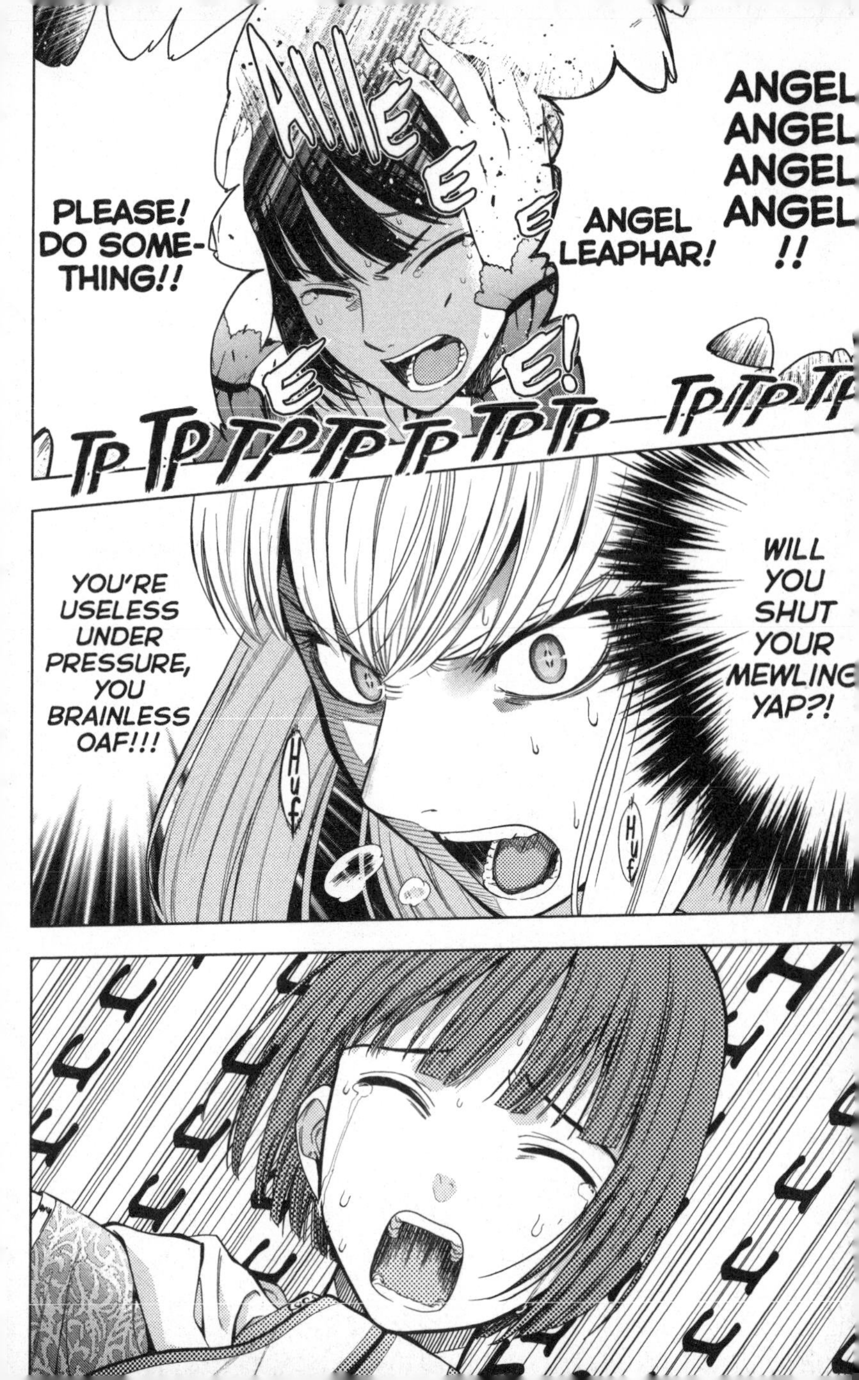
ANGEL ANGEL ANGEL ANGEL!!
ANGEL LEAPHAR!
AIIIEEEE!
PLEASE! DO SOME-THING!!
TP TP TP TP TP TP TP TP TP TP TP
WILL YOU SHUT YOUR MEWLING YAP?!
Huf
YOU'RE USELESS UNDER PRESSURE, YOU BRAINLESS OAF!!!
Huf

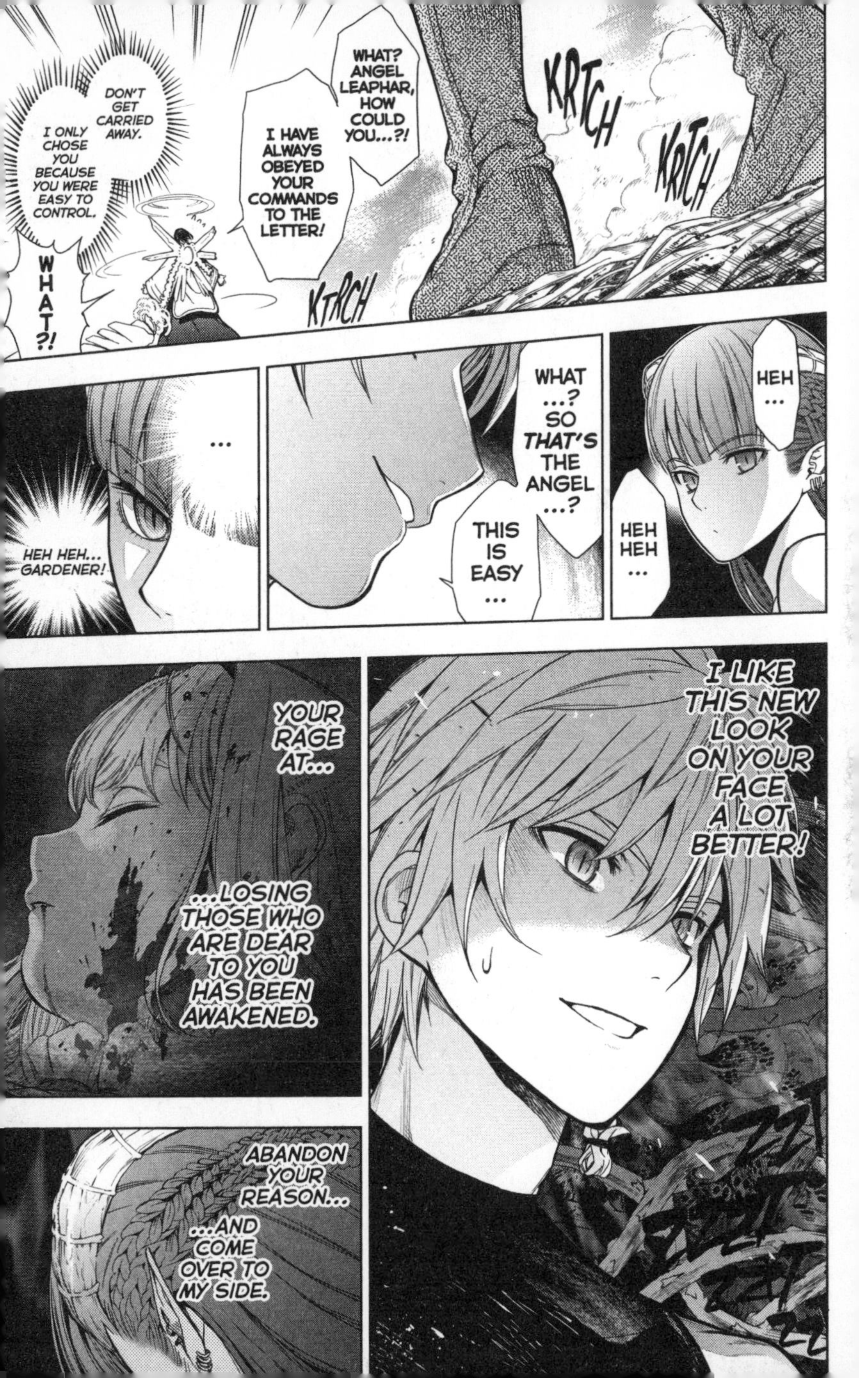
KRTCH
KRTCH
WHAT? ANGEL LEAPHAR, HOW COULD YOU...?!
I HAVE ALWAYS OBEYED YOUR COMMANDS TO THE LETTER!
KTRCH
DON'T GET CARRIED AWAY.
I ONLY CHOSE YOU BECAUSE YOU WERE EASY TO CONTROL.
WHAT?!
HEH...
HEH HEH...
WHAT...? SO *THAT'S* THE ANGEL...?
THIS IS EASY...
...
HEH HEH... GARDENER!
I LIKE THIS NEW LOOK ON YOUR FACE A LOT BETTER!
YOUR RAGE AT...
...LOSING THOSE WHO ARE DEAR TO YOU HAS BEEN AWAKENED.
ABANDON YOUR REASON...
...AND COME OVER TO MY SIDE.

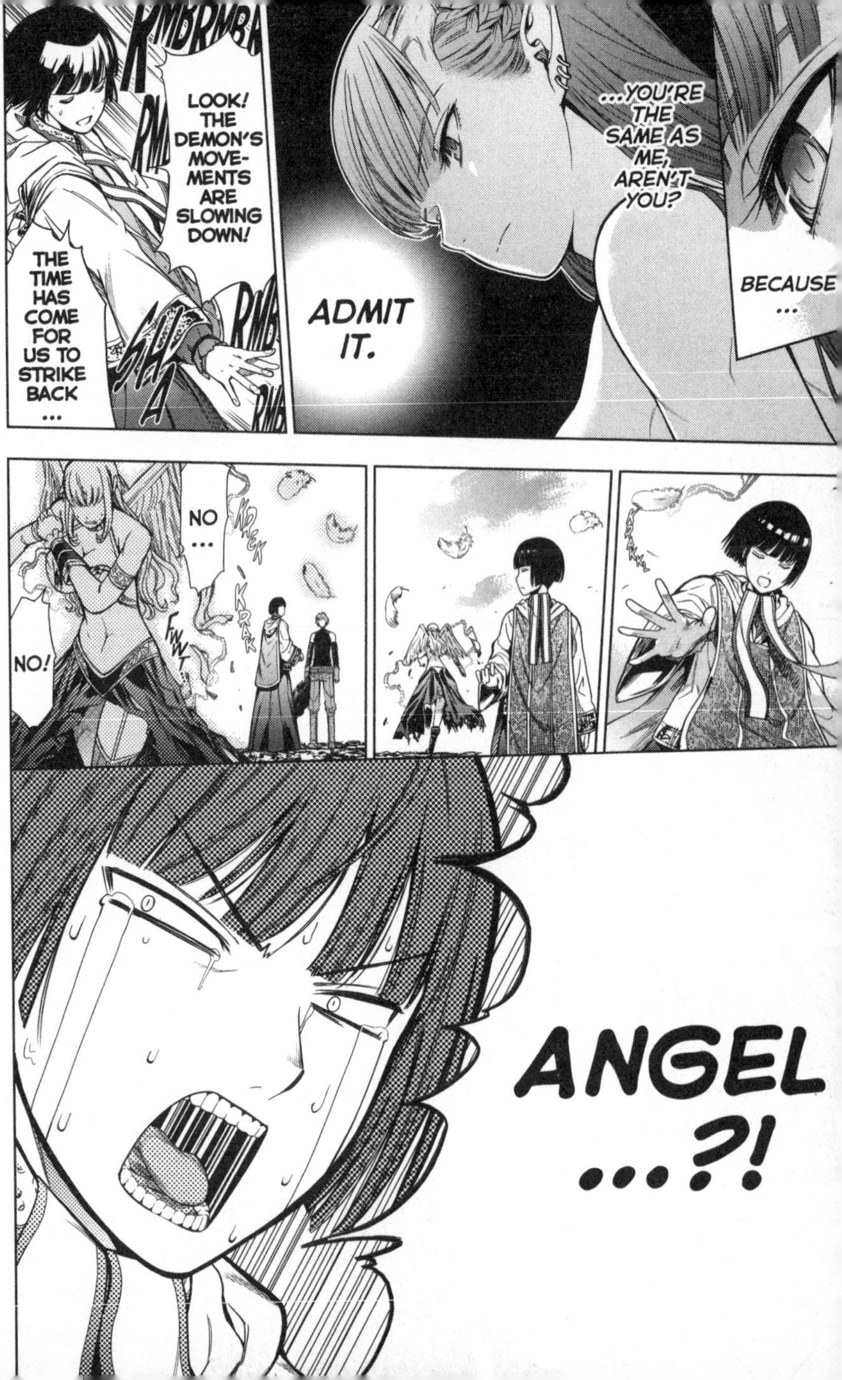
BECAUSE ...
...YOU'RE THE SAME AS ME, AREN'T YOU?
ADMIT IT.
RMBRMBA
LOOK! THE DEMON'S MOVEMENTS ARE SLOWING DOWN!
RMB
THE TIME HAS COME FOR US TO STRIKE BACK ...
KRAKKL
NO ...
KREK
KRAK
FWWT
NO!
ANGEL ...?!

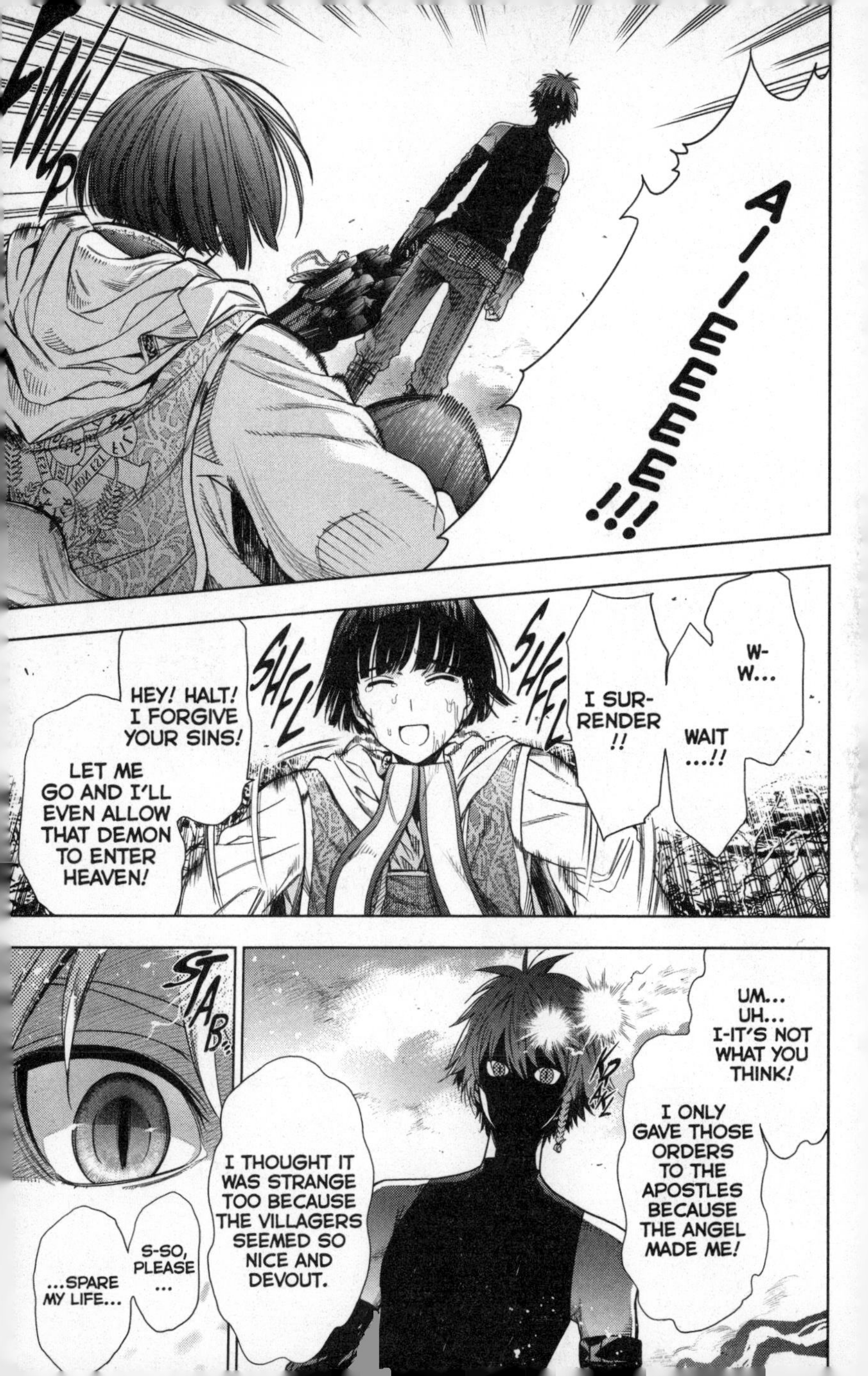
AIIEEEEE!!!
FWUP
W-W... WAIT...!!
I SUR-RENDER!!
SHFFL
SHFL
HEY! HALT! I FORGIVE YOUR SINS!
LET ME GO AND I'LL EVEN ALLOW THAT DEMON TO ENTER HEAVEN!
UM... UH... I-IT'S NOT WHAT YOU THINK!
I ONLY GAVE THOSE ORDERS TO THE APOSTLES BECAUSE THE ANGEL MADE ME!
I THOUGHT IT WAS STRANGE TOO BECAUSE THE VILLAGERS SEEMED SO NICE AND DEVOUT.
STAB...
S-SO, PLEASE...
...SPARE MY LIFE...

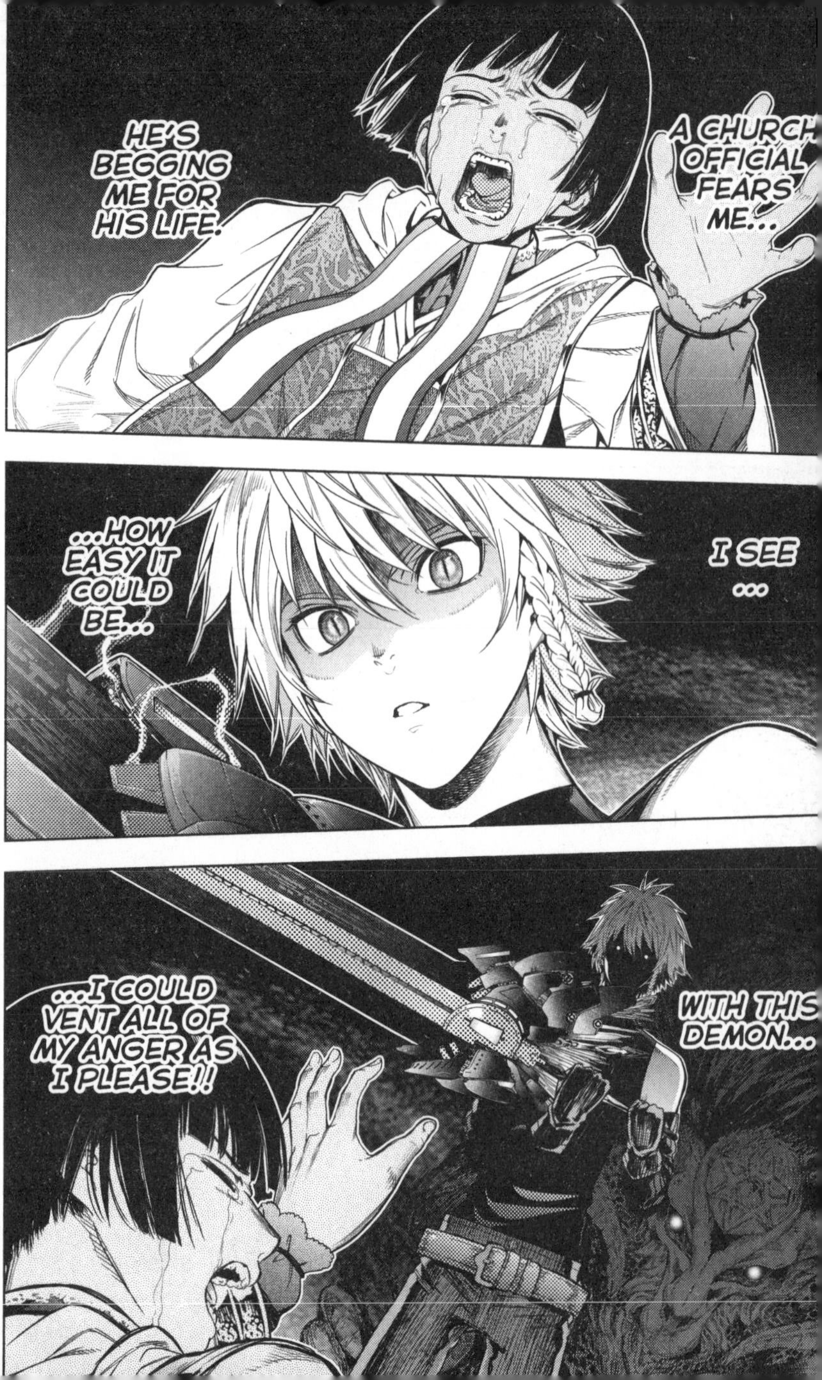
A CHURCH OFFICIAL FEARS ME...
HE'S BEGGING ME FOR HIS LIFE.
I SEE ...
...HOW EASY IT COULD BE...
WITH THIS DEMON...
...I COULD VENT ALL OF MY ANGER AS I PLEASE!!

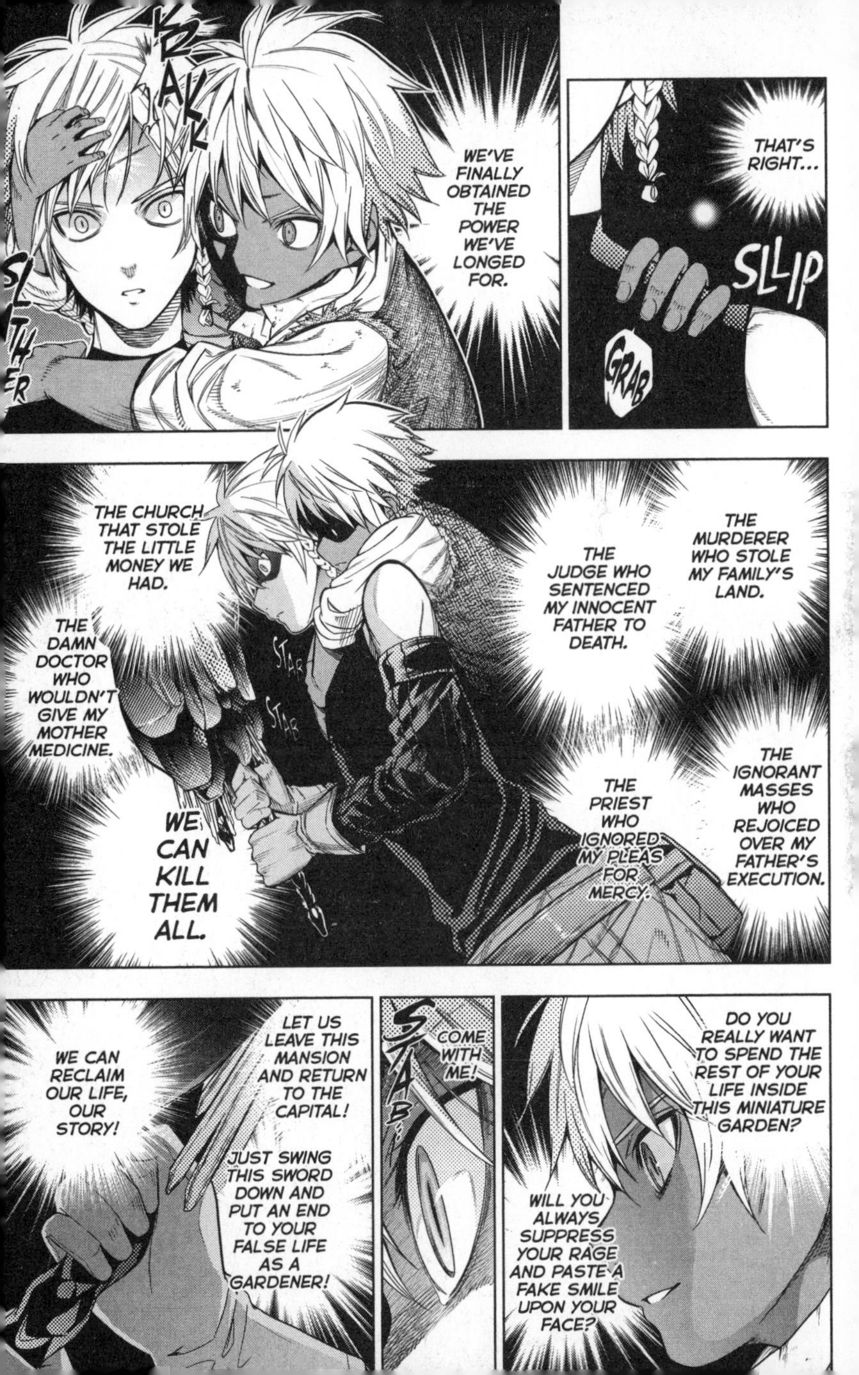
THAT'S RIGHT...
SLLIP
GRAB
KRAKK
WE'VE FINALLY OBTAINED THE POWER WE'VE LONGED FOR.
SLITHER
THE MURDERER WHO STOLE MY FAMILY'S LAND.
THE JUDGE WHO SENTENCED MY INNOCENT FATHER TO DEATH.
THE CHURCH THAT STOLE THE LITTLE MONEY WE HAD.
THE IGNORANT MASSES WHO REJOICED OVER MY FATHER'S EXECUTION.
THE PRIEST WHO IGNORED MY PLEAS FOR MERCY.
THE DAMN DOCTOR WHO WOULDN'T GIVE MY MOTHER MEDICINE.
STAB
STAB
WE CAN KILL THEM ALL.
DO YOU REALLY WANT TO SPEND THE REST OF YOUR LIFE INSIDE THIS MINIATURE GARDEN?
WILL YOU ALWAYS SUPPRESS YOUR RAGE AND PASTE A FAKE SMILE UPON YOUR FACE?
STAB!
COME WITH ME!
LET US LEAVE THIS MANSION AND RETURN TO THE CAPITAL!
WE CAN RECLAIM OUR LIFE, OUR STORY!
JUST SWING THIS SWORD DOWN AND PUT AN END TO YOUR FALSE LIFE AS A GARDENER!

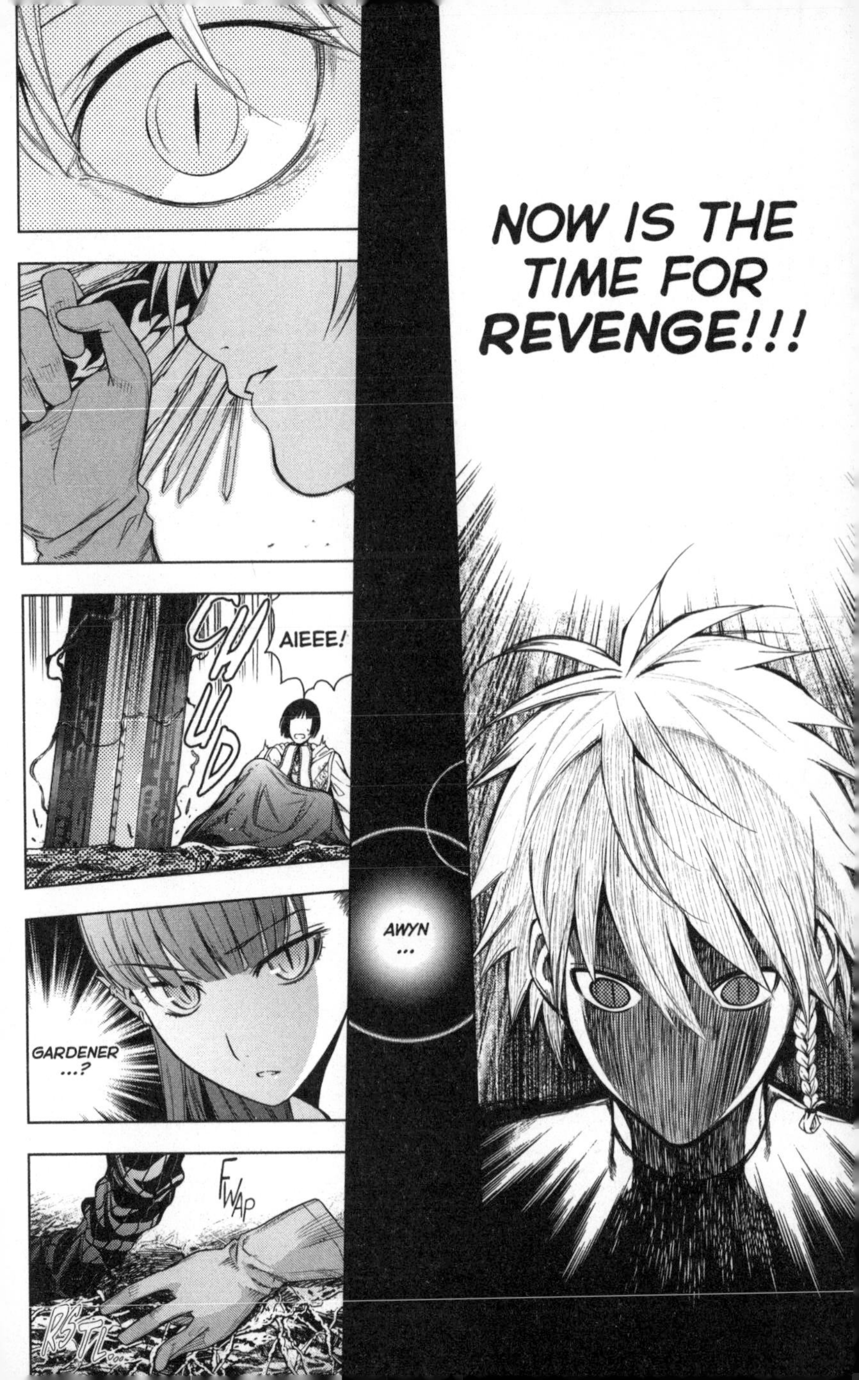
NOW IS THE TIME FOR REVENGE!!!
AWYN ...
CHUD
AIEEE!
GARDENER ...?
FWAP
RSTL...

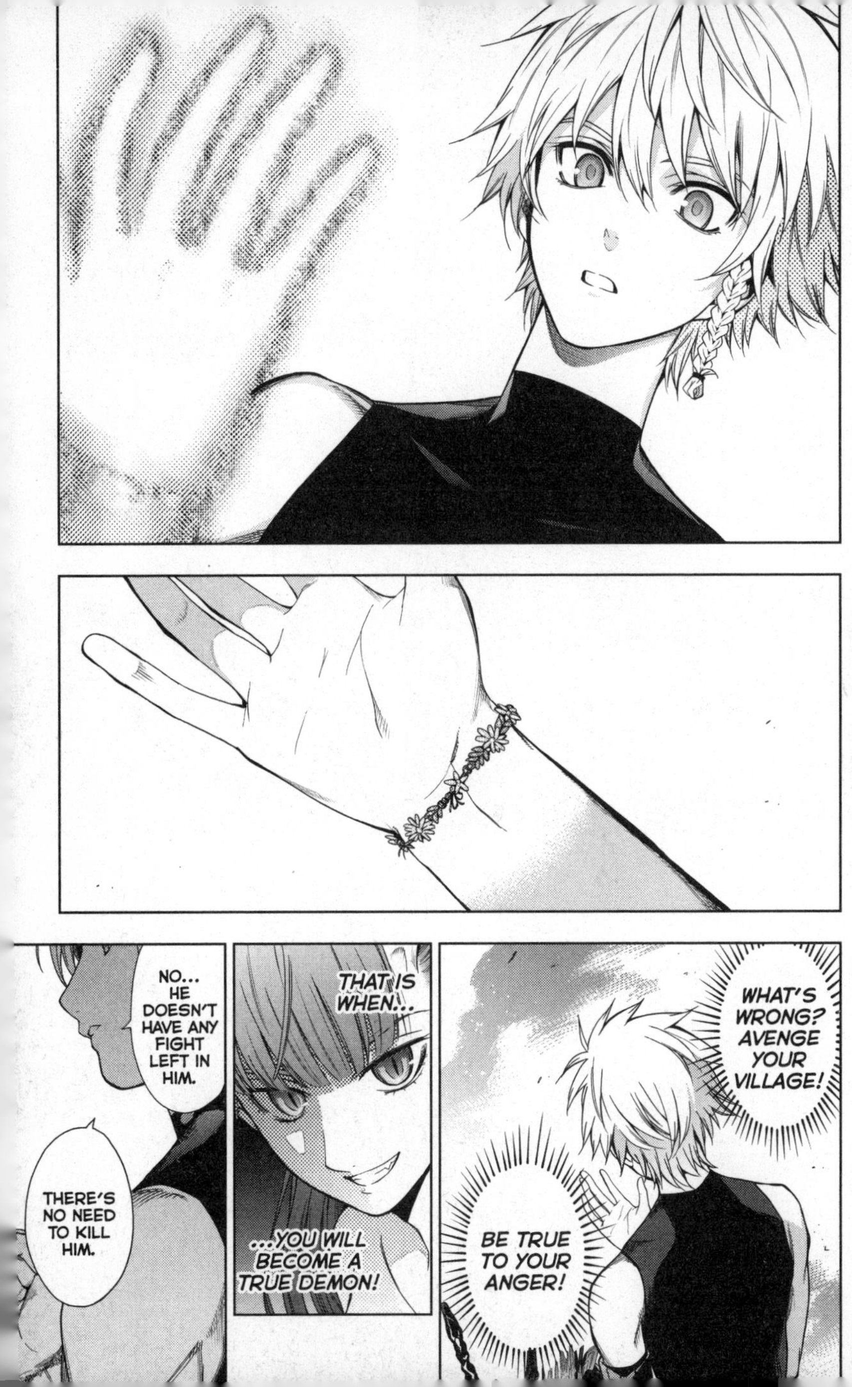
WHAT'S WRONG? AVENGE YOUR VILLAGE!
BE TRUE TO YOUR ANGER!
THAT IS WHEN...
...YOU WILL BECOME A TRUE DEMON!
NO... HE DOESN'T HAVE ANY FIGHT LEFT IN HIM.
THERE'S NO NEED TO KILL HIM.

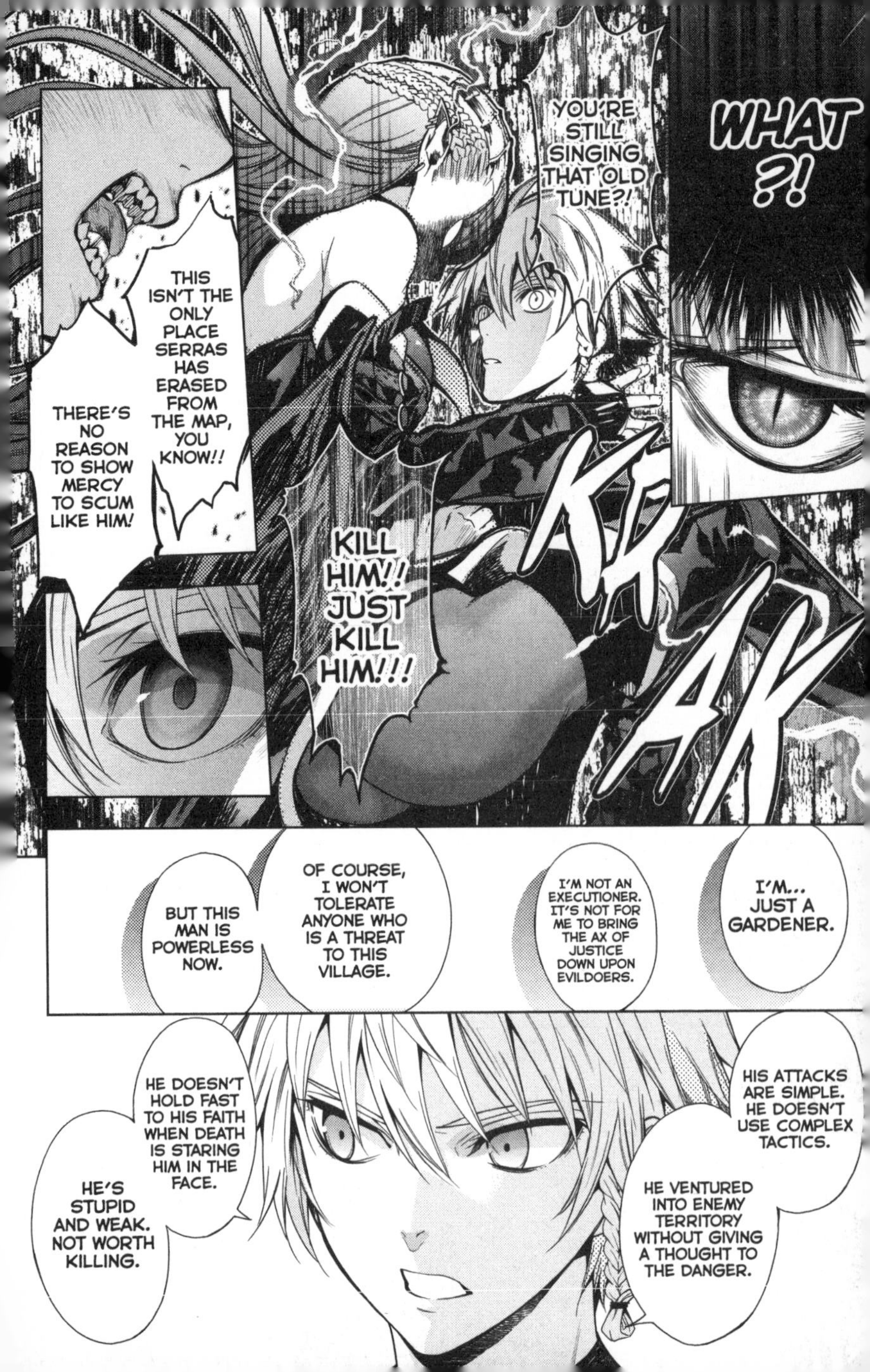
WHAT ?!
YOU'RE STILL SINGING THAT OLD TUNE?!
THIS ISN'T THE ONLY PLACE SERRAS HAS ERASED FROM THE MAP, YOU KNOW!!
THERE'S NO REASON TO SHOW MERCY TO SCUM LIKE HIM!
KILL HIM!! JUST KILL HIM!!!
I'M... JUST A GARDENER.
I'M NOT AN EXECUTIONER. IT'S NOT FOR ME TO BRING THE AX OF JUSTICE DOWN UPON EVILDOERS.
OF COURSE, I WON'T TOLERATE ANYONE WHO IS A THREAT TO THIS VILLAGE.
BUT THIS MAN IS POWERLESS NOW.
HIS ATTACKS ARE SIMPLE. HE DOESN'T USE COMPLEX TACTICS.
HE VENTURED INTO ENEMY TERRITORY WITHOUT GIVING A THOUGHT TO THE DANGER.
HE DOESN'T HOLD FAST TO HIS FAITH WHEN DEATH IS STARING HIM IN THE FACE.
HE'S STUPID AND WEAK. NOT WORTH KILLING.

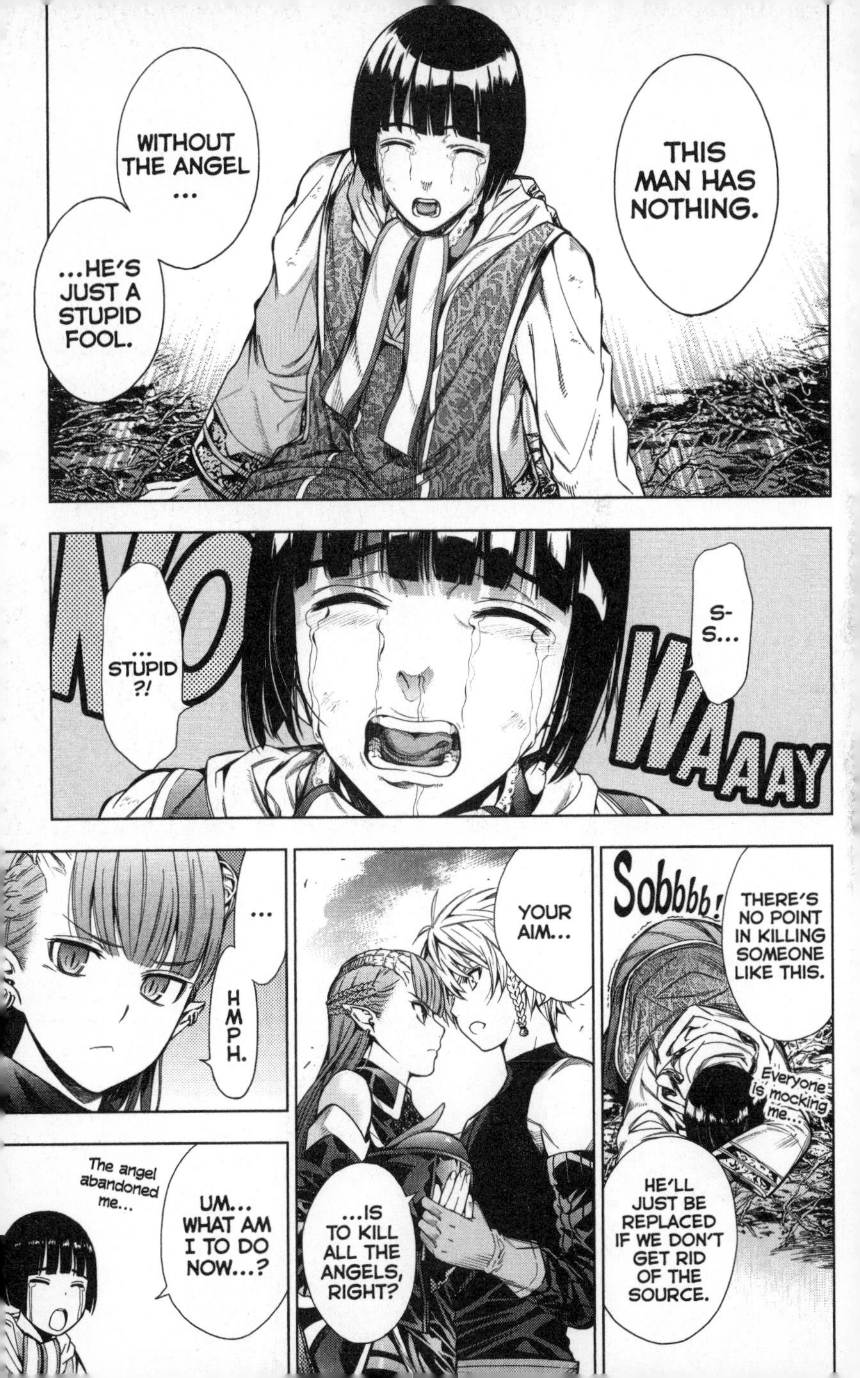
THIS MAN HAS NOTHING.
WITHOUT THE ANGEL ...
...HE'S JUST A STUPID FOOL.
S- S...
WAAAY
... STUPID ?!
Sobbbb!
THERE'S NO POINT IN KILLING SOMEONE LIKE THIS.
Everyone is mocking me...
HE'LL JUST BE REPLACED IF WE DON'T GET RID OF THE SOURCE.
YOUR AIM...
...IS TO KILL ALL THE ANGELS, RIGHT?
...
HMPH.
UM... WHAT AM I TO DO NOW...?
The angel abandoned me...

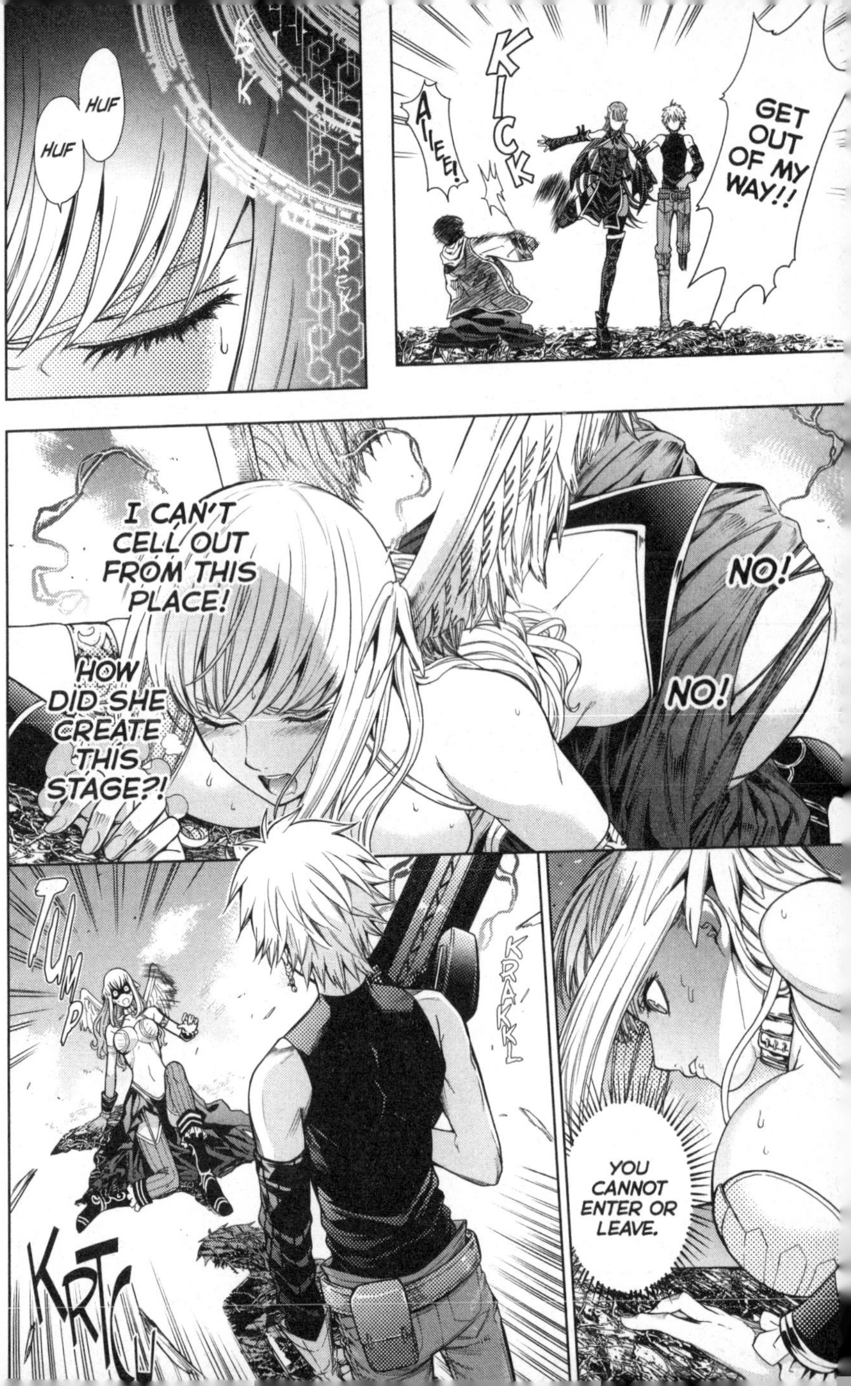
GET OUT OF MY WAY!!
KICK
AIIEE!
HUF
HUF
KRK
KREK
NO!
NO!
I CAN'T CELL OUT FROM THIS PLACE!
HOW DID SHE CREATE THIS STAGE?!
YOU CANNOT ENTER OR LEAVE.
KRAKKL
TUMP
KRTCH

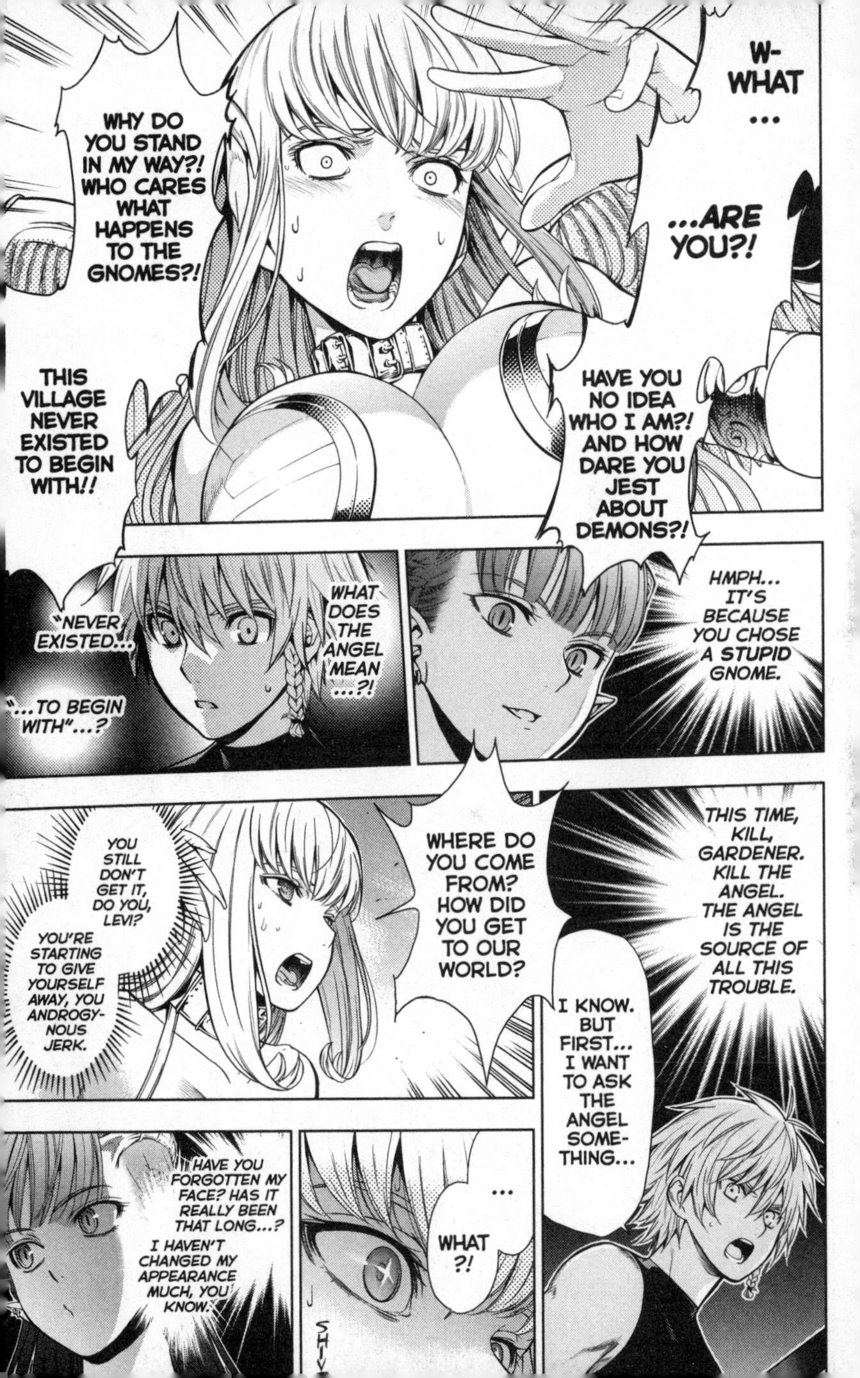
W- WHAT ...
...ARE YOU?!
WHY DO YOU STAND IN MY WAY?! WHO CARES WHAT HAPPENS TO THE GNOMES?!
THIS VILLAGE NEVER EXISTED TO BEGIN WITH!!
HAVE YOU NO IDEA WHO I AM?! AND HOW DARE YOU JEST ABOUT DEMONS?!
HMPH... IT'S BECAUSE YOU CHOSE A STUPID GNOME.
WHAT DOES THE ANGEL MEAN ...?!
"NEVER EXISTED...
"...TO BEGIN WITH"...?
THIS TIME, KILL, GARDENER. KILL THE ANGEL. THE ANGEL IS THE SOURCE OF ALL THIS TROUBLE.
WHERE DO YOU COME FROM? HOW DID YOU GET TO OUR WORLD?
YOU STILL DON'T GET IT, DO YOU, LEVI?
YOU'RE STARTING TO GIVE YOURSELF AWAY, YOU ANDROGY-NOUS JERK.
I KNOW. BUT FIRST... I WANT TO ASK THE ANGEL SOME-THING...
...
WHAT ?!
SHIV
HAVE YOU FORGOTTEN MY FACE? HAS IT REALLY BEEN THAT LONG...?
I HAVEN'T CHANGED MY APPEARANCE MUCH, YOU KNOW.

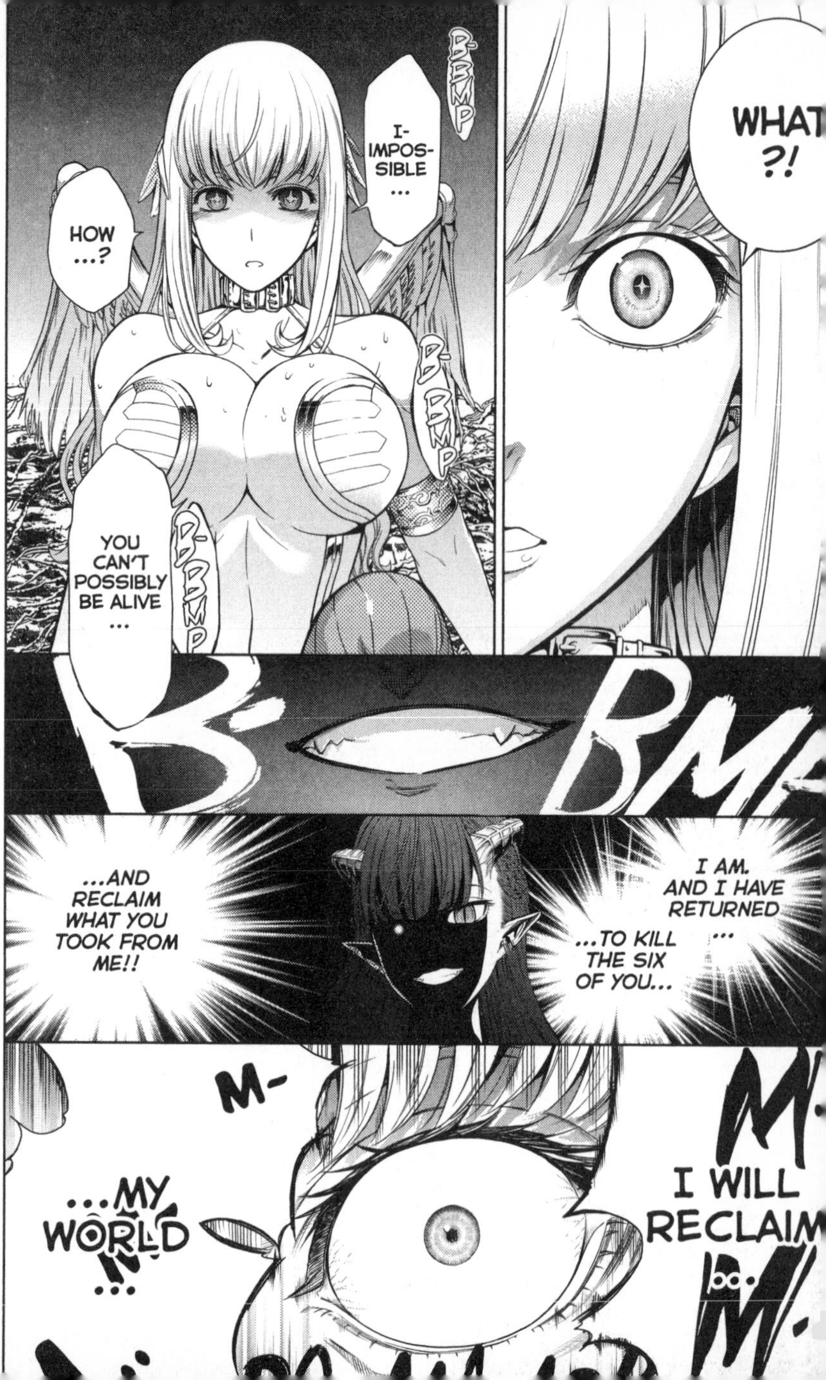
WHAT ?!
B-B-BMP
I-IMPOS-SIBLE ...
HOW ...?
B-B-BMP
B-B-BMP
YOU CAN'T POSSIBLY BE ALIVE ...
BM
I AM. AND I HAVE RETURNED ...
...TO KILL THE SIX OF YOU...
...AND RECLAIM WHAT YOU TOOK FROM ME!!
M-
I WILL RECLAIM ...
M-
M-
...MY WORLD!! ...

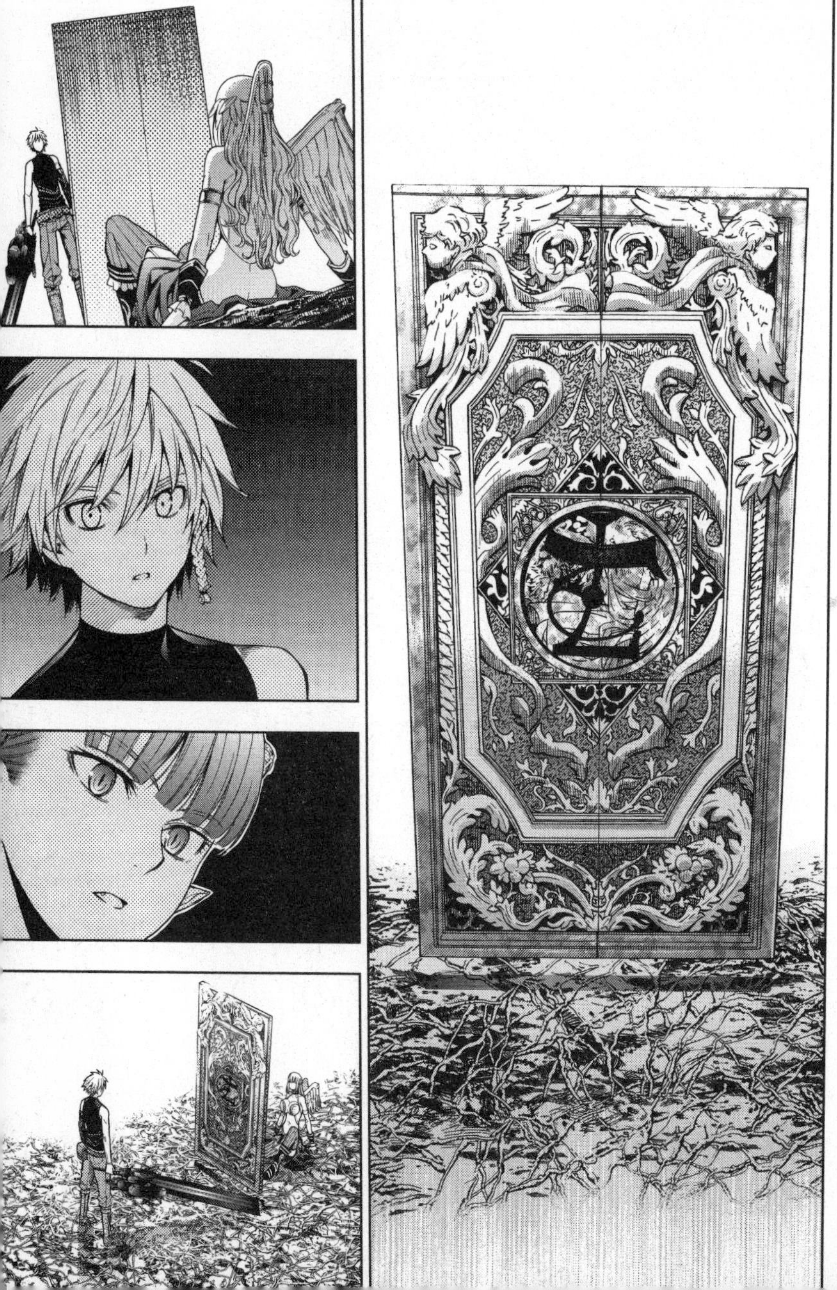

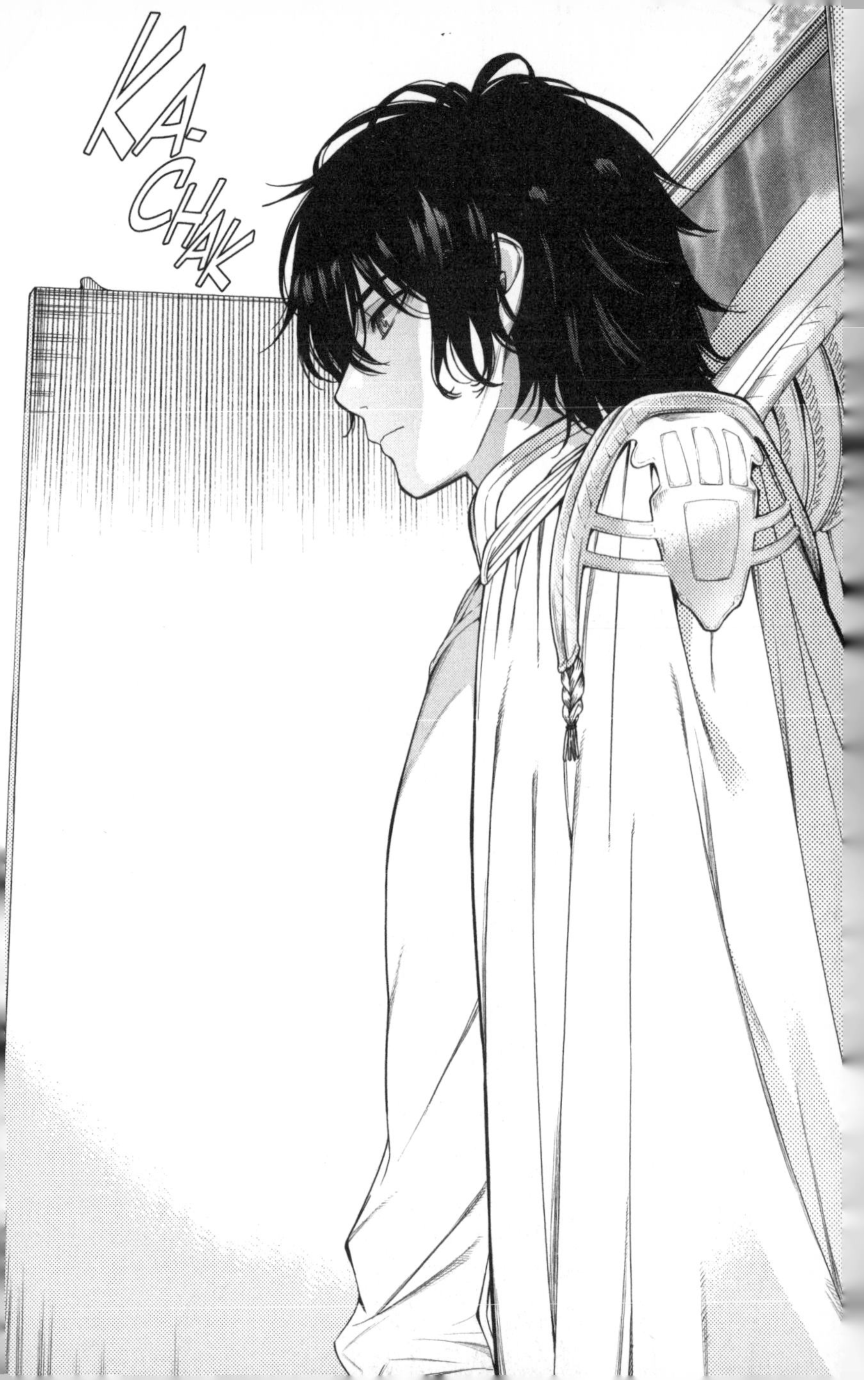
KA-CHAK

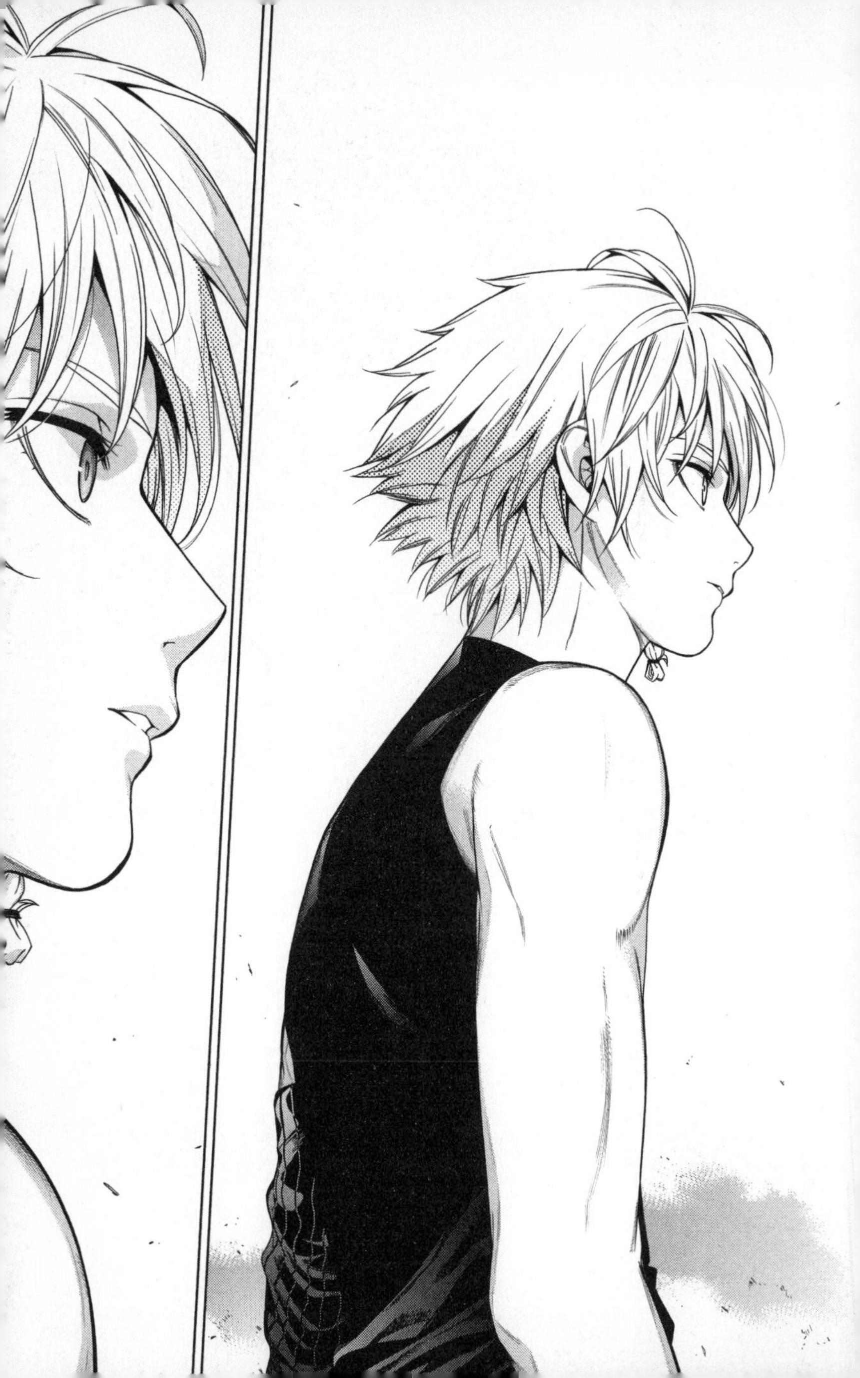

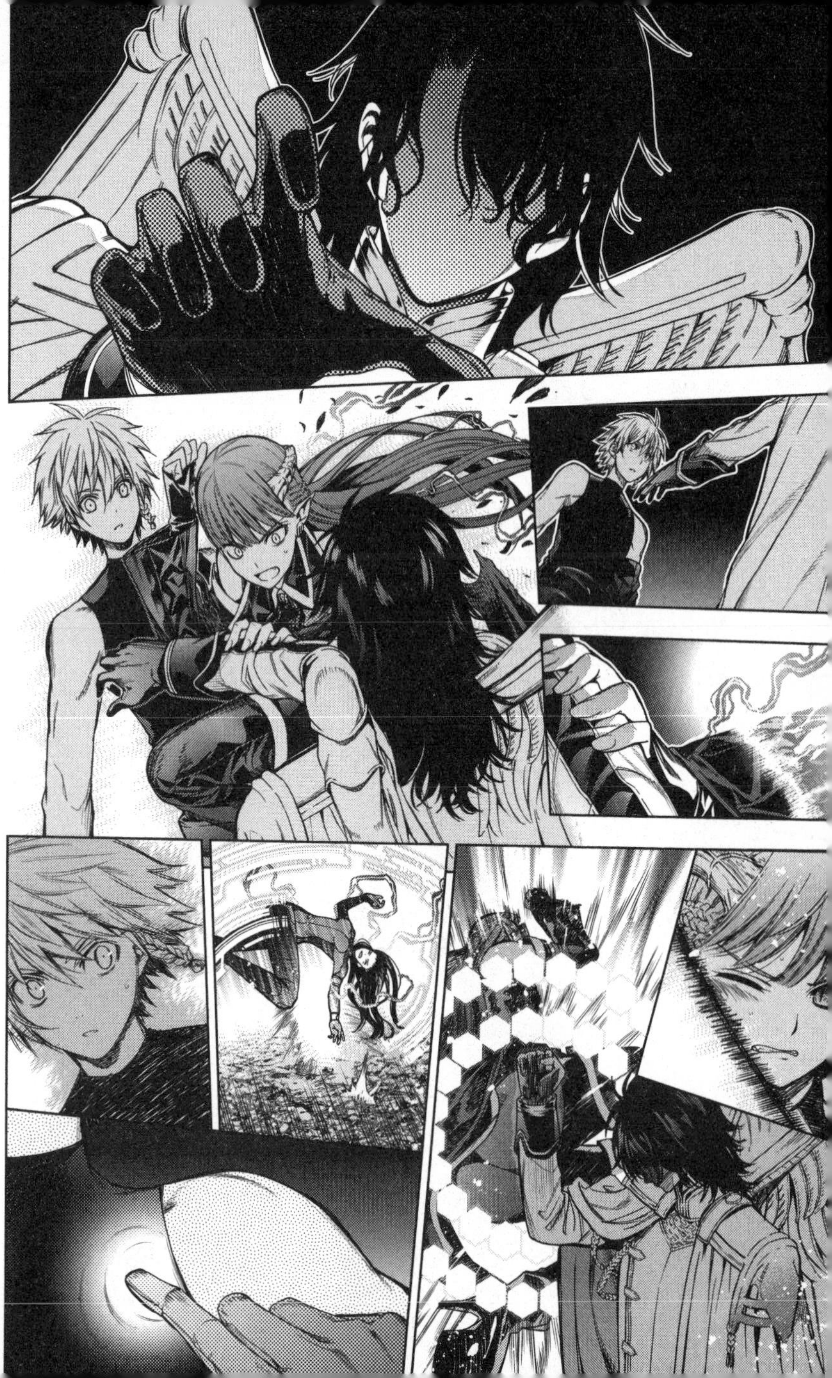

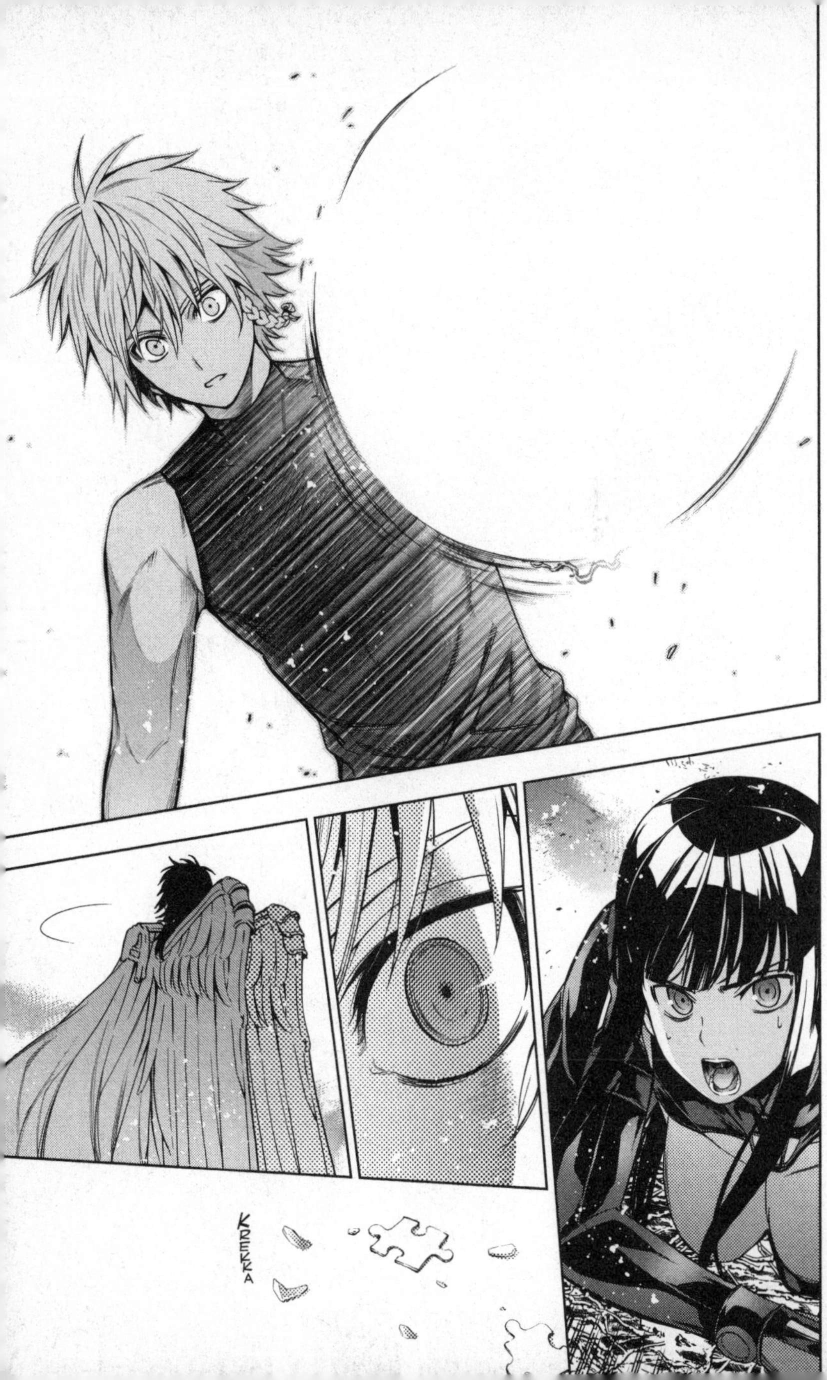
KREKKA

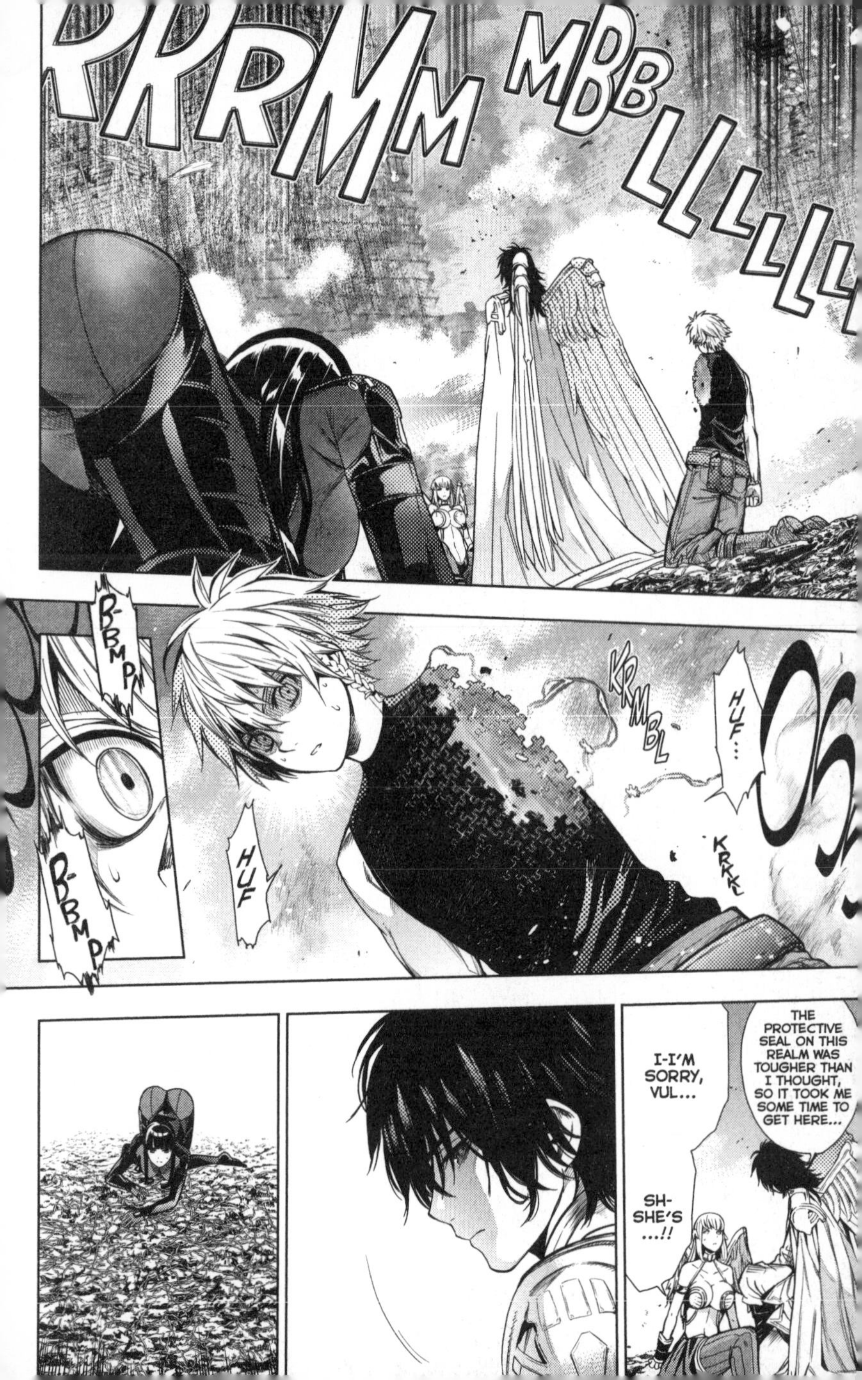
RRRMMM MDBBLLLLL
HUF...
KRMBL
KRAKL
HUF
B-BMP
B-BMP
THE PROTECTIVE SEAL ON THIS REALM WAS TOUGHER THAN I THOUGHT, SO IT TOOK ME SOME TIME TO GET HERE...
I-I'M SORRY, VUL...
SH-SHE'S ...!!

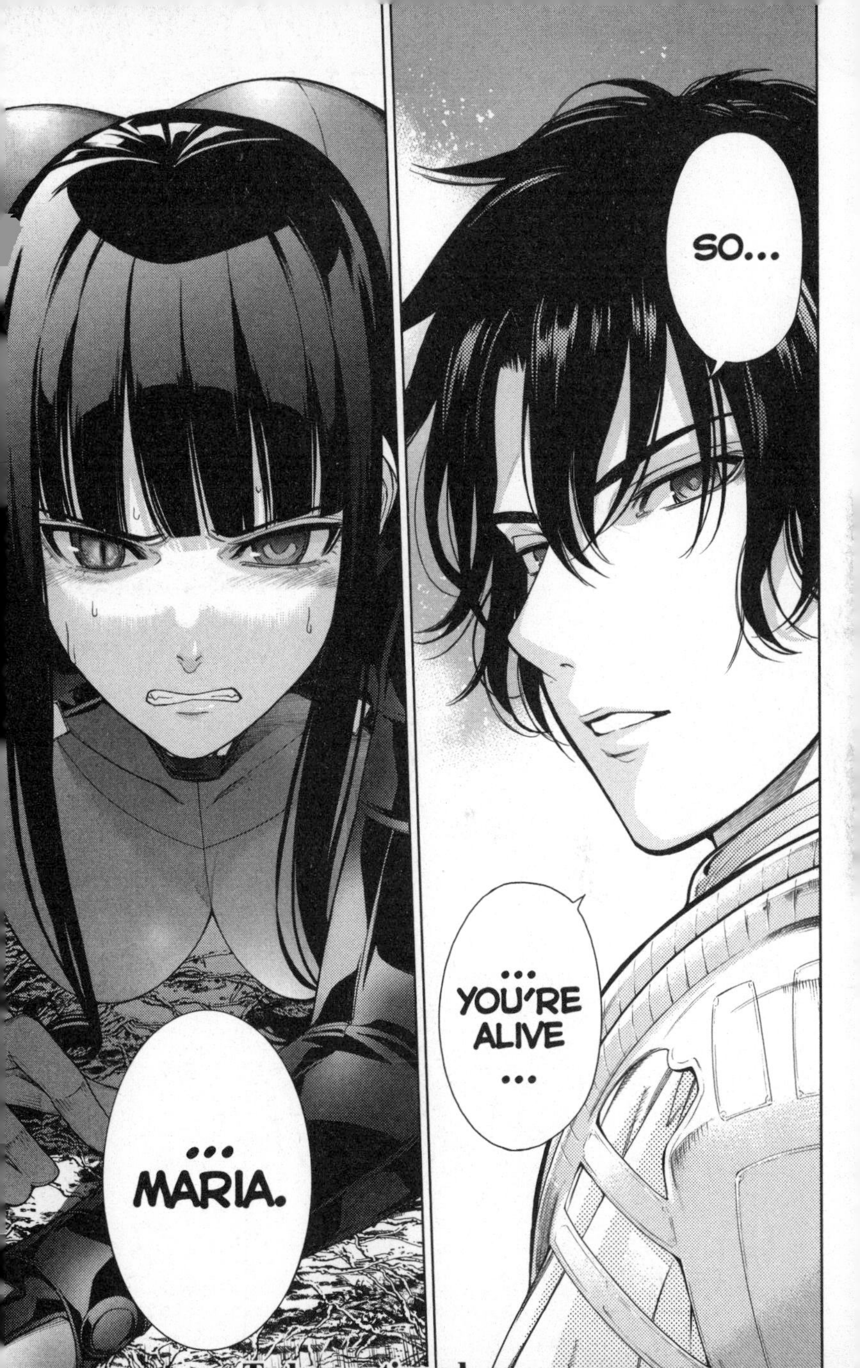
SO...
...YOU'RE ALIVE...
...MARIA.

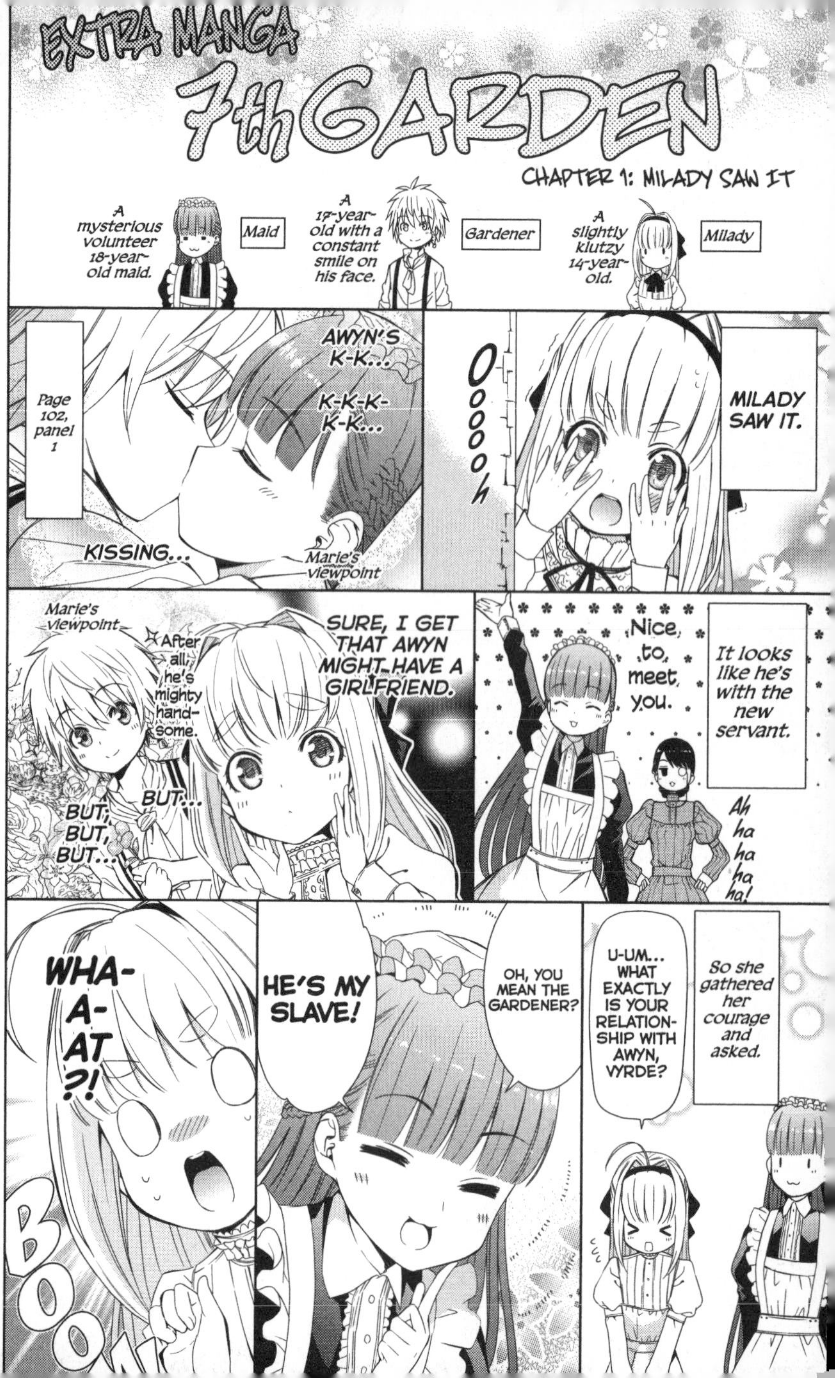
EXTRA MANGA
7th GARDEN
CHAPTER 1: MILADY SAW IT
Milady
A slightly klutzy 14-year-old.
Gardener
A 17-year-old with a constant smile on his face.
Maid
A mysterious volunteer 18-year-old maid.
MILADY SAW IT.
Oooooh
AWYN'S K-K...
K-K-K-K-K...
Page 102, panel 1
KISSING...
Marie's viewpoint
It looks like he's with the new servant.
Nice to meet you.
Ah ha ha ha ha!
SURE, I GET THAT AWYN MIGHT HAVE A GIRLFRIEND.
After all, he's mighty handsome.
Marie's viewpoint
BUT...
BUT, BUT, BUT...
So she gathered her courage and asked.
U-UM... WHAT EXACTLY IS YOUR RELATIONSHIP WITH AWYN, VYRDE?
OH, YOU MEAN THE GARDENER?
HE'S MY SLAVE!
WHA-A-AT?!
BOO

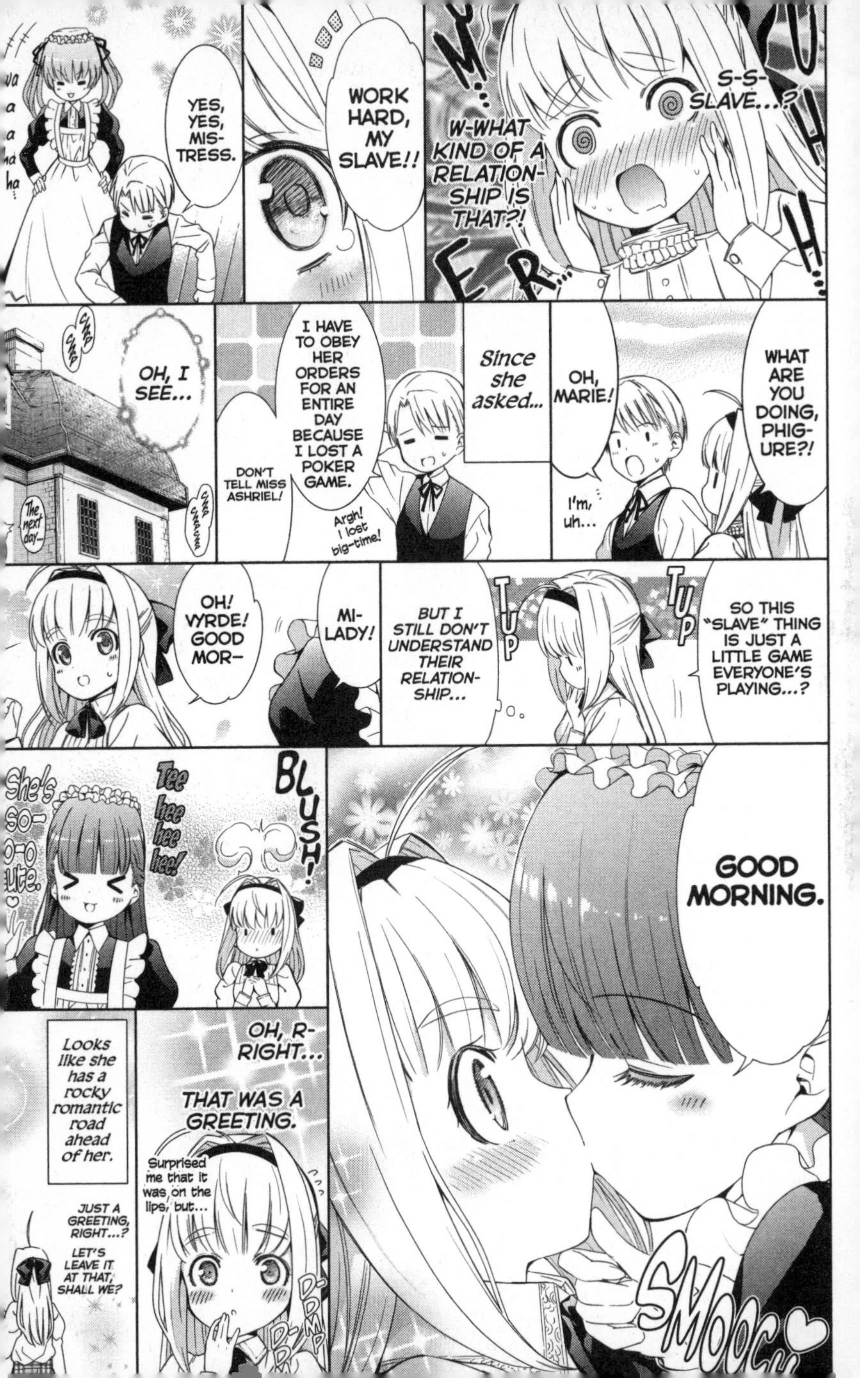
S-S-SLAVE...?
W-WHAT KIND OF A RELATIONSHIP IS THAT?!
HUH!
ERM...
WORK HARD, MY SLAVE!!
YES, YES, MISTRESS.
WHAT ARE YOU DOING, PHIGURE?!
OH, MARIE!
I'm, uh...
Since she asked...
I HAVE TO OBEY HER ORDERS FOR AN ENTIRE DAY BECAUSE I LOST A POKER GAME.
Argh! I lost big-time!
DON'T TELL MISS ASHRIEL!
OH, I SEE...
The next day...
SO THIS "SLAVE" THING IS JUST A LITTLE GAME EVERYONE'S PLAYING...?
TUP TUP
BUT I STILL DON'T UNDERSTAND THEIR RELATIONSHIP...
MI-LADY!
OH! VYRDE! GOOD MOR—
GOOD MORNING.
SMOOCH♥
BLUSH!
Tee hee hee hee!
She's so-o-o cute.♥
OH, R-RIGHT...
THAT WAS A GREETING.
Surprised me that it was on the lips, but...
Looks like she has a rocky romantic road ahead of her.
JUST A GREETING, RIGHT...?
LET'S LEAVE IT AT THAT, SHALL WE?

Mitsu Izumi

Mysterious manga creator Mitsu Izumi was born on February 7 in Kanagawa Prefecture and is the creator of the manga adaptation of *Anohana: The Flower We Saw That Day*, originally serialized in *Jump SQ*.

Is there happiness inside that box?

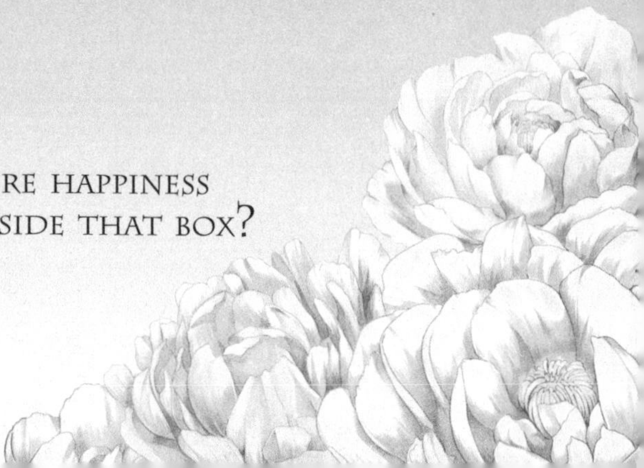

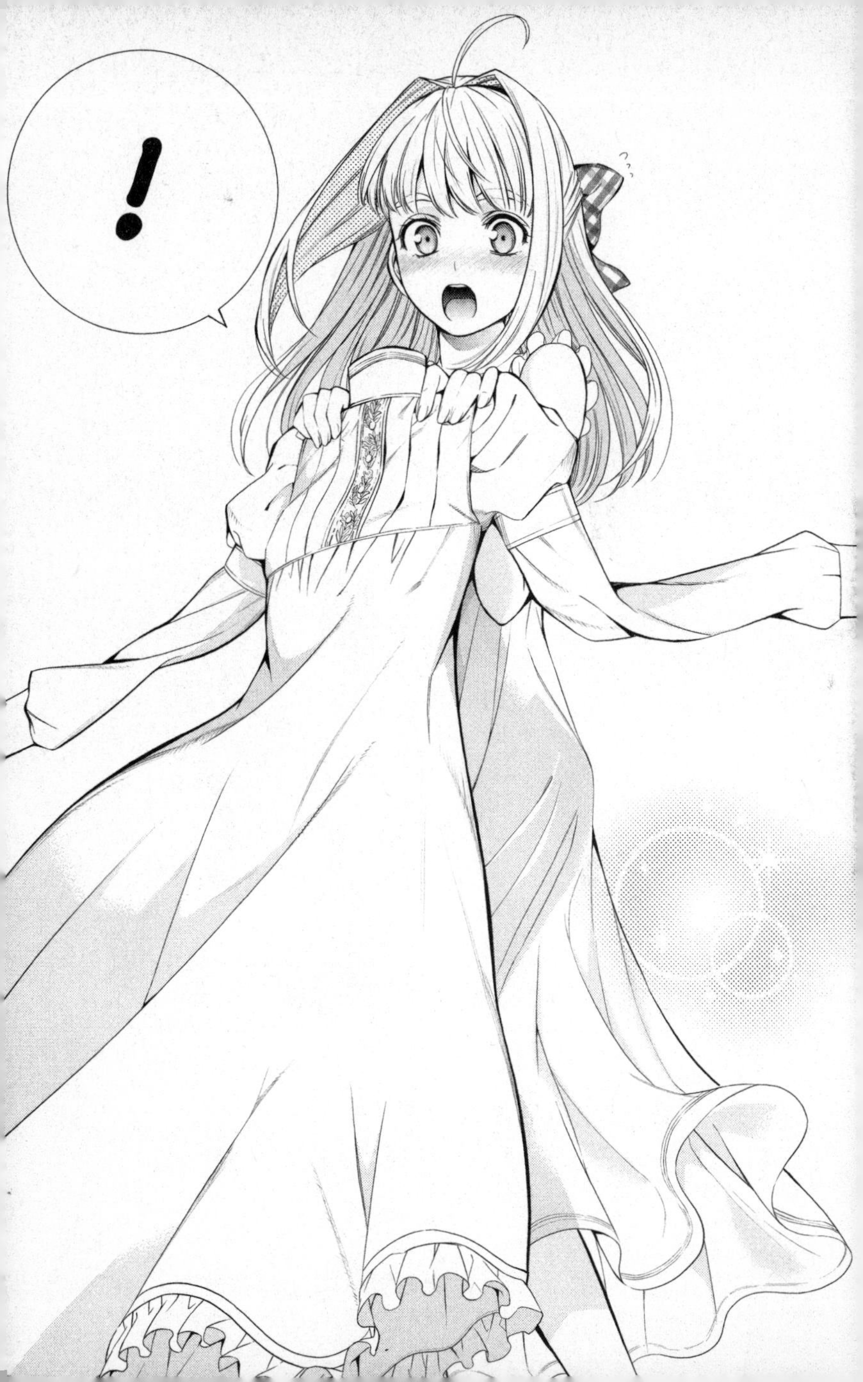
!

7thGARDEN 1
Staff
Kikou Aiba, Yuki Imano
Editor
Takuma Yui
Designer
Kaoru Kuroki + BayBridgeStudi

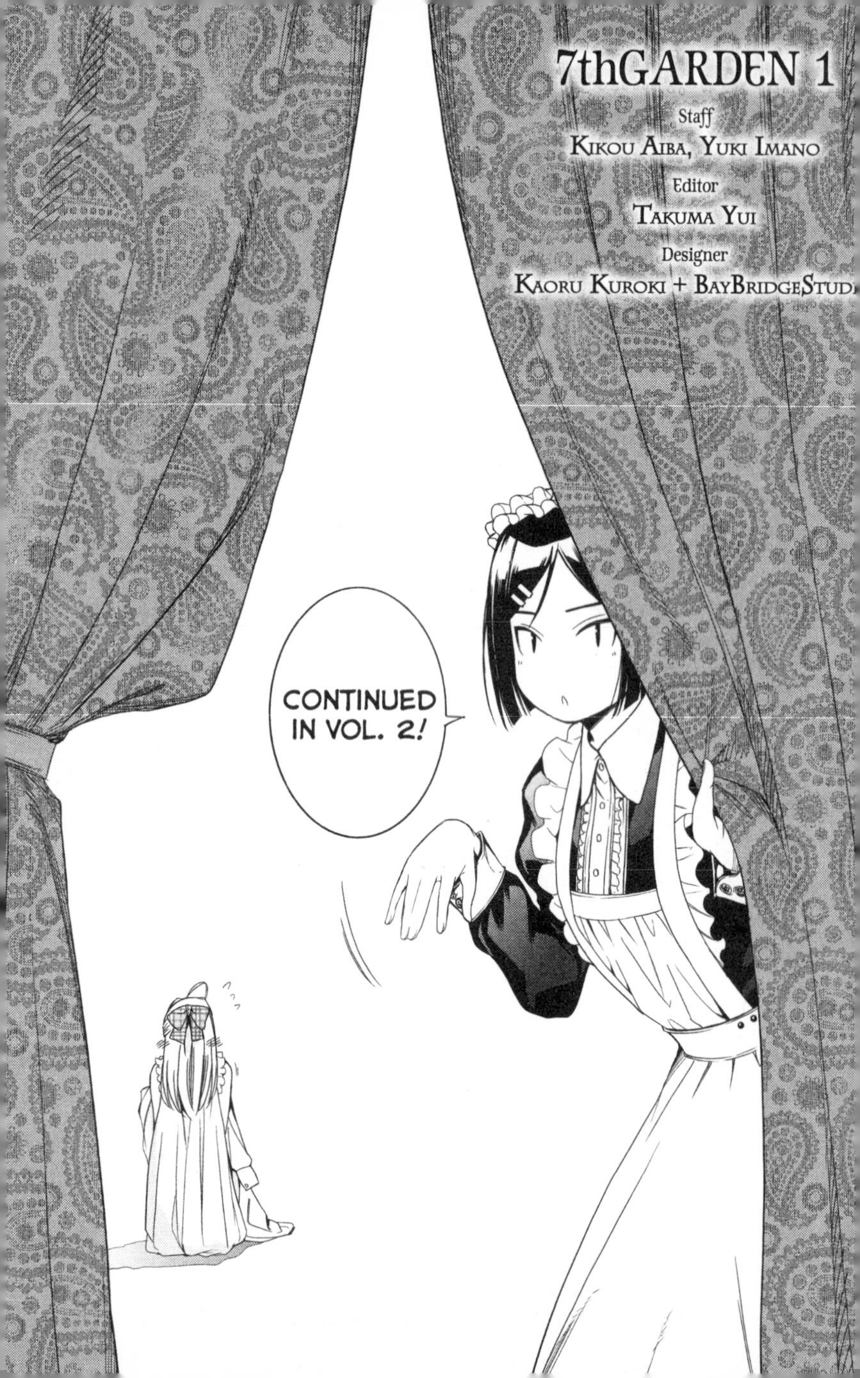
CONTINUED IN VOL. 2!

7thGARDEN
1

SHONEN JUMP Manga Edition

Story and Art by Mitsu Izumi

Translation/Tetsuichiro Miyaki
English Adaptation/Annette Roman
Touch-Up Art & Lettering/Susan Daigle-Leach
Cover & Interior Design/Izumi Evers
Editor/Annette Roman

7thGARDEN © 2014 by Mitsu Izumi
All rights reserved.
First published in Japan in 2014 by SHUEISHA Inc.,
Tokyo.
English translation rights arranged by SHUEISHA Inc.

The stories, characters and incidents mentioned in this
publication are entirely fictional.

No portion of this book may be reproduced or
transmitted in any form or by any means without
written permission from the copyright holders.

Printed in the U.S.A.

Published by VIZ Media, LLC
P.O. Box 77010
San Francisco, CA 94107

10 9 8 7 6 5 4 3 2 1
First printing, July 2016

www.viz.com
www.shonenjump.com

RATED
FOR OLDER TEEN

PARENTAL ADVISORY
7TH GARDEN is rated T+ for Older Teen and
is recommended for ages 13 and up.
It contains fantasy violence.
ratings.viz.com

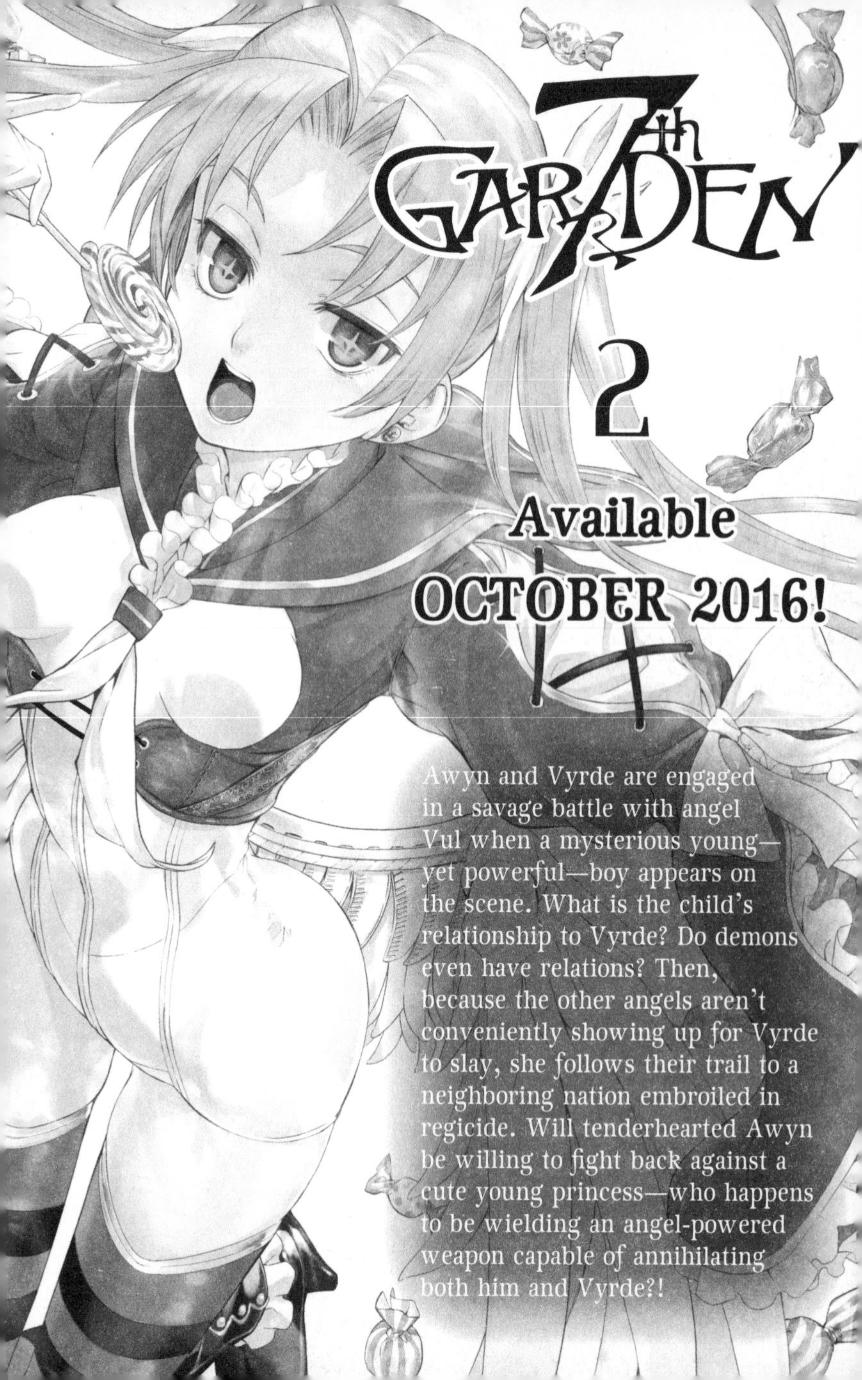
7th GARDEN
2
Available
OCTOBER 2016!
Awyn and Vyrde are engaged in a savage battle with angel Vul when a mysterious young—yet powerful—boy appears on the scene. What is the child's relationship to Vyrde? Do demons even have relations? Then, because the other angels aren't conveniently showing up for Vyrde to slay, she follows their trail to a neighboring nation embroiled in regicide. Will tenderhearted Awyn be willing to fight back against a cute young princess—who happens to be wielding an angel-powered weapon capable of annihilating both him and Vyrde?!

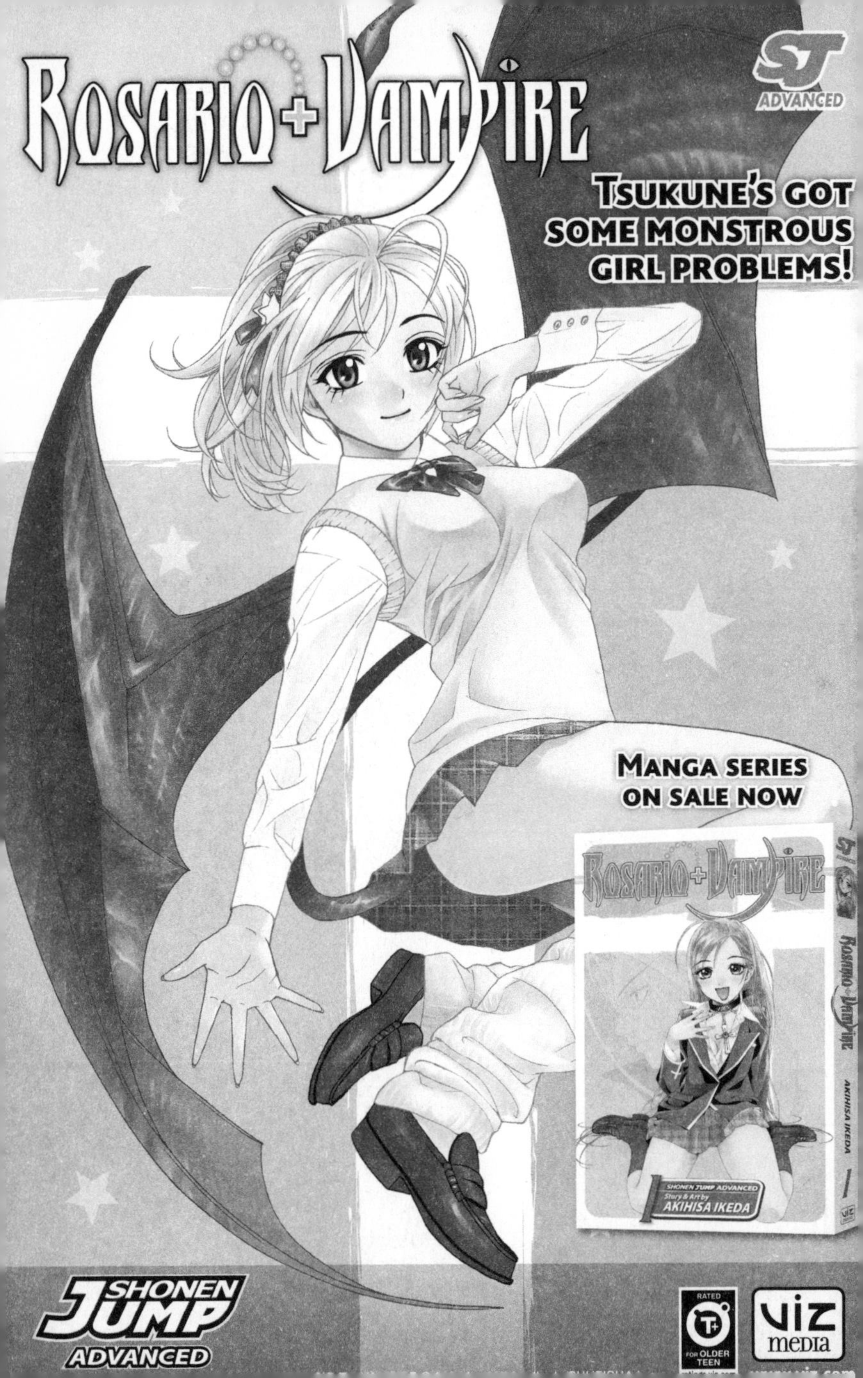
ROSARIO+VAMPIRE
SJ ADVANCED
TSUKUNE'S GOT SOME MONSTROUS GIRL PROBLEMS!
MANGA SERIES ON SALE NOW
ROSARIO+VAMPIRE
AKIHISA IKEDA
SHONEN JUMP ADVANCED
Story & Art by AKIHISA IKEDA
SHONEN JUMP ADVANCED
RATED T+ FOR OLDER TEEN
VIZ media

Seraph of the End
VAMPIRE REIGN

STORY BY **Takaya Kagami** ART BY **Yamato Yamamoto**
STORYBOARDS BY **Daisuke Furuya**

Vampires reign— humans revolt!

Yuichiro's dream of killing every vampire is near-impossible, given that vampires are seven times stronger than humans, and the only way to kill them is by mastering Cursed Gear, advanced demon-possessed weaponry. Not to mention that humanity's most elite Vampire Extermination Unit, the Moon Demon Company, wants nothing to do with Yuichiro unless he can prove he's willing to work in a team—which is the last thing he wants!

THE LATEST CHAPTERS SERIALIZED IN WEEKLY SHONEN JUMP

OWARI NO SERAPH © 2012 by Takaya Kagami, Yamato Yamamoto, Daisuke Furuya /SHUEISHA Inc.

Claymore
クレイモア

Story and Art by
NORIHIRO YAGI

TO SAVE HUMANITY,
MUST CLARE SACRIFICE HER OWN?

In a world where monsters called Yoma prey on humans
and live among them in disguise, humanity's only hope
is a new breed of warrior known as Claymores. Half
human, half monster, these silver-eyed slayers possess
supernatural strength, but are condemned to fight their
savage impulses or lose their humanity completely.

CLAYMORE © 2004 by ... /SHUEISHA Inc.

You're Reading in the Wrong Direction!!

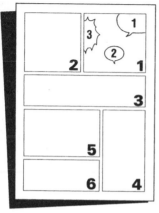

Whoops! Guess what? You're starting at the wrong end of the comic!

...It's true! In keeping with the original Japanese format, **7thGARDEN** is meant to be read from right to left, starting in the upper-right corner.

Unlike English, which is read from left to right, Japanese is read from right to left, meaning that action, sound effects and word-balloon order are completely reversed... something which can make readers unfamiliar with Japanese feel pretty backwards themselves. For this reason, manga or Japanese comics published in the U.S. in English have sometimes been published "flopped"—that is, printed in exact reverse order, as though seen from the other side of a mirror.

By flopping pages, U.S. publishers can avoid confusing readers, but the compromise is not without its downside. For one thing, a character in a flopped manga series who once wore in the original Japanese version a T-shirt emblazoned with "M A Y" (as in "the merry month of") now wears one which reads "Y A M"! Additionally, many manga creators in Japan are themselves unhappy with the process, as some feel the mirror-imaging of their art skews their original intentions.

We are proud to bring you Mitsu Izumi's **7thGARDEN** in the original unflopped format.

For now, though, turn to the other side of the book and let the adventure begin...!

—Editor